SEVEN PSYCHOLOGIES

The Century Psychology Series
Richard M. Elliott, Editor

SEVEN PSYCHOLOGIES

BY EDNA HEIDBREDER, Ph.D.

EMERITUS, WELLESLEY COLLEGE

Prentice-Hall, Inc., Englewood Cliffs, New Jersey

PRENTICE-HALL INTERNATIONAL, INC., *London*
PRENTICE-HALL OF AUSTRALIA, PTY. LTD., *Sydney*
PRENTICE-HALL OF CANADA, LTD., *Toronto*
PRENTICE-HALL OF INDIA PRIVATE LIMITED, *New Delhi*
PRENTICE-HALL OF JAPAN, INC., *Tokyo*

PREFACE

This book has been written not for professional psychologists, but for those interested in psychology who, having made a preliminary survey of the field, are impressed by the fact that there are many different schools of thought in psychology, and wish to inquire further into the matter.

The discussion refers specifically to American psychology; it makes no attempt to picture the situation in the psychological thought of Europe. This does not mean, of course, that American psychology can be considered apart from European influences. As a matter of fact, three of the seven systems here presented—structuralism, *Gestalt* psychology, and psychoanalysis—are outright importations from Europe. They have been treated, however, not as movements in European thought, but as influences in American psychology.

Neither does the account of systems given here attempt to present a complete picture of psychology in the United States. For one thing, it gives only occasional glimpses of that activity which is most characteristic of American psychology, experimental research. For another, it does not consider, nor even enumerate, all the systems now current in American psychology. The names of Bentley, Dunlap, Hunter, Kantor, McDougall, Spearman, Tolman, Weiss, and Wheeler suggest some of the omissions. Finally, it gives only a partial account even of the systems selected for study. Any vigorous school of thought gives rise to interpretations definitely related to, yet divergent from, its own, and these interpretations have not been considered. In the discussion of psychoanalysis, for instance, the systems of Jung and Adler

v

have received little attention; and the treatment of behavior-ism has been restricted to the teachings of Watson, though important modifications of his conception have appeared.

This plan of selection has undeniable disadvantages. To present a system without its fringe of related interpreta-tions might create the impression that its adherents form a single, united, unanimous group, whose ideas are faithful copies of those of their leader. Such an impression would be absurdly false. Similarly, the selection of seven systems might create the impression that American psychology is organized into seven schools; and this impression, too, would be false. The selection might further imply that, of all the systems current in psychology, these seven are most worthy of study; and this implication is not intended.

Still, in spite of its admitted disadvantages, the plan of presenting a few systems and of presenting them as single clear-cut conceptions, leaving out of account, wherever pos-sible, their related conceptions and interpretations, has been adopted, at the risk of oversimplification, as the one most suitable to the present purpose. For that purpose is neither to make an exhaustive study of systems of psychology, nor to present, even in outline, a complete account of American psychology; it is, rather, to enable a reader somewhat new in the field to become acquainted with some of the different points of view from which the facts of psychology may be regarded. With this purpose in mind, it seemed wiser to present seven systems rather than seventy.

The systems, moreover, have been treated as factors mak-ing actual differences in the development of psychology. For this reason, each system has been presented in its historical setting and in relation to the historical continuity that can be discerned running through the various interpretations of psychology. For the same reason, an attempt has been made to estimate the influence of the system on the actual progress of psychology, though the estimates are necessarily premature and tentative. The selection of the seven systems has also been determined by the conception of systems as effective influences in the development of psychology. The systems discussed have been included in some cases because they represent crucial points in the development of American psychology; in others, because they have been associated with important centers of research; and finally, because, when considered together, their differences make it evident that many different approaches to the problem of psychology are possible. Perhaps no one else would have chosen just these seven; the selection admittedly involves personal opinion. But for the purpose which has been indicated it is not important either that all systems be considered or that the most important ones be chosen. To present seven different conceptions of psychology, seven conceptions in actual use, is not only to indicate the function and significance of those particular seven, but to suggest the function and significance of systems in general.

Naturally I offer this book with many misgivings. The difficulties involved in the attempt to portray accurately and to estimate justly the thoughts of others require no comment. The chief of these difficulties is that no objective standard exists by which systems can be judged and compared. Therefore I neither can nor do claim that the account I have written is impartial and unprejudiced. I believe, however, that this fact is not fatal to the usefulness of the book. Discriminating readers will see my partialities more clearly than I can describe them; and by correcting for them, though they must do so not without reference to their own partialities, they will participate in a procedure that, as I have tried to indicate throughout the chapters which follow, is a useful and practically necessary step in the process of bringing objective knowledge into existence.

Many people have helped me to write this book. Some of my students have made suggestions that I have found stimulating and useful. Professors Josephine Curtis Foster, Kate Hevner, and Heinrich Klüver have read portions of the book, and Miss Amy Armstrong and Professor R. M. Elliott have read the entire manuscript. All of them have offered suggestions by which I have profited. Mrs. Nancy Johnson Engene, Miss Dreda Harper, and Miss Marian Greenham have helped enormously in preparing the manuscript for the publishers. The Clark University Press, Henry Holt and Co., the J. B. Lippincott Company, Longmans, Green and Co., The Macmillan Company, and W. W. Norton and Company have given me permission to quote passages from their books. For all these aids I wish to acknowledge my indebtedness and to express my sincere thanks.

EDNA HEIDBREDER

Minneapolis, Minnesota

CONTENTS

SEVEN PSYCHOLOGIES

Chapter I

SYSTEMS OF PSYCHOLOGY: THEIR FUNCTION AND SIGNIFICANCE

IT is something of a paradox that systems of psychology flourish as they do on American soil. Psychology, especially in the United States, has risked everything on being science; and science on principle refrains from speculation that is not permeated and stabilized by fact. Yet there is not enough fact in the whole science of psychology to make a single solid system.

No one knows this better than the psychologists themselves. They see with the eyes of familiar association not only the undeniable poverty of their science, but the flimsiness and shoddiness of much of the material they are asked to accept as genuine fact. Psychologists are continually looking upon the work of their colleagues and finding that it is not good. And with little hesitation, or with none at all, they expose the weaknesses and flaws they discover.

One can hardly cross the threshold of the lively young science without suspecting that all is not peace and harmony under its roof-tree; that the bands of workers one encounters there represent not only a necessary division of labor but a state of internal strife. Perhaps the most assertive of the warring groups is composed of the younger students of animal and comparative psychology, most of whom pride themselves on being hard-headed and realistic and on having discarded the airy nothings of a psychology that deals with minds. They wish above all else to be severely scientific,

3

and some of them seem convinced that they can best realize this ambition by resembling as closely as possible their near neighbors, the physiologists. They are for the most part confident and resolute young men, strong in the faith that by probing into the depths of matter and muscle, they are digging at the roots of things.

A less aggressive group, but one that is no less assured, no less conscious of the integrity of its science, is composed of the experimental psychologists. To these psychologists the term "experimental" is applied not in the sense of including all who conduct research by the experimental method common to natural science in general, but in the special and esoteric sense of designating those who are in the line of descent which derives more or less directly from the world's first active psychological laboratory, that founded by Wilhelm Wundt in Leipzig. Experimental psychology in this sense refers to a particular discipline, developed in Germany, and championed in the United States chiefly by one of Wundt's English pupils, Edward Bradford Titchener. Its typical representatives are the "trained introspectionists," who believe that the true task of psychology is the examination of consciousness. Their work, they are convinced, requires special training and extreme care, and because of the elaborate apparatus they have devised for their assistance, they are sometimes referred to as "brass-instrument psychologists." They represent the established aristocracy of a generation ago. Theirs is the psychology, they are willing to maintain, that has stood and will stand the test of time.

Both these groups look somewhat askance at a third set, those occupied with the testing and measuring of mental traits. For in the workrooms of the mental-testers there is little of the paraphernalia of the older sciences—few brass instruments to suggest the austere dignity of physics, no white rats to suggest the substantial actualities of biology.

There is an abundance of quantitative data, however. For perhaps more than any other single group of psychologists, the mental-testers have developed the mathematical mode of thinking that science finds so congenial; and operating with curves of distribution, correlation coefficients, and more recondite statistical devices, they have undertaken the task of measuring intelligence and other complex mental traits, and of acquiring as much information about them as quantitative treatment will yield.

Closely associated with this group, in fact not clearly distinguishable from it, are the workers in applied psychology. Among them are those who attack the problems of commerce and industry—the selection of employees, the management of personnel, the elimination of industrial fatigue, the most effective methods of advertising, and the lighting and ventilating of factories. Here too are the clinical psychologists, who work in schools, in juvenile courts, in child-guidance clinics, and in institutions for the feeble-minded, the psychopathic, and the insane, attempting, by contributing to a better understanding of the persons under their care, to help them to make their adjustments to life. In applied psychology, too, are the educational psychologists, occupied not only with the many problems of learning and teaching, but more particularly of late with the attempt to measure the capacities and aptitudes of pupils, and the effectiveness of various educational procedures.

These groups, none of which is sharply delimited, together with other groups even less clearly defined and many independent individuals, make up the roll of psychologists. But however imperceptibly each group may merge into the others, all along the line, from the most correct of the experimental and animal psychologists to the newest and crudest of the mental-testers, the workers question the value and validity of the work of other groups. More than that, they question the validity of the work of others of their own group. No one can criticize an animal psychologist as can another animal psychologist; the most pointed attacks upon mental-testers come from other mental-testers. One who is himself engaged in the tricky business of prospecting for facts, knows—and knows with especial conviction as regards his own field—how rarely they are extricated from the matrix of faith and hope and conjecture in which they are embedded, how often they disappear into mere illusion, and how small their value is likely to be, if they survive at all, as compared with their apparent worth in the excitement of discovery. Naturally such a person does not look with immediate credulity upon every large nugget of possible knowledge that a fellow-worker offers as fact. He accepts it only when he has thoroughly assayed it by submitting it to all the critical tests he knows.

All this is a tremendously good thing for the young science of psychology. For anything that emerges from this treatment as a fact, making its way against the opposition of very earnest, very belligerent, very persistent criticism, must have at its core the streak of stubbornness that makes a fact a fact. If intelligence tests, or the laws of learning, or *Gestalten,* or conditioned reflexes survive the manhandling of their active critics, it will be because there is something there in the same sense that there was in the stone that Dr. Johnson kicked in his motor refutation of Bishop Berkeley; because they offer effective resistance to human violence and human cleverness.

And, fortunately, the vigor of the new science expresses itself not only in feuds but in industry. In one respect at least, the clashing groups are alike; they are all relentlessly industrious. With almost incredible diligence they count the errors of their rats, compute coefficients of correlation, and record judgments of lifted weights. And the outcome of all this industry and of all this criticism is the occasional establishment of a fact, or what is far more frequent and almost as good, the overthrow of a dogma.

Furthermore, in the course of the struggle there has grown up a vast respect for science as such. In the presence of the older sciences, psychology feels something of the awe of the novice for the master, something of the abashed admiration of the *nouveaux riches* for an established aristocracy. It feels too the same anxious concern lest its mode of life fail to conform to the standards of the caste, and in its very zeal for maintaining those standards it is sometimes betrayed into a swaggering superiority to the practices it has so recently learned to scorn. But the swagger is compensatory and superficial. For the brash young science, like so many brash young things, is acutely aware of its shortcomings. It looks from its rough graphs and dubious correlations to the elegant precision of physics and doubts whether all is well. For beneath its bluster there is a desire for solid fact and sure technique. The arrogant intolerance it sometimes displays toward anything on which the seal of science has not been set, is in part at least a jealous concern for the integrity of its knowledge, not wholly unlike the fine scorn of Bacon for the pretensions of the Aristotelians of his time. For in the few years of its existence, psychology has acquired not only diligence but the skepticism that for science is the beginning of wisdom. It knows that it knows little and that that little is tentative. Psychology can point to no imposing storehouse of facts; it knows that its greatest virtue is its determination to follow the scientific method, and that at its best, it attempts to push that method into a region which hitherto the inquiries of science have not penetrated. Above all, psychology is aware of a great need for the factual substance of which a science is so largely made, and it has learned to look with disapproval, almost with dread, on speculation that is not steadied by the ballast of fact.

Then why all the system-making? Why does psychology, which is trying so hard to be a science, build structures of speculative thought that it cannot hope for years to verify by established fact?

Briefly, because it has reached a place where such a procedure is all but inevitable. No one can state at present the precise circumstances that stimulate thought—"thought" is used here to denote the reflective and creative activities of the intellect as contrasted with observation and experimentation—but the general conditions are sufficiently well known to make it plain that psychology has not fallen into intellectualistic ways without provocation. It has been subjected to three of the most powerful stimulants to thought: increasing knowledge, grave concern, and persistent doubt.

Knowledge sometimes stimulates thought, but the right amount of it must be present—neither too much nor too little. If a person were in possession of *all* the facts on a given topic, his thought about it would automatically cease. His problem would be solved; the occasion for thought would no longer exist. The educated adult does not have to think when he answers the questions: How many are seven times five? What is the chemical composition of water? What are Newton's laws of motion? The knowledge is either in his possession or is readily accessible. At one time, in the history of the race if not in that of the individual, those questions occasioned a great deal of thought, but at present they simply stir up, more or less readily, the appropriate associations. Similarly, one does not think if he is in possession of *none* of the facts. Most of us, probably, think very little, if at all, about fluxions or uncials or the current political intrigues in Montenegro. In most of us the relevant facts are absent and we therefore lack the very materials with which thought operates. This is doubtless the reason why most of us do not think more about Einstein's theory of relativity, at least about its central concepts. True, there are some aspects of the theory about which we do think; we contemplate it as a revolutionary idea, as a brilliant intellectual feat, as a discovery that demands a revision of fundamental ways of conceiving the physical universe, as another indication of what mathematical thought can accomplish. But that is partly because we do know something about revolutionary ideas, intellectual feats, revisions of fundamental concepts, and the potency of mathematical reasoning. We can go in good spirits as far as this knowledge carries us, but it does not carry us far enough; we know there is something beyond. In fact, the interest that Einstein's theory has set up is an excellent illustration of the degree of knowledge which is likely to stimulate thought. We *know* that there is something stirring; we do *not* know exactly what. Our curiosity is piqued; we have a start; we feel an impulse to go the whole way. And the fact that the impulse does not lead us to acquire sufficient knowledge of physics and mathematics to carry us to complete comprehension, indicates not that the impulse to think has not been aroused, but that it is not sufficiently strong to make us remove the obstacles, or else that the obstacles are too much for us. Not that thought ceases when it reaches the limits of knowledge; it ekes out knowledge with creation; it tends strongly to complete the unfinished picture somehow— anyhow. A little learning is a dangerous thing precisely because it gets creative thought started, and creative thought, though it may sometimes lead to truth, sometimes leads to ridiculous or perilous falsehood.

But thought, of course, is not merely an affair of the intellect. Concern, too, is important. We think about the things we care about, and probably do our freshest and most vigorous thinking on matters that bear most directly on our personal concerns. Hence the bulk of the world's best thought—considering now the thought of mankind in general, not that of a few distinguished thinkers—is probably on such topics as how to carry through some cherished enterprise, what friends and rivals are doing, and how to achieve some sort of salvation, temporal or eternal. The thought that makes the greatest stir in the world is that which has some bearing on the fate of man and his affairs. The Copernican theory arrested attention not so much because it demanded a new view of the universe as because the new view of the universe demanded a new view of man, now no longer the center of the stage. And Darwinism is interesting chiefly because of its implications for humanity; because it presents man not as an object of special consideration, but merely as one of the many forms that protoplasm has assumed in a world not specifically made for any of them. Any question that men see as involving their own welfare has a good chance of stirring up thought, though the quality of the thought is of course determined by other conditions than the nature and magnitude of the feeling involved.

Thought is also related to action, and through action to doubt. We think what to do, particularly when our old ways of doing things are interfered with, or when we discover that they no longer serve. It is then that we doubt, and doubt—the discovery that what has seemed adequate may no longer be adequate—is the signal that a new adjustment must be made. Perhaps in a perfectly adjusted animal thought would be superfluous. But when something goes wrong, thought may be useful and is likely to occur. When a man's motor stops, he tries to understand it; when his work is going badly, he considers the situation; and when his

Weltanschauung is altered so that he sees himself no longer in a cherished rôle, but in one that is ridiculous or insignificant, he is plunged into the *Sturm und Drang* of an intellectual agitation of even greater proportions. Doubt means that a new adjustment must be made, and in the working out of human adjustments thought is often, though not invariably, involved.

There is an abundance of instances outside the field of psychology which show these conditions at work. It is no accident that the great rationalistic systems of Descartes, of Leibniz, and of Spinoza were formulated after the Renaissance had reaped its first harvest of knowledge and doubt about matters closely linked with human happiness and salvation. It is especially interesting that the distrust of medieval intellectualism itself produced an intellectualistic response. Bacon, critical as he was of the rationalistic methods of the Middle Ages, left his mark on science not so much by employing the new method he advocated as by following one far more like the old method he scorned. The *Novum Organum,* though it is a plea and a program for the inductive method, is not itself a good illustration of that method. It is a reflective analysis of what ought to be done if scientific knowledge is to be attained; not the outcome of a systematic accumulation of observed and recorded cases, both positive and negative, of problems actually undertaken by human thought. Even the critical empiricism of Locke and Hume was achieved less by the actual observation of the mind at work than by a retrospective and reasoned analysis of the intellect concerning the pretensions of which those authors were so skeptical. Empiricism discredited the exaggerated claims of the intellect by an examination of those claims which was far more intellectual than empirical in method.

And so it is not surprising that psychology, which, according to its professed code, ought to settle down to the sober acquisition of fact, has indulged at times in riotous thinking and has produced systems of thought for which the factual proof is admittedly lacking and will be obtainable only in the remote future. For psychology is surrounded by the conditions of such thought. Its facts are numerous enough to be suggestive, not numerous enough to be conclusive; its doubts are legion; its subject-matter is close to the personal interests that do not exist for pure science but which are peculiarly likely to arouse the concern of human beings. In these circumstances it is as natural for a psychologist to fall into speculation as it would be for a physicist to fall toward the center of the earth if the center of gravity of his body were not between its points of support.

But what is the bearing of all this on systems of psychology? Fundamentally, that they are to be regarded as productions of living creatures, working in the midst of doubt, concern, and incomplete knowledge, to achieve better adjustments to the particular circumstances that surround them. The nature, the function, and the limitations of systems are all inherent in this manner of conceiving them.

This means, for one thing, that systems of psychology must not be regarded as altogether impartial and unemotional constructions, determined solely by logic and evidence. On no account is it wise to consider systems apart from the particular situations that give rise to them—from the traditions, the conventions, the standards, the prejudices, and at times the rank personal feelings which constitute their background. The most common origin of systems is dissatisfaction with an older system, the disruption of a scientific *modus vivendi;* and the disruption of a *modus vivendi*, involving as it does the disorganization of habit and emotion as well as the stimulation of the intellect, can hardly give rise to an altogether calm and disinterested activity. The regular response to the discovery that one's way of life has failed is to try another way, in spite of the fact that the new way must be based on incomplete knowledge, as was the old. Perhaps the purely rational method of meeting the situation would be to suspend judgment until all the evidence is in, but to suspend judgment indefinitely is a highly sophisticated procedure, not always appropriate to the rough and ready pioneering ways of a new science. Actually scientific progress has often been achieved by accepting wrong or partial or tentative answers on the basis of the available data, and correcting the answers as more data came in. Psychology, at least, has had little success in arresting its thought in mid-career; it has answered its questions by producing systems, each of which is to its adherents a foreshadowing of the truth and a program of action—at once something to work by and something to work for. A system of psychology, therefore, is not only a basis of procedure but a basis of morale. Perhaps to the adherents of a system the justification for its acceptance is to be found in something like Vaihinger's philosophy of "as if." But the person who observes and studies the system must see it as the psychologist sees the activities of a rat in a maze: as a set of varied and complex performances that are more or less effective means of reaching a goal.

This means in turn that systems of psychology are to be regarded not as statements of scientific knowledge, but as tools by which scientific knowledge is produced; not as accounts of scientific fact, but as means of acquiring scientific fact. They are the scaffolding within which the structure of the science of psychology is being erected, as necessary as the scaffolding and as impermanent; not to be identified with the structure itself, which however could not exist without it. They are the tools by which knowledge is extracted, but as different from knowledge as are the instruments from the ore that they expose. They provide zeal for the work, but are as different from work as inspiration is from production. They offer a specific and sometimes glamorous program of action, but the program is not to be confused with accomplishment. It is difficult to know which to emphasize more: the indispensability of the instrument or the fact that it is an instrument.

Perhaps the former, considering the temper of psychology at the moment. For psychology, with its determined devotion to the scientific method, becomes at times almost bitterly anti-intellectualistic. It recognizes, of course, that speculation plays a legitimate part in scientific thought, that the distinction between observation and speculation is not absolute, and that the two are really complementary. But its active attitude is not so calmly rational. Perhaps because of the recency of the separation of psychology from philosophy, perhaps because of an acute sense of need for observed facts, many psychologists regard speculation with suspicion and distaste, almost with resentment and dread. For many of them are still somewhat afraid of being metaphysical, and by being metaphysical they mean, whether rightly or wrongly, spinning theories out of the head without verifying them by fact. What they fear, of course, is not thought, but thought that runs away from fact, beyond the reach of fact. But all thought runs ahead of fact; it is the very nature of thought to do so; and the difference between scientific thought and "mere speculation" is the difference in the relation of the creations of thought to the facts by which they must be tested. Thought that keeps its line of communication with fact open and active is scientific thought; that which fails to do so is "mere speculation."

No system of psychology can or does claim at present that it is established by fact. Neither does any system proceed in total indifference to fact. The simple truth is that psychology does not at present possess enough facts with which to test its systems. Its need of facts makes it disparage speculation; its lack of facts makes it resort to the practice, and it does so at times with a bad conscience.

And so again the question arises: Why does not psychology turn from its systems and devote itself to collecting the facts it so sorely needs? The answer to this question is the justification of systems: that without the systems few facts would be forthcoming. For scientific knowledge does not merely accumulate; it is far more likely to grow about hypotheses that put definite questions and which act as centers of organization in the quest of knowledge. As a matter of historical fact, science has not grown by following the method Bacon described—that is, by the steady amassing of data and the emergence of generalizations. Bacon himself said that mere accumulation is not enough; but not even the watchful and systematic accumulation Bacon outlined, with its careful comparisons of positive and negative cases, and its notations of varying degrees of quality in varying circumstances, has actually been the source of most of the insights of science. More often than not, the insight *precedes* the systematic evidence; is tested rather than suggested by it; is, indeed, the occasion for the acquisition of the evidence. Frequently the victories of science are won through the use of conjectures not yet established by fact, conjectures that become the basis of active and ingenious research especially directed toward that particular body of evidence which will prove or disprove the point at issue. Guesses on the basis of inadequate evidence have proved to be powerful and, in actual practice, indispensable tools, which science regularly employs.

It is for this reason that systems figure so prominently and so pertinently in contemporary psychology. A system may fulfil its function by proving itself either right or wrong, or, as is far more likely to be the case, by proving itself partly right and partly wrong. The very errors of systems, especially if they are clean-cut and decisive, may further the cause of science by revealing mistakes that need not be repeated. Systems give form and definiteness and direction to an enterprise that without them would be vague and aimless; and more, they provide interest and zest for the venture. For science does not live by facts alone, nor even by facts and hypotheses alone. It needs the joy of combat and the hope of achievement, and evidently at times even the spice of malice and the excitement of running with the pack; and for psychology at present this means schools and systems.

Considered from this point of view, as programs of action and as bases of morale, systems may be regarded as significant symptoms of the condition of psychology in particular places, at particular times, and in the hands of particular sets of workers; as indications of those aspects of psychology which are probably receiving *more* than their share of emphasis in a given set of circumstances. Not that it is in the least regrettable that overemphasis should occur. It attracts attention to important issues, it stimulates criticism, and it is almost certain to be counteracted by overemphasis in the opposite direction at other times or at other places. For the development of science cannot be regarded as the work of one man or of one group of men; science is a vast social enterprise in which an individual's most valuable contributions may be his brilliant mistakes.

It is from this point of view, then, that systems of psychology will be considered in this study; not as right or wrong, not as more or less complete approximations to knowledge, but in terms of their influence on the actual development of a science of psychology. They can best be understood not as statements of scientific fact, not as summaries of existing knowledge, but as ways and means of arriving at knowledge, as temporary but necessary stages in the development of a science, as creations of workers who, in a confusing and sometimes depressing enterprise, must keep not only their poise but also their verve. For it can hardly be repeated too often that science does not proceed in the light of reason alone, but like other human enterprises is a muddled adventure working itself out

> "as on a darkling plain
> Swept with confused alarms of struggle and flight
> Where ignorant armies clash by night."

Chapter II

PRESCIENTIFIC PSYCHOLOGY

IT is almost necessary, in studying systems of psychology, to inquire into their past. The very fact that they appear late in human thought means that the problems they represent have had long years in which to form obscure affinities and entangling alliances, quite unsupervised by the watchful care of science. The young science of psychology is continually discovering that its favorite problems have histories; that its very terms have implications which connect them with preëxisting points of view, and that its conclusions are often determined by custom and association. Its path is anything but a straight line; it is always being pulled this way and that by the attraction of some body of knowledge or opinion of which it may hardly be aware. Often the turns of its thought and the very content of its concepts are determined by historical accidents that occurred hundreds of years ago.

Ideally and in its finished form a system of psychology is an envisagement of the total field of psychology as a consistent and unified whole. It assumes that the apparently chaotic particulars which lie within its domain can, if properly understood, be brought into order and clarity: that the subject-matter can be defined, the central problem stated, the methods of investigation agreed upon, the relations to other bodies of knowledge determined, the elements or basic processes identified, the distinctive features brought into relief, the general outline or characteristic movement indicated.

To know a system is to know how it stands on all these matters, and especially to know the point of view from which it regards them. For the essential fact about a system of psychology is the position from which it surveys its field, the vantage-point from which it examines the concrete data of the science and from which it discerns a coherent pattern running through them and giving them unity.

But whatever systems of psychology may be, they are not static, finished, purely logical structures that may be considered as so many separate, complete, and independent objects, to be analyzed apart from the conditions that gave rise to them. For the systems of psychology that actually exist—the bodies of fact and conjecture which function as systems—are often not systems at all in the strict sense of the term, certainly not closed and finished constructions of thought, worked out to consistency to the last detail.[1] On the contrary they are products of long and sometimes obscure lines of historical development; for psychology, like any other enterprise of the human intellect—perhaps more than most—has been subject to confusions, entanglements, and misunderstandings, many of which have their roots in the remote past.

It is particularly significant that psychological interest develops not only late but incidentally. Thought apparently works from without inward; philosophy begins with cosmology, and science with astronomy and physics. This does not mean that human beings are not from the first interested in themselves. They are interested in the world primarily because they are in it, because it contains the things

---

[1] The term "system of psychology" as used in this book does not necessarily denote a closed and finished construction. It refers, rather, to any attempt to survey the field of psychology from a definite point of view and to organize the facts from that standpoint. Consequently, some interpretations of psychology are included that the authors themselves do not regard as "systems" in the strict sense of the term.

they find important. But at first their own existence and nature, though they form the center from which all human interests radiate, are quite simply taken for granted. Thought is unself-conscious in the beginning, for self-consciousness implies a way of observing the self somewhat as one observes other objects, an awareness of self that is by no means free from self-concern but which nevertheless shows the beginnings of intellectual disengagement. To require an explanation of the self and its ways is to have raised questions concerning them, and that can be done only after the first freshness of taking the self for granted has in some measure been lost.

Hence psychology, which at first is human psychology, begins in observations that are at the time secondary to the major occupations of the intellect. In philosophy, psychology is likely to be encountered as epistemology. In their attempts to comprehend the universe, philosophers are sooner or later arrested by the thought "How can we know?" and this question gives rise to an examination of human ways of knowing. Psychological inquiries arise, too, in ethics and in social and political theory; questions concerning man's conduct in relation to his fellow-men and to the state easily direct attention to the nature of man himself. In science, psychology emerged chiefly from physiology, particularly from the physiology of the sense-organs, which seemed the paths of connection between the external world and the world of private and personal experience. Then too, in their everyday lives and in their dealings with others, human beings are forced to learn, at least in the rough and ready manner of common sense, something about human ways. Furthermore, from whatever starting-point human beings begin to consider themselves, they are almost irresistibly drawn into questions concerning their own value and welfare—their place in nature, their origin and destiny, the significance of their existence, their chances of salvation. From the first, human observations of human nature are likely to be colored—from the standpoint of pure science, tainted—by human hopes and wishes and fears. Even when psychology emerges as a separate discipline, it comes trailing clouds of philosophy and ethics and common sense. Consequently, a first step toward understanding the psychological systems of to-day is a survey, however brief, of some of the outstanding psychological views of the past.

Not that it is possible to go back to the beginning. Even in the early Greek cosmologies, before the distinction had been made between mind and body, many of the conceptions found in modern psychology, many of its characteristic ways of dealing with its material, were present and in general outline mature. One of these is the attempt that runs through the whole cosmological period to reduce the universe to its elements. The early Greeks, with the utmost directness, wanted to know what the world was made of. Their answer was found when they had analyzed the complexity of the world as they saw it into some one element —water, air, atoms—or into a system of elements. The task they set themselves was that of reducing the complex to the simple, and their assumption was that the complex and the manifold form the world of appearance, in distinction to the underlying reality, which is simple. This task and this assumption have never ceased to appeal to the human intellect. They imply that the universe, or that part of it which one is investigating, can be understood by discovering the units of which it is made. Physics has found such units in atoms; biology, in cells; and psychology, depending upon the point of view adopted, in simple ideas, sensations, or bits of behavior involving elementary stimulus-response connections. But whatever the unit, the principle of construction is always the same; it involves in some form, coarse or subtle, the conception of the universe as a composition of parts, a mixture of simples. To a manipulative animal like man, this is a long step toward making the world intelligible. He knows what it is made of; he can see how the parts are put together; if he had the parts, he could put them together himself. It is true that the engaging simplicity which characterizes this view at first glance grows less apparent on examination; difficulties emerge that are not immediately evident. But so long as one does not pry too curiously below the level of common sense, the method is satisfying and useful. It has repeatedly proved its effectiveness by achievement; and it is beyond question one of the readiest and most dominant responses of human beings faced with complex situations. It is a method that appears over and over, in one form after another, in the attempt to deal with psychological material.

Democritus, the last of the ancient cosmologists, represents this way of looking at things in the most finished form it assumed in Greek thought. The nimble-witted Greeks had not permitted the cosmological speculations to go their ways without criticism. Early in the sixth century b.c., Thales, the first Greek philosopher known to history, had found his unit in a concrete substance, water. But this position was only a starting-point, and the story of the development that followed is one of speculation submitted to criticism, and of fresh speculation submitted to fresh criticism. Out of this development, about a century and a half later, came the formulation of Democritus, free from the more obvious difficulties of the earliest speculations, clear, intelligible, complete, and abstract. According to Democritus the universe is made of atoms. The atoms are small particles of matter in motion; they move in different ways; they are different in size and form, but they move according to necessity or law. Man, like the rest of the world, is composed of atoms, of soul atoms and body atoms, which are alike material but which differ from each other in that the soul atoms are finer and more active. Man's thoughts and deeds, all the events of his life, are determined as rigidly as the courses of the stars. In Democritus, atomism is definitely allied with materialism and determinism, which in his thought appear in their clearest and least ambiguous forms and with their logical implications for human actions and destinies fully recognized.

A second development rose as a criticism of the first. Long before the time of Democritus, there were philosophers who saw difficulties in the apparently simple device of reducing the world to elements. One of these was Heraclitus, who expressed his dissatisfaction somewhat paradoxically in the thesis that the element which constitutes all nature is fire. But though Heraclitus apparently meant fire in the literal sense—as literally as Thales meant water—he saw as its significant characteristic, impermanence or change. At the core of the universe he found no lasting substance, nothing solid, nothing enduring, nothing that could serve as a stable element. The very mountains, he pointed out, are not the same from age to age, nor from day to day; one cannot step into the same stream twice. Only change is real: "Everything flows" is his central teaching. Essentially this doctrine is a critique of common sense. "Things" are not real; they are forever vanishing, passing into their opposites. The senses may reveal what seem to be substantial objects, but thought, transcending appearance, perceives reality, which is change. Whereas common sense sees *things,* Heraclitus saw processes, and in doing so employed a conception similar to that used in the physics of to-day, which is depriving matter of its stability and solidity. The relevance to psychology of this mode of thinking is immediately apparent. A psychologist cannot have even a slight first-hand knowledge of his subject-matter without realizing that he is not dealing with bits or particles of anything stable and substantial, but with transient processes. Even in those systems of psychology which reduce their material to elements, the elements, whether bits of consciousness or bits of behavior, are defined as processes. It is true that, having been defined as processes, they are often, in actual practice, treated as fixed units, for the habit of thinking in terms of fixed units is tenacious. But when attention is turned upon psychological material directly, the character of change presents itself as an inescapable fact. Psychology is continually emphasizing the point that it is dealing with processes and events.

A third development was that started by Anaxagoras. Like Heraclitus, Anaxagoras believed that a reduction to elements did not completely explain the world, but his criticism was less radical than that of Heraclitus. He was not troubled by the thought that there is no substance, and that therefore no elements exist. Anaxagoras in fact postulated an indefinite number of qualitatively different elements. His problem rose from the consideration that, granted one knew the elements, one would still be unable to account for the world as we see it. The *arrangement* of the elements he found as important as their existence. The *order* of the world must be explained as well as its constituents, and the ordering principle he found in *nous,* something corresponding to human intelligence or reason, but not yet contrasted with matter. This doctrine is significant to psychology partly because it singles out a psychological process for special attention and partly because, in emphasizing the question of arrangement, of order, of pattern, it brought up a problem that repeatedly recurs in psychology. It is the latter point— the protest against a reduction to elements as a complete explanation—that gives the philosophy of Anaxagoras its chief significance for modern psychology. It is a view closely related to the persistent protests against the various forms of sensationalism, and it is not unlike the revolt that the *Gestalt* movement, one of the newest of the psychologies, is directing against psychological atomism to-day.

A fourth movement represents a very different way of accounting for the universe. Its origin is associated with the name of Pythagoras and its doctrine is that reality can be understood through number. In the Pythagorean school, this doctrine took on the character of a cult. It was surrounded by mystical and fantastic and sometimes trivial teachings, and was accompanied by such specific and apparently meaningless rules of conduct as the prohibition against eating beans. But the attempt to know the world in quantitative terms is itself of the highest importance, and it is interesting that such an attempt made its appearance as early as it did. Science, striving for exact knowledge, has always eagerly joined hands with quantitative thought and, as will appear later, the successful application of quantitative methods to psychological material was historically one of the decisive factors in making psychology a science.

But gradually, in the course of these inquiries into the nature of the universe, in the midst of all these theories, each claiming to be right and each supporting its claim with a degree of plausibility, there arose a question of another sort—the question "How can we know?" Primarily this was not a psychological question; it was not "How *do* we know?" but "How *can* we know?" and it was occasioned less by curiosity about the *process* of knowledge than by concern for the *validity* of knowledge. Still, this concern for the validity of knowledge led to inquiries into the processes of knowledge. Very early, philosophers had distinguished between knowledge gained by the senses and knowledge achieved by reason. They had noted, too, that knowledge is relative, that our knowledge is *human* knowledge, gained from a human point of view, colored by human ways of knowing. The next step was to inquire whether any human mode of conceiving the world can have objective validity; whether inquiry into the ultimate nature of reality is not, after all, quite futile.

The Sophists, starting from this point of view, gave a radically new direction to Greek thought. They turned definitely from cosmology to human affairs, and thus became interested in matters that may be termed, in a broad sense, psychological. Furthermore their approach was practical. It was inevitable that the very wealth of speculation about the universe, the spectacle of successive explanations of all but equal plausibility, should impress some minds chiefly with the uselessness of such speculation. The Sophists, at any rate, refused to occupy themselves with attempts to understand the fundamental nature of reality. They turned instead to their business, which was the teaching of philosophy as a way of life, and of rhetoric and dialectic as practical skills. Deliberately superficial and adroitly practical, they undertook, for pay, to train young men in the arts of persuasion—arts that were distinctly useful in the Greek city-state where men rose to power by convincing their equals and swaying the populace. There were, of course, Sophists and Sophists, representing a range of intellectual integrity from delight in the unhampered exercise of critical intelligence to the wish to "make the worse appear the better reason." But whatever their views on the usefulness or uselessness of dialectic, the process itself interested them. In it they found something with which to busy themselves, something that could be exercised and cultivated and controlled, something, furthermore, which—whatever the ultimate nature of reality might be—was important in the world of affairs. With an attitude curiously similar to that of modern applied psychology, they turned to specific performances and concrete situations, far more interested in manipulating the immediate and the actual than in delving into the fundamental and the profound. It would be a mistake, of course, to ascribe wholesale to modern workers in applied psychology the views associated with the Greek Sophists, but whatever the theoretical starting-point of their activities, something in their temper is similar. The great virtue of applied psychology is its healthy association with the actual and the immediate, its practice of keeping close to, or at least within sight of, materials that human beings can manipulate and control.

An indirect consequence of the teachings of the Sophists was the philosophy of Socrates, one of the most picturesque figures in the brilliant society of the Athens of the fifth century B.C. Socrates was ugly, charming, eccentric, convivial, and high-minded, a man who made it the serious business of his life to inveigle young men into philosophical conversations and to lead them, by artful questioning, to see that their ideas about the most fundamental and even the most commonplace affairs of life were confused and self-contradictory. His aim was to confront his listeners with the necessity of defining their terms exactly, and to urge them to discover what reason revealed as true. His success in making his hearers question apparently obvious truths was so great that as an old man he was tried and condemned to death on the charge of undermining the religion of the state and corrupting its youth.

Like the Sophists, Socrates believed that inquiry into the nature of the cosmos is futile, but unlike them, he believed that one kind of knowledge is obtainable—knowledge of the self. Furthermore, he believed that it is this kind of knowledge that men really need, knowledge that will reveal their duty and enable them to lead virtuous lives. Socrates believed that virtue is the outcome of knowledge and that evil is fundamentally ignorance—an early instance of the belief repeatedly encountered in psychology that the intellectual or rational principle is dominant in man. Socrates believed, too, that truth is implicit in the human intellect; that it needs only to be drawn out and clarified. To demonstrate this point, he led an untaught slave, aided only by skilful questions, to discover for himself that the square on the hypotenuse of a right-angled triangle is equal to the sum of the squares on the other two sides.

And yet, Socrates was more interested in the total nature of man than in any of his particular abilities. Essentially, his interest in human beings was ethical, and this fact is responsible for one of the distinctive features of his psychological approach. He considers men not as isolated units but always in relation to their fellows and to the state. In a sense, this view is like that of the modern behaviorists, who believe in studying the whole organism in its relations to its environment. It is true that behaviorism in its early days tended to be interested largely in the physical environment, whereas Socrates was interested chiefly in the social environment; but of late behaviorism has been placing more and more emphasis on the social influences in human life and is coming into closer and closer relations with ethical problems.

Socrates' most distinguished pupil was Plato, who formulated for the first time the clear-cut distinction between mind and matter that has figured prominently in psychology down to the present time. Both by birth and by temperament Plato was an aristocrat, a man who had little interest in the common affairs of everyday existence, and who gave himself over as completely as possible to the life of reason. For Plato believed that in the life of the intellect man was expressing his highest possibilities. In his life of contemplation, he was deeply impressed by the difference between *ideas,* which are revealed by reason, and *things,* which are revealed by the senses; and placing ideas in a world by themselves, he regarded them as far more real than the world known to the senses. Ideas, Plato noted, have a perfection that is never present in concrete things. The idea of beauty, for instance, is permanent, flawless, immutable, absolute; whereas beautiful things, which are beautiful only in relation to something else, are imperfect, changing, and impermanent. To Plato it seemed evident that the permanent, the perfect, the changeless, and the absolute must be more real than the perishable, changeful, imperfect objects which, however much of beauty they may contain, can only approximate pure beauty as such. He therefore posited a world of ideas, of which the "real" world—the world revealed by the senses—is only an imperfect copy. Matter is the substance in which ideas express themselves, but its very nature makes their perfect expression impossible, for it imposes its own limitations upon them and robs them of their purity. Thus Plato not only established a distinction between mind and matter, but associated those terms with opposed sets of values. Mind was identified with the good and the beautiful. Matter was the enemy, the baser part of man and of the universe, something to be struggled against and subdued. This distinction, along with the values with which Plato invested the terms, has persisted to the present time. There is still a tendency in everyday thought to regard mind as lofty and matter as ignoble. In some quarters, however, there has been a curious inversion. The triumphs of modern science have been triumphs of physical science; the scientific method and point of view have been associated with the study of physical nature; and to those who have acquired a set of values different from Plato's—who contrast the scientific and the unscientific, not the noble and the base—mind and matter have changed places in the scale of values. It is matter that lends itself to the ways of science; it is mind that is disturbing and untractable. By easy stages mind is identified first with the highest good, then with the ineffable and the unattainable, and finally with the mystical and the unscientific; and in consequence the Platonic distinction, largely through the values that cling to its terms, even to-day determines attitudes in science.

When Plato considered men, he naturally thought of them from the standpoint of his own interest in the life of the intellect. Ranking men's powers from highest to lowest, he named first reason, which resides in the head; then courage, which resides in the chest; and last sense and appetition, which reside in the abdomen. Plato looked upon these powers as parts of the soul and thus employed a mode of thought similar to that which was later to be called faculty psychology. Plato also recognized individual differences among men. In the ideal state, the Republic, men were to be chosen for their several duties with reference to their abilities. Those endowed with superior reason were to be rulers; those endowed with courage, warriors; the rest of mankind were to be artisans, tradesmen, laborers, and slaves—necessary to the state, but lower in rank than warriors and statesmen, as the appetites and senses are lower than courage and reason. This part of Plato's thought, however, has had relatively little effect on modern psychology. The chief source of his influence is his distinction between mind and matter aiid his identification of mind with the unearthly—a distinction that still lives in the belief held by some psychologists that the mental can never be an object of scientific knowledge.

But the Greeks themselves did not despair of understanding the mind. Aristotle, Plato's pupil and successor, and to some extent his rival, in attempting to make a comprehensive survey of being, addressed himself to the things of the mind in much the same manner as to anything else in the natural order. However, his distinction between mind and matter was not the same as Plato's. He thought rather in terms of matter and form. In outlook and temperament, Aristotle was very different from Plato. He was interested in the concrete and the actual as Plato was not, and turning his attention in that direction, he found no sharp distinction between matter and mind or, as he put it, between matter and form. It seemed to him that neither existed apart from the other. Form exists in the concrete object, he said, not as a separate entity. Matter is potential form; the actual object is form realized in matter, it is the union of form and matter. Marble is matter to the statue; the statue is form realized in marble. Furthermore, the distinction between form and matter is not absolute; the marble that is matter to the statue is form to lower organizations of matter. Thus concrete reality arranges itself in a series in which it is impossible to indicate a point and say that on this side there is matter, on the other, form. This concept of continuity, too, though in a context very different from Aristotle's, is one that is often encountered in the psychology of to-day. Like Aristotle, modern psychologists, when confronted with concrete data, find it impossible to fix hard and fast boundaries; they cannot point to a dividing line between conscious and unconscious processes, between intelligence and feeble-mindedness, between anger and fear, between sanity and insanity, between instinct and reason, between childhood and maturity, between psychology and physiology. They deal far less in absolute distinctions than in series in which there are continuous gradations between extremes.

Closely related to the concept of matter and form is the practice of explaining phenomena in terms of final causes. Aristotle made one exception to the rule that form never exists alone. The final form, the Supreme Being, can be matter to nothing beyond. It is therefore pure form; and

since all matter strives to realize itself in form, this final
form is the goal toward which all nature moves. Therefore
all nature, including human nature, is explained teleologically
as tending toward an end or goal. But since science deals
with proximate causes, with the events immediately antecedent to a given effect, it has not been hospitable to the
notion of teleology. Another implication of Aristotle's general scheme, however, has very definitely appeared in modern
psychology. In the world of nature, Aristotle finds, matter and
form are always related. If the whole body were an eye, the
soul would be seeing. The body exists for the sake of the soul,
but the soul exists only in and through the body. The activities of the soul, in other words, are activities of bodily
organs. It is as impossible to desire and strive without the
appropriate physical structures as to see without eyes. He
regards particular psychological processes as activities or
functions of physical structures, existing in a world where
such activity is definitely related to a particular physical
constitution.

But in the soul, Aristotle distinguished between a mortal
and an immortal part. Activities that are functions of bodily
structures perish with the body, but there is in man an
active intellect that is not a function of the body. It is this
active intellect which Aristotle declares to be simple, immaterial, and immortal; and it was this part of Aristotle's
teaching, his recognition of the active intellect, which claimed
the greatest interest of the schoolmen of the Middle Ages.

In addition to his treatment of psychological processes
in the general scheme of things, Aristotle made a specific
contribution to psychological theory in his discussion of memory, particularly in his famous statement of the principles
of association. These principles—association by contrast, by
similarity, and by contiguity in time and space—were given
as empirical rules. In the apparently fortuitous way in which

ideas present themselves, Aristotle saw not chance, but law. Both the general conception of association and the particular rules he formulated exerted a great influence on the development of psychology centuries later.

Aristotle was the last of the major philosophers of antiquity. His death, in the last quarter of the fourth century, B.C., marks the close of the most original and productive period in Greek thought. Among the philosophies that flourished during the closing centuries of the ancient world, the views held by the Stoics and the Epicureans are the most interesting to psychology because of the contrasting attitudes they took on what might be considered a practical application of psychology. Both schools were occupied primarily with the problem of making the most of human life. In general, the Stoics stood for suppression, the Epicureans for expression of natural impulses. The Stoics believed in subduing desire to reason in the interests of virtue, which was to be sought for its own sake; the Epicureans believed in so ordering the expression of the natural impulses as to achieve happiness and tranquillity. It is interesting to see the attitudes of these rival schools persisting down to the present day in modern theories about the control of human nature and the achievement of happiness and virtue.

Thus, while psychology was still a part of philosophy, many of the patterns of thought that were to become prominent later had already appeared. This means neither that the later modes of thought were consciously borrowed from the earlier, nor that the discoveries of modern science were implicit in ancient speculations. It means rather that the same problems arose in human affairs, that they were perceived in the same ways, and that they gave rise to the same methods of attack. Then, as now, there were the problems of elements and form, of the parts and the whole, of the relation of mind and body, of function and structure, of process and substance, and of the control and management of human nature in the interests of achievement, virtue, and happiness.

From the standpoint of positive contributions to a scientific psychology, the Middle Ages are relatively unimportant. Their characteristic approach to psychological problems is found in the scholastic discussions about the nature and attributes of the soul. But, as every one knows, these dis cussions have often been cited as the very antithesis of scientific procedure. They began not with questions, but with accepted truth, based on authority. They proceeded not by using observation and induction, but by the elaborate unfolding of the implications of concepts and the logical deduction of consequences. Their final appeal was not to factual evidence, but to logical validity. Their method of thought has been used as the example *par excellence* of speculation in the air, of reasoning operating without the ballast of empirical fact. Yet the negative consequences of just this practice were of the utmost importance to science. Many of the characteristics of science—not, it is true, its essential nature, but an appreciable number of its accidental features—can be explained as a revolt from the excesses of that procedure. Its disgust at dogmatism and its dread of untested speculation are clearly survivals of emotional attitudes developed in the necessarily violent struggle against the appeal to authority and the practice of empty deduction that medieval scholasticism had made the accepted intellectual fashion.

The modern period in philosophy, however, is full of anticipations of the psychologies of the present. It contains, in fact, so many previsions of problems and theories which are being considered to-day that it is impossible to attempt a comprehensive survey of them. Many points of view interest ing and suggestive in themselves must be passed over, and attention limited to those lines of thought which have some obvious historical relationship to the development of the scientific point of view in psychology. The most consecutive of these is the line of critical inquiry which ran through Descartes, the British empiricists, and Kant, and which had among its by-products the growth of two schools of prescientific psychology, associationism in Great Britain and Herbartianism in Germany.

Very near the source of this movement was René Descartes, whose work in the first half of the seventeenth century is altogether typical of the early modern period in its revolt against the dogmatism of the scholastic tradition. Descartes himself, however, was anything but a rebel by temperament. He was a candid, very cautious, extraordinarily reasonable man who, though he had devoted himself to the pursuit of learning, discovered upon reaching maturity that there was nothing that he knew with certainty. Finding that he could doubt some of man's strongest beliefs, he deliberately undertook to use doubt as a method—to doubt everything it was possible to doubt, in the hope of arriving at the self-evident and the indubitable. He found that he could doubt a good deal: he could doubt the existence of God, the existence of the world, even the existence of his own body. The one thing he could not doubt was the fact that he was doubting, and the certainty that his doubt—i.e., his thought—existed gave him the foundation of his system. He stated his conviction in the famous formula *"I think, therefore I am,"* and treated the proposition as an axiom. He thereby established the belief in his own existence as a thinking being, and then by a process of deductive reasoning, in the existence of God and the world, including his own physical body. His proof of the existence of God consists in the argument that he, the doubter **and**

an imperfect being, nevertheless has the idea of God, a per
fect being. And since the perfect cannot be dependent on
the imperfect, it is necessary to assume the existence of God
to account for the idea of God. Then, if God exists, the world
must exist, for the ideas we perceive clearly and distinctly
to be true—not the ideas we accept merely on the evidence
of imagination and the senses—must be true, "for otherwise
it could not be that God, who is wholly perfect and veracious,
should have placed them in us." Thus Descartes came out
at the end of his reasoning with everything that his doubt
had destroyed. The difference between his first state and his
last was not a difference in the objects of belief, but in the
fact that they were now rationally established.

This point is significant. It means that though Descartes
struck at the dogmatism of scholastic thought, he did not
attack its intellectualistic procedures. His appeal was not to
experience but to reason. If there is anything in Descartes
more remarkable than his deliberate attempt at a thoroughgoing skepticism, it is his sober faith in the power of the
human intellect to straighten out the existing confusion. Apparently Descartes did not consider the possibility that reason might be inadequate to the task. When he discovered
that he could be sure of nothing, he summoned the aid of
reason as a matter of course, and systematically set about
the task of constructing a secure intellectual foundation
for the universe. He struck a telling blow against medieval
subservience to authority, but in doing so he utilized the
deductive procedure that is as characteristic of medieval
thought as is its dogmatism.

There are several of Descartes's specific views that are
of particular interest to psychology. The most far-reaching
of these is his dualism, which, though different from Plato's
in its derivation, is similar in its effects. According to Descartes, there are two substances: mind and matter, the think-

ing substance and the extended substance. This conception involved him in some interesting and enlightening difficulties; he had separated mind and matter so completely that he found it hard to bring them together again into any working harmony. One outcome of this situation was the theory that animals, since they have no *res cogitans*, or thinking substance, are automata—an interpretation of complex living organisms that is especially interesting in the light of recent mechanistic interpretations of animal and human behavior. Descartes was, in fact, a thoroughgoing mechanist so far as the whole material world is concerned. He believed that all the actions of the human body—the movements of the muscles and tendons, the activities of respiration, even the processes of sensation—can be explained according to mechanical principles. It was Descartes, indeed, who introduced the concept of reflex action, which has been so widely used ever since in mechanistic explanations of bodily processes. Yet Descartes stopped short of making human beings *mere* automata; he believed that in each person there is a reasonable soul, a thinking substance, which has the power to direct and alter the mechanical course of events. This soul operates through the pineal gland at the base of the brain, and influences the movements of the body by acting on the animal spirits in the blood, which by entering one nerve or another determine which movement shall occur. But the action of the body itself, though subject to the direction of the soul, is strictly mechanical. The relation between mind and body, as Descartes saw it, is thus one of interaction. The mind acts on the body in the manner just described, and is acted upon by the body through its modes of sensation, emotion, and action. Just how two substances so totally different can influence each other Descartes failed to explain, but he stated the position of dualism and interactionism with the utmost clearness and thus reaffirmed the distinction between mind and matter in modern thought.

Another point in Descartes's teachings that has a rather direct bearing on psychology is his belief in innate ideas. Descartes, who was a mathematician as well as a philosopher, assumed that there are certain necessary truths or axioms which constitute the basis of demonstrable knowledge. These truths, he assumed, are inherent in man's nature, and when perceived are self-evident. Despite his intention to doubt everything, Descartes had not questioned the existence of innate ideas. The question, however, was raised by some of his critics, and attained such importance that it became the starting-point of the long line of inquiry about which the philosophers of Great Britain developed their critical empiricism.

One of these, an older contemporary of Descartes, was Thomas Hobbes, a blunt, hard-headed British Royalist, who wrote a number of treatises on human nature in which he paid particular attention to man's relations to the state. The *Leviathan*, published in 1651, two years after the execution of Charles I, was probably the most important of these. This book is primarily a political treatise, but running through its treatment of political problems is a tendency that is of special interest to psychology, the tendency to overrationalize human conduct. Hobbes's main purpose was to justify the absolute power of the ruler. He did so by explaining that first of all there is a natural impulse in all men to take what they want and what they can get. This impulse, however, leads inevitably to conflict. Every one is at war with every one else; nobody is safe; every one is to some extent defeated in his purposes. This intolerable situation is terminated when men, prompted by fear and self-interest, see that they can gain security, and more of the goods of life, by giving up their natural right to take whatever they can, and by receiving in return the assurance of protection from the aggressions and depredations of their fellow-men. But this state of affairs can be maintained only if there is a power strong enough to enforce it, and this power is created when the members of the state agree to hand over their rights and powers to one central authority. This voluntary agreement is the justification for the absolute power of the ruler.

From the standpoint of psychology, a significant point in Hobbes's discussion is the use it makes of the notion of the "rational man," the notion that human conduct is dominated by reason. Though fear and self-interest, it is true, are regarded as the motives of action, reason suggests the "convenient articles of peace" and guides the course of conduct. The fear and self-interest are calculating, not blindly impulsive. It is, in other words, reason that manages the situation. Hobbes thus supplies another illustration of the common tendency to think of man as the reasoning animal, to explain the course of his actions as planned and foreseen, rather than as determined by chance; as directed finally by intellectual considerations, rather than by anything so unrational as feeling, emotion, and the accidents of life. Psychology is continually discovering that human beings like to assign reason the major rôle in their affairs; and it is peculiarly indicative of the strength of this tendency that it should appear in the realistic and cynical Hobbes, who has never been accused of attempting to draw a picture of human nature that is even mildly flattering.

But Hobbes's attitude toward the rational man was less an expression of himself than of the current mode of thought. It is significant in fact *because* it is an expression of the current mode. Hobbes's other contributions to psychology, however, mark out new paths. One of these is a general treat ment of psychological processes which places them unequivocally in the stream of natural events. Hobbes had evidently been impressed by the work of Galileo, and seizing upon the suggested possibility of a naturalistic explanation, he attempted to account for all human activity, not excepting the psychological, in terms of motion. Sensation, which is the source of knowledge, is motion communicated by the external object to the brain. Imagination and memory are continuations of that motion; "decaying sense" is Hobbes's term. The mind has no content, however complex, that is not reducible to these terms. Even the sequences of thought, however accidental they may seem, are matters of natural law. Just as ideas themselves are determined by objects acting on the senses, so the transitions from one idea to another are determined by the relations they bear to each other in the original experience. This, of course, implies the basic principle of associationism: that one idea succeeds another not by chance but according to law. It was in this connection that Hobbes made a distinction between the two kinds of thought which have since been called free and controlled association. In the former, "thoughts are said to wander and seem impertinent to one another as in a dream"; in the latter there is some "passionate thought to govern and direct those that follow to itself." And yet, even in the apparently "wild ranging" of free association, Hobbes regarded the course of thought as determined. His psychology was materialistic, mechanistic, and deterministic throughout, a psychology in which even the most casual imaginings of man take their place in the orderly stream of events that constitute the world of nature.

It was not Hobbes, however, but his successor, John Locke, who raised the specific question that gave the impetus to British empiricism. From the standpoint of psychology, Locke stands at the starting-point of two movements. One, a line of critical inquiry carried on by Berkeley, Hume, and Kant, led to the destruction of the old rational psychology, that system of thought which, claiming a knowledge of the soul that was based on intuition and deduction, held that its knowledge was demonstrable as absolutely valid. The other was a more positive movement, which, expressing itself partly in the common-sense philosophy of the Scottish school, and partly in the teachings of the British associationists, led to a psychology that, though it was empirical as opposed to rational, stopped just short of becoming experimental.

The origin of Locke's problem is singularly appropriate. During a discussion with a few friends, it occurred to him that, since they were making no progress toward a solution, their first task ought to be to inquire into the nature of the understanding itself; to find out what matters it was capable of coping with, and what matters lay outside its scope. He suggested the problem, therefore, and agreed to present his thoughts on the topic at the next meeting of the group. Accordingly, he assembled his reflections on the subject for a brief paper, but this question, so shrewdly put, occupied him at intervals for twenty years of his very busy life. His final answer was given in the *Essay concerning Human Understanding,* published in 1690, when the author was fifty-eight years old.

Locke's problem, it will be noted, was not strictly psychological. Like the Greek philosophers, he was interested chiefly in the *validity* of knowledge; he was not examining the process of knowledge for its own sake. Only incidentally was his question "How *do* we know?" Essentially it was "What are we justified in accepting as genuine knowledge?" Primarily Locke's enterprise was an epistemological inquiry, but it turned attention to psychological problems.

When Locke examined the constitution of knowledge, he

became convinced that all knowledge is derived from a single
source, experience. But experience itself is of two sorts:
some of it comes through sensation, some through reflection;
some, in other words, comes through impressions from sensible objects in the external world, some through our awareness of the operations of our own minds. There are no
other sources of knowledge. There are no innate ideas. That
we do not start with a stock in trade of axioms or necessary
truths is a point on which Locke is especially insistent. For
page after careful page, he wages war against the notion
that the mind is equipped with ideas which are independent
of experience. Originally the mind is "white paper, void of
characters, without any ideas." "Nothing in the intellect
which was not first in the senses" is sometimes given as a
statement of Locke's theory of knowledge. Sensation and reflection give us simple ideas, and simple ideas are the stuff
of which all human thought is made.

To Locke all this was interesting and important because
it indicated the capacities, and especially the limitations, of
the human understanding. It gave him a criterion for testing the validity of knowledge. If an idea could be traced to
its legitimate source, experience, it was acceptable; if no
basis in experience could be found, it was specious—it had
slipped in surreptitiously and had no foundation in fact.
Locke's analysis of knowledge, however, had a psychological as well as an epistemological significance. It established
in the thought of the time an atomistic conception of mind
—a conception of mind as composed of units combined in
various ways. It provided a set of simple ideas and a plan
of mental organization which suggested that it is necessary
only to discover how the simple ideas are put together in
order to understand the human mind and all its possibilities.
It is this positive side of Locke's teaching, this promise of
making the mind intelligible in terms of units and their com-

binations, which led to the development of the school of psychological associationism.

But the negative or critical sides of Locke's thought also had important consequences. Locke's explanation of knowledge as composed of simple ideas, together with his attempt to account for knowledge of a real external world, drove him to a distinction between primary and secondary qualities. Primary qualities are those like motion, extension, figure, solidity, and number, which exist in the object itself. Secondary qualities are those like colors, tastes, and sounds, which depend on the sensory equipment in the organism. Thus, solidity really exists in the external world, but color does not, for color is something we ourselves contribute because our sense-organs are what they are.

But is there any real difference between primary and secondary qualities? This question was raised by George Berkeley, a brilliant young Irishman, who later became Bishop of Cloyne. Berkeley put this question in 1710, in *A Treatise concerning the Principles of Human Knowledge.* In entire agreement with Locke, he pointed out that our knowledge of the external world comes through the senses. All that we know about an apple, for instance, is what our senses tell us. We know that it is red and sweet and fragrant because we have sensations of vision and taste and smell; we know that it is solid and extended because we have sensations of touch—because we feel sensations in the skin and muscles when it offers resistance to pressure, and when we make movements of the muscles in handling it. Is there any difference, then, between our knowledge of solidity and extension, which are primary qualities, and of redness and fragrance, which are secondary? All are derived from sensation and from no other source. Locke himself said: "Let the eye not see light or colors, nor the ear hear sound; let the palate not taste, nor the nose smell; and all colors, tastes,

odors, and sounds, as they are such particular ideas, vanish
and cease." Berkeley simply carried Locke's reasoning a step
further. Solidity, extension, and all other primary qualities
are likewise known only through perception, and are in exactly the same case as are the secondary qualities. The
apple is *all* sensation; it is *nothing but* sensation; its *esse* is
percipi. That *to be* consists in *being perceived* is Berkeley's
central doctrine, and in making his point, he appeals directly
to experience. Confident that the feat is impossible, he asks
the reader to imagine any of the qualities of objects—primary as well as secondary—without a mind that perceives
them. Take away the perception, he says, and the quality
disappears. As there can be no red without the perception
of red, there can be no hardness without the perception of
hardness. To put the point plainly, there is no material
substance. We know only sensory qualities; we never get
beyond them; and if we try to get beyond them and infer
that there is a substance underlying them, something that
supports them and in which they inhere, we are really adding nothing. We are simply making an empty declaration,
utterly gratuitous and baseless, and in the end inconceiv-
able. Locke, who stuck to common sense, retained a core
of material substance in the external world; Berkeley, who
stuck to a course of logical reasoning, waved it aside.

Or hardly that, for Berkeley did not blink the difference
between perceived objects and imagined ones. The former,
he said, are independent of our volition; they are there
whether we choose or not; furthermore, they have an order
and a coherence and a steadiness that we do not impose upon
them. They are not subject to our own whims; they have
a reality outside us. But this reality, Berkeley insists, cannot be corporeal. His analysis has shown that material substance is unreal; that the existence of things depends on
their being perceived; that external objects have no core of

bodily substance; that no such core is necessary or even imaginable. Still, the coerciveness, independence, order, and stability of objects are facts that must be accounted for; and Berkeley explains these qualities by saying that they reside in the perceiving mind of God—a concept that to him is free from the contradiction and the emptiness which he finds in the notion of material substance. As our ideas are to our minds, the whole order of nature is to God's mind. The existence of things, finally, consists in God's perception. To Berkeley, this was the essential point of his whole treatise. Like Locke, he was interested in his psychological analysis chiefly for the sake of its metaphysical outcome. But from the standpoint of historical development, the positive side of his thinking has had little influence. It was the critical, destructive side of his philosophy that bore fruit in subsequent thought.

And yet, in spite of the fact that his interests were primarily metaphysical, Berkeley is the author of what is probably the first strictly psychological treatise—it may almost be said, of the first psychological monograph. His *New Theory of Vision*, published a year before the *Treatise*, attacks a psychological problem for its own sake, the problem of showing how "we perceive by sight, the distance, magnitude, and situation of objects." Berkeley undertakes in this study to show how we perceive distance or the third dimension, and he does so not because of any ethical or philosophical implications of the problem, but simply because the problem exists. Berkeley remarks that we cannot see distance directly because "distance being a line directed endwise to the eye, it projects only one point in the fund of the eye. Which point remains invariably the same whether the distance be longer or shorter." His explanation is that we perceive distance as a result of experience; more specifically, that certain visual impressions become associated with the sensations of touch and movement which occur when we make the necessary ocular adjustments in looking at near or far objects, and when we move our bodies or parts of our bodies in approaching or withdrawing from seen objects. This is probably the first application of the principle of association to a strictly psychological problem. Perhaps it should be mentioned parenthetically that Berkeley seemed to an unusual degree aware of the rôle of tactual and muscular sensations in psychological processes. For some reason, the sensations that make us aware of our own bodily movements are more likely to be overlooked than are those from the eye and the ear, and they attracted general notice rather late in the development of psychology. And yet Berkeley utilized these sensations not only to account for the perception of distance, but to show that primary qualities, like secondary ones, consist ultimately in being sensed or perceived. The recognition of tactual and muscular sensations was therefore involved in the central doctrine of his philosophy.

Berkeley raised still another distinctly psychological problem, that of the existence of abstract ideas. In this case, however, the problem was undertaken because of its bearing on his metaphysical position. Locke, who had attacked the notion of innate ideas, had nevertheless recognized the existence of abstract ideas. But Berkeley denied the existence of abstract ideas, and he did so avowedly because of the bearing of this question on his contention that the notion of material substance is, when closely scrutinized, unthinkable. Berkeley's discussion is interesting from the standpoint of psychology, because he evidently identifies idea and image. Since he cannot frame the idea of a man unless it be of "either a white, or a black, or a tawny, a straight or a crooked, a tall, or a low, or middle sized man," since he cannot form an idea of motion that is distinct from the body moving, and which is neither swift nor slow, curvilinear nor rectilinear, he considers the belief in abstract ideas a "delusion of words." Though the point did not come out explicitly in the discussion, the difference between Berkeley and Locke on the possibility of abstract ideas really involved the question of the possibility of imageless thought. In the background were the questions: Must our ideas be copies of the things we are thinking about? Or if not that, must they contain some sensory content that in some way represents them? Can there be thoughts that have no sensory content at all, and which nevertheless have a genuine function as thought? Such questions as these were implied in Berkeley's inquiry; but they did not emerge as strictly psychological problems until two centuries later, when the imageless-thought controversy gave them the clearness of formulation that an experimental setting made possible.

Berkeley, of course, had carried Locke's critical analysis much farther than Locke had intended, but it was carried still farther by the Scottish philosopher, David Hume. Berkeley had disposed of the concept of material substance, denying the objective existence of things or objects outside experiencing minds or Mind. He had not, however, doubted the existence of mind itself, nor had he questioned the principle of causality. Rather he had assumed both, giving as the cause of the characteristics that distinguish percepts from images, the divine mind which perceives them. As Berkeley left it, the universe still had some support; it was not a mere kaleidoscope of ideas. This support Hume proceeded to remove by questioning both the existence of the thinking self and the principle of causality.

Hume's criticism of the self is strikingly like Berkeley's criticism of material substance. When he tries to examine the self, Hume explains, he finds nothing but particular perceptions—love or hate, pleasure or pain, light or shade—

nothing to correspond to the self that the philosophers describe as a simple substance persisting through all change. In the idea of the self he sees a baseless and unnecessary addition to observed facts, the same kind of groundless notion that Berkeley found in material substance.

In a similar manner, Hume disposes of causality. The idea of cause, he explains, contains the idea of necessary connection, but when he traces the idea back to the experiences from which it is presumably derived, he finds nothing of necessity, only contiguity and succession. Experience gives us nothing more than invariable temporal sequence; all that we actually see is that when A happens, B follows. The necessity that the notion of causality implies is nowhere to be found in experience. The idea of causation therefore has no objective validity. It is produced in the mind; it is not discovered in the object. The fact remains, however, that we have a strong belief in causality, a fact which Hume never denies, and which he attempts to explain. Our belief in causality he finds to be a matter of custom, or habit, or very strong association. All that we observe is that certain sequences invariably occur, but these sequences, repeated again and again, produce in the mind a strong disposition to connect the events that form them. If A has always been followed by B, the occurrence of A leads us to expect B. The principle of causality therefore is based on a habit or tendency or disposition in ourselves; there is no warrant that it is objectively valid.

Thus under Hume's criticism, the world collapsed into an aggregate of ideas, supported by no substance and connected by no necessity. Berkeley's criticism had removed material substance, but had left a world of orderly events, dependent on a spiritual substance. By applying the same kind of criticism that Berkeley himself used, Hume demolished whatever of order and substantiality Berkeley had left in the world. The world as Hume saw it was a drift of ideas, without connection, without permanence, without unity, without meaning, simply present and passing. Even to its author, there was something strained and unnatural in this conception. No one saw more clearly than Hume the discrepancy between the extreme skepticism to which his reasoning had led him and the demands of everyday life; and he offered no logical reconciliation. "I dine, I play a game of backgammon, I converse, and am merry with my friends"; so runs one of his comments, "and when, after three or four hours' amusement, I return to these speculations, they appear so cold and strained, and ridiculous, that I cannot find it in my heart to enter into them any farther."

Hume's successor in the critical movement was Immanuel Kant. But Kant found it impossible to accept with Hume's equanimity the outcome of Hume's destructive speculations. Kant could not stop with a situation in which the cogitations of the philosopher's study led to one view of the world and the demands of daily life to another. After all, Kant insisted, the world as we know it *is* a world of order; and this order, as Hume has clearly shown, cannot be derived from experience. Neither can it be denied. It must then be derived from the mind itself, which, instead of reflecting the order of an external world, imposes its own laws upon nature. This is the thesis which in 1781 Kant announced in the *Critique of Pure Reason,* a book that made its author, up to that time an obscure professor in the University of Königsberg, the leading figure in the philosophical world of the day.

Experience, according to Kant, is derived from two sources: things as they are in themselves, and the mind. Experience is a product, a creation, of the two. Experience begins when things in themselves act upon the senses, but the moment this happens, an elaborate machinery is set going that makes it forever impossible for us to know things as they are, independent of our ways of knowing. Not only is the content of our experience determined by our modes of sensation—a fact that had been sufficiently recognized—but its very form and arrangement, its order and organization, are determined by the mind that receives and molds it. Nothing can enter into our experience without arranging itself according to the laws of our nature: [2] first, according to the forms of immediate perception or intuition, space and time, which are purely subjective; second, according to the logical order imposed by the categories of the understanding, of which causality is one; and finally, into that unified world which is made necessary by the logical unity of the ego that apperceives all the contents of experience. The order and coherence that we see in nature are the order and coherence we impose upon nature. Things in themselves, therefore, can never be known as they are; they can be known only as they appear in experience, determined by the forms of our thought. Nature can never be discovered; reality, as it exists outside our experience, is forever beyond our reach. True metaphysical knowledge is impossible; only empirical knowledge is obtainable. We can never know the world as it is in itself, as it exists outside our ways of knowing. But neither can we know the experiencing soul directly—and this is the point which is particularly significant for psychology—for we know it not as it is in itself, but only as it appears in time, one of our forms of intuition. It is as impossible to know the soul as to know the world. Therefore rational psychology, the psychology that claimed to have direct knowledge of the soul, is as impossible as metaphysics. There remains only an empirical psychology, which cannot attempt to answer ultimate questions, any more than can an empirical science of physical nature. Neither the world nor the self

[2] Kant refers to a logical, not a temporal, order

can be known to the human mind in its true nature. It is useless to try to attain ultimate and absolute truth about either. Psychology, like physics, is an empirical science, or as Kant would say, a *mere* empirical science. Kant himself wrote, under the title of *Anthropology*, what amounted to an empirical psychology; but in his opinion psychology could never take high rank even as an empirical science, because its material is not reducible to quantitative terms and is therefore not susceptible of the exactness of treatment that characterizes true science. It was not as a psychologist, however, that Kant influenced psychology. It was as a critical philosopher announcing that the pretensions of rational psychology are groundless. His importance to psychology lies in the fact that he stands at the end of a line of critical inquiry in which, by examining its own instrument, the human intellect, philosophy made it increasingly clear that psychology, whatever it may be, is not metaphysics. Descartes started the movement by his appeal from authority to reason. Hobbes, Locke, Berkeley, and Hume, carrying their analyses through successive stages, arrived at a point where no absolute justification could be given for the authority of the intellect. Kant, while affirming the rôle of intellect in experience, asserted that it was valid only *within* the realm of experience, and that all knowledge which pretended to transcend experience, which pretended to be absolute and ultimately certain, was groundless. Rational psychology was part of this baseless knowledge. There was no more hope in psychology than in physics for absolute and certain knowledge. Psychology, like physics, could exist only as an empirical science.

In the meantime, the interest in the psychological aspects of experience itself did not wait for this metaphysical justification. It will be remembered that side by side with the critique of knowledge, there was another movement, more positive in character, which had its source in the empirical analysis of knowledge that Locke and his successors employed. One part of this movement expressed itself in the common-sense philosophy of the Scottish school. Its point of departure was Hume, as was Kant's, but the Scottish philosophers disposed of their distinguished fellow-countrymen far more summarily than did the painstaking Kant. The sturdy Scotch realists took their stand in a solid world that refused to be dispelled by subtle speculations. Subtle speculation was far less real to them than the objects of sense and of daily life, and if rational analysis left a picture of things so obviously at variance with reality as it appears to common sense, they considered it so much the worse for rational analysis. Thomas Reid, professor of philosophy at Edinburgh and a contemporary of Hume, was the founder of the school. He grounded his position on "instinct" and "common sense." The senses, he declared, make us immediately aware of an external world and they arouse in us an "invincible belief" in the existence of external objects. Though it is true that no reason can be given for our belief, its presence is indisputable, and the belief itself must therefore be explained as due to an original and instinctive tendency implanted in the human constitution. It has been suggested that the views of Hume and Reid are not after all very different, since both men hold that belief has no rational basis, but nevertheless exists. The story is told that when this point was suggested to Dr. Thomas Brown, one of Reid's followers, Brown replied: "Yes, Reid bawled out we must believe in an outward world; but added in a whisper, we can given no reason for our belief. Hume cries out we can give no reason for such a notion; and whispers, I own we cannot get rid of it." [3]

[3] G. H. Lewes, *The Biographical History of Philosophy*, 521.

But the difference in emphasis had tremendous practical consequences. The attitude of the common-sense school not only turned attention to the world of empirical fact, but legitimized that direction of attention. In doing so, it adopted the position that is essentially the one science shares with common sense—that of taking for granted, as a starting-point, the world as it appears to naïve perception. The common-sense philosophy also took up the case for revealed religion. It was, indeed, one of the aims of the Scottish school to protest against those implications of Hume's skepticism which might undermine religious faith. To assert that faith and belief are legitimate and necessary attitudes toward the external world was to take a step toward justifying those attitudes toward religion. Religion for the Scottish school meant Calvinism, and since the Scottish school a little later joined forces with British associationism, an alliance was formed that is of special interest to American psychology. For a psychology that blended harmoniously with Calvinism was peculiarly adapted to the needs of the first American colleges. It was, in fact, this psychology—British associationism tinged with Scottish common sense—which was generally taught in the early, devout days of American education, when psychology was included in the college curriculum as mental philosophy, when philosophy was, as a rule, taught by the president of the college, and when the president was extremely likely to have been trained for the Christian ministry in one of the Calvinistic denominations. It was this kind of psychology which was in possession of the field when James and Titchener introduced their respective innovations.

But British associationism was derived even more directly than was the philosophy of the Scottish school from the mode of thought that characterized Locke and his successors. It is difficult to name the founder of associationism—it may

have been Hobbes or Locke or Berkeley or Hume—but there
can be no doubt that in the work of Daniel Hartley the basic
doctrine was formulated with all the definiteness and ex-
plicitness that any school could require. Hartley, like Reid,
was a contemporary of Hume. By profession he was a physician, and perhaps he gained from his profession the interest,
not always found in other associationists, in the physiological aspects of the problem. According to Hartley, there are
two orders of events to be taken into account, the mental and
the physical. These two orders are not identical, but run
parallel to each other, so that a change in one is accompanied
by a change in the other. On the mental side, there are
sensations and ideas; on the physical side, there are vibrations and vibratiuncules. Vibrations are exceedingly small
motions in the particles of the nervous system; vibratiuncules
are even smaller motions of the same sort, which occur only
in the brain. While sensations involve the action of both
nerves and brain, ideas require the action only of the brain.
The vibrations, which are active in sensation, initiate the
vibratiuncules, which are active in ideation. There is thus a
direct connection between sensation and idea. The general
law of association is that if sensations have often been experienced together, the corresponding ideas will tend to
occur together; if A has been associated with B, C, and D
in sensory experience, the sensory experience A, occurring
alone, will tend to arouse the ideas of b, c, and d, which accompanied it. Association may be either successive or simul-
taneous. The former determines the course of thought in
time; the latter accounts for the formation of complex ideas.
These few principles form the basis of associationism. Naturally, the associationists differed among themselves in particulars. Some inclined to one form of association, some to
another; some recognized association by similarity, others
did not; and some attempted to reconcile a belief in the

unity of the self with an account of mental processes derived from a Lockian atomism. But whatever the modifications introduced by individuals, the main line of development was an attempt to show, sometimes in great detail, that starting with ideas and the general principle of association, it is possible to account for all mental formations, whatever their degree of complexity.

In Dr. Thomas Brown, the Scottish school and British associationism were very definitely combined. Brown, who had studied under Dugald Stewart, Reid's successor at Edinburgh, himself became professor of philosophy there. Following the Scottish school, which accepted selves as it accepted an external world, Brown upheld a psychology that emphasized the unity of the mind. At the same time he believed that the analysis offered by the British empiricists had much to contribute to the knowledge of the particular ways in which the mind works. He is known in psychology chiefly for his attempt to formulate the specific conditions under which the general principle of association operates. The laws of recency, frequency, and intensity—that much-used trio—are among them.

After Brown, the main line of succession runs through Sir William Hamilton to the Mills, Spencer, and Bain, who represent associationism at its height. Sir William Hamilton, a remarkably able man, was primarily a philosopher and a logician. He is best known in psychology for his concept of "complete redintegration," the tendency of an idea to reinstate in the mind all its concomitants in the original experience. James Mill is sometimes cited as the associationist *par excellence*, for in his writings the associationistic principles were applied with such thoroughness and in such detail that their limitations became apparent along with their possibilities. Mill was indefatigable in his endeavor to show that the associative processes are adequate to the

highest complexities in mental life. His remarks on the idea
of Everything are often quoted as an example of the lengths
to which he was willing to push his principle.

"Brick is one complex idea," he wrote, "mortar is another
complex idea; these ideas, with ideas of position and quantity, compose my idea of a wall. My idea of a plank is a
complex idea, my idea of a rafter is a complex idea, my idea
of a nail is a complex idea. These united with the same ideas
of position and quantity, compose my duplex idea of a
floor. In the same manner, my complex ideas of glass, wood,
and others, compose my duplex idea of a window; and
these duplex ideas, united together compose my idea of a
house which is made up of various duplex ideas. How many
complex, or duplex ideas, are all united in the idea of furni-
ture? How many more in the idea of merchandise? How
many more in the idea called Everything?" [4]

   John Stuart Mill, the son of James Mill, found difficulty
in explaining complex ideas in terms of simpler ideas "united
together" even if it were granted, as his father granted,
that the elements do not retain their distinctness. The
younger Mill, however, remained an associationist, at least
nominally, and overcame his difficulty by means of the concept of "mental chemistry." Complex ideas, he said, are not
always matters of composition; they may be said to *result
from* or to be generated by the simple ideas, not to consist
of them, just as in chemical compounds something appears
in the compound that is not present in the elements taken
separately. As the sensation of white is not *composed* of the
seven prismatic colors, but is *generated by* them, so a complex idea may be generated by, not composed of, simple
ideas. In the Mills, too, the principles of Bentham's utili-
tarianism were combined with the doctrines of associationism,
with the result that associationism carried along, as part of

   [4] James Mill, *Analysis of the Phenomena of the Human Mind*, I, 115.

itself, a conception of motivation that explains human conduct in the somewhat overrational terms of "enlightened self-interest," a belief that human actions can be accounted for in terms of seeking pleasure and avoiding pain.

Herbert Spencer, twelve years younger than John Stuart Mill, is important in associationism chiefly because he adopted the standpoint of evolution in his psychological thinking. Spencer, who believed in the inheritance of acquired characteristics, maintained that complex traits are evolved in the race as complex ideas are developed from simple ones in the individual—that instincts, for example, are built up from reflexes. Alexander Bain, a contemporary of Spencer, is best known for his two volumes *The Senses and the Intellect* and *The Emotions and the Will*. His importance lies not so much in any specific contribution, not so much in any particular theory or doctrine, as in the fact that his two books constitute a systematic and scholarly exposition of classic associationism at its height. These books, published just after the middle of the nineteenth century, mark the culmination of British associationism and therefore may be regarded as one of the landmarks in the history of psychology.

In a sense, associationism was the first "school" of psychology. Its adherents were a group of men who worked from a common point of view and who saw the major problems of psychology in very much the same way. They did not agree on all points—on the relation of idea and sensation, for example, and on such points as whether association by similarity should be recognized along with association by contiguity—but they were all occupied with the same kinds of materials and their thought represents a continuous development. And very definitely, the associationists were writing psychology rather than philosophy. They surveyed their problems in the matter-of-fact manner of natural science, seeking their subject-matter in actual experience, in observable formations of thought. In their hands, the mind lost much of its aura of mystery and ineffability, and psychology became downright, unpretentious, and empirical. The main business of the school was that which everywhere occupies science—the attempt to discover natural laws in a world of observable, natural events.

So far little has been said of the Continental philosophers. Only Descartes and Kant have been mentioned, and they have been included because of the connections they made with the critical and empirical thought of Great Britain. Even more than their British contemporaries the philosophers of the mainland were interested only incidentally in psychology. Certainly there was, on the Continent, no continuous line of psychological inquiry persisting, as did British empiricism and associationism, through changing personalities and problems. Still, many of the conceptions of the Continental philosophers, though they were evolved in attempts to solve problems not in themselves psychological, have definitely influenced psychology.

One of these conceptions is the parallelism of Spinoza, a contemporary of Descartes, and like Descartes, the author of one of the great rationalistic systems of the seventeenth century. In some of his writings Spinoza dealt with distinctly psychological problems; but, strangely enough, it is only through his metaphysical doctrine of parallelism that he is represented in psychology at present. And even this doctrine has been used in psychology in a manner by no means representative of its author's thought. For Spinoza's parallelism was part of his conception of reality as an all-embracing unity, of a reality that, though it has an infinite number of attributes, is itself one, and appears to human perception through only two of its attributes, matter and mind.

Fundamentally Spinoza was a monist; the belief in the unity of the world, a belief that lay at the basis of his philosophy, was something for which he felt both an emotional and an intellectual need. But in psychology, the concept of parallelism, taken out of the context that gave it its significance to its author, has been used by some schools as a convenient device for disposing of the mind-body problem. Its merit, as such a device, lies in the fact that it enables an investigator to take into account both physical and mental happenings and to note their relationship empirically without becoming involved in the metaphysics of their ultimate relation. Spinoza's parallelism, in fact, has been found useful in psychology precisely because it can be taken apart from its context and used without regard to its metaphysical implications. The mental and the physical can be treated as two streams of events, neither acting as the cause of the other, but together constituting a system in which a change in one is regularly accompanied by a change in the other. This conception makes it possible to preserve the dualism of mind and matter and yet to avoid the difficulties of interactionism. A somewhat similar mode of thought is found in the occasionalism of Malebranche and the preëstablished harmony of Leibniz, both of whom, like Spinoza, represent the rationalism of the seventeenth century.

Leibniz, in fact, following Descartes and Spinoza, produced the last of the three great rationalistic systems of the century. His conception of reality was that of a "pulverized universe," composed of an infinite number of unextended, immaterial centers of force called monads. His mental habit of "pulverizing" is also present in his contributions to the special sciences; in the infinitesimals of the calculus, of which he was one of the inventors, and in the *petites perceptions* that are involved in one of his contributions to psychology. This doctrine of *petites perceptions* is virtually a doctrine of the unconscious, and of the continuity of the unconscious with the conscious. As the visible world is reducible to invisible monads, so our clear consciousness goes back to obscure consciousness or even to unconscious mental states. Leibniz used the roar of the sea to illustrate his meaning. That we hear this sound is an undeniable fact, yet the "little sounds" of which it must be composed—the sounds made by the individual waves that make up the sea—would not be heard if each one occurred alone. Nevertheless we must be affected a little by each single wave, for "otherwise we should not have a perception of a hundred thousand waves, for a hundred thousand nothings cannot make something." Perhaps modern psychology would, on the whole, prefer to explain this phenomenon in terms of the summation of stimuli, rather than in the terms of the summation of unconscious perceptions. But the significant point is that in Leibniz there is a definite recognition of unconscious mental processes, a realm of psychology that, it is hardly necessary to state, has occasioned the liveliest interest in the psychology of to-day. The doctrines of the psychoanalysts, however much they may differ in texture and character from the speculations of Leibniz, nevertheless have something in common with the precise reasonings and acute perceptions of one of the founders of the calculus.

Leibniz was interested, too, in the question of innate ideas. Locke, it will be remembered, denied their existence, but he based his argument on the assumption that such ideas are either present or absent, fully formed or non-existent. Locke made much of the fact that the basic axioms are not present in the minds of children, of savages, and of the uneducated, and that they appear only when the individual has encountered the experiences that are capable of producing them. To Leibniz, all this might be true, and yet the concept of the mind as "white paper" or "tabula rasa" might not be the only possible explanation. He suggested "veined marble" as an alternative. As a block of marble may be so marked with veins as to make it more suitable for the figure of Hercules than for any other, so the human being may come into the world not with ideas fully formed, but with tendencies and predispositions that make the development of certain ideas highly probable and highly suitable to his nature. This conception is not unlike that of the loosely organized instincts, which is held by a number of psychologists to-day—the conception that certain modes of behavior are native, not in the sense that they emerge fully formed, perfect, and with the machinelike regularity of a chain of reflexes, but in the sense of existing as tendencies to reaction, the details of which are acquired by a process of trial-and-error learning in response to the particulars of concrete situations. According to this way of thinking, the modes of action known as instincts are produced by two sets of factors, those involved in native constitution and those supplied by the environment.

In the eighteenth century, the rationalism of the seventeenth persisted, not as a tendency to form closed systems like those of Spinoza and Leibniz, but in the formalism, classicism, and pleasure in logical construction that characterized the thought of the period. In France, the two main lines of psychological thinking were attempts to push existing theories to their logical conclusions. One of these was represented by Lamettrie and Cabanis. Descartes, it has been noted, explained animals as automata and to a very striking extent employed mechanistic principles in explaining human behavior. In 1748 Lamettrie in *L'Homme Machine* took the step that Descartes had not been willing to take and asserted that *all* the actions of human beings can be explained mechanistically. Fifty years later, Cabanis, a physician, reasserted and developed the same position. He declared that mind is merely a function of the body, more specifically of the brain, and that man's actions, including the most complicated operations of his intellect and the most exalted expressions of his moral nature, are nothing but the inevitable consequences of natural law operating in his physical being. Materialism and mechanism were wholeheartedly accepted as constituting a thoroughly adequate explanation of human conduct.

Similarly Condillac, the Abbé of Mureaux, writing in the middle of the century, carried Locke's theory of knowledge to the extreme of absolute sensationalism. Locke had recognized two sources of knowledge: sensation and reflection. Condillac reduced all knowledge to one source: sensation. In presenting his case, he imagines a statue, constituted internally like a human being, but covered with a layer of marble. He first removes the marble from the nose and places a rose before it. The statue now has a sensation of smell; the fragrance of the rose constitutes its whole consciousness. The rose is removed and the sensation becomes memory. Other objects are placed before the statue—a violet, jasmine, asafetida. Their characteristic odors are now compared with the memory image of the rose and with the memory images of each other, with the result that some are perceived as agreeable, others are disagreeable. In this way desire occurs for some, aversion for others, and the passions and the will arise from the comparison of sensations pleasant and unpleasant. In a similar manner, all the operations of the intellect are produced; from the comparison of sensations arise reflection, judgment, abstraction, generalization, and reasoning. When other sensations are permitted the statue— sensations of taste, audition, vision, and touch—its psychic life becomes enormously more complex. The sense of touch is especially important, since it provides the basis of the idea of an object, and consequently of the external world. But all along, there is nothing that happens in the mind, there is no idea that the mind produces, which is not derived from sensation. The whole content of the mind, including its operations, is nothing but sensation that transforms itself in different ways. Condillac's thesis is the last word in sensationalism, and also in empiricism, in so far as that term denotes a theory of human knowledge as constituted by, and developing through, experience. But it is important to note that the system of Condillac is not empirical as opposed to rational. It is through and through a logical construction; it is not an account of observed facts. Perhaps it should be noted, too, that Condillac was not a materialist. Starting with his conviction that all mental facts are but transformed sensation, he might easily have believed, with the French materialists of his day, that sensation is produced by the operation of the sense organs and the brain. But the Abbé of Mureaux did not take this step. Clearly and definitely, he posited a soul, which though distinct from the body was, so far as his psychology was concerned, nothing but the bare capacity for sensation. This point, however, is not especially important in his teachings. Condillac is remembered chiefly for his claim that sensation alone is sufficient to account for the most complex operations of the human mind.

In the same century, Jean Jacques Rousseau struck out on a radically different line of psychological thought. Rousseau's outstanding contribution to psychology was his insistence on the rôle of feeling and emotion in the human make-up. All along psychology had tended strongly to be intellectualistic. Empiricists and rationalists alike had analyzed the human being as if he were a creature whose primary business was knowing and thinking and discovering the truth. But to Rousseau, it was evident that man's true self is his emotional nature. The notion that man is essentially a creature of ideas and reason Rousseau regarded not only as false, but as a falsehood allied with all the evils of civilization, for Rousseau believed in the "noble savage" and a "return to nature," and regarded civilization as synonymous with slavery. In his eyes, the conventions and restrictions of society were false to man's deepest being; and by his very outrageousness in the eyes of his contemporaries —outrageousness that expressed itself in both words and deeds—Rousseau stood out in conspicuous protest against the formalism and artificiality of his age. His influence on psychology, however, is not easy to trace, for it was primarily as a political theorist and as an untrammeled individualist that he impressed the world. Certainly he does not fit into any of the well-defined lines of development that led to the science of psychology. But the man who sowed seeds of revolt in the France of the eighteenth century, and who protested against cold intellectualism in philosophy as against artificial conventionality in human society, made it impossible for psychology, even academic psychology, to remain wholly inattentive to the emotional side of man's nature. Emotion was to remain for a long time a dark and little-explored field, and psychology was to remain for many years predominantly intellectualistic. Still, the field of the emotions had been conspicuously indicated and its vast importance recognized.

But the currents that were sweeping psychology toward empiricism and naturalism were by no means without competition. They were in fact reactions against the thought that was officially established. In Germany, for example, there was Christian Wolff, a very paragon of rationalism, formalism, and dogmatism, whose school of thought flourished during the first half of the eighteenth century. Wolff is important to modern psychology largely because his teachings so clearly exemplify two habits of thought that had to be eradicated if psychology was ever to become a science. The first is the assumption that rational psychology has directed access to truth and reality in a way inaccessible to natural science; that absolute and demonstrable truth about the soul is attainable by the exercise of pure reason. This is the belief which, as has already been noted, Kant attacked from the standpoint of critical philosophy. The second is the conception of faculty psychology, the theory which holds that the soul is endowed with a number of powers—reasoning, remembering, and judging, for example—and which explains the specific performances of the mind in terms of the exercise of these faculties. There had been murmurs against faculty psychology from various quarters. The whole trend of British empiricism was obviously opposed to the conception, and Locke in particular raised his voice against it. But the faculty psychology of Germany in the eighteenth century, faculty psychology as it was represented by Wolff, met its most direct and effective adversary in the Herbartian psychology that displaced it. For Johann Friedrich Herbart aroused German interest in a mode of thought that definitely opposed and dispensed with faculties or powers of a soul. Herbart's psychology dealt with ideas or *Vorstellungen*, mental units somewhat similar to the simple ideas employed by the British associationists and also resembling the monads of Leibniz.

Herbart was Kant's successor at Königsberg, and as Kant's thought is a development of the critical side of British empirical philosophy, so Herbart's theories resemble the more positive side of the same movement. Like the British associationists, Herbart undertook to explain the most complex mental phenomena in terms of simple ideas. He was impressed by the thought that each idea has a certain degree of force, and emphasized the phenomena of inhibition as well as of association. Some mental facts he explained in terms of ideas that form compounds or blends, but he made inhibition, rather than association, the key-note of his system. Every idea, according to Herbart, has the tendency to maintain itself and to drive out ideas with which it is incompatible; and ideas vary in strength. When an idea encounters a stronger idea or group of ideas with which it is incompatible, it is thrust below the threshold of consciousness. The idea is not destroyed, however, but persists, though for the time it is unconscious. An idea that is in itself weak may gain admittance to consciousness, and maintain itself there, if the ideas above the threshold are congenial with it. Ideas already in possession of the field regularly repel uncongenial ideas; but uninhibited ideas, following the tendency of all ideas to rise to consciousness, are assimilated to the ideas in consciousness at the time. This process Herbart calls apperception, and the group of ideas into which the entering idea is introduced is known as the apperception mass. Mental life is thus mainly a struggle between ideas, each of which is active, each of which strives to attain and maintain a place in consciousness, and each of which tends to repel all ideas except those with which it is compatible.

This conception made it possible for Herbart to think of mental phenomena in terms of mental mechanics, and also in quantitative terms. Ideas vary both in time and in force or intensity; therefore psychological material offers two measurable independent variables. Applying his principle, Herbart wrote mathematical formulæ to state the laws of the mind. He did not believe, however, that psychology could ever become experimental. It is interesting to note this fact as an indication of the very gradual manner in which the conception of psychology as a science evolved. Kant, in the latter half of the eighteenth century, though he regarded psychology as an empirical science, held that it could never become

quantitative. Herbart, in the first half of the nineteenth
century, believed that, though psychology might become
quantitative, it could never become experimental. And yet
it was partly through Herbart's conception of a quantitative
psychology [5] that psychology developed as an experimental
science during the half-century following his death.

Herbart was also interested in education, and the widespread interest in applying his theory to the technique of
teaching represents an important step toward the recognition
of psychology as a science having something to contribute to
the practical affairs of everyday life. For a time teachers
everywhere were made acquainted with the famous five steps
of the Herbartian technique, a method designed to build up
in the pupil's mind an apperception mass suitable to the
reception of the new material to be presented. Since Herbart's time, education and psychology have been closely related, and even to-day education is probably the most extensive branch of applied psychology.

It is important to note, too, that Herbart's psychology
required the recognition of active unconscious processes. His
conception of ideas as active, as persisting below the threshold of consciousness when inhibited, as continually striving
to gain complete expression, and as contending against other
ideas, is remarkably similar to the theories of the unconscious held by the psychoanalysts.

One of Herbart's disciples in psychology, W. F. Volkmann,
wrote a textbook that bears much the same relation to
Herbartian psychology as do Bain's two volumes to British
associationism. It marks the culmination and presents the
main contributions of a distinctive line of thought. Until experimental psychology was well established, Volkmann's
Lehrbuch was widely used as a text in Germany. The date

[5] Especially through the influence of Fechner, who will be discussed
in the next chapter.

of its publication is 1856, a year after the appearance of *The Senses and the Intellect* and four years before the publication of *The Emotions and the Will*. It is interesting that, in about the middle of the century, Germany and Great Britain each produced a treatise presenting preëxperimental psychology in its most developed form. It is convenient, therefore, to consider these books as marking the close of one period in the history of psychology. William James, in commenting on the psychology of this period—a psychology as yet untouched by the experimental method—characterized Bain's work in words that might equally well be applied to Volkmann's, as "the last monument of the youth of our science, still untechnical and generally intelligible, like the Chemistry of Lavoisier, or Anatomy before the microscope was used."

In the middle of the nineteenth century, then, the long era of prescientific psychology came to a close. But during this era, psychology had come a long way. Beginning in speculations incidental to the practical problems of men and societies and to the search for ultimate truth, it had emerged as a body of knowledge studied for its own sake and existing in its own right. Among the Greeks, before psychology existed as a separate discipline, cosmology and epistemology, ethics, political theory and practical affairs, had all encountered questions concerning human nature. In this setting, however, such questions were not objects of a truly psychological interest. They were studied not for their own sake, but for the light they threw on other problems; they were studied because they were involved in attempts to understand the universe, or to work out a rational way of life. Besides, they were answered less on the basis of observation than on that of speculation, and the formulations that grew up about them were general and abstract. But for this very reason the early formulations stand out in the clear-cut outlines of rational concepts, as yet unblurred by the factual minutiæ which are subsequently revealed by detailed observation, and which, as often as not, do not quite fit the conceptual mold. As a consequence, many of the problems that occupied the Greeks—problems of substance and process, of the parts and the whole, of mind and matter, of the individual and society, of proximate and final causes, of the mathematical approach to understanding, and of the general problem of knowledge—were formulated in such a way that they have served as fixed points of reference and as conceptual tools in the thought of psychology ever since.

In modern times, in western Europe, psychological problems again presented themselves. For a time philosophy was immensely concerned with the critique of knowledge, and out of that concern grew a lively psychological interest. In its broadest outlines the critical movement proceeded first from an appeal to ecclesiastical authority to an appeal to reason, and then from an appeal to reason as represented by metaphysics to an appeal to factual evidence as represented by science. One of the by-products of this movement was an interest in psychology for its own sake, an interest that eventually expressed itself in the formation of two schools, associationism and Herbartianism. In the meantime particular psychological problems had arisen—problems of the possibility of innate and abstract ideas, of the nature of space perception, of the laws of association, of the relation of conscious and unconscious processes. A few fairly definite tendencies had emerged, among them the possibility of explaining human activities mechanistically, and of analyzing human experience atomistically. For the most part, during this period, psychology had overintellectualized and over-rationalized its material, but it had also received strong intimations that the affective life of man might be very important, and had occasionally glimpsed the possibility that attention to the motor side of human nature might be enlightening. All this had taken place in a fashion far from systematic; still, a definite attitude and a definite method of approach had been evolved. By the middle of the nineteenth century psychology had learned to look upon its subject-matter as a part of the world of nature and to seek to explain it in naturalistic terms. It was learning, too, to observe its material as well as to reflect upon it. In short, psychology was on the verge of becoming a science. In both subject-matter and method it had become empirical; there remained only the step of becoming experimental.

Chapter III

THE BEGINNINGS OF SCIENTIFIC PSYCHOLOGY

THE first psychological laboratory was founded by Wilhelm Wundt in Leipzig in 1879.

This statement is included, almost inevitably, in any account of the development of psychology as a science. It is not altogether accurate, and the truth it contains may easily become misleading, but it so closely approximates an important fact that it has found a secure place in the lore that surrounds psychology. For whatever its exact significance, the founding of the Leipzig laboratory is a conspicuous and indispensable point of reference in any survey of the events that led to scientific psychology.

From the standpoint of mere chronology, the first psychological laboratory was probably that which William James started almost casually at Harvard about 1875. At the time, James was an instructor in anatomy in the Harvard Medical School, but he was already displaying his characteristic disregard of the boundaries of academic fields. Having become greatly interested in sense physiology, he began at some time during the period from 1874 to 1876 to take into his laboratory problems in sensation that were distinctly psychological. James's laboratory, however, had nothing of the historical importance of Wundt's. James himself was not greatly interested in it, and it was not until the laboratory came under the direction of Hugo Münsterberg, a pupil of Wundt, that experimental psychology at Harvard really flourished. Wundt's laboratory, if not the first, was undoubtedly the first that made a stir.

But even so, it would be a mistake to regard the founding of the Leipzig laboratory as the beginning of experimental psychology. Experimental psychology was in the air; it existed long before it housed itself in laboratories, and it housed itself in other laboratories almost as soon as in the one at Leipzig—in laboratories, furthermore, that did not derive from Wundt's. Ebbinghaus, Stumpf, and G. E. Müller, all younger contemporaries of Wundt and all active in experimental psychology, can hardly be considered his faithful followers. Neither can Galton and Pearson, nor Charcot and Janet and Binet, who furthered important movements in psychology in England and France. Not even Hall and Cattell, pupils of Wundt who had much to do with the founding of the first laboratories in America, can be said to have followed closely in the footsteps of their master. Certainly the Leipzig laboratory was not the point upon which all lines leading to experimental psychology converged and from which all subsequent developments took their rise. But just as certainly its founding was an event of the utmost importance. Its formal establishment at a great German university was the outward and visible sign both that psychology had become definitely experimental and that it had become an independent science, existing in its own right.

But it is a far cry from the psychology that culminated in Bain and Volkmann to the psychology that began in the laboratories. Before psychology could speak with the accent of science, before it could even pretend to produce results that bear the hall-mark of knowledge as distinguished from opinion, it had to acquire new methods of collecting and elaborating its data. It had, in short, to learn the scientific method and in doing so to move from its arm-chair to the laboratory.

The difference between laboratory psychology and arm-chair psychology is not the difference between observation and no observation. Neither is it the difference between good observation and bad observation. It is the difference between two methods of observation. Occupants of arm-chairs are sometimes very acute observers—witness Hobbes, Locke, and Hume—but when they answer a question on the basis of observation, they utilize observations which have already occurred, observations, that is, which have not been made specifically for the sake of bringing out the relevant facts on a particular problem. In such circumstances, where the data are necessarily limited to cases which have occurred spontaneously, and which have been noted and remembered, it is obvious that even in the best-intentioned observers, such factors as direction of attention, limitation of experience, accidents of environment, and faults of memory may influence the selection of evidence. It is the distinguishing mark of a scientific *experiment* that it is a means of *acquiring* just the information that is relevant—not simply using what is already on hand—and of acquiring it in circumstances that rule out as completely as possible the accidental and private factors in observation. Therefore, the experimenter begins by formulating his question definitely, and proceeds by arranging that particular set of conditions which is best calculated to bring out the pertinent facts. He repeats his observations carefully, both to increase accuracy and to minimize chance; he varies the conditions systematically, both to broaden his view and to check his hypotheses; and he controls the whole situation as rigorously as possible in order that, knowing precisely what he has put into the experiment, he may not be misled as to what has come out of it. Whenever possible, he reduces his results to quantitative terms and submits them to statistical treatment, scrupulously taking account of negative as well as positive cases. And he does all this to minimize as much as possible the influence of his own peculiarities and the accidents of his situation—his own wishes and hopes, his preferences and aversions, his susceptibilities to impressions of a particular kind, his very motives in undertaking the problem. For in a very real sense, the scientific method is a device for protecting the investigator from the influence of his own interest in his own research. The conditions are arranged so that the facts will emerge as cleanly impersonal as possible. The importance of this practice in psychology, which deals with a subject-matter on which people are so likely to have preconceived notions and subtly determined preferences, is too obvious to require comment. Scientific psychology is but the extension of the scientific method into a region where disinterested observation has been peculiarly difficult.

Once the physical sciences were started and well under way, it was inevitable that scientific psychology should arise. The older sciences themselves made it necessary. Investigators were repeatedly having their attention drawn to the observing organism and to the necessity of taking its reactions into consideration in order to make their own accounts exact and complete. The classic example is found in astronomy, in an incident that every student of psychology learns about sooner or later. In 1796 Maskelyne, the astronomer royal at the Greenwich observatory, noticed that his young assistant, Kinnebrook, reported observations of stellar transits that differed from his own by over half a second. When they continued to differ even after the younger man had been told of the discrepancy, Maskelyne felt it necessary to dismiss him. About twenty years later, the German astronomer Bessel took note of the incident. Suspecting its significance, he compared the observations of a number of astronomers of established reputation and found that slight discrepancies in observation were the rule; in other words, that there are individual differences among observers in the reaction-time required for the highly complex process of noting and estimating to a tenth of a second the instant at which a star crosses a given line in the field of the telescope. Bessel called the phenomenon the personal equation. He investigated it experimentally, emphasizing the importance of correcting for it, and thus made astronomy distinctly aware of the rôle of the observer between the physical event and the psychological perception.

It was chiefly in physiology, however, that investigators were confronted with the fact that elaborate processes intervene between the physical object and the psychological perception. The facts of color-mixture, which were receiving considerable attention at the time, form as good an illustration as any. If two complementary colors, blue and yellow, for example, are presented in proper proportions on a rapidly rotating disk, the observer sees neither blue nor yellow, but gray. But how does it happen that when physically two colors are put together, the observer sees something that is colorless? Evidently there is no simple point-for-point correspondence between the immediate perception and its physical object. The most probable hypothesis is that the answer must lie in the nature of the responding organism, particularly in the action of the sense-organs interposed between perception and its external stimulus. Other researches pointed to the same problem. Plateau in his study of the persistence of sensation after stimulation, Brewster and Wheatstone in their investigations of stereoscopic vision, and Purkinje in his observations of the peculiarities of twilight vision all made it clear in an increasingly detailed and concrete fashion that it is impossible to ignore the eye that sees in accounting for the thing seen. And certainly the theory of the specific energies of the nerves contained the same implication. According to this doctrine, a nerve always reacts in its own special way, no matter how it is stimulated; the optic nerve, for example, even when stimulated mechanically, leads to the sensation of light. It is plain that, according to this theory, the sensation cannot be conceived as a copy of the stimulus, and that the impression the human being receives of the external world must be regarded as determined largely by his own organization. Johannes Müller, one of the great pioneers in the new science of physiology, formulated and supported the theory of specific energies, and largely because of his enthusiasm for it, he stimulated a mass of researches in sense physiology that in a very direct way determined the course of psychology. Thus physiology, itself a new science, by turning attention to the rôle of the reacting organism in sensation and perception, did much to prepare the way for the still newer science of psychology.

It is interesting to note that, in both philosophy and science, interest in psychology developed late and was at first incidental. Philosophy, setting out to account for the universe at large, began as cosmology, and only when it became involved in the problems of epistemology did it address itself seriously and directly to psychological material. Science, too, started as an attempt to explain the world at large, beginning with physics and astronomy. And physical science, like philosophy, first became seriously attentive to psychology when it met in science the counterpart of the problem of epistemology—the necessity of considering the observing organism in order to give a complete account of the observed universe.

Historically, the work of Ernst Heinrich Weber was of special importance to psychology. Weber, a contemporary of Müller, and like him a pioneer in physiology, was especially interested in the sense of touch. Or rather, he was one of the physiologists who were demonstrating that there is no single sense of touch; that there are instead many senses of touch; that different sensations such as those of pressure, temperature, and pain can be distinguished; and that the muscles, the skin, and interior of the body all make separate and special contributions. (Incidentally, the fact that it was no longer proper to speak of the old five senses appealed to the popular imagination as one of the more revolutionary discoveries of modern science.) While Weber was investigating the relative sensitivity of the cutaneous and muscular senses, he undertook an experiment that was destined to be of crucial importance in the development of psychology. His problem, which seemed prosaic enough, was to discover to what extent the muscle-sense figures in the discrimination of weights. His experiment was made primarily to determine whether differences in weight can be detected more accurately when the weights are lifted by the subject or when they are placed on his hand by the experimenter—that is, with or without the active participation of the muscles.

The investigation yielded two discoveries. The first was the direct answer to the main question of the experiment: sensitivity to weight is much finer when the muscular sense is included. The second was the discovery subsequently formulated as Weber's law, a discovery that became the starting-point of a series of experiments which led straight to experimental psychology.

This discovery was, in brief, that there was not a simple one-to-one relation between the magnitude of a difference and the subject's ability to perceive it. If a standard weight of thirty-two ounces was placed on the subject's hand, and the subject was asked to compare with it other weights similarly presented, he was likely to detect an increase in weight when eight or nine ounces [1]—approximately one

---

[1] These quantities are used illustratively; they are not the exact values obtained by Weber, though the standard weights referred to, thirty-two ounces and four ounces, were those used in Weber's experiment. The reader will find a discussion of Weber's experiments in E. B.

fourth of the standard weight—had been added. This value has been called the just noticeable difference. But if a standard weight of four ounces was used, an increase in weight could be detected when approximately one additional ounce was added. In other words, a much smaller absolute increment gave rise to a just noticeable difference in the one case than in the other; but again the difference was about one fourth the standard weight. Apparently the perception of the difference depended *not on the absolute* size of the difference *but on the ratio* of the difference to the standard. The ratio was different, about one to forty, when the muscle-sense was included, but again fairly constant. And within each of the two sense-fields studied, the results for the four persons who served as subjects were roughly the same. Furthermore, the results were confirmed in a subsequent, more carefully controlled experiment. Was it not possible, then, to express, within a given sense-field, the just noticeable difference in terms of a constant ratio? Weber was willing to consider the generalization. To test it, he extended his observations to the discrimination of visual lengths and found that in general his results confirmed his speculation. He also believed,[2] though he was mistaken in doing so, that the work of Delezenne in acoustics confirmed his view in the field of pitch-discrimination; and on the available evidence he advanced the hypothesis that within each sensory field the ability to discriminate barely noticeable differences is dependent not on the absolute magnitude of the difference involved, but on a constant ratio between the difference and the standard of comparison.

Here was the same fact that had presented itself unob-

Titchener's *Experimental Psychology, Instructor's Manual,* II, "Quantitative Experiments," XIII-XX.
    [2] . . . "Mistakenly—since Delezenne made no comparative determinations of the D.L." E. B. Titchener, *op. cit.,* XVIII.

trusively, but repeatedly and inescapably, in the work of other scientists. It cannot be assumed that there is a simple, literal, point-for-point correspondence between the physical stimulus and the perception of it. To Weber, this was an interesting physiological fact but no more. He did not announce it as Weber's law, nor regard it as having a far-reaching philosophical significance. In his eyes the generalization was as important as, but not more important than, any other empirical rule.

But the discovery was seized upon almost as a revelation by Gustav Theodor Fechner, who placed it in the very center of the psychological movement by his ardent and unwearying interest. To Fechner, its significance lay in the fact that it revealed a connection between the physical and the psychical —an exact mathematical relationship—and a connection of some sort between the two worlds was what Fechner had been seeking for long, anxious years with all the terrible earnestness of his unity-loving nature. He literally devoted his life to the testing of Weber's law, and in doing so worked out methods of investigation that helped to make the science of psychology possible.

Fechner is sometimes called the father of modern psychology, but the paternity of this infant among the sciences is doubtful. It has been vaguely ascribed to Helmholtz, Wundt, and Galton. But if psychology is looking for a picturesque ancestor, it can hardly make a happier choice than Fechner, a simple, subtle, profoundly learned man, in the grip of an irresistible impulse to take ideas seriously, and utterly at the mercy of his intellectual sincerity. Fechner was at once a scientist and a mystic. Torn by rival intellectual claims, he was totally incapable of giving up one for the other and equally incapable of peace without victory. As a scientist his interests were both broad and deep. He began his career as a student of medicine, but very early his activities shifted to physics, chemistry, and mathematics. It was chiefly in physics that he made his reputation, partly by his researches in the properties of the electric current, and in 1834, when he was thirty-three years old, he was appointed professor of physics at Leipzig. And not only was he identified with the scientific movement as one of its active investigators, not only was he thoroughly conversant with the science of his day; he was profoundly impressed, both emotionally and intellectually, by science as such—by its exact and rigorous methods, by the orderly nature of the world it revealed. He found its views and its ways impossible to ignore. But over against the world of science he set the world of values, which science did not heed, but which he found equally real, equally legitimate, and equally compelling as an object of intellectual concern. In his youth, Fechner had been deeply impressed by the philosophy of Schelling, and the experience left him with a lasting sense that to ignore the immediate appeal of life and mind was to turn aside from immediately felt reality. When he was only twenty, he wrote, under the name of Dr. Mises, a paper on the thesis that the moon is made of iodine, the first of a number of essays in which under the same pseudonym he expressed, usually in the form of satire on science, the side of his nature that science did not satisfy. The conflict, at the same time subtle and severe, was almost a deadlock. As professor of physics Fechner taught the official science of the day; as Dr. Mises he found an outlet for the feeling that science was unsatisfying and incomplete. Under the strain his health gave way, but in spite of his illness, he conducted experiments on positive after-images—border-line phenomena, it is to be noted, between the mental and the physical worlds. In doing so he injured his eyes nearly to the point of blindness. His health broke completely. He resigned his position and lived for three years almost completely cut off from the world, a victim of illness, pain, and depression.

He recovered, no one knew quite how, least of all himself; but on the morning of October 22, 1850—he carefully notes the date—he came upon an idea that satisfied both the scientific and the humanistic demands of his nature. It occurred to him that there might be an observable, even measurable relationship between the stimulus and the sensation and therefore between the physical and the mental worlds. He noted that sensation and stimulus apparently do not increase in intensity at the same absolute rate. For example, if one candle is burning in a room and another is lighted, the difference is immediately noticed; but if ten candles are burning and one more is added, the difference is scarcely appreciated. It is possible, then, that sensation may increase in arithmetical progression as the stimulus increases in geometrical progression. Sensation itself cannot be measured directly, but the stimulus can, and it may be possible to show that an increase in the stimulus by a constant fraction of itself is regularly correlated with every discernible increase in the sensation. In other words, an exact quantitative relation may be found between the physical and the mental worlds. To Fechner, the conception was an utterly satisfying one; if confirmed, it would bind together what had seemed disconnected and irreconcilable; it would give him the sense of world-unity that he had always craved—a world-unity, moreover, that he would be able to demonstrate by exact, mathematical evidence.

There remained, however, the task of testing his hypothesis experimentally, and it was not until this task was actually started that he encountered Weber's discovery. To Fechner it seemed a confirmation of his hopes. He gave Weber's results mathematical formulation, called the generalization Weber's law, and devoted himself unreservedly to the task of verifying it by experiment. So he lifted weights, literally thousands of them, attempting to compare his immediate impressions of weight with the physically determined weights of the objects lifted. He made similar studies of degrees of brightness, and of visual and tactual distances, always believing that if sensation, the point of contact between the physical and the psychical, could be shown to have a definite mathematical relation to the stimulus, the world-unity he sought would be established.

He found the constant ratios, at least in sufficient quantity and in sufficiently close approximation to ideal requirements to encourage his hopes and his efforts. But his significance for psychology lies not at all in the world-view he hoped to establish by his researches. It lies, rather, in the exact, quantitative, experimental procedures he developed in pursuing them. Fechner himself worked out three of the psychophysical methods—called psychophysical because of his conception of a science of psychophysics dealing with the relationship between the physical and psychical worlds. The number of technical and controversial points that arise in an apparently simple experiment on lifted weights is truly amazing, yet such points contain in little the essentials of some of the most fundamental and persistent problems in experimental psychology: the difficulty of controlling both the external conditions and the subject's attitude, the necessity for repeated observations, for refined quantitative analysis, and for ingenious arrangement of setting and procedure so that now one disturbing factor, now another, shall be ruled out. The techniques that Fechner developed were soon utilized by other workers, modified, made points of departure for other techniques, and applied to other fields than sensation. Fechner himself extended them to the field of esthetics, comparing stated preferences with objective situations, e.g., rectangles of different proportions, linear relations of different sorts, in a manner roughly similar to that utilized for sensation. In fact, to Fechner's contemporaries, the remarkable feature of the psychophysical methods was the fact that they were quantitative. To measure mental processes was considered a startling innovation; to experiment with them in a manner that gave quantitative data marked the dawn of a new day. The publication in 1860 of *The Elements of Psychophysics,* the book in which Fechner reported his work and his views, ranks with the founding of the Leipzig laboratory as one of the outstanding events in the development of psychology. As a serious, original, carefully executed attempt to treat psychological processes in the manner of the exact sciences, the book is sometimes taken as marking the first definite achievement of the science of psychology. The psychophysical methods themselves aroused the greatest interest. They were carefully examined by leading scholars of the day, and though they were criticized adversely as well as favorably, the promise they held triumphed over the skepticism they aroused. It was not long, indeed, before Fechner's methods, along with others added by his followers, became a regular part of the stock in trade of what was rapidly becoming the new science of psychology. They have persisted down to the present day and they still hold a place among the recognized tools of research in psychology.

But widespread as the use of Fechner's methods has been, the interpretation of his data has been of a character very different from that which he intended. The mystical interpretation, which was for him the chief outcome of his experiments and their very reason for being, has never been accepted in psychology. Even in the more restricted and technical sense, his interpretations of his experiments have not received general assent. There has been and still is much disagreement as to precisely what processes the psychophysical experiments measure. And there has been at least one distinguished critic who considered the whole movement started by Fechner as utterly worthless. William James writes:

"The Fechnerian *Maasformel* and the conception of it as an ultimate 'psychophysic law' will remain an 'idol of the den,' if ever there was one. Fechner himself indeed was a German *Gelehrter* of the ideal type, at once simple and shrewd, a mystic and an experimentalist, homely and daring, and as loyal to facts as to his theories. But it would be terrible if even such a dear old man as this could saddle our Science forever with his patient whimsies, and, in a world so full of more nutritious objects of attention, compel all future students to plough through the difficulties, not only of his own works, but of the still drier ones written in his refutation. Those who desire this dreadful literature can find it; it has a 'disciplinary value'; but I will not even enumerate it in a footnote. The only amusing part of it is that Fechner's critics should always feel bound, after smiting his theories hip and thigh and leaving not a stick of them standing, to wind up by saying that nevertheless to him belongs the *imperishable glory*, of first formulating them and thereby turning psychology into an *exact science,*

" 'And everybody praised the duke
Who this great fight did win.'
'But what good came of it at last?'
Quoth little Peterkin.
'Why, that I cannot tell,' said he,
'But 'twas a famous victory!' " [3]

But however plausibly James may put the case, the historical fact remains that one of the sources of modern psychology lies in the patient and perhaps dull researches of the "dear old man" who carried out the first attempt actually to measure psychological processes, however ill-defined, and to correlate them with physical events. Even if not a scrap of his specific doctrines should remain, the founding of the science

[3] William James, *Principles of Psychology*, I, 549.

of psychology would still be to an impressive extent the work of his hands.

The founding of the new science was also, to an impressive extent, the work of Hermann von Helmholtz, by twenty years Fechner's junior. Like Fechner, Helmholtz was first a student of medicine, and then a physicist whose interests were by no means limited to physics. But Helmholtz was not given to brooding concern about the unity of the universe. He wanted to know, among many other things, exactly how the eye and the ear worked, and to this end he plunged into the series of researches which brought together the tremendous mass of fact and theory, constituting the two great works, *A Handbook of Physiological Optics* and *Sensations of Tone*. From the standpoint of sheer amount of work done, the achievement is stupendous. Helmholtz carefully worked over all existing knowledge on the subject, tested it experimentally, devised new experiments, discovered new facts, and suggested new theories. With equal facility, he invented apparatus, devised experimental methods, and constructed theories. He was extraordinarily gifted in dealing with both things and ideas. His powers of observation, visual and auditory alike, were said to be exquisitely accurate and sensitive. No aspect of his subject failed to interest him; his investigations ranged from the anatomy of the eye and ear to the history of the development of harmony.

Helmholtz's researches on the eye and the ear rank among the greatest achievements of science. The fundamental and pioneer studies in the field, they belong to physics, physiology, and psychology. Their importance in the development of psychology can hardly be overestimated; not only did they disclose the enormous complexity of such apparently simple psychological processes as seeing objects and hearing sounds, but at the same time they brilliantly demonstrated the possibility of studying these processes by the methods of the natural sciences. In his work on acoustics, Helmholtz showed how an apparently simple tone like that produced by a single vibrating string contains overtones in addition to the fundamental; how two tones, sounded together, may give rise to summation tones, difference tones, and the "beats" that he considered the cause of discord. He determined the highest and the lowest audible pitches and the distinguishable intervals between them. He also advanced his resonance theory of hearing, the theory that the ear is like a harp. In optics, he dealt with such problems as refraction by means of the lens, methods of stimulating the retina and the optic nerve, after-images, the retinal image, optical illusions, eye movements, monocular and binocular vision, and the perception of distance. After exploring the facts of color-vision, he advanced the theory that all the phenomena of color-vision can be explained in terms of three primary colors, red, green, and blue—a theory for which he felt party indebted to the British investigator Sir Thomas Young, and which is now known as the Young-Helmholtz theory. In explaining space-perception, he adopted the empiristic as opposed to the nativistic view. That is, he did not regard spacial perception as "given," but as a product of experience. In opposition to the Kantian view that space is one of the forms of intuition, Helmholtz maintained that the experience of space is a construction of the mind, the product of unconscious inferences from numerous and various experiences not spatial in themselves. The controversy between nativism and empiricism, in its many forms, has had a long history in psychology and is by no means settled; but it was fortunate that, in the special set of circumstances in which he worked, Helmholtz threw the great weight of his influence on the side of empiricism; for his action in this case meant the analysis of fundamental processes which would otherwise have been taken for granted. It was largely because of his attitude on this question that Helmholtz demonstrated the possibility of making exact scientific observations on sensation and perception, processes that in his day were regarded as constituting the groundwork of mental life. As Fechner solidly established both the idea and the practice of measurement in psychology, so Helmholtz proved, by his successful researches in sensation and perception, that it is possible to apply exact observation and experimentation to specifically psychological material.

Another experiment performed by Helmholtz, which had its inception in the consideration of a physiological problem, had important results in psychology. Helmholtz was the first person to measure the speed of the nerve-current. At the time it was generally believed, partly on the authority of Johannes Müller, that the velocity of neural conduction could not be measured because there is not room enough in any animal organism to determine a speed so rapid. Helmholtz measured it in the leg of a frog. He first stimulated a motor nerve near the muscle that it innervated, and measured the time between the stimulation of the nerve and the contraction of the muscle; next he stimulated the nerve at a point farther from the muscle, and measured as before the time between neural stimulation and muscular response; then he subtracted the first measurement from the second, and so obtained the time it had taken the neural current to traverse the distance between the two points stimulated. A series of such measurements was taken, of course. Finding the results consistent, Helmholtz placed the speed of conduction in the motor nerve at thirty meters a second,[4] a surprisingly low figure considering the expectations of most scientists of the

---

[4] The rate of conduction, at present, is given as about 123 meters per second.

time, some of whom thought of the speed of neural conduction as comparable with the speed of light.

The next step, now that the motor-nerve impulse had been measured, was to see whether the rate of conduction in sensory nerves was different. The procedure for this problem involved the use of the intact organism and therefore the essentials of the reaction-time experiment in its present ιorm. A sense-organ was stimulated, the subject was instructed to react as soon as the stimulus was perceived, and the time between the application of the stimulus and the contraction of the muscle was measured. The same general plan as that used for measuring the rate of the motor-nerve impulse was followed: stimulation was given at different points, the knee and the thigh, and the rate of conduction obtained by subtraction. In this case, however, the results were extremely variable, and Helmholtz was unwilling to draw any definite conclusions from them.

Up to this point, it will be observed, the problem had been purely physiological; Helmholtz was interested simply in measuring the speed of the neural impulse. But the psychological possibilities of the experiment caught the attention of other investigators, and the method of measuring the rate of conduction in sensory nerves—the method, that is, which involved the intact organism—soon became the reaction-time experiment, which made possible a flourishing line of distinctly psychological research.

Donders, a Dutch physiologist, turned to the experiment in the hope of getting measurable psychological "constants." His general plan was to use the simple reaction-time experiment of Helmholtz as a basis; then to introduce complicating factors involving discrimination and choice; and, by subtracting the simple reaction-time from the time required for the more complex reactions, to obtain definite measures of such psychological events as discrimination and choice.

The plan was simple. First a series of measurements was to be taken in which the subject reacted in the usual way to a designated signal—for example, a flash of red light. This would give the simple reaction-time. Then, in another series, the subject was to react only after he had distinguished between a red light and a green one, reacting if the red light appeared, not if the green one was shown. These reactions, it seemed reasonable to suppose, would involve not only everything that the simple reaction contained, but in addition, discrimination. In still another series, the subject was to react with his right hand to the red light, with his left hand to the green. These reactions, it was assumed, would include everything involved in the discriminatory reaction, and in addition, choice. Then by making the obvious subtractions, it would be possible to obtain measures of "discrimination-time" and "choice-time." The result would be a number of distinguishable mental events which could be measured in time and which would give the psychologist definite units to work with.

The idea was attractive, promising as it did the gratifying simplification that comes from reducing complex material to fixed, identifiable, quantitative units. But the subsequent analysis of reactions, simple and complex, gave little or no evidence of psychological "constants." On the contrary, it threw considerable doubt on the legitimacy of the basic assumption that the more complex reaction can be conceived as a composition in which the simple reaction is retained in its essentials, with the addition of the one designated factor. Donders himself, it is true, carried out his plans and obtained results that gave longer times for choice-reactions than for discrimination-reactions, and longer times for discrimination-reactions than for simple reactions; and this gross result has been repeatedly confirmed. But as reactions and reaction-times were studied more thoroughly, it became increasingly apparent that even in this small bit of human activity, the situation is enormously complex. It became evident that reaction-time varies with the sense-organ stimulated, with the intensity of the stimulus, with the number of items to be "discriminated" or "chosen," with the degree of difference between them, with the amount of practice the subject has received, and with a hundred other factors. One of the most suggestive contributions was made by Lange, who found that reaction-time varied with the subject's attitude. If the subject attended mainly to the stimulus, the reaction-time was slightly longer than if his attention was fixed primarily on the movement he was to make. This discovery of the difference between sensorial and muscular reactions, as they were called, led to a mass of interpretation, controversy, speculation, and research of really astonishing proportions. Wundt, who had analyzed the reaction into perception, apperception, and will, as its psychological components, believed that the muscular reaction was incomplete, that it was a reaction in which apperception had not been allowed to develop. Exner and Cattell suggested that the reaction-time experiment measured in the practised subject something strongly analogous to a reflex; that the organism which is prepared to react is "set" in a certain way and that the ensuing reaction is itself an automatic neural event, the resultant of several factors; in other words, that the reaction is not a train of successive processes such as perception, apperception, and will, but a unitary neural process determined by a particular set. Later Ach's introspective study of reaction tended to confirm this view. It indicated that the period of reaction proper is almost bare of psychological content, and that such processes as awareness of instructions, of stimulus, of movement, and of errors either precede or follow the movement itself. The studies on this point are extensive and controversial, but whatever their specific import, they give little evidence to justify the subtractive procedure and the theory on which it is based. They form one of the many instances in the history of psychology in which an *a priori* analysis of a situation fails to be confirmed by subsequently observed facts, and in which the actual situation is found to be less clear, less simple, and of far less obvious rationale than the preliminary intellectual analysis indicated.

But this discussion of reaction-times runs far ahead of the main story of the development of psychology, and forms but a single illustration of the vital way in which Helmholtz stimulated psychological research. Not only had he made possible the reaction-time experiment; he had demonstrated, by his researches on the eye and the ear, that the experimental methods in use in physiology were applicable to the psychological processes of sensation and perception. By placing the resources of the physiological laboratories at the disposal of students of psychology, he had made the development of an experimental psychology all but inevitable. Certainly his work had put provocative questions. Had he not shown that sensation can be studied experimentally, and may not sensations be the raw material, the elemental stuff, of which the psychic life is made? Then is not the study of these processes and their relations an obvious means of pushing scientific knowledge farther into the realm of the psychological? And with the psychophysical methods at hand, may not exact, quantitative knowledge be attainable? It was some such reasoning as this, tentative but hopeful, with reservations, qualifications, and elaborations, which was vaguely afloat when psychology was about to take form as an i)dependent discipline. Already there was on hand a respectable amount of scientific work, specifically psychological in character. Techniques, methods of investigation, and apparatus had been invented, important books had been written, and widespread interest had been aroused. The parts were ready to be assembled, and when assembled they would form a new science.

The final touch that brought the parts together was given by Wilhelm Wundt, who thereby became the next conspicuous figure in the history of psychology—though to apply the adjective "conspicuous" to Wundt is somewhat misleading, since neither the work nor the character of the man has the bold simplicity and distinctness of outline which make for a single, memorable impression. To understand Wundt's work is to understand an intricate network of relationships, in which emphasis and clarity are regularly subordinated to completeness of detail. For Wundt was so keenly conscious of the qualifications which hedge about a stated fact that he has been described as a man who "never said a foolish thing or a brilliant one." Learned, logical, industrious, and systematic, he was admirably suited both by training and by temperament to the task of centralization, organization, and integration, which for psychology was the great need of the moment.

As a young man, Wundt's chief interest was in physiology, and naturally he became thoroughly familiar with physiological research in the tradition of Weber, Fechner, and Helmholtz. He had, in fact, been personally associated with both Helmholtz and Fechner; at Heidelberg, the scene of his early academic career, with Helmholtz; at Leipzig, which witnessed its culmination, with Fechner. These personal associations, however, seem not to have played a decisive or even an important part in determining his thought. His relations with Helmholtz, never close, were not even particularly cordial, and his work had taken its characteristic form before he became acquainted with Fechner at Leipzig. While still at Heidelberg, he produced his *Physiological Psychology,* the treatise that is generally considered more than any other single book to draft the first constitution for psychology as an independent science. In some of his earlier writings, it is true, there had been anticipations of his conception of an experimental psychology; but in his *Physiological Psychology* the conception was definitely formulated and elaborated, and much that had been vaguely implicit in the psychology of the physiological laboratories was treated explicitly and systematically. The book in fact attempted two tasks: the first, a comprehensive presentation of the known facts of the psychology of the day; and the second, the formulation of the principles of a system. This system, though repeatedly modified in the many subsequent editions of the book, was in general outline the one to which Wundt subscribed throughout his life. Expressing as it did his fundamental conviction that psychology is the study of mental contents and that it is a science which approaches these contents chiefly through introspection and experimentation, his *Physiological Psychology* became one of the major influences in determining the character of the first experimental work in the new science.

The book contains, in fact, Wundt's conception—a conception that had likewise appeared in his earlier writings—of exactly what a psychological experiment should be. As he describes it, the psychological experiment is plainly patterned after the physiological experiment: it is a procedure in which the process to be studied is kept very close to a controllable stimulus and very close to an objective response, and in which introspection is an intensive, short-range, carefully prepared act of observation. It is of special interest that, for all his faith in introspection and experimentation, Wundt never believed that those methods were applicable to the study of the higher mental processes; and that later, when some of his pupils—notably Külpe—made the attempt to study the higher thought processes by introspection under controlled conditions, he characterized their procedures as "mock experiments." The higher mental processes, he believed, can be studied only by means of "social products"; [5] they are accessible only to the historical method. Only by tracing the development of man through his language, his art, his laws, his customs, his institutions in general—only, in short, by a study of "social products"—is it possible to discover the nature of the mental processes by which those products have been formed.

The publication of the *Physiological Psychology* marked a turning-point in the career of its author, as well as in the development of psychology. In 1874 Wundt went to Zürich as professor of philosophy, a step which, according to the scheme of organization in the German universities,[6] meant a movement from physiology to psychology. A year later he became professor of philosophy at Leipzig, where after four years—that is, in 1879—he founded his famous laboratory for psychological research.

Naturally Leipzig became the Mecca of students who wished to study the "new" psychology—a psychology that was no longer a branch of speculative philosophy, no longer a fragment of the science of physiology, but a novel and daring and exciting attempt to study mental processes by the experimental and quantitative methods common to all science. For the psychology of Leipzig was, in the eighties and nineties, the newest thing under the sun. It was the psychology for bold young radicals who believed that the ways of the mind could be measured and treated experimentally—and who possibly thought of themselves, in their private reflections, as pioneers on the newest frontier of

[5] Wundt himself applied this method in his *Folk Psychology,* a work in ten volumes, which he completed shortly before his death.

[6] In the German universities, psychologists hold positions in the departments of philosophy.

science, pushing its method into reaches of experience that it had never before invaded. At any rate they threw themselves into their tasks with industry and zest. They became trained introspectionists and, adding introspection to the resources of the physiological laboratories, they attempted the minute analysis of sensation and perception. They measured reaction-times, following their problems into numerous and widespread ramifications. They investigated verbal reactions, thus extending their researches into the field of association. They measured the span and the fluctuations of attention and noted some of its more complex features in the "complication experiment," a laboratory method patterned after the situation that gave rise to the astronomer's problem of the "personal equation." In their studies of feeling and emotion they recorded pulse-rates, breathing-rates, and fluctuations in muscular strength, and in the same connection they developed methods of recording systematically and treating statistically the impressions observed by introspection. They also developed the psychophysical methods and in addition made constant use of resources of the physiological laboratory. And throughout all their endeavors they were dominated by the conception of a psychology that should be scientific as opposed to speculative; always they attempted to rely on exact observation, experimentation, and measurement. Finally when they left Leipzig and worked in laboratories of their own—chiefly in American or German universities—most of them retained enough of the Leipzig impress to teach a psychology that, whatever the subsequent development of the individual's thought, bore traces of the system which was recognized at Leipzig as orthodox.

For along with the laboratory, there was a system. The system, in fact, preceded the laboratory and then developed with it. Wundt's *Physiological Psychology*, it will be remembered, was written before its author left Heidelberg, but the system it outlined was revised and developed as the laboratory became more and more productive. To an order-loving mind like Wundt's, it was essential that the items of information that were coming into psychology be duly arranged as they entered; and as the science grew, he prepared edition after edition of his formulated system—a system in which the subject-matter of psychology was defined, the methods outlined, the problem stated, the elements of the mental life isolated and classified, their modes of combination described, and the fundamental principles of the science enunciated. Evidently Wundt never tired of trying to find a place for everything and of trying to keep everything in its place. A prolific writer, he devoted a large part of his work to the task of keeping his systematic exposition abreast of the discoveries of the new science and of the development of his own thought; at times he strongly suggests the careful housewife, industriously picking up after a growing science that had not learned—and has not yet learned—to be neat. His *Physiological Psychology* went through six revisions and the *Groundwork of Psychology,* a more popular exposition of his views, through ten. The labor involved must have been enormous, but the task was important. For a recognized body of doctrine that kept pace with the rapidly growing science was distinctly helpful in giving form and definiteness to the mass of material which was beginning to be called psychology.

It seems, at times, that Wundt was the kind of person who is particularly likely to be underestimated. His personality was not sufficiently picturesque to make him stand out on that account; and his work shows no single, brilliant contribution to knowledge that can be readily circumscribed and labeled with a phrase. His great achievement was the bringing into effective relations of many things which, it is true, had existed before, but which had not been integrated into an effective organization; and somehow human beings are prone to regard such achievements as less striking and less creative than those of the order of Helmholtz's and Fechner's. But the man who sensed the movements of scientific thought as Wundt did, who embodied them in the first laboratory, who gave them form in an influential system, and who imparted them to enthusiastic students who were proud to carry on his work, has no small claim to the title often accorded him, that of father of modern psychology. Wundt himself was not unaware of the debt psychology owed him, and not altogether indifferent as to whether or not it was recognized. In his rôle as father, he inclined toward the patriarchal, almost toward the papal; he reserved the right to speak with authority, to pronounce *ex cathedra* on psychology and psychologists, and to draw a distinct line of demarcation between authentic psychology and psychology of which he did not approve. Even to-day, so great have been his influence and prestige, the term "experimental psychology" to many still has as its first connotation the kind of psychology which was taught in Wundt's laboratory or which Wundt recognized and approved.

But Wundt and Leipzig, despite their deserved prestige and their evident determination to maintain it, had no monopoly on psychology, even in Germany. In other places and under other masters the new science was flourishing. Hermann Lotze, a contemporary of Helmholtz, had done much to turn attention to the problems that were to become psychology. Though Lotze had taken his degree in medicine, he was an artist and a philosopher as well as a scientist, and it is significant that his first publication after his doctor's dissertation was a volume of poems written during his student days. His influence in psychology was due principally to his *Medical Psychology, or, The Physiology of the Soul,* a book in which he attempted to reconcile human values and the naturalistic ways of the new science of experience, and in which he combined the acuteness and penetration of the scientist and metaphysician with a sympathy toward human hopes and desires not always found in the critical temperament. Lotze believed that there are no mental states which are not related to physical processes, but he also believed that this fact leaves the values of life unaltered. His best-known specific contribution to psychology is a theory of space-perception which assumes that on a native capacity for perceiving spatially, human beings build up their perceptions of space through experience. The raw data are non-spatial characteristics of visual and tactual sensation—specifically, the particular complexes of intensities that accompany the stimulation of the skin and muscles and which, in the case of vision, are aroused by eye movements. These complexes of intensities Lotze thought of as "local signs" which, regularly associated with the stimulation of particular points, serve to distinguish them from each other. This theory, it is evident, can be claimed by either nativists or empiricists.

Of Wundt's own academic generation was Franz Brentano, a priest whose scruples in the matter of intellectual integrity were always bringing him into crises in the academic world, and eventually led to an open break with the church. Brentano's chief influence was in establishing act psychology— a psychology which maintains that psychic processes are essentially acts which refer to or are directed toward contents. This conception is in striking contrast with the Wundtian view that the psychic processes themselves are contents. The difference may be illustrated by the process of hearing a tone. According to Brentano, it is necessary to distinguish between the tone one hears and the hearing of a tone. It is the *hearing* of a tone, he maintains, that is a psychological process or act; the *tone heard* is the act's content. To hear middle C is a psychological process; middle C as heard is not. The content, however, is indispensable to the psychological process, for a psychological process by its very nature refers to a content. It is, in fact, the distinguishing feature of a psychological process that it refers to something not itself—that it "intends" an object. A true psychological process therefore is act, not content. According to Wundt, however, it is the sensational content of middle C that is the psychological process; it is, in fact, just such processes of which the psychic life is made, which constitute its elements. Besides, it is content alone that can be studied by introspection. Acts cannot be made the objects of direct observation and therefore cannot constitute the subject-matter of a science; but processes like hearing tones are sensational contents, and are commonplaces of the physiological laboratory. It is, in fact, the study of such processes by the approved methods of natural science that must constitute the groundwork of psychology. Thus the difference in subject-matter involves a difference in method. Acts do not lend themselves to the analytical introspection that was regarded at Leipzig as essential to an experimental psychology. The students of mental acts used observation in a larger, less esoteric, though not necessarily less careful sense than that approved by orthodox introspectionists. This kind of observation has been called phenomenological, and has been distinguished from introspection in the technical sense; in consequence act psychology has been characterized as empirical as opposed to experimental. It should be noted, however, that the movement represented by Brentano, though contrasted with the experimental psychology of Wundt, was not a return to the old speculative psychology. The empirical method was a method of observation, though not a method of experimentation. Brentano's statement of his position in *Psychology from*

the Empirical Standpoint appeared in the same year that
Wundt completed the first edition of the *Physiological Psychology*. Thus from the first a line of cleavage was established in the growing science; from the first a contrast was
set up between contents and acts, between analytical introspection and phenomenological observation, between experimental and empirical psychology.

The next generation of German psychologists is represented by men who, though about twenty years younger than
Wundt, are nevertheless counted among the pioneers in psychology. Of these, probably the most influential were Carl
Stumpf, Theodor Lipps, Hermann Ebbinghaus, and G. E.
Müller, all of whom worked in complete or almost complete
independence of Wundt.

Stumpf was definitely a rival of Wundt. As a student, he
had worked with Lotze and Brentano and was therefore
outside the Wundtian fold. As a mature psychologist, he was
called to the chair of philosophy at Berlin, a position generally considered the highest a German psychologist can hold,
and one for which Wundt seemed the logical candidate from
the standpoint of both priority and prestige. Stumpf, like
Lotze, was a philosopher and an artist, as well as a psychologist. From childhood he had been intensely interested
in music, and his musical bent was undoubtedly strongly
implicated in turning him to the research that resulted in
his masterpiece *The Psychology of Tone*. This book, which
is recognized as a classic in its field, second only to Helmholtz's *Sensations of Tone*, is the work on which Stumpf's
reputation is mainly based. It was Stumpf's musical interest,
too, that led him into the famous controversy with Wundt
on tonal distances—famous not so much for what the com-
batants said about tonal distances as for what they said
about each other. For the discussions, becoming both personal and bitter, developed into one of the famous scandals

of modern psychology, a scandal that has steadily afforded amusement to the many who find irresistible comedy in the spectacle of learned psychologists at the mercy of primitive feelings which have obviously escaped control. Stumpf, because of his connection with Brentano and because he regarded mental functions as typical psychological processes, is classified with the act psychologists.

Lipps, another important figure in the new psychology, was not to any considerable extent an experimentalist. Interested chiefly in problems of perception and esthetics, he formulated his theories in *Æsthetics,* his best-known book. His most famous contribution is his doctrine of *Einfühlung* or "empathy," the theory that the observer tends to "feel himself into" the object he is contemplating and that the slight and almost unnoticed muscular responses he makes in doing so form the basis of the esthetic experience. The theory is interesting, aside from its specific relation to esthetics, for calling attention in a novel way to motor reactions, in this case slight and incipient. It is significant that the tendency to take motor reactions into account grows increasingly prominent as psychology depends more and more on observation and less and less on contemplation. For the recognition of movement came into experimental psychology through sensations of movement; sensations of movement, like other sensations, found their way into psychology through introspection; and thus even introspection illustrates the tendency of observation to work from without inward. Sensations referred to the external world, like those of sight and hearing, attract attention more strongly than those by which the subject becomes aware of his own activity.

Ebbinghaus, too, was independent of Wundt. He was, in fact, independent of any school, having found his way into psychology by pursuing his own interests and following the course of study they directed. In his day it was being said

that though the new psychology might reduce simple processes like sensation and perception to measurement and experiment, it could never deal with the higher mental processes
—with processes, that is, connected less directly than are
sensation and perception with controllable, external stimuli.
It was Ebbinghaus's chief contribution to psychology to disprove this idea by bringing memory under experimental control, and to do so by means that were so simple, so effective,
and so precisely suited to the needs of the situation that they
seemed obvious after they had been invented. Using specially
prepared nonsense syllables as the materials to be memorized, Ebbinghaus provided an unlimited supply of units for
memorizing which were presumably of equal difficulty and
with which no habitual associations had been formed. Then,
acting as his own subject, he put himself through a series
of experiments that a brother-psychologist has characterized
as heroic. His task included the learning of literally hundreds
of lists of nonsense syllables—one of the most tedious occupations, as any one who has gone through the discipline will
testify, ever contrived either inside or outside a psychological
laboratory. His general plan was to control the processes of
memorizing and retention, systematically varying the conditions, measuring the number of repetitions required for
learning and relearning specified lists, and thus accumulating quantitative data obtained under known conditions on
the processes involved in remembering and forgetting. For
purposes of comparison, he memorized also meaningful material under experimentally controlled conditions. Throughout all his work, Ebbinghaus exercised the utmost care, even
arranging the events of his life about the routine of his experiments in order to keep as constant as possible all the
conditions that might affect his efficiency as a subject. His
results are presented in his monograph *Memory*, and though
they were based on the records of only one subject, they

have been confirmed in the main by subsequent investigation. This work on memory is unquestionably Ebbinghaus's greatest achievement, but he has to his credit also a general treatise on psychology. This book is commonly regarded as the most readable handbook on the subject in German, for Ebbinghaus was characterized by a pleasing personality as well as by unusual scientific competence, and both find expression in his book. The book as he planned it was, however, interrupted by his death. The first volume was so successful that he was called upon to make two revisions for new editions while he was still at work on the second volume, which after his death was completed by Dürr. Finally, it is a fact of some interest that Ebbinghaus invented the completion test. As early as 1897, in a study of the possible effects of fatigue, and of the most satisfactory arrangement of working-hours for school-children—an investigation that he was requested to make by the city of Breslau —Ebbinghaus used this device, which has since proved one of the most useful in testing programs.

The influence of G. E. Müller on the new psychology was exerted partly through his own personal contributions, and partly through the very active laboratory he directed at Göttingen. Müller's work, characterized by extraordinary thoroughness and keen critical insight, centers about three main topics: vision, memory, and psychophysics. In vision, his best-known work is his modification and amplification of the Hering theory of color-vision—a theory that explains the phenomena of color-vision in terms of three pairs of complementary colors, blue-yellow, red-green, and black-white. Müller, accepting Hering's classification as basic, advanced a slightly different physiological explanation, and added "cortical gray," which occurs when the sensory processes underlying color-sensations are excited to the point of neutralizing each other. In his work on memory, Müller took over the methods of Ebbinghaus, revised them in an attempt to control conditions more minutely, introduced new methods, and with his pupils conducted exhaustive researches, noted for careful planning and painstaking execution. The work included a study of the various "aids" used in memorizing. The results of these researches, published in three large volumes, form the most exhaustive treatise on memory in existence. In psychophysics, too, Müller carefully reviewed the existing material, subjected it to a thorough and critical analysis, and introduced changes in procedure. One of Müller's discoveries, incidental to his main work on psychophysics, was that which led to the concept of "motor set." In his study of lifted weights, he included careful introspective observations of the process by which the subject judged one weight to be heavier than another. It had seemed reasonable to suppose, on the basis of an intellectual analysis, that in forming a judgment of "lighter" or "heavier" the memory image of the previous weight was compared with the sensation or memory after-image of the present weight. This analysis, however, turned out not to correspond to the observed facts. A subject, as he was lifting the weight, usually knew immediately whether it was lighter or heavier than the one just lifted; his arm sprang up quickly if the weight was lighter, more slowly and with more difficulty if it was heavier; he had unconsciously "set" himself for a given pull, and the weight either confirmed his set or proved that it had over- or under-prepared him. In other words, his judgment was the outcome of immediately felt muscular reaction, not of intellectual comparison. This apparently trivial fact is significant as further evidence that an *a priori* intellectual analysis of psychological material may lead to a picture of the facts that is false. Such an analysis is particularly likely to overintellectualize the situation, and it is dangerously unlikely to be challenged until actual observation shows that the facts in the case are otherwise. Müller's explanation of the observed situation in terms of motor set is further significant as still another indication that the motor side of reaction was gradually receiving notice. In this case, Müller's interpretation led to the general concept of the "set" of the organism, a concept that has proved extremely useful—sometimes it seems a shade too useful—in the interpretation of conduct. It is interesting to note that in Müller's case as in that of Lipps the recognition of the rôle of muscular activity came as a result of introspection.

These men and many others were devoting themselves to psychology in Germany. Some were more philosophical than psychological in their interests, others more physiological, but out of their labors a branch of knowledge was growing that was neither philosophy nor physiology. The "new" psychology was not a study of the soul, certainly not an inquiry by rational analysis into its simplicity, substantiality, and immortality. It was a study, by observation and experiment, of certain reactions of the human organism not included in the subject-matter of any other science. The German psychologists, in spite of their many differences, were to this extent engaged in a common enterprise; and their ability, their industry, and the common direction of their labors all made the developments in the German universities the center of the new movement in psychology.

It was not only in Germany, however, that a new point of view in psychology was developing. In England too men were observing man naturalistically. Here the outstanding scientific event of the century was the publication in 1859 of Darwin's *Origin of Species,* a book that forced upon the attention of the scientific world the possibility of looking on humanity not as a special and favorite creation, not as a race set apart, not as an object of special concern in the universe, but merely as one of the many animal species evolved in the course of natural events. For psychology, as a science of living creatures, the Darwinian theory has obvious implications. It means first of all that it is not sufficient to study man in and by himself, but that it is necessary to consider him also in relation to the many forces that mold him—to know his history and surroundings, his development both genetic and phylogenetic, his position in the array of the animal species, and the means by which he adapts himself to his environment. Genetic psychology, comparative psychology, and folk psychology all become vastly important, and at the same time the concept of mental activities as adaptive functions is thrust into the foreground. In a sense, the scientific psychology of Germany was patterned on physics. Growing in large measure from the attempt to understand the sense-organs as mechanical models, and influenced by this fact in its mode of attack upon the psychic life, it undertook the task of discovering into what elemental parts mental states can be analyzed, and of determining the ways in which these parts are combined. German psychology, to a considerable extent, was a psychology that kept a mechanical model before it; but Darwin gave psychology another pattern. In the light of his conception, man was not merely something to be minutely analyzed; he was also a unit in a system external to himself, to be studied in relation to his history and surroundings.

Darwin's cousin, Sir Francis Galton, was the first representative of this view in psychology. Unlike his German confrères, Galton was not a professional psychologist. He was a man of leisure whose active curiosity and extraordinarily keen intelligence were attracted by several sciences. Coming upon psychological problems in the course of his varied intellectual interests, he naturally saw them from points of view somewhat different from those of the experimenters in the German laboratories. One of Galton's chief interests was eugenics, and through eugenics he was led to consider the problem of the inheritance of mental traits, a problem toward the solution of which *Hereditary Genius, English Men of Science, Natural Inheritance,* and *Inquiries into Human Faculty* are his principal contributions. In his studies in this field, Galton developed several methods that have come into common use, of which the biographical method, the family-history method, the study of twin-resemblances, and the comparison of races may be mentioned. On the basis of his investigations he came to the conclusion that mental ability is something inherent in the individual, something that is not fundamentally dependent on training. He believed that men who attain eminence possess exceptional ability, and also that really able men become eminent in spite of adverse circumstances.

In these studies, Galton was naturally impressed by the variations within the human race, in mental as well as in physical traits. He therefore turned his attention toward the subject of individual differences, a topic which has assumed great importance in psychology, and which has been studied with particular enthusiasm in America. As Wundt and the Wundtians were interested in the generalized human mind, Galton was interested in the fact that individual minds show a wide range of variations. In the study of individual differences two kinds of tools are required: first, tests for revealing differences in capacity between individuals: and second, statistical methods for analyzing the large mass of quantitative data which such tests yield. Galton devised tools of both kinds and did much to get them firmly established in psychology. He is sometimes called the father of mental tests. A "test," it should be observed, is a device for revealing an individual's ability in a given performance, not for analyzing the process. It thus differs in intention from the typical experiment, which is directed toward finding out something not about the individual, but about the process that is being examined. The difference may be illustrated by means of the reaction-time technique. If used as a test, the reaction-time procedure simply determines an individual's position on a scale, showing where he stands with relation to other members of a group with respect to the one item, speed of reaction. If used as an experiment, the reaction-time technique involves such elaborate analyses, objective and subjective, as those described above. As an experiment its purpose is to discover not a single fact about an individual, but everything possible, within the conditions of the experiment, about the process itself. Galton also had recourse to statistical tools. He took account of the probability curve in his studies, arranged his cases on scales that have been considered the ancestors of the modern rating scales, and worked out a procedure for representing graphically and stating quantitatively the degree of relationship between two variables, thus obtaining what he called the "index of co-relation." His studies in the theory of statistics were developed by his pupil, Karl Pearson, who worked out the now widely used product-moment formula for obtaining the coefficient of correlation.

No account of Galton would be complete without special reference to his famous study of imagery and to his less famous but equally important work on association. In the latter, he served as his own subject and attempted an analysis of a group of actual associations. He used seventy-five stimulus words, recorded his first two associations to each of them, measured the amount of time required for the two associations, and tried to account for their content in terms of his own past experience. The "associations" that Galton used were either single words, or mental images, which of course had to be described. The method was almost immediately taken over by Wundt, who simplified and altered it somewhat, chiefly by requiring that each stimulus word be responded to by a single response word, by controlling the conditions more adequately, and by reducing the whole to a more uniform procedure which would obtain responses that could be measured in time, classified, and treated quantitatively. Galton's study thus gave rise to the experiments in free and controlled association that have constituted one of the more fruitful methods of investigating the more complex mental processes, intellectual and emotional, in both normal and abnormal subjects.

The study of imagery involved the use of a questionnaire, said to be the first employed for a large-scale investigation in psychology. It required the subject to "think of some definite object—suppose it is your breakfast table as you sat down to it this morning—and consider carefully the picture that arises before your mind's eye." The subject, in reporting, was to consider such questions as whether the image was clear or dim, colored, sharply defined or blurred. The results showed not only that individuals varied greatly in their imagery, but that there was no necessary correspondence between imagery and ability—that a painter, for example, might have no visual imagery, or that a scientist or scholar might have no concrete pictures of the facts on which he was an authority. It had been popularly assumed, more or less vaguely, that images were the materials employed by thought, and as a corollary, that clear and abundant imagery accompanied superior mental ability. But again the facts ran counter to predictions based on *a priori* analysis; again observation gave no evidence for what, according to such speculation, ought to be the case. And here, too, as in the study of association, the methods used in this experiment have been widely utilized, with modifications, in psychology.

Thus Galton, who was not a psychologist, and whose interest in psychology was largely incidental, contributed more to the growing science than did many a diligent professional. He made definite inroads into the fields of association, imagery, and mental heredity, in all of which he introduced new or nearly new methods of research. He is largely responsible for a flourishing branch of modern psychology, the study of individual differences. Besides, his whole approach to psychology was different from that of the German scientists. Studying intact processes and intact organisms much as they appear to common sense, he supplemented the method of minute analysis practised in the German laboratories with a method of observation which took larger wholes as its units, which revealed problems of a different range, and which set those problems forth in a new perspective.

The characteristic influence of the French upon the development of psychology was exerted chiefly through their interest in psychiatry and abnormal phenomena. The list of Frenchmen prominent in this field includes such distinguished names as those of Pinel, who as early as the 1790's convinced the world that the insane are ill, not devil-ridden; of Charcot, who, working in the middle of the next century, turned the attention of his colleagues and pupils to the scientific study of hysteria and similar disorders; of Bernheim and Liébeault, who contended that hypnotism or mesmerism was nothing more mysterious, nor for that matter more pathological, than suggestion; of Pierre Janet, one of Charcot's pupils, and like Charcot a student of hysteria and of dissociation in general; and of Ribot, who tried to view disturbances in mental life in the light of the new physiological psychology. The study of the insane, who through long ages had been regarded as utterly different from normal human beings, gradually led to the view, now generally accepted, that abnormal reactions are only exaggerations of normal ones, and that, as such, they are due to conditions similar to those which produce their less disruptive counterparts in normal persons. As a result of the serious study of abnormal states, man came to be regarded as a complicated organism that sometimes got out of order; his weirdest vagaries were believed to be explicable in terms of the laws that operated in his sanest living; the "unity" of his "soul" was no longer thought of as absolute and indissoluble, but as subject to disintegration not only by death but also by the stress and strain of living. Psychiatry, with its increasing emphasis on the essential similarity between the normal and the abnormal, strongly reinforced the growing tendency in psychology to regard all human behavior as conforming to natural law.

All these movements, in Germany, in England, and in France, were involved in the highly complex process by which the psychology of to-day came into being. Psychology as a science was the work neither of any one man nor of any one group. It did not rise inevitably from any one problem or from any set of problems. Rather, it was but one of the many manifestations of the scientific mode of thought that characterized the intellectual life of the nineteenth century. Unquestionably, the center of the movement was in the German universities, and the "new" psychology, as it was beginning to be known, was usually associated with that developed in Germany, particularly with that of the Leipzig laboratory. But elsewhere there were signs that scientific thought had found its way into psychology. During the second half of the nineteenth century, psychology was conducting operations in many different fields. It was acquiring techniques, equipping laboratories, producing research, and developing schools and systems. As a consequence, it had secured academic recognition as an independent discipline, and by the closing decade of the century, psychology as a science had made a definite start in life. Wherever students set themselves to observe rather than to reflect on psychological material—however they might differ in their formal definitions of it—wherever they looked upon their subject-matter as part of the natural world, wherever they attempted to note with the aid of experimental and quantitative methods the conditions in which psychological processes occurred or failed to occur, there psychology as a science had begun.

Chapter IV

TITCHENER AND STRUCTURALISM [1]

THE new psychology was very early imported into the United States. Several young Americans were among the first students at the Leipzig laboratory, and when they returned to America, they soon presided over laboratories of their own, and taught psychologies which, however they might differ from each other and from the Wundtian model, bore unmistakable signs of their Leipzig origin. Hall, Cattell, Wolfe, Pace, Scripture, and Frank Angell were the first of this number. But the most ardent champion of the new psychology in America was not himself an American. Edward Bradford Titchener, a brilliant young Englishman, who in 1892 became director of the laboratory at Cornell University, worked so vigorously and so consciously in the Wundtian tradition that he became the recognized representative in America of that point of view. Despite deviations on particular points, Titchener was definitely on the side of the Wundtian orthodoxy. It was Titchener who strove most valiantly to establish the new psychology in the new world and, with something of the zeal of a prophet for the integrity of his message, to keep it unspotted from that world.

[1] Throughout this chapter, Titchener's psychology is referred to as structuralism. Strictly speaking, this practice is not correct, since the term "structuralism" was used primarily to contrast the system with functionalism, a rival system that developed a little later. For convenience, however, and because there is no one term that is in general use to designate Titchener's psychology, "structuralism" is used for that purpose in this book.

The position of Titchener in American psychology is extraordinary and unique. In a country in which he was an alien, in which he always remained an alien, his influence for years was all but dominating; and even when his prestige had visibly diminished, his school remained an essential point of reference in American psychology. His was the psychology *against* which many of the distinctively American movements asserted themselves. When he died, E. G. Boring, a former pupil and colleague, wrote:

"The death of no other psychologist could so alter the psychological picture in America . . . he was a cardinal point in the national systematic orientation. The clear-cut opposition between behaviorism and its allies on the one hand, and something else, on the other, remains clear only when the opposition is between behaviorism and Titchener, mental tests and Titchener, or applied psychology and Titchener. His death thus, in a sense, creates a classificatory chaos in American systematic psychology." [2]

It is significant that Titchener was never in the slightest danger of being Americanized, though he came to the United States when he was only twenty-five and remained until his death, thirty-five years later. And yet only two years at Leipzig had Germanized him. He even looked like a German and was sometimes mistaken for one; the science for which he labored was German to the core; and in what must have seemed to him a crude university on the wrong side of the Atlantic, he preserved with sturdy and punctilious devotion the ceremonial with which he had seen psychology surrounded in a German university. Evidently he found in the German culture, in German science at least, something deeply congenial to his nature. But with his American surroundings Titchener was never quite compatible. He both withdrew from and opposed the characteristically American enterprises in psychology which, bearing all the signs of being indigenous growths, took root and flourished on American soil. Applied psychology, the study of individual differences, the movement toward mental testing, in all of which American interest was spontaneous and keen, seemed to him second-rate, from the standpoint of pure science even a little cheap; and when definite schools like functionalism and behaviorism arose and prospered, he fulminated against them in a manner truly Jovian. Certainly he did not drift with the American current. He even found it difficult to remain a member of the American Psychological Association, an organization of which most qualified psychologists in America are members as a matter of course. On one occasion he failed to secure its support in a measure which he thought involved a matter of professional ethics. He therefore resigned his membership, and though he renewed it several years later, he never attended the meetings of the association—not even when it met at Ithaca—and eventually permitted his membership to lapse. In the meantime he had formed a group of his own, known as the Experimentalists. This group could hardly be called an organization. It had no officers and no constitution, its membership was determined by Titchener's invitation, and its papers and discussions were limited to topics that met his approval or at least escaped his genial but authoritative *"Verboten!"* It was his own creation and he held it in the hollow of his hand. Both the existence of this group and his pleasure in its existence are indicative of Titchener's relation to American psychology. Apparently he regarded the Experimentalists as a band of the elect, a chosen few worthy or almost worthy to serve psychology as a pure science—a saving remnant set apart by his approval from the ruck of the native psychologists.

As a result of this attitude, this habit of contrasting pure experimental psychology with American psychology generally, a curious situation developed. In one sense, conditions in the new country were distinctly favorable to the development of an experimental psychology. In so far as the experimental method implied a tendency to prefer facts to theories, to appeal to evidence rather than to speculation, to try things out and be "shown" rather than to accept them on faith, the American temper was thoroughly hospitable to the experimental movement. And yet experimental psychology in America, in the sense that managed to get itself accepted as authentic, was carefully sheltered from the more characteristic American influences. It became a thing apart, almost precious, definitely aloof from the main stream of American interests. The very phrase "experimental psychology" took on a special significance. In America, experimental psychology could almost be described as the psychology that was made in Germany and imported by Titchener. Its adherents were of course American students, but for the most part Americans who had been trained under Titchener's influence and under a system of imported academic *mores* that they could hardly fail to find impressive.

There could be no doubt at Cornell that psychology was a matter of grave importance. Titchener himself gave the lectures to the beginning classes to insure their proper induction into the science. Those lectures are famous, not only for their content and influence, but for the unchanging ceremonial that surrounded them. Titchener lectured in his Oxford master's gown. "It confers the right to be dogmatic," he explained. The custom that grew up about the lectures has been described by Boring, who was for a time Titchener's assistant.

"In the first semester on Tuesday and Thursday at eleven he lectured to the undergraduates in the new lecture-room in Goldwin Smith Hall, the room with a psychological demonstrational laboratory and an office built off it, and with the pitch of the seats determined by Titchener's stature. The demonstration was set out the hour before and Titchener arrived shortly after ten to inspect it. Later the staff gradually gathered in his office. When the time for the lecture arrived, he donned his gown, the assistant brushed his coat for fear of ashes from the ever present cigar, the staff went out the door for apparatus and took front seats, and Titchener then appeared on the platform from the office door. The whole rite was performed pleasantly and sometimes jokingly, yet it was scrupulously observed. After the lecture the staff gathered in Titchener's office for an hour for talk and at one o'clock dispersed for lunch." [3]

The whole procedure was patterned on that which Titchener had witnessed at Leipzig as a student of Wundt. Though he had brought his psychology into a far country, he preserved not only the matter but also the manner of the Leipzig tradition.

The lectures themselves were trenchant and powerful, and year after year they attracted crowds of students. Not only did they present pure academic psychology in the strictest sense of the term, but also they included injunctions to beware of false prophets. The staff listened with at least as much interest as the students, for in these lectures they sometimes heard Titchener's first pronouncement on a new theory or discovery, and on the way it was to be assimilated, if accepted at all, to the main body of psychology.

All this was for beginners. The graduate students, too, found psychology at Cornell impressive. During the second semester, Titchener conducted a seminar attended by the staff and advanced graduate students where, it goes without saying, he dominated the situation. Except for these meetings, for doctor's examinations, and those occa-

[3] E. G. Boring, *op. cit.*, 500.

sions when he was acting as host to distinguished visitors, he did not come to the laboratory. On the rare occasions when the students conferred with him, they did so at his house, by appointment. His working-hours at home were carefully protected, and it was understood that only a real emergency justified an attempt to reach him by telephone.

But Titchener was a man of charm as well as of power, and the admiration his students felt for him was not wholly for his prowess in his special field. He was a man of varied and infectious interests, a brilliant conversationalist, and a gracious host. He could be genial as well as imposing, and helpful as well as authoritative. There is no doubt that the feeling he aroused in his students and associates was more than mere respect.

Though he was rarely seen at the university, Titchener's influence was all-important; and psychology at Cornell became psychology as interpreted by a single dominating person, by an all but invisible presence. In the background there was always a final authority who held the fate of men and theories in his hands, who drew a sharp line between orthodoxy and heterodoxy, who made the distinction one of academic caste, and who ordered the events of his academic world for the defense and advancement of the new psychology—of *the* new psychology in all its purity.

In his writings, too, Titchener speaks in character. Especially in the books he wrote for students his tone is the tone of authority. For Titchener's textbooks are hardly more remarkable for scientific competence and expository power than for sheer lack of pedagogical tact. He rarely takes a chance on the reader's intelligence. He assumes that he, the author, must point out everything to the last detail; that he must tease out the implications; that he must explain, to the uttermost, the qualifications and reservations. Not for a moment does he ask the reader to accept his views without evidence or argument, but his very manner of marshaling facts, of heaping explanation on explanation and argument on argument, is didactic. Beyond a doubt, much of the meticulous care that characterizes Titchener's exposition is due to his own passion for clarity and explication, to an insistent demand for thoroughness in his own nature. One suspects, too, that some of it has its source in an unusually sensitive appreciation of all the considerations which might be urged against his position; that his convictions did not come with the untroubled ease which characterizes less critical temperaments; and that his conclusions, when formed, were stated the more clearly and maintained the more vigorously because they were not achieved without inner resistances. But over and above this, there is more than a suggestion of the copy-book style of teaching. After all, Titchener's characteristic way of presenting a topic is to expose his own intellectual operations upon it; and the implication is that the reader will observe closely, and produce the best reproduction he can. In discourses intended for his professional colleagues and for audiences in which he can assume some technical psychological knowledge, he is less the schoolmaster, but not less the authority. Even here—in the two series of lectures published as the *Experimental Psychology of the Higher Thought Processes* and *Psychology of Feeling and Attention,* for example—he does not really ask his public to consider the matter with him; he surveys the field, organizes the facts, and points' the way.

And the system itself? The psychology that was the reason for the whole impressive setting, the object of all this careful exposition and vigorous defense? It is a psychology that has no generally accepted name, but which is referred to sometimes as structuralism, sometimes as introspectionism,[4] sometimes as existentialism,[5] and occasionally as Titchenerism. Stated in its most complete and systematic form in Titchener's *Text-book of Psychology*, it is the psychology which, in America, especially since the rise of behaviorism, has often been characterized as "traditional" and "reactionary." It has sometimes been pronounced animistic because it deals with the mind. It has also been called metaphysical as opposed to scientific, apparently on the rather curious set of assumptions that the mental is synonymous with the supernatural, that the distinction between science and metaphysics is the distinction between matter and mind, and that any inquiry which addresses itself to mental processes is *ipso facto* outside the field of natural science.

It would be difficult, however, to find an attitude that would more surely obscure the significance of the whole movement of which Titchener's psychology is a part, or which would serve better as an example of the historical fallacy. Nothing could be more misleading than to apply the term "unscientific," as it is used by a particular group of psychologists to-day, to a school that a half-century ago helped to fight and win the battle for the independence of psychology from metaphysics. The whole point of the new psychology was that it was an extension of the scientific method into a new field. When it is remembered that in the nineteenth century even the physical sciences were relatively new, that physiology was considered a daring venture in the application of scientific principles to *living* matter, and that mental processes such as sensation and perception were

[4] Because of the importance it attached to introspection as a method of study.

[5] "Existentialism," like "structuralism," is a term used to contrast Titchener's psychology with psychologies which, like functionalism and act psychology, attempt to study mental processes as acts and functions, not merely as conscious contents or existential realities.

in good repute in the physiological laboratories, it becomes apparent that logically the next step was to extend the scientific method to *mental* processes—to treat them as natural events in the natural world and to submit them to the kind of experimental investigation that characterized other scientific disciplines. The new psychology was based on the utmost faith in the scientific method, specifically in its power to reveal the laws of mental processes as it had discovered and was still discovering those of physical nature. It was for this reason that the new psychology regarded itself as the boldest and farthest thrust of the scientific movement, and that it became consciously, even self-consciously, scientific. In defining its subject-matter, in determining its methods, and in formulating its tenets, its followers kept the question constantly in the foreground: Is this science? The key-note of the whole enterprise was the attempt to treat psychological material as science regularly treats its data. To fail to recognize this attempt as fundamental to the whole endeavor is to lose sight of the deepest significance of the movement.

Titchener's initial task, then, in presenting his system,[6] was to show that the subject-matter of psychology is a legitimate object of scientific study. Perhaps the shortest way to his meaning is to say that he regards psychology as the science of "consciousness," or "mind," and then to hasten to add that one must not read into these terms the meanings that common sense is likely to put there. Titchener unhesitatingly assures the reader that his old notions of mind are unfit for scientific use. What science means by mind and consciousness can best be understood by

---

[6] The following account is based mainly on the *Text-book* and *A Beginner's Psychology* and does not purport to take into account later views not formally included in the system.

showing how the subject-matter of psychology is distinguished from that of physics.

All science, Titchener explains, has its starting-point in experience. Fundamentally, the subject-matter of physics and that of psychology are the same. The two sciences differ not because they deal with different objects, but because they regard their common subject-matter, the world of experience, from different points of view. Physics studies the world without reference to man. Psychology studies the world with reference to the person who experiences it. The subject-matter of physics is experience independent of the experiencing person; the subject-matter of psychology is experience dependent on an experiencing person. In physics, for example, space, time, and mass are always the same; the centimeter, the second, and the gram are constant units, unaffected by the person who experiences them. In psychology, however, a space may be large or small, an hour long or short, a weight light or heavy, according to the conditions affecting the experiencing person. The same holds true of heat, sound, and light. Psychologically they vary with the factors affecting the person who experiences them; but physically, heat is always molecular motion, sound a wave-motion in the air, light a wave-motion in the ether. In the world of physics, there are no colors, no sounds, no tastes and smells and "feels," for all these are dependent on the person who experiences them. From the standpoint of psychology, a particular datum in the world of experience is red; from the standpoint of physics, it is ether vibration of a specified wave-length. So it is with all the stuff of experience. Conceived as independent of the experiencing person, it is the subject-matter of physics; conceived as dependent on the experiencing person, it is the subject-matter of psychology. Hence Titchener's formal definition of the subject-matter of psychology is "experience dependent on an experiencing person," or what amounts to the same thing, "the world with man left in." This experience, or this world, it must be noted specifically, consists of contents that can be observed and described. Titchener further explains that the "experiencing person" means the living body and that, for the purposes of the psychologist, the living body may be reduced to "the nervous system and its attachments." He also distinguishes between mind and consciousness. Mind refers to "the sum total of mental processes occurring in the lifetime of the individual," consciousness to "the sum total of mental processes occurring *now*, at any given present time." But mind and consciousness are both to be thought of as human experience, dependent upon a nervous system, and describable in terms of observed facts.

In defining his subject-matter in terms of point of view, Titchener was following Wundt; in defining it as "experience dependent on an experiencing person," he was introducing modifications, but modifications derived from his student days at Leipzig. Wundt, too, had distinguished the subject-matter of psychology from that of physics only after he had insisted that both are derived from the same source, human experience, and that both are subject to human observation. Wundt's distinction, however, was based on the difference between immediate and mediate experience. A person is directly and immediately aware of his sensation of red; the ether-waves that explain it, considered as objects in the physical world, are constructed on the basis of the sensation and are known only through the sensation. The sensation red, which is known immediately, belongs to psychology; the ether-waves, which are known mediately, belong to physics. Wundt did not labor the point sometimes made in this connection that psychological knowledge is therefore safer and more certain, less subject to the slips of inference, than is the mediate knowledge of physics. His primary purpose was to show that psychology, like physics or any other natural science, has a subject-matter that is given in experience, and his chief concern was to justify the claim that psychology is a natural science. But some of the pupils of Wundt, as thoroughly convinced as he that a science of psychology is possible, preferred another explanation. Külpe, influenced by the writings of Mach and Avenarius, believed that the distinction between physics and psychology can best be made in terms of experience as independent of, and dependent on, a nervous system; and it was this view which Titchener accepted.[7] It is interesting to note that both theories express the same fundamental conviction, the conviction that consciousness or mental processes can be made the object of scientific observation. At basis, both are attempts to show that psychology is a science of experience and as such distinct from metaphysics.

But for Titchener, it was not enough to keep the subject-matter of psychology pure of metaphysics; it was necessary too to keep it pure of common sense. He plainly regarded the common-sense notions of mind and consciousness as enemies, perhaps the strongest enemies scientific psychology has to encounter. Common sense, he explains, thinks of the mind as "an unsubstantial manikin living inside the head," a kind of ghostly inner man who directs the actions of the visible outer man, and who is in turn affected by the experiences the outer man encounters. This, Titchener insists, is what the common-sense notion of mind really amounts to, when put plainly, and he never tires of

[7] To avoid confusion, it should probably be mentioned at this point that Titchener did not follow Külpe in the views that he (Külpe) later developed on the use of introspection. Certainly Titchener did not accept the interpretation Külpe placed on the introspective studies he directed.

poking fun at its inconsistencies and absurdities. Against the manikin conception of mind, a conception absolutely inimical, in his opinion, to any real understanding of psychology, he never ceased to wage war.

And just as he strove to keep the subject-matter of psychology pure of metaphysics and pure of common sense, so he strove to keep it pure of utilitarian interest. Titchener was brusquely intolerant of the point of view that psychology, probing the depths of the human heart, exists to bring aid and comfort to "sick souls." The business of psychology, he asserts, is not to relieve suffering or to effect improvement, but to discover facts about its subject-matter and to understand them. To Titchener, science has nothing to do with values. For science, the struggling human self conceived as common sense conceives it, with its appeal to human interest and to human sympathies, simply does not exist. In the same impersonal and detached manner in which a physicist studies a block sliding down an inclined plane, the psychologist studies mental processes. To be sure, the results of science may be utilized in everyday life and may thus acquire value in the eyes of common sense; but to science as such, their values are irrelevant. No one should be less occupied with personal and private interests than the trained psychologist who is trying to discover exactly how one sensation differs from another in quality, or what an allegedly imageless thought is made of.

From every point of view, in fact, Titchener was in favor of pure as opposed to applied psychology. Like Wundt, he was interested in "the generalized human mind"—not in particular human minds as such, nor in the individual differences that are matters of undeniable importance in the practical affairs of everyday life. It is true that both Wundt and Titchener formally recognized that psychology may include the study of animals, of children, of societies, and of madmen, but for both of them the point of departure and the final point of reference was always the adult human consciousness of which the psychologist is immediately aware. Psychology may gather its material from many sources, but its aim is to understand the generalized human mind; to *understand* the mind, Titchener always insisted, not to alter it or improve it, or to attempt to operate on it in any way. And it is indicative both of his tastes and of his power that, in a country which tends rather strongly to value knowledge less for its own sake than for what it can accomplish, he upheld the idea that the only work proper or fitting for true science is disinterested study of its subject-matter.

For Titchener, then, the subject-matter of psychology is consciousness; consciousness not as common sense conceives it, not as a manikin animating the body, not the stuff that ghosts are made of, but "experience as dependent on the experiencing organism." Such experience consists of observable processes in the world of nature, purged of human interest and detached from the practical involvements of daily life. It is something that can be studied in the same impersonal manner which science regularly adopts toward its data. In no sense is it allied to the supernatural. Nothing could be more free from the taint of animism than the consciousness that Titchener inspects and analyzes.

The definition of the subject-matter as "experience dependent on an experiencing person" was accompanied by the doctrine of psychophysical parallelism, which Titchener took over specifically from Wundt.[8] Evidently Titchener

---

[8] As a matter of fact, Titchener took over the doctrine from Wundt quite uncritically, apparently without considering that this conception —which Wundt had formulated in connection with a distinction between immediate and mediate experience—might not apply without alteration to the distinction between experience as dependent on and independent of an experiencing person.

was not greatly interested in the mind-body problem for its own sake; but having made a distinction between the mental and the physical, he found in this theory the most convenient way of conceiving the relation between them. According to this conception, mental processes and physical processes run along side by side as parallel streams. Neither one causes the other, there is no interaction between them, but a change in one is always accompanied by a change in the other. It is possible, therefore, to refer the one to the other; even, as Titchener points out, to "explain" the one by the other—that is, to explain the mental processes by bringing them into relation with the events of the physical world, which form a coherent and self-contained system. Titchener therefore accepts psychophysical parallelism as a scheme that permits him to take cognizance of both mental and physical data, and thus to do justice to all the facts of experience with the minimum of attention to metaphysics. Apparently this was his sole interest in the matter. His emotions were not involved in the problem for its own sake, as are those of some of his fellow-psychologists. As he used the conception, psychophysical parallelism was a convenient explanatory device—and nothing more—for a man who was sufficiently faithful to the data of experience to insist on including both physical and mental facts, and sufficiently alive to rational considerations to be uncomfortable without a systematic explanation. The fact that he did not argue about it, and the fact that he made no other claim for it than that of expediency, show how clearly psychology, as he conceived it, had emerged from its metaphysical setting. He is almost perfunctory in his discussion of the topic. Obviously he found the whole problem far less interesting than such purely psychological questions as whether images and sensations are different in texture, and

whether there are any elementary affective processes besides pleasantness and unpleasantness.

The question of the methods that psychology may legitimately employ is one of the important points in Titchener's
system; and since the system is sometimes called introspectionism, it may seem sufficient to say without further
ado that the characteristic method is introspection. But
such a procedure would be as misleading as to say without
comment that the subject-matter is consciousness. For here
again Titchener finds it necessary to indicate with great
exactness what science means, and what it does not mean,
by the term.

The method common to all science, Titchener notes, is
observation, and introspection is a form of observation. Introspection, or observation of the contents of consciousness, may be distinguished from inspection, the observation
of the physical world; but fundamentally, the two methods
are the same. Introspection, Titchener maintains from first
to last, is a form of *observation*.

Introspection, moreover, is observation of a very special
sort. For a time, much was heard in the new science about the
"trained introspectionist." As psychology grew conscious of
its status as a science, it strongly tended to emphasize introspection, which, in substituting observation for speculation,
set it apart as different from the rational psychology of its
prescientific past. Apparently some of the psychologists of the
period delighted in the possession of a method, technical and
esoteric, that marked off psychology from the other sciences
and yet made it one of their distinguished company. They
insisted, therefore, that introspection must not be taken
lightly. They emphasized the difficulty of observing conscious processes—processes which do not stand still to be
watched, which are so enmeshed in other conscious proc-

esses that it is difficult to single out one of them for examination, and which if they are to be seen in their own character demand an attitude that runs counter to the habits of a lifetime. For the ordinary habits of observation dispose one to see the objects and events of common sense and of daily life, not the contents of consciousness. To see the thing, rather than the conscious content, was subsequently called the "stimulus error." When a person observes naïvely, in the manner of common sense, he sees, for example, a table; but if an introspectionist sees a table while making a scientific observation of his perception of a table, he is committing the stimulus error. He is attending to the stimulus instead of to the conscious process the stimulus occasions in him; he is reading into the process what he knows about the object and, in doing so, is failing to distinguish what he, as a person, knows about the stimulus from what he, as an observer, is immediately aware of in his experience. All that his immediate experience gives him is color and brightness and spatial pattern. The rest is interpretation, not observation, and is the result of reading meaning into what is immediately present in his experience. He may be irresistibly led to the perception of a table, but the trained introspectionist distinguishes between his immediate and his elaborated experience—and even he is not infallible. For this reason, introspection requires special training; it involves not only the difficulties inherent in all exact observation, but difficulties peculiar to itself. "Hard introspective labor" is a phrase Titchener once applied to the discipline. Hence there grew up among the adherents of the early experimental psychology an attitude that true introspection is something to be practised only by those who have gone through a very special and rigorous preparation.

From this explanation, it should be apparent that introspection is not to be confused with the moody self-attention, the solicitous concern with personal thoughts and feelings, which common sense sometimes calls by that name. Very definitely Titchener repudiates the popular notion of introspection that is likely to be accompanied by the adjective "morbid." One of his comments runs:

"So we find that the hero of yesterday's novel was not given to introspection. His external interests in life were too engrossing for him to think deeply or continuously about himself. Such a habit of mind he used vehemently to deprecate as morbid, egotistical. But now—now the fateful girl is on the scene; the hero begins to think about himself; and flatters himself, poor man, that he is to turn psychologist. Unfortunately, neither a keen appreciation of his own virtue nor a rooted distrust of his own powers makes a man into a psychologist." [9]

It is impossible to do justice to Titchener's system without realizing fully his position on this matter. It is an essential and explicit part of his teachings; yet some of the criticisms directed against his school are based on a misunderstanding of this very point. One almost gets the impression from some objectors that introspection consists in dreamily recalling thoughts and feelings in the manner of pleasant reverie before an open fire. But whatever the objections to introspection may be—and serious objections can be urged against it—the charge of being lax and generally tender-minded cannot be included among them. That it is beset with dangers and difficulties, no one, least of all the "trained introspectionist," will deny. By far the best accounts of the difficulties of introspection are written by those who have tried it at first hand. In his directions to both students and instructors in his *Experimental Psychology*, Titchener points out so clearly what particular obstacles will be encountered that the heated objections of

[9] E. B. Titchener, *A Beginner's Psychology*, 21-22.

most of his critics seem irrelevant and amateurish by contrast.[10]

Scientific observation at its best is experimental; and as insistently as he maintained that introspection is observation, Titchener stood for the experimental method in psychology. A scientific experiment, providing as it does for observation that is careful, systematic, and controlled, is calculated to secure the two essentials of all good observation, attention to the phenomena and a record of the phenomena.

"An experiment," Titchener says, "is an observation that can be repeated, isolated and varied. The more frequently you can repeat an observation, the more likely are you to see clearly what is there and to describe accurately what you have seen. The more strictly you can isolate an observation, the easier does your task of observation become, and the less danger is there of your being led astray by irrelevant circumstances, or of placing emphasis on the wrong point. The more widely you can vary an observation, the more clearly will the uniformity of experience stand out, and the better is your chance of discovering laws. All experimental appliances, all laboratories and instruments, are provided and devised with this one end in view: that the student shall be able to repeat, isolate and vary his observation." [11]

There is nothing in which Titchener and his school took greater pride than in their scrupulous observance of the rules of scientific experimentation. They were keenly conscious, too, of the fact that their psychology was experimental as opposed to empirical, and they thus kept alive the distinction that goes back to the difference between Wundt and the act psychologists. Titchener's emphasis on

[10] E. B. Titchener, *Experimental Psychology; Qualitative Instructor's Manual,* XIX-XXXIII; *Student's Manual,* XIII-XVIII.
[11] E. B. Titchener, *A Text-book of Psychology,* 20.

the experimental method requires little comment when it is remembered that in America the very phrase "experimental psychology" came to connote, in the minds of many, the particular kind of psychology that he sanctioned.

With the subject-matter defined, the mind-body relation stated, and the methods understood, the problem of psychology, as Titchener saw it, can be definitely stated. All science, he says, asks three questions about its subject-matter: "What?" "How?" "Why?" The question "What?" is answered by analysis, by reducing the material to its elements and finding out precisely what is there. The question "How?" is answered by synthesis, by showing how the elements are arranged and combined, and by discovering the laws of their sequences and combinations. The question "Why?" inquires into the cause. The first two questions are answered by description; the third seeks explanation.

Explanation in psychology, according to Titchener, is made in terms of the nervous system. Even if we had a description that fully answered the questions "What?" and "How?" our knowledge would be incomplete until the phenomenon in question had been traced to its cause. But how can this final step be taken in psychology? One mental state cannot be considered the cause of another if only because a change in physical surroundings may be attended by entirely new conscious contents. "When I visit Athens or Rome for the first time," Titchener writes, "I have experiences which are due, not to past consciousnesses, but to present stimuli." Nor can conscious experience be caused by processes in the nervous system, or by other events in the physical world; the doctrine of psychophysical parallelism rules out this possibility. Still, Titchener maintains, though the nervous system is not the cause of mind, it can be used to explain it. "It explains mind as the map of a country explains the fragmentary glimpses of hills and rivers and towns that we catch on our journey through it." For mental processes do not form the un-broken chain of events that a causal explanation requires. Their continuity is broken by such events as sleep and coma and lapses of memory. But the physical world, pre-cisely because it is independent of the experiencing individ-ual, contains no such gaps and breaks. Because of this fact—and also because the physical and mental streams run parallel to each other—it is possible to note what physi-cal events regularly attend given mental processes and thus to assign each mental process to a definite place in a regu-lar and unbroken series. It is in this sense, but only in this sense, that reference to the body explains mental events.

It is important to note that this method of explanation does not imply either that the nervous system is funda-mental to consciousness or that it is in any sense more real than consciousness. Titchener makes it clear that knowl-edge of the nervous system is not itself psychology; that it adds nothing whatever to the data of psychology, which are the contents of consciousness open to introspection. Psychology, it is true, seeks its explanations outside the world of its own subject-matter; but it does so not because the world of physics is more real or more fundamental, but because it is more continuous and unbroken than the world that introspection reveals.

This, then, is the groundwork of Titchener's system: the subject-matter is consciousness; the mind-body relation is parallelism; the distinctive method is introspection; and the problem is to discover the "What?" "How?" and "Why?" of its data. The next task is to reduce the material to its elements.

Obviously the task is one of tremendous importance, for the elements are the very stuff of which consciousness is made. It is also a task of great difficulty and delicacy, for psychology is incomplete and the important choice must be made on the basis of partial knowledge. The choice must be made, nevertheless, and on the basis of the available evidence Titchener decides on three elementary processes: sensation, affection, and image. Sensations are defined as the characteristic elements of perceptions; they occur in the sights, the sounds, the smells, the tastes, the tactual and muscular "feels," and kindred experiences of actually present physical objects. Images are the characteristic elements of ideas; they occur in the mental processes that picture, or in some way represent, experiences not actually present, such as memories of the past and imaginings of the future. Affections are the characteristic elements of emotion; they are found in such experiences as love and hate and joy and sorrow. Titchener is not absolutely certain that sensation and image belong to different classes. He even believes that affection has some important resemblances to sensation, enough at least to suggest that they have a "common mental ancestor." But on the whole he prefers to regard them as distinct and to recognize three kinds of elementary processes—sensation, image, and affection.

As the simplest processes to which consciousness can be reduced, elements, from the standpoint of psychology, are absolutely simple. Elements, however, have attributes. Sensations and images always have at least four attributes: quality, intensity, duration, and clearness. Affection has the first three, but lacks the attribute of clearness.

Quality is defined as the attribute that distinguishes every elementary process from every other. Cold, blue, salt, and b♭ are examples. Intensity is the attribute that places an experience of a given quality on a scale running from the highest to the lowest degree of its particular kind, the attribute that makes it possible to say that one sensation is stronger or weaker, brighter or duller, louder or fainter, than another. Duration is the attribute that gives a process its characteristic course in time—its "rise, poise, and fall." The attribute of clearness determines the place of a given process in consciousness; whether it is near or far from the center of the stage. If clear, the process is dominant and outstanding, as are the tones to which one is listening attentively; if unclear, it fades into the background, as do the irrelevant noises that one is hardly aware of when absorbed in an interesting task. Affection, however, lacks clearness. It is impossible to attend directly to pleasantness or unpleasantness; when we try to do so, the affective quality itself disappears. Pleasantness and unpleasantness are felt most keenly when we attend to the sensations and images with which the affective qualities themselves are connected.

These attributes, however, do not make an exhaustive list. Particular processes have attributes peculiar to themselves. Sight and touch, for instance, have the attribute of extensity; they are spread out in space. Besides, there are "attributes of the second order," formed by the concurrence of two or more attributes. One of these is "insistence," which Titchener finds in the "penetratingness of odours like camphor and naphthaline; the urgency or importunity of certain pains or of the taste of bitter; the obtrusiveness or glaringness of certain lights and colours and tones." Insistence, however, he regards not as a new primary attribute, but as a combination of two or more primary attributes—clearness and quality perhaps, or clearness and quality and intensity together.

Thus it becomes apparent that the elements with their attributes are the units of which the whole psychic structure is made. The elements, however, are not static units.

They are processes; their "essence is processence." They form a mosaic, but a mosaic in motion, in which intricate and fleeting patterns are formed. And yet, in the midst of all the complexity, there is a simple principle of organization. Everything that occurs in consciousness is reducible to three sorts of elements and their combinations. Clearly an understanding of the different kinds of elements becomes the next step toward the understanding of psychology.

The bulk of the *Text-book* is devoted to this task. Sensations are considered first and are treated at greatest length because they constituted one of the most thoroughly worked fields in the new psychology of the day. Each class is studied in turn—the visual, the auditory, the olfactory, the gustatory, the cutaneous, the kinæsthetic, the organic; and for each class the plan of study is the same. The procedure is regularly from description to explanation. First, the sensory qualities themselves are analyzed and described; and then, by way of explanation, the experiences are related to their physiological correlates. As a means of getting the feel of the orthodox psychology of their day, these chapters in the *Text-book* are probably unsurpassed. For here are discussions of the color pyramid and the tonal pencil, of pressures that are "bright" or "tremulous" or "granular," of taste blends and twilight vision, of cold spots and heat spots, and of punctiform pain. Here are references to the classic apparatus—color-mixers and adaptation frames, tuning-forks and resonance boxes, olfactormeters, variators, perimeters, and Galton whistles. Here, too, are the current theories of vision, audition, and the other forms of sensation, with descriptive accounts of the structures involved. Weber's law is included in the chapter on the "Intensity of Sensation," where it is interesting to find, under the caption "Mental Measurement," a consideration of such matters as liminal and terminal stimuli and just

noticeable differences, instead of the i.q.'s and m.a.'s that
the phrase now suggests. The references for further reading at the ends of the chapters are as characteristic as anything in the book. Bristling with German titles and with
the great names of the time, they bring very distinctly to
mind the earnest, hopeful, productive days when psychology was establishing itself as an independent science.

There is little to be said about the image. In the *Text-
book*, it is treated in a single scant section. Its great similarity to sensation is admitted and even emphasized, but
its "textural difference" from sensation—the fact that it is
"more filmy, more vaporous, more transparent"—is made
the basis for its recognition as an elementary process distinguishable from sensation.

Affection is treated at greater length than image, but not
so fully as sensation. The affective processes constitute one
of the most confused and controversial fields in all psychology, and nobody was more aware than Titchener of
the intricacies of the subject. He stated his position, however, with characteristic clearness. "Affection," he insisted
over and over again, "is not sensation." It differs from
sensation partly because it lacks the attribute of clearness,
and partly because its two elementary qualities, pleasantness and unpleasantness, are not merely different from
each other, but are opposites; they are "incompatible" in
consciousness, as sensations like red and blue are not. The
elementary affective qualities are pleasantness and unpleasantness, and these are the only elementary qualities. This
view Titchener held in opposition to Wundt's tridimen-
sional theory of feeling: the theory that "feeling moves,
first between the opposite poles of pleasantness and unpleasantness; secondly, between the opposite poles of excitement and depression; and thirdly, between tension and
relaxation." After a detailed consideration of this theory,

Titchener rejected it on the grounds that it is not logically constructed and that it is not supported by the experimental evidence. Titchener's view of affection led him, too, to repudiate the James-Lange theory of the emotions, a theory which claims that emotion is the sum total of the *sensations* set up by the bodily commotion that is reflexly aroused by certain exciting situations. Emotion is thereby reduced to sensation, particularly organic sensation. Though Titchener admitted that organic sensation is present in emotion, that it is an important constituent of the emotional experience as a whole, he did not believe it possible to dispense with the affective element as such. Organic sensation, he declared, is simply organic sensation and is quite different from affection itself. Organic sensation cannot account for pleasantness or unpleasantness as such, and these are the qualities which give the emotional experience its distinctively affective tone. Affective processes themselves are not reducible to anything else. Pleasantness and unpleasantness are conscious elements, coördinate with sensations and images.

Out of these elements—sensation, image, and affection— is made the whole structure of the psychic life; and in this notion is implied the general plan, the basic architectural scheme, of the system as a whole. The scheme itself is simple in the extreme—simple, that is, in general conception; the concrete details are often enormously complex. The fundamental assumption is that in some way the more complex states of consciousness are always made up of elementary processes, that different combinations of elements, brought together in different degrees of intimacy, constitute such conscious experiences as perception, imagination, emotion, and thought. Sometimes the blends are very close, as in the fusion of the fundamental and the overtones in a musical tone; sometimes the connections are less intimate, as in the perception of a melody which is both qualitatively and temporally a pattern; and sometimes the association is rather loose, as in the recall of the name of a melody that is being played. But always the more complex states are in some sense compositions of the elements; and the task of psychology is to show how the higher mental processes can be accounted for in this way.

At the threshold of this task lies the problem of attention. Titchener's treatment of this problem is strongly characteristic, revealing as it does the distinctively "structural" features of his psychology. In attention, if in any mental process, there seems to be something actually working, hence the "power of attention" of popular psychology, and the "faculty of attention" of prescientific psychology. But there is no place in Titchener's psychology for "powers" and "faculties" nor, for that matter, for the "acts" and "functions" of rival contemporary schools. In his hands, even attention becomes a matter of content; and introspection is consulted as a matter of course in order to discover its nature. The typical attentive consciousness, he finds, has as its characteristic feature an *arrangement* of conscious contents such that those attended to are prominently in the foreground. In the state of attention, consciousness falls into focus and margin, the essential difference between the two being a difference in clearness. Attention, then, is essentially clearness, and by reference to an attribute of sensation and image, Titchener is able to picture attention without resorting to "powers" or "acts," without calling on anything not given in the elements and their attributes, and thus to describe it wholly as content. Attention, in short, is a *patterning* of consciousness. This idea goes back to Wundt's concept of apperception. According to Wundt, consciousness is not evenly disposed over the entire field. There is a focus, in which processes are apperceived, within a total field that includes the total range of consciousness. It is this Wundtian pattern, this arrangement into focus and margin, which Titchener adopts in explaining attention. As to the precise nature of the pattern, he is not altogether certain, but that it is a pattern, he is in no doubt. On the whole, he inclines to the belief that the pattern is one of two levels, with a well-defined difference between the level of clearness and the level of obscurity. That there may be a gradual shading-off from the focus to the margin he entertains as a possibility, but on the whole he casts his vote on the side of two main levels and suggests that where more degrees of clearness exist, they are differences within one of the two main levels, "wrinkles" on their surfaces, and no more. From the standpoint of the system as a whole, however, the important point is the recognition of attention as arrangement—as content and clearness—without recourse to anything that the elements and attributes cannot supply; without reference, that is, to anything which is not "structural." The point is significant because attention, which more than any other mental process seems actually to do something, is particularly likely to slip out of the terms of content.

With equal consistency, Titchener deals with other mental processes. The difficult problem of meaning, for example, he reduces to a matter of context. Psychologically, the meaning of a mental process is the constellation of processes in which it stands; that and nothing more. For instance, a perception means danger if it occurs in a context of the kinæsthetic sensations that accompany the tendency to flee and of the organic and affective processes that characterize fear. Thus meaning, like attention, can be described as content. So can emotion, which is a temporal process, "suddenly initiated," "highly complex," "strongly affective," "insistently organic," and "predetermined" in the sense of proceeding toward a natural terminus. Emotion, too, is a pattern; it is one of extreme complexity, to be sure, and one in which the temporal factor is extremely important, but it is, nevertheless, a pattern of conscious contents. Even action, psychologically considered, is, as he shows by reference to the "action consciousness" in the classic experiments, an affair of conscious content. Even here, though he is dealing with an event which most people would take primarily as an overt movement, Titchener works his way unerringly toward the conscious experiences which he regards as the core of the process. In the early reaction-time experiments, he explains, there was little interest in the *psychological* aspects of the problem. But in his opinion, the simple reaction, which is action reduced to skeleton form, provides an excellent opportunity for the study of action consciousness. In action consciousness he finds "a preliminary phase in which the prominent things are kinæsthesis and the idea of end or result; a central phase, in which some object is apprehended in relation to, in the sense of, the idea of end; and a final phase, in which the perception of result is set on a background of kinæsthesis, of the sensations aroused by the actual movement." Thus even in the study of reaction-time, where the obvious approach—and in this case, the actual historical approach—is quite different, Titchener attacked the problem by means of introspection and in terms of conscious content.

It is unnecessary to multiply illustrations. The treatment is always essentially the same. The subject-matter of psychology is consciousness; its characteristic method is introspection; its phenomena must be explained by reference to bodily processes; but the conscious contents themselves hold the center of the stage. This statement is, of course, oversimplified and would be utterly false if it conveyed the impression that Titchener was capable of ignoring complexities. For, with his sensitiveness to the subtle difficulties that enter into even the simplest of psychological problems, he had something of Wundt's reluctance to make a statement without surrounding it with qualifications. But Titchener never permitted the qualifications to obscure the main outline; he strove, it would seem, to make his main course clear partly *because* he was aware of the many considerations that might have made it different. Consequently, in spite of the paragraphs of fine print that safeguard the main text; in spite of the careful explication of considerations and counter-considerations; in spite of the repeated reminders that psychology is incomplete, that it cannot make statements dogmatically, that its conclusions must stand ready to be modified by the experimental evidence which it so sorely needs; in spite of all this, the general plan is unmistakable. The incompleteness of psychology is admitted again and again, but not with the implication that the main program will be altered. Future experiment will fill in the gaps in knowledge and settle controversial points, but the plan of attack is known. The *Text-book* ends on a confident note. "The experimental method, having conquered the whole domain of nature and of life, is pressing forward to the highest reaches of mind, to thought itself. It needs no gift of prophecy to foretell that the first half of this century will mark an epoch in the history of scientific psychology." And it needs no gift of divination to suspect that, in Titchener's opinion, those epoch-making advances would require no profound changes in the basic conceptions of his system.

So much for what the system is. It is important to note, too, what it is not. To the last, Titchener withheld his blessing from the work on intelligence tests, an enterprise that American psychologists, with their practical interest in individual differences, had promptly taken to their hearts. Applied psychology, another enterprise that American psychologists were developing energetically and enthusiastically, also remained outside the pale. And apparently Titchener did not even consider including in his general psychology what McDougall has called "snippets of abnormal psychology," materials which are finding their way into many courses in general psychology, and which appeal strongly to the interests of disturbed adolescents. He was opposed, too, to the James-Lange theory of the emotions, which accounted for emotion without recognizing a specific affective element. He was also, on the whole, antagonistic to the imageless-thought movement, which cast doubt on the interpretation of thought from the standpoint of sensations, images, and conscious contents generally, and which used a method of introspection [12] unorthodox to say the least. And it goes without saying that he opposed the schools of functionalism and behaviorism,[13] which were definitely directed against his interpretation of psychology. "I see less prospect of gain from a revolution than from persistent work under the existing régime," he said in commenting on the new work on the higher thought-processes, and the comment holds for his attitude toward his psychology as a whole. He saw no reason for radical change or expansion; his was a "right little, tight little" system.

[12] Toward the close of his life, Titchener was greatly interested in phenomenology, but he made no formal statement of a change in his attitude toward this topic.

[13] Titchener's attitude toward functionalism may be found in his "Postulates of a Structural Psychology," *Philosophical Review* (1898), **7**, 449-465, and in "Structural and Functional Psychology," *ibid.* (1899), **8**, 290-297. His reply to Watson's announcement of behaviorism was given in a paper entitled "On 'Psychology as the Behaviorist Views It'," *Proceedings of the American Philosophical Society*, **53**, 1-17.

It was, indeed, as a clear-cut conception and as a positive attitude that Titchener's psychology exerted its greatest influence in America. It was a system with a definite form and a definite code. Aggressively pure, pointedly aloof, consciously correct, it stood out conspicuously as a fixed and unambiguous point of reference in the rapidly changing scene of American psychology.

But for all his stanchness and power, Titchener could not stem the tide of the times. New psychologies, of various degrees of heterodoxy, grew up everywhere about him. At Columbia, Cattell persistently encouraged the study of individual differences and openly asserted that most of the studies carried on in his laboratory could dispense with the services of the trained introspectionist. Thorndike, also at Columbia, experimented on animals and school-children, admittedly preferring large-scale researches that dealt with hundreds of cases to the minute observations of a few trained psychologists. At Chicago, there developed a new movement known as functionalism, a school that treated mental processes as functions of living organisms. To Titchener, such a view of psychology meant an easy lapse into common sense as contrasted with scientific ways of thinking, an evasion of the demands of a strictly experimental psychology, and a dangerous dalliance with teleology; it meant a confusion of science with technology on the one hand and with philosophy on the other. He saw it as the kind of psychology that Brentano represented, a mode of thought which he habitually contrasted with the truly scientific psychology of Wundt. Behaviorism, too, rose and prospered in spite of his declaration that it was logically irrelevant to psychology and that, though it might make valuable contributions to the knowledge of bodily mechanisms, it could never displace psychology as such.

Particularly disquieting was the work of those who de-

ciared for "imageless thought," for here were men, some
of them trained in the school of which he himself was a
product, announcing discoveries that made the accepted
psychology of that school seem inadequate. Külpe and his
pupils in Germany, Binet in France, and Woodworth in the
United States had independently and almost simultaneously
presented evidence suggesting that thought is not an affair
of images and sensations, as had been supposed. Their
studies, based on the direct examination of various thought-
processes, indicated that thought may go on at times without any observable sensational or imaginal content, and
that what can be observed at such times is likely to consist
of attitudes or "awarenesses," usually vague and unanalyzable, and quite different from the expected conscious "contents." It was suggested by some writers that a thought
element must be introduced. Titchener could not accept
this point of view. He believed that the "unanalyzable"
states of consciousness were merely "unanalyzed"; and on
the basis of his own introspections and of studies made in
his laboratory, believed that these "awarenesses," "feelings
of relation," and "imageless thoughts" were really complexes of easily overlooked kinæsthetic sensations and
images, which are the representatives in consciousness of
motor attitudes. He thus assimilated the discovery to his
system without altering the system itself: conscious thought,
though still a matter of images and sensations, contained
stretches in which the contents were largely kinæsthetic;
he also recognized "motor sets" and "determining tendencies"
which have no conscious accompaniments. But though Titchener had thus, in one sense, disposed of the difficulty, many
psychologists believed that the significant fact in the imageless-thought movement was that, even in thought, motor
activity and neural sets seem to be of the utmost importance, and that introspection may not give the most perti-

nent clues to what is actually happening. At any rate, the imageless-thought controversy revealed a willingness, even an eagerness, among American psychologists to attempt methods of studying and interpreting their material that were not strictly orthodox.

Whatever the reason, Titchener's influence, and apparently even the vigor of his interest in psychology, declined during the last decade of his life. He was at the time working on his *Prolegomena,* a book that, intended as a final formulation of the basic principles of his system, was to be his *magnum opus.* But the work remained unfinished at his death, and the four completed chapters, constituting an exposition, even more thorough than his previous statements, of what he regarded as the fundamental principles of psychology, contain nothing essentially new. It was almost as if psychology as he conceived it was inadequate to sustain the working-power of the man who had labored so zealously in its behalf. He turned to the study of ancient coins and with characteristic thoroughness became an expert in the field. Having devoted himself to one of the newest adventures of human thought, he spent the last years of his life, though he was not an old man, occupied with relics of dead civilizations.[14]

But whatever the inner and outer resistances he encountered, Titchener combated them to the extent of producing an enormous amount of work. At different periods of his career he wrote four of the most influential textbooks of his day, *An Outline of Psychology,* a *Primer of Psychology,* a *Text-book of Psychology,* and a *Beginner's Psychology.* Of these the *Text-book* is of outstanding importance because it contains the most completely worked-out statement

[14] Titchener died Aug. 3, 1927 of a brain tumor, but there had been no indication of any impairment of his intellectual abilities.

of his system as a whole. His *Experimental Psychology: A Manual for Laboratory Practice* is usually considered his greatest single achievement. It consists of four volumes, two on qualitative and two on quantitative experiments, a student's manual and an instructor's manual in each set. This work, a monument to its author's erudition, is often pointed to as a kind of documentary evidence for the actual existence of a science of experimental psychology. The *Psychology of Feeling and Attention* and the *Experimental Psychology of the Higher Thought Processes* display his characteristic manner, both conscientious and authoritative, of dealing with large masses of intricately interrelated evidence on highly controversial topics. In addition to his books, he wrote numerous articles, polemical and otherwise, and through his influence on his students and their work, and on psychological discussion generally, played a dominant rôle in shaping psychology in the United States.

There can be no doubt that the chapter Titchener wrote in American psychology is an important one. Perhaps his main achievement was to give the system he represented a thorough tryout. This statement refers not only to his own personal formulation, but to the general type of psychology his system represented, to the psychology that was "experimental" in the narrow sense of the term, the product of the particular scientific movements that culminated in the German laboratories. To Titchener this kind of psychology was *the* scientific psychology. Essentially it was an attempt to study, not by the speculations of philosophy, not by the rough tools of common sense, but by exact observation and experiment, the phenomena of consciousness. It has been pointed out earlier in the chapter that this was almost inevitably the next step for science to take. Science, having revealed first the ways of inorganic matter, then of living bodies, was now to reveal those of mental processes. And since the possibility presented itself so pointedly, it was desirable that it be tested whole-heartedly. What the new psychology was good for could best be revealed by some one who accepted it in all faith and pushed it as hard as he could as far as it would go. If psychology as Titchener interpreted it could not maintain itself in the United States under the leadership of a man of his ability; if, with the prestige of priority and of an honorable academic tradition, it could not establish itself as the basis of future psychology and assimilate future developments to itself—that fact itself was significant. And to have revealed the fact is no small achievement. If psychology as Titchener defined and directed it had done nothing more than reveal its own limitations by stretching its powers and its claims to the utmost, the attempt would have been worth while. To have shown by its own example, by making a thorough and courageous and clean-cut experiment, that scientific psychology as first conceived was inadequate to the demands of its material, was to have rendered a distinct service to a growing science.

That the school made important contributions to psychology is not in question. It is a simple historical fact that it was the kind of psychology which Titchener taught, the enterprise which centered in the German laboratories, that first gained recognition for psychology as a science. And it is also a simple matter of fact that this discipline, imported from Germany, was one of the means by which American psychology made the transition from mental philosophy to science, learning to rely less on speculation and more on observation, to be less preoccupied with values, ethical and otherwise, and to pay more attention to facts as facts. Besides, the method advocated by the new psychology was justified by the careful studies that came out of its experimental laboratories. In sensation and perception, it had distinct achievements to its credit; it made some progress in exploring the affective processes; to some extent it even penetrated the difficult fields of memory, thought, and volition. And yet, experimental psychology as Titchener understood it did not remain *the* scientific psychology in America; and what is more significant, the new enterprises in American psychology were not outgrowths of its way of thinking, but protests against its restrictions.

Perhaps the fundamental reason for this state of affairs lies in the passion for formal correctness that characterized the Titchenerian school. In its very zeal to be scientific, it set up restrictions that hampered its development. Having defined certain materials and methods as scientifically correct, it limited itself to problems within the scope of those definitions. But curiosity, even scientific curiosity, starts with concrete situations, not with formal definitions; and if lively and genuine it will not be curbed by definitions. If there is a strong and genuine desire to know, for example, how human beings act and why, and if those questions lead beyond the limits set by a particular scientific code— into investigations of muscles and glands, for instance, or of animal behavior, or of individual differences, or of the functions and utilities of mental activities—true curiosity will not be stopped by the assertion that its interest is unscientific. However vaguely the question is formulated— and the chances are that the formulation will be vague at first—the crude curiosity at the basis of the question will not be satisfied by something off the line of its main interest. After all, such curiosity is the basis of science and must not be too sternly repressed. If it becomes involved in a struggle with a particular scientific code, it is extremely likely to win, partly because science cannot live without it, and partly because a particular code, upheld by a particular group at a particular time and place, is determined not only by the basic and essential demands of science, but also by the local and more or less accidental circumstances of the situation. It was in such a conflict between curiosity and formal correctness that Titchener's psychology became involved. When faced with the alternative of either sticking to problems that suited its constitution or revising its constitution to suit new problems, it unequivocally chose the former. It recognized the new problems as problems, but not as psychology; and it was largely this attitude that made the movement Titchener represented in the United States a school of psychology rather than the starting-point of American psychology in general.

Indeed, the most relevant comments on Titchener's psychology are those implied in the successful revolts against it. Many of the statements against his doctrines are, it is true, overdrawn; and some of the reactions against them are based on misunderstandings of the system itself. There has been difficulty, for example, in seeing the subject-matter he describes as belonging to the natural order, in accepting introspection as genuine observation, in interpreting the system as one of "elements" and "content" and yet one in which the elements are processes. At times there has been a tendency to overemphasize the thinness of the factual content of the system and to see in its disinterestedness only irrelevance and futility. There has been a tendency, too, to overemphasize Titchener's intolerance; to forget that he is willing to acknowledge the worth of rival movements, provided only they do not call themselves psychology. But the general direction of the movement he represented is clear; and it was against a movement in that direction that new schools protested—schools which believed that a strictly structural psychology failed to do justice to psychological material as it occurs in experience; that a psychology which was too pure might be sterile; that existing formulations must not be taken so seriously as to exclude relevant problems they were not framed to meet. True, many of the objections could be met on logical grounds by the Titchenerians; others, irrelevant to its position as formulated, left it untouched and unmoved. But it was against the system as it worked itself out in going enterprises and in active exclusions, not merely as it might be stated and defended on paper, that the newer psychologies rose in successful protest.

And yet the movement that Titchener directed in America represents a definite achievement in making psychology a science. In so far as its subject-matter was something actually present in experience, and in so far as its purity turned attention to facts rather than to values, Titchener's psychology marked a genuine advance toward the scientific point of view. If it took its definitions and restrictions too seriously, it did so in an attempt to establish itself as an enterprise distinct from common sense, from technology, and from metaphysics. If it tried unsuccessfully to force all psychology into its mold—or rather to maintain that its boundaries and the limits of true psychology coincide —its failure revealed both the possibilities and the limitations of its principles. Beyond question, the psychology of Titchener played a major rôle in the development of American psychology, not only as a distinct and lasting achievement, but also as a gallant and enlightening failure.

Chapter V

THE PSYCHOLOGY OF WILLIAM JAMES

IN the meantime, there was William James. In a sense, James both precedes and follows Titchener in American psychology. He was older than Titchener by twenty-five years; he published *The Principles of Psychology,* his major contribution, in 1890, two years before Titchener came to Cornell; and he died in 1910, when Titchener's power was at its height. Yet the two men stood for influences which were parallel rather than successive, and which have in fact never really met.

Unquestionably the teachings of James reach farther back into the past than do Titchener's, into the old metaphysical psychology that Titchener so cleanly leaves behind; but apparently they are destined to extend farther into the future, for they continue to flourish with a vigor and freshness that makes them relevant to the newest problems. The psychology of James is psychology in transition. It shows the marks of metaphysics, but it is a movement toward science. For James, less intent on formal correctness than on getting directly at the material he was studying, turned naturally in his inquiries toward concrete experience both for cues and for evidence. Whereas Titchener was intent chiefly on making the new psychology a science, James was more concerned that the new science be psychology.

It is impossible to place James in any of the well-marked lines of psychological development in progress in his day. He was neither the founder nor the adherent of any school.

Primarily he was an individual, and it was primarily as an individual that he exerted his influence on psychology. However engrossed he became in a movement, however enthusiastic about its import, he was never overwhelmed by it; he remained incorrigibly himself. He was keenly alive to all the psychological enterprises going forward in his day —always interested, and by turns sympathetic, amused, critical, and admiring. He discriminated and appraised, rejected and accepted, but he never lost himself, either in his enthusiasms or in his aversions. Yet he was not in any sense aloof. He was in the thick of psychology in its turbulent and factious youth, but he never lost his individuality and his independence.

The relation of James to the new experimental psychology of the Wundtian school is strongly characteristic of his attitude. To most psychologists of the time, the experimental psychology that Wundt sanctioned was in some way decisive. Either as adherents or dissenters, they were drawn into the current of its thought. Even men like Brentano and Stumpf derive part of their importance from their relation to it, and their positions are significant with reference to it. It is the psychology with which their views are compared and contrasted. But such statements can hardly be made of James. His thought developed independently of the new experimental psychology, took full cognizance of it, dismissed parts of it, included and assimilated large masses of it; but it was not transformed by it. There is a trace of Yankee isolation in James's psychology, and more than a trace of Yankee independence in his good-humored refusal to succumb to prestige suggestion.

A similar attitude marks his relations to other schools— in particular to British associationism and to French psychiatry. The pages of *The Principles* are dotted with the names of the British writers and strewn with acknowledgments of indebtedness to their insights and observations. Yet James did not write in the British tradition; and he was definitely not an associationist. In the same spirit of appreciation, generously enthusiastic yet judicial, he turned to the work of the French psychiatrists. He believed that in their dealings with psychopathic personalities, especially in their work with dissociation and multiple personality, they were making discoveries of the utmost importance; he was strongly convinced that the psychology of the morbid· has much to contribute to psychology in general. But though he plunged into the lore of the abnormal and the not quite normal, he never limited his attention to its problems. Again he showed that blend of appreciativeness and independence which has made him at once the most catholic and the most individual of psychologists.

There is, in fact, something of the same independent attitude in James's dealings with psychology as a whole. James ranks with the greatest psychologists—some place him first— yet even professionally psychology did not occupy him exclusively. He began his career, it will be remembered, not as a psychologist, but as a biologist, and it was while he was teaching anatomy in the Harvard Medical School, that he made a place in his laboratory for psychological experiments and thus started almost by accident the first psychological laboratory. The definite shift of his interest toward psychology is marked by his undertaking in 1878 to write *The Principles of Psychology,* a task which occupied him for twelve years. During this time, however, he became interested in philosophy; or rather, philosophy, which had attracted him from his early youth, claimed more and more of his attention. Naturally enough, his official positions at Harvard did not quite keep pace with his changing interests. While he was an instructor in anatomy, he was conducting psychological experiments. While he was work-

ing on *The Principles of Psychology,* he was made professor of philosophy. A year before *The Principles* was published, his title was changed to professor of psychology;
but by that time his interest had so definitely shifted to
philosophy that his title was changed back to professor of
philosophy. There is no doubt that after publishing *The
Principles,* James ceased to be chiefly interested in psychology. All the questions worth answering, he said, were in
philosophy. For him, psychology had been a phase. Though
he was one of the most potent influences in shaping the
new science of psychology, and though for a time he served
it ardently and well, in the end he called it a "nasty little
science."

It is not surprising, therefore, that to some psychologists
James is at times disconcerting. He is recognized as one of
the greatest of their number, yet he openly violated some
of their strongest prohibitions. For one thing, he wandered
into fields of investigation not considered above suspicion
—into the doubtful region of psychical research, for example, which has always been regarded as faintly disreputable.
James was never overawed by academic taboos. If he
wanted to investigate the possibility of communication with
a spirit world, he did so; if he felt impelled to discuss freewill in a chapter on attention, he followed his impulse; and
if he was faced by a question on which there were as yet
no conclusive experimental or statistical data, he did not
cautiously refrain from speculation. He was far more likely
to observe shrewdly, and then to guess at the drift of the
available evidence, trusting his intellect to fill in the gaps
—sometimes rather large—and to get the hang of the situation as best it could. In following this method, he had a
way of developing conceptions, like the James-Lange theory
of the emotions, that were enormously stimulating to research. He also had a way of anticipating future discov-

eries; his chapter on the stream of thought contains excellent descriptions of the "imageless thoughts" subsequently discovered in psychological experiments. And in spite of this practice, James could not be accused of playing fast and loose with facts. He stated fact as fact and speculation as speculation, and though he often broke through the particular restrictions of the science of the day, he was fundamentally of a scientific turn of mind. Whatever his subject-matter, he addressed himself to it with an eye to raw facts and with a gift for faithful observation that the most austere scientists have recognized. But he also had a way of coming out on the side of the angels on a question that science could not answer. He was so alive to human hopes and desires that he could not help giving them a chance.

Indeed, the personality of James permeates his thinking, and his writings bear the unmistakable stamp of his temperament. But this does not mean that his thought was swamped by emotion. No one could recognize more surely than James the difference between intellect and emotion or that between fact and preference. It was indeed a perception of the difference, not a confusion regarding it, that made him so insistent on the recognition of the rôle of temperament and preference in intellectual activities. His loyalty to facts made him recognize this fact among others, but it also made it impossible for him to accede to the pretensions of the intellect to pure and absolute rationality.

It is not easy to describe the personality of James. Perhaps as good a starting-point as any is his stand on this very matter of the rôle of the intellect in human affairs. On the question of intellectualism versus empiricism, James was for empiricism and against intellectualism, to put the matter in terms of unqualified contrast. He was strongly convinced that experience must serve both as the starting-point and as the verification of thought. This belief appears

in his philosophy as well as in his psychology, for the
appeal to the immediately given lies at the basis both of
his logic and of his metaphysics—of pragmatism and of
radical empiricism; and though the publication of *The Principles* antedated the working-out of these theories, the tendencies they represent were distinctly present in his psychological thinking. For reasons related to this same point of
view, James was opposed to determinism as contrasted with
freewill; he was inclined to trust the immediate feeling that
something is actually being decided in attention and will,
that human life is not the "dull rattling off of a chain."
Determinism he recognized as an enormously convenient
simplification of the universe and as, therefore, a tool that
appeals strongly to the intellect. But to James the intellect,
as but one of the many phenomena in a complex world,
had no right to impose its demands on the character of
reality in general. He recognized the intellect as one of
man's ways of dealing with his environment; but he recognized it as one among many, and one that had a definite
and limited place in human nature as a whole. His refusal
to take the claims of the intellect too seriously—especially
any expression of those claims in an officially sanctioned
academic opinion—often made him the champion of lost
causes against the entrenched intellectual respectability of
the day. It was his opinion that nothing that presented itself
as a possibility should be dismissed without a hearing.
Santayana, one of his colleagues in philosophy at Harvard,
said of him:

"Philosophy for him had a Polish constitution; so long as
a single vote was cast against the majority, nothing could
pass. The suspense of judgment which he had imposed on
himself as a duty, became almost a necessity. I think it
would have depressed him if he had had to confess that
any important question was finally settled. He would still

have hoped that something might turn up on the other side, and that just as the scientific hangman was about to despatch the poor convicted prisoner, an unexpected witness would ride up in hot haste, and prove him innocent." [1]

All this goes back to a radical democracy in James's nature. Every man, every idea, every moment of experience, must have its chance to speak out and be recognized. This democracy, this unfeigned desire that all be counted somehow—all experiences, all men, no matter how disreputable in the eyes of the savants—was probably his fundamental prejudice. He seemed actuated by a desire to be faithful to all, and the desire appears not only in his relations to people—his colleagues, his pupils, his friends —but also in his dealings with ideas.

For James's attitude toward ideas is above all democratic. He receives them with courtesy and entertains them with interest, genuinely bent on knowing them as they are. He cannot accept them all, he does not pretend to like them all, but he is determined that all shall have a hearing; and when he dismisses those he must, he takes leave of them, sometimes almost regretfully, with knowledge of their strength as well as of their weakness. He has the same engaging manner of dealing on terms of equality with people, including his reader. He flatteringly assumes that the reader is his intellectual equal and that the reader, the author, the learned scholars whose views are under discussion, are all engaged in the common enterprise of trying to get to the bottom of whatever absorbing topic is being considered. Because all are equals, it is possible to be both generous and unsparing. In a society of equals, no one need be overtender of another's feelings. Any one may be called to account, for every one can defend himself. The tone of James's controversial writing is that of justice between

[1] George Santayana, *Character and Opinion in the United States,* 82.

equals, of fair play on an intellectual plane. For this reason James, as has frequently been said, can state an opponent's position better than can his opponent himself; and for the same reason he can criticize it with relentless thoroughness. In criticism, as in everything else, his thoroughness does not permit him to stop short of doing his utmost. He does his foeman the honor of exerting his full strength against him.

Perhaps the thoroughness with which James treats a question requires a word of comment, chiefly because the rapidity and freshness of his style sometimes give the impression that his statements are unconsidered. His swift characterizations, his sharply illuminating insights, his quick thrusts, all suggest something going at top speed, directed only by the impulse of the moment. But no impression could be farther from the truth. James's writing is exquisitely careful. He was almost painfully conscientious about it. He kept his manuscripts and labored over them, refusing to let them go until they said exactly what he wanted them to say. He always resented the criticism that his writings were not carefully planned. For all his delight in the insight of the moment, he spared himself no drudgery, whether of working through masses of factual material he considered dull, or of following long lines of argument and speculation he thought pompous and empty. In spite of his feeling that much of the work of the German laboratories was laborious futility—he used to call some of the dissertations "elaborations of the obvious"—he became thoroughly conversant with that branch of psychological literature. Any one who goes through the foot-notes of *The Principles* will see how completely James was master of the psychology of his day; and any one who examines the argumentative portions of the book—his consideration of the automaton theory, the mind-stuff theory, freewill, and brain localization—will see how carefully James considers hypotheses suggested by other points of view than his own. There is a surprising carefulness in the work of James, a carefulness which is undoubtedly related to the fact that he found it difficult to accept anything as proved and final. His breadth, his thoroughness, his carefulness, and his high seriousness are as much a part of his complex personality as are his vivacity and acuteness.

In his direct personal relationships James was as effective as in his writings. His *Letters* [2] show how many lines of communication he kept open with friends; and they reveal, too, the scope of his interests. His students found him extraordinarily stimulating. In his class-room, as in his books, he assumed a society of equals. It was not his custom to deliver formal lectures, and often he plunged into brilliant digressions suggested by the situation of the moment. Sometimes he went rather far afield in his pursuit of a topic that he found absorbing, and one day a student, attempting to bring him back from one of these excursions, burst out, "But, Professor, to be serious for a moment . . ." Plainly the atmosphere of James's class-room was such as to make one forget the ordinary class-room formalities. It is as characteristic of James as anything about him that he did not found a school. He stimulated students to think —not necessarily to think *his* thoughts. He preferred to throw his thoughts and theories out into the world and let them take their chances with other thoughts and theories. He did not seek to give them the backing of a school; he let them rely on their own naked strength.

James's psychology is set forth in its most complete form in the two volumes of *The Principles of Psychology*. It is often said that this work is unsystematic, that it lacks

[2] *The Letters of William James,* ed. by his son, Henry James.

organization, or, at least, that whatever organization it possesses is not a matter of first importance. Certainly the book does not create the impression of a closely articulated structure; rather it suggests a series of insights, of penetrating flashes into the depths of the subject. Almost every chapter can be read by itself as a separate treatise on its special topic; and with few exceptions each chapter reads as if its subject-matter were the most important part of psychology, as if just here, by this approach, the way to the very heart of the subject is to be found. James himself believed that he was primarily a "creature of *aperçus*," and *The Principles* is clearly the work of such a creature. Though it was the most exhaustive treatise on general psychology in its day, it is, at its best, a series of acute perceptions and penetrating insights into a new and little-explored department of knowledge.

All this is true, yet the lack of organization must not be overemphasized. For throughout the book there is a pattern, faintly indicated and never obtrusive, but nevertheless significant. Undoubtedly some of the comments that the book was not carefully planned rose from the fact that it did not follow the conventional plan of beginning with units like sensations or simple ideas and, out of those units, constructing the more complex states of consciousness. But it was an essential part of James's teaching that this procedure is unjustified; that the proper starting-point is experience as it is immediately given, the stream of consciousness as it flows before perception, not the simple sensation. The "simple sensation" or "simple idea," James always insisted, is not to be found in unanalyzed, unintellectualized experience; it is a product of abstraction, arrived at after long and sophisticated study. Besides, he believed that before psychology proper could be discussed, it was necessary to clear the ground. For he could not take it for granted, as Titchener did, that psychology was already a science, write a brief statement of the mind-body relation, and without further ado, write psychology. James was an American and a philosopher as well as a psychologist, and he knew too well the philosophical tradition in America to believe that it could be disposed of lightly. He took American psychology not as it ought to be, but as he found it; as mental philosophy based on associationism, often allied with Calvinism, and sometimes, in its more sophisticated forms, with transcendentalism and absolute idealism. James not only knew the American tradition, but it was a part of himself. For him it was impossible to sweep aside the problems of the mind as they presented themselves to the American public of his day.

Briefly, the outline of *The Principles* is this. The first six chapters of the first volume serve largely to clear the ground for psychology proper. Regarding it as his first task to get the necessary biological conceptions before the reader, James discusses those aspects of nervous activity which he considers most relevant to mental life; and in this connection he introduces his famous chapter on habit —a chapter which develops the thesis that mental life, in fact, all human conduct, is largely determined by the tendency of the nervous system to be so modified by each action that every subsequent action of the same sort is a little easier than its predecessor. James next prepares the reader for the scientific point of view by discussing the chief metaphysical conceptions of mind. He considers the automaton theory, the mind-dust theory, the material-monad theory, and the soul theory; but he ends by rejecting all metaphysical hypotheses concerning the mind-body relation, and by contenting himself, for the purposes of psychology, with "a blank unmediated correspondence, term for term, of the succession of states of consciousness with the succession of total brain processes." In other words, he accepts both states of consciousness and brain-processes as phenomena in the natural world; and he believes that since psychology is a natural science, not a system of metaphysics, it may note and accept whatever relationships it finds without feeling obliged to account for their existence.

In the rest of the volume, James deals with psychology proper. He discusses methods of investigation in a chapter at once shrewd and tolerant, significantly entitled "The Methods and Snares of Psychology." A chapter called "The Stream of Thought"—in about the middle of the volume, it is well to notice—describes the subject-matter of psychology as James sees it. The theme of the chapter is that consciousness is not composed of discrete bits joined together, but that it is a continuous, flowing current. The stream of thought is described as having five chief characteristics: it is personal; it is changing; it is sensibly continuous; it deals with objects not itself; and it is always choosing among them, welcoming, rejecting, accentuating, selecting. In a sense, the rest of the first volume is a development of this chapter. The immediately personal character of consciousness is discussed in a chapter on the self—a chapter which directly follows that on the stream of thought, instead of being placed at the end of the book, where the chapter on the self is usually found in treatises on psychology. The selective nature of consciousness is treated in the three chapters, "Attention," "Conception," and "Discrimination and Comparison"; and the rest of the volume deals with various aspects of the change and continuity of the stream of thought. The chapter "Association" treats the associative processes not as couplings of "simple ideas" or discrete bits of consciousness, but as merging physiological processes in the nervous system. This chapter, in its attack on the theory that consciousness is composed of discrete bits, repeats and

emphasizes the statement that consciousness is sensibly continuous and changing. In the chapter entitled "The Perception of Time" James again emphasizes change and continuity, pointing out that in our direct and immediate experience
of time—time as we sense it, not as we conceptualize it—the
past, the present, and the future are all contained in "the
specious present." The last chapter, "Memory," deals with
events in conceived time, not in immediately given time.
This chapter is important chiefly for its claim that native
retentiveness is given once and for all and cannot be improved by exercise. In support of this contention, James
reports one of his few psychological experiments, the only
one that has been influential. Though this experiment, one in
memory-training, was not well controlled, it aroused great
interest and led to further research on the problem.

In the second volume, the organization seems at first
glance to follow the conventional order. The first chapter
deals with sensation, and successive chapters treat of perception, belief, reasoning, instinct, and volition, in what
seems to be the usual manner of proceeding from the simple
to the complex. But the arrangement is deceptive if it suggests that James believes in the compounding of complex
states of consciousness out of simple elements. It is the road
to and through and from the central nervous system that
gives him the scheme of the book. Sensation is taken up
first because it corresponds to the nervous process most immediately aroused by the stimulation at the periphery and
presumably the first nervous process in the brain. Perception
corresponds to the first stages in the elaboration of the
sensory processes; belief and reasoning, to their further
elaboration. In a short chapter on the production of movement, the general fact is presented that incoming currents
find their way out through efferent pathways and occasion bodily movements, large or small. From this point

on, processes related to outgoing currents are considered. Emotion and instinct are both treated from the standpoint of bodily movement, and volition is discussed as an activity involving movement under conditions that may become peculiarly complex. This is the bulk of the book. So far as the general organization is concerned, the last two chapters are almost appendices. One is a chapter on hypnotism, a topic which at the time James wrote was attracting a vast amount of attention. The final chapter, "Necessary Truths," deals with psychogenesis. Here James takes up the problems of racial and individual development, attempting to discover how some of the more stable characteristics of the cognitive functions have come to be what they are.

This is the framework within which James's psychology is presented. Though the scheme of organization is not emphasized, it is present and it carries a special significance. Not only does James say in words that consciousness is not a composition of discrete units; he says it in the total movement of his thought. Not only does he formally recognize the intimate relation between psychology and biology; a recognition of that relation underlies the organization of his material. Not only does he write that psychology is departing from metaphysics and becoming a natural science; the transition is visible in his treatment.

The two volumes of *The Principles* are so solidly packed with particulars—with observations, arguments, theories, experimental findings, interpretations, insights—that it would be folly to attempt a comprehensive survey of their teachings. The best that can be done is to select a few portions which are most characteristic of the whole.

Perhaps the shortest route to an understanding of James's conception of psychology is to consider his stand on the basic questions of subject-matter and methods, and of the relation of mental life to the rest of the natural world. Concerning both subject-matter and methods, James's tendency was to be inclusive rather than exclusive. The book opens with the sentence, "Psychology is the Science of Mental Life, both of its phenomena and of their conditions." The words "phenomena" and "conditions" are both important: "phenomena" because it indicates that the subject-matter is found in experience, and "conditions" because to James the immediate conditions of mental life are in the human body, particularly in the human brain. From his point of view, the physical structures that constitute the conditions of mental life form an actual part of psychology; they are not merely the subject-matter of an allied science. James wrote with an eye to the whole human being; the center of his interest was the stream of consciousness, but consciousness as it exists in its natural setting, the physical man. This biological turn of thought, in fact, is one of the distinctive features of James's psychology. Out of the new and controversial material that constituted brain physiology—for James wrote when brain physiology was new and when the whole subject was even more unsettled than it is now—he adopted the conception of the nervous system as an apparatus in which currents initiated by stimulation of the sense-organs traverse the sensory nerves to the central nervous system, there pass through connecting pathways of various degrees of complexity, and then flow out through the motor nerves to the muscles. It is the action of the cerebrum that, in James's opinion, is immediately associated with consciousness.

The other term in his definition, "phenomena," also has important implications, for to study the phenomena of mental life is to study consciousness as it is given in immediate and actual experience. This meant to James the "stream of thought." He believed that the true starting-point of psychology is immediately felt experience—not a soul or mind that manifests itself in and through consciousness, not bits of conscious stuff pieced together, but experience as we know it at first hand. James's account of the stream of consciousness is one of the most famous passages in all psychological literature. It is a classic partly because it describes with vividness and fidelity something that it is extremely difficult to describe at all, partly because it is historically important as an attack on the atomism of associationism and Herbartianism.

James notes as the first characteristic of the stream of consciousness that it is *personal,* and this characteristic he accepts as a primary fact about it. We do not begin with thoughts and end with selves. The self is there from the first, not as a soul, nor immanent spirit, nor bundle of ideas, nor logical construction, but as a patent empirical fact— the fact that "every thought tends to be part of a personal consciousness." Every thought, to be sure, is not *invariably* a part of a personal consciousness. Janet had shown that thought may be dissociated from the main personality. But even these split-off portions of consciousness, if they have any considerable amount of content, tend to assume a personal form and to become secondary personalities that exist side by side with the main personality.

In noting the second characteristic of the stream of thought, that it is always *changing,* James gets nearer the heart of his doctrine. He means literally that we never have the same thought or idea or feeling twice; that "no state once gone can ever recur and be identical." We may see the same object, hear the same sound, even consider the same ideal reality over and over again, but we must not confuse the object of thought with the thought itself. It is, in fact, a physical impossibility for the same bodily sensation to recur; for every sensation corresponds to some cerebral activity, and to be identical with its predecessor, the activity would

have to occur the second time in an unmodified brain, a condition that is impossible. All this means that "a permanently existing 'idea' or *Vorstellung'* which makes its appearance before the footlights of consciousness at periodical intervals, is as mythological an entity as the Jack of Spades."

The third characteristic, that thought is *sensibly continuous,* leads James to the important distinction between substantive and transitive states of consciousness, and to the
far-reaching doctrine of the "fringe." His main contention
is that there are no breaks or cracks in the stream of
consciousness; that there is a felt, experienced continuity.
What gives the appearance of breaks and cracks, what makes
us think in terms of objects and events with intervals between them, is the different *pace* of different parts of the
stream. When the rate of change is slow, we are aware of an
object or event that thought can dwell on; when the rate is
rapid, we are aware of a passage, a transition, a relation.
James refers to the two rates of change as "resting places"
and "flights," as "substantive" and "transitive" states of
consciousness. The substantive states—the perception of a
table, or of a man walking—are the ones we notice easily and
naturally. They are literally arresting. But the transitive
states, James insists, are equally real, and by recognizing
them, he is able to discover relations as well as things in the
actual stuff of experience. "We ought to say a feeling of
'and,' a feeling of 'if,' a feeling of 'but,' and a feeling of
'by,' quite as readily as we say a feeling of 'blue' or a
feeling of 'cold.'" Feelings of tendency are also transitive
states. The feelings of "Wait!", "Hark!", "Look!"; the feeling that a forgotten name is almost within reach; the feeling
of "twigging" a meaning before it is uttered in words—
these are examples of feelings of tendencies. Such states are
not exceptional. Every substantive term, in fact, is surrounded by a fringe of relations, which may not be conscious

but which are nevertheless effective. This doctrine of the fringe is extremely useful. By means of it, James explains general and abstract ideas, for the fringe makes it possible for an idea to have a bearing or meaning, in fact, a vast store of latent connotations, without all the concrete and explicit details that Berkeley and his school demanded. James uses the same conception to account for the psychological experience of time, showing how the past, the present, and the future may all exist together as the "specious present." He also uses it to show why the course of thought takes the surprising turns it sometimes does, how something a moment ago vaguely present in the fringe may develop and become dominant and give the whole course of thought new direction.

The fourth characteristic of the stream of consciousne. the fact that thought *deals with objects other than itself,* James regards as an ultimate fact from the standpoint of psychology. He refers elsewhere to the "irreducible dualism" between the mind and its objects which as a psychologist he simply accepts. But the object must be taken, psychologically, in a less simple sense than the popular one. When asked to name the object of the thought expressed by the words "Columbus discovered America in 1492," most people answer "Columbus," or "America," or "the discovery of America." In other words, they choose some term corresponding to a substantive state of thought and ignore the fringe. But actually, the object of thought, James insists, is neither Columbus, nor America, nor the discovery of America; it is nothing less than the complete content, "Columbus-discovered-America-in-1492" with its whole fringe of relations. And yet, for all its complexity, the state of mind that knows the object is single. It is not an idea of Columbus, joined to an idea of discovery, joined to an idea of America, joined to an idea of 1492. Again James insists on the unity and continuity of thought, however complex its object.

Finally, the fifth characteristic of the stream of thought is that it is always *choosing*. The very sense-organs are selective apparatus; they respond only to vibrations of limited range. Perception too is selective; out of all the views of a rectangular table-top, possible and actual, one view emerges as typical and the table-top is seen as rectangular. The same kind of selectivity goes on through the higher processes and becomes most conspicuous in the activities that we know as deliberation and choice. It must be understood, however, that James does not read into all the selective activities of the mind, those at the level of sensation and perception, for instance, the characteristics of acts of volition. His point is that always the mental stream is cluttered with content and that at every moment there is a wealth of possibilities, only a few of which are made actual.

This stream of thought is the subject-matter of psychology as it appears to adult human introspection. But James did not limit the subject-matter of psychology to what can be observed in this way. He recognized as psychology the studies of animals, of savages, of children, and of the insane. He was always interested in the psychology of the abnormal; he said repeatedly that much could be learned from sick minds. Plainly, he wished to make room for everything that could possibly add to the sum total of psychological knowledge. The study of physiology, the examination of consciousness, the inquiries into minds mature and immature, normal and abnormal, human and animal—all these investigations he welcomed as possible sources of knowledge. He had his preferences and his aversions, but there was no report to which he refused to listen.

When James considers the problem of methods, he very significantly entitles his chapter "The Methods and Snares of Psychology." For though he accepts psychology as a natural science, he fully appreciates the difficulties its subject-matter presents to scientific observation. Of the methods of investigation, he mentions introspection first. This method he looks upon as absolutely fundamental. That we discover states of consciousness when we examine our own minds he accepts as a basic fact that has never been doubted. The belief in this fact he regards as the most fundamental postulate of psychology, and he discards "all curious inquiries about its certainty as too metaphysical for the scope of this book." His statement that "the existence of states of consciousness has not been doubted by any critic" has a strange sound in the ears of students of psychology to-day. But it is important to notice that such doubts are, to James, *too metaphysical* for a book on natural science; for to him nothing could be more real, more self-evident, less in need of metaphysical justification, than the stream of consciousness as it is immediately given.

But though James regarded introspection as the basic method in psychology, and was to that extent in agreement with Wundt and Titchener, the kind of introspection he advocated was not the same as that of the "trained introspectionist." With James, introspection was the exercise of a natural gift; it consisted in catching the very life of a moment as it passed, in a fixing and reporting of the fleeting event as it occurred in its natural setting. It was not the introspection of the laboratory, aided by brass instruments; it was the quick and sure arresting of an impression by a sensitive and acute observer. But James was no less aware of the difficulties of introspection than were the most stanch adherents of the orthodox faith. He considered both extremes of the attitude toward introspection. The one extreme, represented by Brentano among others, is the belief that introspection is infallible; that in our awareness of our own states of consciousness, we experience reality immediately and without distortion, not in the reconstructed form in which we know. the objects of the external world. The other extreme is represented by Comte. "The thinker," Comte says, "cannot divide himself into two, of whom one reasons while the other observes him reason. The organ observed and the organ observing being, in this case, identical, how could observation take place?" James adopted neither of these extreme views. He accepted introspection as a form of observation that is neither infallible nor impossible. He admitted that it is beset with difficulties, and with difficulties peculiar to itself, but he believed that, like other forms of observation, it can be verified by using appropriate checks and by comparing the reports of various observers. This kind of verification science regularly accepts, and the kind of knowledge attained in this way is all that James claims for introspection.

Though he was not himself an experimentalist, James believed also in the experimental method in psychology. His own description of the method shows his attitude as nothing else can.

"But psychology is passing into a less simple phase. Within a few years what one may call a microscopic psychology has arisen in Germany, carried on by experimental methods, asking of course every moment for introspective data, but eliminating their uncertainty by operating on a large scale and taking statistical means. This method taxes patience to the utmost, and could hardly have arisen in a country whose natives could be *bored*. Such Germans as Weber, Fechner, Vierordt, and Wundt obviously cannot; and their success has brought into the field an array of younger experimental psychologists, bent on studying the *elements* of the mental life, dissecting them out from the gross results in which they are embedded, and as far as possible reducing them to quantitative scales. The simple and open method of attack having done what it can, the method of patience, starving out, and harassing to death is tried; the Mind must submit to a regular *siege,* in which minute advantages gained night and day by the forces that hem her in must sum themselves up at last into her overthrow. There is little of the grand style about these new prism, pendulum, and chronograph-philoso- phers. They mean business, not chivalry. What generous divination, and that superiority in virtue which was thought by Cicero to give a man the best insight into nature, have failed to do, their spying and scraping, their deadly tenacity and almost diabolic cunning, will doubtless some day bring about." [3]

It need hardly be said that this half-amused attitude was not the one generally adopted by the devotees of the new psychology. But to James, much of this effortful and organ- ized attack, much of the grim business of discriminating element from element, seemed forced and artificial. The experimental method, however, he recognized as one of the possible means to psychological knowledge. "Facts are facts," he said, "and if we only get enough of them they are sure to combine." As always, he was determined to ignore no possible source of information.

The comparative method James included as supplementary to the introspective and experimental methods. Its useful- ness, he believed, lies in the fact that it reveals mental life in its variations. It undertakes inquiries into the psychology of animals, of children, of primitive races, of the defective and the insane, and into the history of such institutions as language, custom, and myth. The method, however, is in- exact, and the interpretations made on the basis of its find- ings are subject to many a slip. In this connection, James makes an observation that subsequent experience has found to be true: that comparative studies, if they are to give definite results, must be made to test some specific hypoth- esis. And he adds "the only thing then is to use as much sagacity as you possess and to be as candid as you can."

[3] William James, *The Principles of Psychology*, I, 192-193.

In his comments on these various methods, James shows repeatedly that he is distinctly aware of difficulties in their use: introspection is often inaccurate; experiment is sometimes ponderous and futile; the interpretation of the results of comparative psychology may become "wild work." But there are two difficulties in method which he found so pervasive and so serious that he felt it necessary to consider them by themselves.

One of these arises from the use of language. Our words were forged by common sense, not by science; they were made to serve the practical needs of everyday life, not to mirror thoughts and feelings. Consequently, no reliable correspondence exists between words and the facts of consciousness, and words distort our vision of psychological material. If there is no word for a mental fact, we tend to overlook the fact itself; we find it hard even to believe that such a fact exists. On the other hand, if there is a word that purports to denote a mental process, we tend to believe in the process even if there is no introspective evidence of its existence. Furthermore, since the words of common sense usually have an objective reference, we are likely to think that our thoughts are like the objects they represent. Thus we tend to regard the thought of several distinct things as several distinct bits of thought; and because the objects of thought come and go again and again, we think of thoughts themselves as coming and going, persisting and retaining their identity as we believe that objects do. This fallacy, according to James, lies at the basis of the whole of the associationistic and Herbartian schools and of the atomistic conception of psychology generally—a fallacy against which the psychologist must forever be on guard.

The other great difficulty is "the psychologist's fallacy." Essentially this is a confusion of the psychologist's standpoint with that of the mental state he is studying. The psychologist, as a psychologist, is outside the mental state he studies, even if it is his own. He knows not only the mental state, but its object, and the world of reality in which the thought and object exist. He may therefore read into the mental state, for example, the perception of a tree, what he, outside the perception, knows of the tree; that is, he may suppose that everything he knows about the tree is in the present perception of the tree. He may even suppose that the perception of the tree resembles the tree. Furthermore, he may assume that the perception is aware of itself as he, the psychologist, is aware of it; that instead of knowing itself only from within, it knows its own relations to other thoughts and things as he, the psychologist, knows them. But if we look upon consciousness itself and see it as it is, we discover that consciousness of an object does not have to be like the object it refers to, and that, in itself, it does not have to be aware of its external relations. Again James was urging an appeal to immediate experience. That appeal, in fact, lies at the very basis of his warning against the "psychologist's fallacy." What he was urging psychology to do was to examine its subject-matter at first hand—to see all that is there and only what is there, and to see it undistorted by custom, or learning, or the uncritical habits of common sense.

The mind-body relation, as James saw it in psychology, can be stated briefly. As a natural science, psychology must begin at the starting-point common to all science, the world as it appears to naïve, everyday observation. From this point of view, the minds the psychologist studies are objects in a world of objects; they are the minds of particular individuals, existing in time and space. "With any other sort of mind, absolute Intelligence, Mind unattached to a particular body, or Mind not subject to the course of time, the psychologist as such has nothing to do." That the immediate conditions of minds are living bodies and brains is accepted simply as an empirical fact; the ultimate nature of the relation between them is a problem for metaphysics, not for psychology.

Minds have another relation to the world of objects in which they exist—that of being aware of those objects, of knowing them, and of welcoming or rejecting them. Concerning this relation nothing can be said beyond the bare statement that it exists. To the psychologist, knowledge is an "ultimate relation that must be admitted whether it is explained or not, just like difference or resemblance which no one seeks to explain." True, there are problems that center about the relation of knowing, but they are epistemological, not psychological, problems. The psychologist's attitude is simply that the relation of knowing exists, that it cannot be reduced to any simpler or more intelligible terms, and that it must be accepted as science accepts any other relation which from its point of view is ultimate.

It is important to note that it was James the psychologist who took this stand on the mind-body problem. James the philosopher was tremendously interested in the problems he dismissed from psychology as metaphysical. In his theory of radical empiricism—specifically in his essay "Does Consciousness Exist?" [4]—he put forward, as a philosopher, an original conception of the mind-body relation. But though many of the attitudes that were later to be made explicit in his philosophy can be discerned in his psychology, James as a psychologist, and as the author of *The Principles*, maintained the position stated.

So much for James's attitude toward the fundamental problems of subject-matter and method, and of the relation

[4] William James, "Does Consciousness Exist?" *Essays in Radical Empiricism*, 1-38.

of minds to the world in which they exist. His treatment of special problems must next be considered. Here, even more clearly than in his discussion of the basic principles of psychology, his characteristic manner is revealed. It would be impossible to appreciate both the freshness and the exhaustiveness of his treatment without observing his manner of dealing with some of the special topics of psychology.

In the chapter on the self James exhibits some of his most distinctive habits of thought. He does not treat of the self as a bare abstraction, persisting through experience and giving it unity; he deals with the perceived selves that live in the actual world. In its most obvious form, the self is material, but the material it includes is a fluctuating stuff. The material self is the body, but it is more than the body; it includes clothes and house and property and bank-account—all the possessions the self can call its own. All these things arouse the same kinds of feeling, though not necessarily to the same degree. When they flourish and prosper, they bring elation and a sense of triumph; when they diminish or die, they bring dejection and depression, and a feeling of "partial conversion . . . to nothingness, which is a psychological phenomenon by itself."

In addition to the material self, there is the social self—or rather, there is a throng of social selves, for every one has as many social selves as there are persons who recognize him and have some opinion or idea of him. But since these people fall into classes or groups, it is possible to say that a person has as many social selves as there are groups of people whose opinion is important to him—a family self, a professional self, a club self, a self he shows to his contemporaries, to his elders, to his employers, to his employees, to all the people he knows. Even his "fame" and "honor" are social selves. The triumphs and misadventures of his social selves cause the same kinds of rises and falls in emotion, the same kinds of elation and depression, as do the fortunes of the material self.

More intimate than any of these selves is the spiritual self—the intellectual capacities, the sensibilities, the will, "all the psychic faculties or dispositions taken together." It is the spiritual self that one feels to be most truly himself, and by that self James means something which is actually felt in experience—not a mere abstraction, not a logical necessity of thinking, not anything outside or beyond immediately felt reality. Its very center he finds in a sense of activity, something internal even to thoughts and feelings, something that seems *to go out* to meet all the qualities and contents of experience, while they *come in to* it and are received by it. But this spiritual self James finds not to be spiritual at all in the commonly accepted meaning of the term. He does not deny that the sense of activity is present; nor does he doubt for a moment the genuineness of the experience; but when he observes the experience psychologically, he finds that the feeling is always one of physical activity, for the most part taking place within the head. Adjustments of the sense-organs, the openings and closings of the glottis, the contraction of the muscles of the jaws and forehead, the movements used in breathing—these and similar processes contribute to the feeling. And the sense of such activities, obscure but ever present, constant as compared with other activities, adequately accounts for the characteristics we feel as the innermost nature of the self—for the self as an activity persisting through all other activities, but not identifiable with them. The fact that the processes are obscure, monotonous, and uninteresting in themselves explains why they are not recognized for what they are, why they almost pass unnoticed, and yet constitute a background of genuine feeling that we know as the spiritual self.

Taken together, the material self, the social self, and the spiritual self form the empirical self, thus constituting a heterogeneous company, in which the various members are not always at peace. No one has portrayed more vividly than James the multitudinous impulses, the possibilities for rivalries and conflicts, within a single self:

"With most objects of desire, physical nature restricts our choice to but one of many represented goods, and even so it is here. I am often confronted by the necessity of standing by one of my empirical selves and relinquishing the rest. Not that I would not, if I could, be both handsome and fat, and well dressed, and a great athlete, and make a million a year, be a wit, a *bon-vivant,* and a lady-killer, as well as a philosopher; a philanthropist, statesman, warrior, and African explorer, as well as a 'tone-poet' and saint. But the thing is simply impossible. The millionaire's work would run counter to the saint's; the *bon-vivant* and the philanthropist would trip each other up; the philosopher and the lady-killer could not well keep house in the same tenement of clay. Such different characters may conceivably at the outset of life be alike *possible* to a man. But to make any one of them actual, the rest must more or less be suppressed. So the seeker of his truest, strongest, deepest self must review the list carefully, and pick out the one on which to stake his salvation. All other selves thereupon become unreal, but the fortunes of this self are real. Its failures are real failures, its triumphs real triumphs, carrying shame and gladness with them. . . .

"I, who for the time have staked my all on being a psychologist, am mortified if others know much more psychology than I. But I am contented to wallow in the grossest ignorance of Greek. My deficiencies there give me no sense of personal humiliation at all. Had I 'pretensions' to be a linguist, it would have been just the reverse. So we have the paradox of a man shamed to death because he is only the second pugilist or the second oarsman in the world. That he is able to beat the whole population of the globe minus one is nothing; he has 'pitted' himself to beat that one; and as long as he doesn't do that nothing else counts. He is to his own regard as if he were not, indeed he *is* not." [5]

Obviously the empirical self, as James sees it, lacks that absolute unity which popular thought, theology, and many systems of philosophy have found as its essential characteristic.

All that has been said, however, applies to the empirical self, the self that is directly known in experience. There remains the pure ego, the self as thinker, not as the object of thought. But even when he turns his attention to the pure ego, James finds no evidence of absolute oneness. The impression of unity is created, to be sure; there seems to be something at the very center of one's being that is the same through all shifts of experience. But this impression of unity James explains in terms of certain transitive states of consciousness, certain feelings of relation in the stream of thought. Each moment of experience comes into experience on the heels of the one that, though passing, has not completely passed; it senses its continuity with its predecessor, appropriates it to itself, and is in turn appropriated by its successor. There is thus a continuous feeling of ownership, but the feeling is not due to a unitary something *behind* experience, it is due to relations of appropriation *in* experience which transmit the feeling of ownership from one moment to the next. This explanation of the feeling of personal identity James maintains against the theory of a substantial and immaterial soul, against the associationist's doctrine of the self as successive states of consciousness "gumming themselves together," and against the Kantian doctrine of a transcendental ego of apperception that is logically implied in all thinking. All that is necessary to account for the unity of the self he finds in the stream of consciousness, specifically in

[5] William James, *The Principles of Psychology*, **I**, 309-310.

relations of appropriation that are transitive states discoverable in immediate experience.

James concludes his chapter on the self by reporting cases
of striking changes in personality—those phenomena of alter-
nating personality, split-off states of consciousness, and
dissociation which always interested him. To him, they
seemed to constitute empirical evidence that the self is not
the absolute unity it is often said to be. The phenomena of
dissociation seemed to him to have far-reaching implications
concerning the organization of actual selves.

This summary has necessarily omitted much of the concrete detail that gives the chapter its distinctive tone. In no
portion of *The Principles* is James's manner better displayed
than in his treatment of the self. The shrewd and sympathetic
observations, the picturesque portraits, the empirical approach, the explanation of the unity of the self in terms of
transitive feelings of relation, the careful explication of his
own position with due regard to current theories, both psychological and metaphysical, the interest in the recently investigated phenomena of abnormal personalities—all reveal
his characteristic touch. And throughout the length of the
chapter, which runs the gamut from direct observation to
abstract metaphysical speculation, from minute scrutiny to
broad generalization, the self stands out as a living thing.
It is treated not as an abstraction, not as a soul, not as a
string of simple ideas, not as a logical necessity of thinking,
but as a psychological actuality, not merely conceived but
felt.

Another of James's characteristic attitudes is found in his
treatment of the intellectual processes. It was one of his
strongest beliefs that psychology had overintellectualized its
material; and at times it seems that his chief concern in
discussing man's rational nature was to show how largely it

is non rational. At the basis of his treatment of conception, belief, and reasoning lies a profound conviction that the intellectual activities are present in the human animal because they have biological utility; that they are among the practical means by which the human creature maintains himself in the world.

Thus, conceptions are creations of living beings bent on particular enterprises and aims. They are sections cut out of the flux of experience, fixed with names, and fashioned to suit human purposes. They are human ways of dealing with experience, which itself never stands still. Conceptions themselves, however, are fixed and immutable; they are *made* fixed and immutable by the intellect. They form the very "keel and backbone" of our thinking, since only by reference to their stability are we able to deal with experience which otherwise would forever escape us. When, for example, we conceive of paper as something to write on, we single out and fix that one fact about paper, and in doing so we make it something we can operate on in a particular way. But such a conception is our own construction; it is a tool fashioned by a particular need; it does not mean that paper *is* essentially something to write on. There is, James insists, no property absolutely essential to any one thing. While we are writing, paper is conceived as a surface for writing, but if we are using it to light a fire, it is conceived as combustible material. The same paper may be conceived in an indefinite number of ways: "a thin thing, a hydrocarbonaceous thing, a thing eight inches one way and ten another, a thing just one furlong east of a certain stone in my neighbor's field, an American thing," are some of his suggestions. Conception, he adds, is necessarily partial.

"Whichever one of these aspects of its being I temporarily class it under, makes me unjust to the other aspects. But as I always am classing it under one aspect or another, I am always unjust, always partial, always exclusive. My excuse is necessity—the necessity which my finite and practical nature lays upon me. My thinking is first and last and always for the sake of my doing, and I can only do one thing at a time." [6]

That there is no one quality absolutely essential to a thing, no one essence which it most truly *is*, James admits is an idea repugnant to common sense. Common sense assumes that there must be something at the core of a thing which constitutes its essence and of which its various characteristics are merely properties. The essence of the thing is what gives it its name. The thing *is* paper, and its rectangularity, its combustibility, its distance from a particular stone, are properties that inhere in it. But this attitude is itself due to one of our particular and practical purposes, that of naming things. It is a tremendous convenience to have names for things, something by which they can always be represented even if they are absent. Consequently the practice of naming has become so habitual that the commonest name comes to stand in our minds for what the thing really is beneath the less common ways of conceiving it. Or if we adopt the attitude of popular science, we may think of water as really and essentially H_2O. But water is no more truly H_2O than it is something to drink, or something that will keep flowers fresh. To conceive it under its chemical formula is useful in some circumstances, to conceive it under other forms, in others; but no one conception invariably represents its reality independent of particular purposes. "This whole function of conceiving, of fixing, and holding fast to meanings has no significance apart from the fact that the conceiver is a creature with partial purposes and private ends." [7]

Reasoning, like conceiving, is grounded in non-rational

[6] William James, *op. cit.*, II, 333.
[7] William James, *op. cit.*, I, 482.

needs, and from the first it is subject to non-rational conditions. Certainly reasoning is not an affair of a disembodied intellect. It is, for one thing, a matter of association; it must utilize what the associative processes offer, and it is therefore dependent on the machinery of the brain. It is also a matter of selection. Out of all the materials presented, some one character is extracted as essential. This process of selection has just been discussed as conception; and the ability to conceive a matter properly, to seize upon and isolate the elements relevant to the needs of the situation, is the most important step in the whole reasoning process. To conceive properly presupposes the ability to break up a total situation into parts, to see what is essential and—what is just as important—to ignore the rest. The extracted character then arouses associations that lead to the conclusion. These associations are, of course, products of learning. Thus, if heat is conceived as motion, the facts already known about motion are now associated with heat. In understanding heat mechanically, then, there are two steps. One involves what James calls sagacity; it is the conception of heat as motion. The other involves learning; it is the arousal of the knowledge associated with the idea of motion. In terms of the syllogism, the act of conceiving gives the minor premise, that heat is motion. The major premise, the proposition about motion, is aroused by association.

Not that James gives the impression that reasoning, psychologically considered, follows the pattern of the syllogism. Since reasoning is dependent on association, it is subject to all the accidents, checks, irregularities, and irrelevancies of association. Association by similarity is especially important in reasoning because it assists in conception, in the perception of essence. Selection, too, plays an important rôle in reasoning. It is present primarily in conception—that is, in the selection of essentials; but the process by which associations relevant to the selected element are aroused also involves selection. And selection, it cannot be repeated too often, is an activity of creatures of partial and practical purposes who are pursuing private ends. James is emphatic upon the point that reasoning occurs for the sake of action.

Finally, belief, like conception and reasoning, is determined by non-rational factors. To James, belief is more akin to emotion than to anything else; and credulity, the immediate and unquestioned sense of reality, he regards as our primary response to our own perceptions and thoughts. Credulity is not the outcome of proof; it occurs before the need of proof arises. We tend strongly to accept as real whatever presents itself; only when something interferes with the belief it arouses, or runs counter to it, do we begin to doubt. This means that there are many possibilities of reality, many candidates for belief, and that we must choose one as real and disregard the others. We must decide, for example, whether in a particular perception we are seeing a ghost or a mist or a hallucination. There are, indeed, several orders of reality that most people recognize and discriminate from each other. There is, first of all, the world of sense or physical things as we immediately perceive them, with their colors, sounds, and temperatures. There is also the world of science from which colors, sounds, and the other secondary qualities are excluded. There are worlds of abstract relations, of which the worlds of logic and mathematics are examples. There are various supernatural worlds, such as the Christian heaven and hell and the world of classic mythology. There are worlds of intentional fiction, such as the world of the *Pickwick Papers,* which, though recognized as fiction, have a reality of their own so distinctive that a suggested addition is immediately sensed as appropriate or inappropriate. There

are all the worlds of individual opinion. There are even
worlds of madness, which have their special sort of reality.

In the presence of so many possibilities, there must be
selection. The possibilities, however, are not mutually exclusive. We accept the world of sense, and the world of
science, and the world of the *Pickwick Papers* in different
moods and for different purposes. Yet we are continually
confronted with the task of discriminating the real from the
unreal, the more real from the less real; and in doing so,
we have not one criterion but several. James writes:

"As a rule, the success with which a contradicted object
maintains itself in our belief is proportional to several qualities which it must possess. Of these the one which would
be put first by most people, because it characterizes objects
of sensation, is its—

"(1) Coerciveness over attention, or the mere power to
possess consciousness: then follow

"(2) Liveliness, or sensible pungency, especially in the way
of exciting pleasure or pain;

"(3) Stimulating effect upon the will, i.e., capacity to
arouse active impulses, the more instinctive the better;

"(4) Emotional interest, as object of love, dread, admiration, desire, etc.;

"(5) Congruity with certain favorite forms of contemplation—unity, simplicity, permanence, and the like;

"(6) Independence of other causes and its own causal
importance." [8]

But underlying all these conditions of belief is the fact
that a thing, to be believed, must have some vital relation
to the self. It must bring pleasure or pain, or arouse action.
From the standpoint of the intellect alone, we give a certain
reality to any object we think about; we accept it as real, at
least as an object of thought. But we are not mere intellectual
beings; we are emotional and volitional creatures as well;

[8] William James, *op. cit.*, II, 300.

and we attribute a higher degree of reality to those things
which arouse our emotional and volitional natures. Only
that is truly real which makes some living connection with
the self, which touches it with some "stinging" term, which
stirs it emotionally, and which rouses it to action. The
relation of will and belief is to James especially significant.[9]
He maintains that the object of belief is not determined
solely by evidence, but largely by wish, and finally by the
decision of the believer. What we wish to believe, what
we will to believe, determines to an enormous extent what
we do believe.

Thus the processes of thought, as they appear to James,
are by no means rational in any absolute sense. Conceptions
are formed from the standpoint of particular purposes;
reasoning is undertaken for the sake of action; and beliefs
are determined by wish and will quite as much as by proof
and evidence. Thought is an activity of creatures who are
pursuing practical and limited programs of action. The
human intellect is rooted in the needs of living organisms
that have their way to make in the world.

In his chapter on instinct, James comments on another
of the non-rational aspects of human conduct.

*"Now, why do the various animals do what seem to us
such strange things,* in the presence of such outlandish
stimuli? Why does the hen, for example, submit herself to
the tedium of incubating such a fearfully uninteresting set
of objects as a nestful of eggs, unless she have some sort of
a prophetic inkling of the result? The only answer is *ad
hominem.* We can only interpret the instincts of brutes by
what we know of instincts in ourselves. Why do men always
lie down, when they can, on soft beds rather than on hard
floors? Why do they sit around the stove on a cold day?

[9] Cf. William James, *The Will to Believe and Other Essays in Popular
Philosophy,* 1-32.

Why, in a room, do they place themselves, ninety-nine times out of a hundred, with their faces towards the middle rather than to the wall? Why do they prefer saddle of mutton and champagne to hard-tack and ditch-water? Why does the maiden interest the youth so that everything about her seems more important and significant than anything else in the world? Nothing more can be said than that these are human ways, and that every creature *likes* its own ways, and takes to following them as a matter of course. Science may come and consider these ways, and find that most of them are useful. But it is not for the sake of their utility that they are followed, but because at the moment of following them we feel that that is the only appropriate and natural thing to do. Not one man in a billion, when taking his dinner, ever thinks of utility. He eats because the food tastes good and makes him want more. If you ask him why he should want to eat more of what tastes like that, instead of revering you as a philosopher he will probably laugh at you for a fool. The connection between the savory sensation and the act it awakens is for him absolute and *selbstverständlich,* an '*a priori* synthesis' of the most perfect sort, needing no proof but its own evidence. It takes, in short, what Berkeley calls a mind debauched by learning to carry the process of making the natural seem strange, so far as to ask for the *why* of any instinctive human act. To the metaphysician alone can such questions occur as: Why do we smile, when pleased, and not scowl? Why are we unable to talk to a crowd as we talk to a single friend? Why does a particular maiden turn our wits so upside-down? The common man can only say, '*Of course* we smile, *of course* our heart palpitates at the sight of the crowd, *of course* we love the maiden, that beautiful soul clad in that perfect form, so palpably and flagrantly made from all eternity to be loved!'

"And so, probably, does each animal feel about the particular things it tends to do in presence of particular objects. They, too, are *a priori* syntheses. To the lion it is the lioness which is made to be loved; to the bear, the she-bear. To the broody hen the notion would probably seem monstrous that there should be such a creature in the world to whom a nestful of eggs was not the utterly fascinating and precious and never-to-be-too-much-sat-upon object which it is to her." [10]

This passage, showing the impulsive, non-rational nature of instinct, contains the essential point of James's teaching on this subject. Perhaps it should be noted that to emphasize instinct in James's day carried a meaning quite different from that which a similar emphasis carries to-day. There is at present, in psychology, a tendency to sheer off from the concept of instinct, to distrust it because it may possibly imply innate ideas, or even a mysterious force, unanalyzable by science, that compels an organism to behave in particular ways, something that discourages investigation because it is accepted as "given." But in James's generation, an emphasis on instinct, especially if coupled with his views on the nature of the intellectual processes, meant calling attention to the fact that the species which human psychology studies is after all a biological species; it meant a departure from the psychology of simple ideas and *Vorstellungen,* and a step in the direction of considering man as a living organism in the world of nature.

Indeed, it is interesting to note that some of James's comments on instinct, published over forty years ago, are closely in line with the tendencies of the psychology of to-day. James held that instincts are not necessarily "blind and invariable," as the historical concept of instinct implied, and that they can be modified by habit. In this respect his observations are in harmony with the best experimental evidence available to-day, which shows that when the activities usually classified as instinctive are submitted to observation under controlled conditions, they are not found to be the inevitable, unmodifiable, "perfect" performances that the older concept would lead one to expect. Furthermore his view

[10] William James, *The Principles of Psychology,* II, 386-387.

that human beings have a large number of instincts—more, in fact, than do the lower animals—is also in harmony with contemporary criticisms, for it tends in the direction of specificity. The breaking-up of instinct into specific ways of behavior was, indeed, the first step toward overthrowing the old notion of instinct as a vague, vast force, charged with mysterious potency. Vague, vast forces that are by definition mysterious do not lend themselves to the matter-of-fact ways of science; but in the presence of definite and specific performances, science can immediately get into action. Consequently, when investigators began to break up such large entities as the instinct of self-preservation into particular activities like locomotion and vocalization, or even into less specific activities such as constructiveness and curiosity and pugnacity, wonder and awe in the presence of the unknown began to give way to investigations of definite, concrete occurrences.

In his treatment of the emotions, James developed the theory that is probably his most famous single contribution to psychology. This is the conception known as the James-Lange theory of the emotions. James, considering the problem from the psychological point of view, became convinced that emotion is nothing but the feeling of bodily activity that is reflexly aroused by certain exciting situations. Lange, the Danish physiologist, studying specifically the circulatory system, came to the conclusion that feelings of vasomotor changes constitute the essentials of emotion. The two men announced the theory independently and almost simultaneously.

James states his theory by contrasting it with the view of common sense:

"Common-sense says, we lose our fortune, are sorry and weep; we meet a bear, are frightened and run; we are insulted by a rival, are angry and strike. The hypothesis here to be defended says that this order of sequence is incorrect, that the one mental state is not immediately induced by the other, that the bodily manifestations must first be interposed between, and that the more rational statement is that we feel sorry because we cry, angry because we strike, afraid because we tremble, and not that we cry, strike, or tremble, because we are sorry, angry, or fearful, as the case may be. Without the bodily states following on the perception, the latter would be purely cognitive in form, pale, colorless, destitute of emotional warmth. We might then see the bear, and judge it best to run, receive the insult and deem it right to strike, but we should not actually *feel* afraid or angry." [11]

In the coarser emotions, such as rage, fear, grief, and love, the bodily disturbances are obvious; in the subtler emotions, the bodily responses, though not so easy to detect, are nevertheless present. Unless we actually smile at a witticism, unless we actually tingle at an act of justice or courage, we have no emotional appreciation of the situation; we merely have an intellectual perception that the object of attention is witty or just or courageous. Without the bodily disturbance, gross or slight, there is no emotion.

This theory, as James explicitly states, runs directly counter to the conception of common sense. According to common sense we first see the bear, then feel afraid, then run; the order of events is perception, emotion, bodily movement. James reverses the temporal sequence of the last two events; the bodily movement *precedes* the emotion and is its basis. What we actually feel as emotion is the mass of sensation occasioned by the bodily movements. The feeling of the bodily movements *is* the emotion.

But this is putting the theory in its crudest and boldest form. Certain qualifications are necessary to make the statement portray James's thought more exactly. In the first

[11] William James, *The Principles of Psychology*, II, 449-450.

place, James does not mean that there are three discrete psychological events—the perception of the stimulus, the bodily movements, and the feeling of the bodily movements —separated by appreciable intervals of time. The sequence is so rapid, and the overlapping so great, that no accurate introspection of the temporal order is to be expected. What he does mean is that the emotion has an organic basis, that without the feeling of bodily movements there would be no emotion, that over and above the feelings aroused by the stir-up in the body there is no mind-stuff or purely mental constituent of emotion. In the second place, though he insists on the immediate connection between the perception and the bodily movements, James does not deny the rôle of the cortical response in influencing the total reaction. Rather, he insists on it. A bear in the woods and a bear in a cage produce different reactions. They do so because they constitute different situations, and it is the total situation that counts. James without doubt assumes an instinctive and immediate connection between the object and the reaction; he declares that "objects do excite bodily changes by a pre-organized mechanism"; but he also insists that it is the total situation, not a particular item in it, that produces the result; and the apprehension of the total situation implies a cortical response. James is vague, to be sure, in regard to the exact nature of the connection between the stimulating object and the bodily disturbance; but considering that both the concept of instinct and the knowledge of the nervous system were very indefinite at the time he was writing, that fact is not surprising. Obviously, however, in emphasizing the immediacy of the connection between perception and movement, he relates emotion to the instinctive rather than to the intellectual side of human nature. The fact he wishes to make clear is that though the idea or intellectual appreciation of danger may be present and, if present, will make its own peculiar contribution to the emotional tone, that idea is not itself the basis of fear.

James's view has been adversely criticized by both psychologists and physiologists. The principal objection from the psychology of his day rose from the fact that it abolished a specifically affective element. If James had been a psychologist who compounded states of consciousness from elements, he could have built up an entire system from a single element, sensation; for he had reduced emotion and feeling to sensations of bodily changes, organic and otherwise. Some of his contemporaries strongly objected to this procedure, Titchener,[12] for one, fought to defend an affective element, insisting that affection is intrinsically different from organic sensation or sensation of any sort. He held that the theory confused affection and organic sensation, and he was convinced that an irreducible difference between affection and sensation of any kind is unmistakably revealed by introspection.

Naturally the James-Lange theory interested physiologists as well as psychologists. Sherrington [13] and Cannon,[14] to mention two of the best-known workers, undertook to test it by means of laboratory experiments. Sherrington, operating on dogs, severed the spinal tracts that communicate to

[12] E. B. Titchener, *A Text-book of Psychology*, 473-487.

[13] C. G. Sherrington, *The Integrative Action of the Nervous System*, 255-268.

[14] W. B. Cannon, *Bodily Changes in Pain, Hunger, Fear and Rage;* "The James-Lange Theory of Emotions: a Critical Examination and an Alternative Theory," *American Journal of Psychology* (1927), **39,** 106-124. Cannon's own theory of the emotions is one which emphasizes the rôle of the thalamus in emotion and which gives a more detailed explanation, based on experimental researches, of the nervous processes involved in emotion. A brief statement of Cannon's theory and a summary of the experimental evidence supporting it may be found in a paper by Philip Bard, "The Neuro-Humoral Basis of Emotional Reactions," *The Foundations of Experimental Psychology,* ed. by Carl Murchison, 449-487.

the brain the nervous impulses from the viscera in the trunk. Finding that vocalization, facial expressions, and movements of the sort generally associated with emotion occurred after the operation in situations that would normally arouse emotion, he concluded that emotion could not be produced in the manner James described. Cannon found the usual signs of rage and fear in cats, after he had removed the portion of the automatic nervous system that is involved in the stimulation of the visceral reactions normally present during those emotions. Cannon discovered, too, in a series of experiments, that the same physiological changes were present in fear, rage, hunger, and pain; in other words, that the different emotions could not be differentiated on the basis of distinctive physiological characteristics. This fact he regarded as additional evidence against the theory.

Defenders of the James-Lange theory contend that these experiments are not crucial. They criticize those which attempted elimination by surgery as not eliminating *all* possible sources of bodily sensations that might serve as the basis for the emotion. They grant that what James considered the main organic basis was eliminated, but they believe that possibly less obvious physiological bases were left intact and that these may have been sufficient to initiate the emotional responses observed. They point out, further, that the observed emotional responses may have been associated with given situations through learning, and that at the time they were observed, they may have involved no actual emotion. It has been suggested, too, that Cannon's failure to find physiological conditions that differentiate the emotions from each other does not necessarily count against the theory; that there may be physiological conditions not investigated in his researches—differences due to bodily attitude, posture, facial expression, or very slight physiological changes—that distinguish the emotions as we habitually think of them.

It has also been suggested that the disturbances Cannon found are those common to emotions in general, which after all are not so sharply differentiated as our habits of thought imply.

As a matter of fact, though the James-Lange theory has been neither absolutely proved nor absolutely disproved by the experimental evidence, the consensus of opinion to-day is that it does not adequately explain the known facts; in particular, that it does not account for the relation between perception and feeling, and that it is either vague or flatly wrong about the neural connections between the brain and the viscera. There is no question, however, that the theory has been enormously influential. That the organic side of emotion is tremendously important is generally admitted, even by those who disagree with the fundamental contention that emotion is the feeling of bodily disturbance alone. The theory has been welcomed, too, in its general outline, because it gives emotions a biological reason for being, and assigns them a place and function in the total economy of man's nature. Above all, it has stimulated research on the emotions as has no other conception. Whatever the answer of the experimental evidence may be, the James-Lange theory will have played an important part in bringing it into being.

James's method of dealing with these topics has shown the main tendencies of his thought. Almost any other topics might have been chosen. His famous chapter on habit might have been used to illustrate his strong physiological bent, showing as it does how enthusiastically he defends the thesis that the pathways formed in the nervous system by our own actions determine the very structure of our conduct—the accent with which we speak, the clothes we wear, our professional peculiarities, our social behavior, our sympathies, our judgments, even our moral characters. The chapter on association might have been chosen to illustrate the same point, for in it he treats of association in terms of neural pathways. Having first reduced association by similarity to a special case of association by contiguity, he then reduces association by contiguity to functional connections in the nervous system.

There are several chapters that might have been used to illustrate the author's inveterate habit of appealing to immediate experience for the answers to his questions. His "nativism" in both time and space perception is a case in point, for he regards the continuity of time as "given" in the "specious present" and the perception of depth as derived from a "crude extensity" in our immediate impressions. James, indeed, is inclined to give a nativistic interpretation to many human reactions. Belief, for example, is based on native credulity; even will in its higher manifestations is but a modification of ideomotor action, which is after all a native impulsiveness in ideas, a tendency to get themselves expressed in action. At present the trend in psychology is away from nativism; many investigators feel that to accept a thing as "given" is almost equivalent to accepting it as a miracle. But James's nativism was determined by a distaste for what he considered the miracles that the intellect was called upon to perform in the empiricist philosophy. It was not clear to him, for example, just how the peculiar qualities of spatial voluminousness could be evolved out of nonspatial data, and his loyalty to the experienced quality, as experienced, made him refuse to reduce it to terms other than itself. It is significant that when confronted with this situation and others like it, he preferred to recognize a datum provided by immediate experience rather than to accept a product created by the intellect.

Finally, there are topics in which James's treatment shows a tendency that has been too little stressed in this presentation—a tendency toward voluntarism. To some extent, his position on this problem is implicit in his account of conception, reasoning, and belief as closely allied to man's emotional and active nature. But in his chapter on attention, he attacks the problem more directly. Here he points out that if, by voluntary attention, a given idea could be prolonged for but a moment—long enough to permit its reinforcing associations to enter and do their part—the victory of that idea would be assured. The effort of will would then accomplish what it seems to accomplish, and James puts forward the possibility that it does. The problem of freewill, he points out, is outside the province of science; science can declare neither for it nor against it. But James, as a person, preferred the theory of freewill to that of determinism, and therefore he was at great pains to show that the one is scientifically as reputable as the other.

The publication of *The Principles* was hailed both at home and abroad as an event of the first magnitude in the psychological world. Not only was it a comprehensive survey of a new field of learning, not only was it a new synthesis of the facts of psychology; it was itself a contribution to psychology. From the first, it was recognized as more than a mere book about psychology. Because of its freshness and power, because of its definite attitudes and stimulating suggestions, it was itself an event in the history of psychology.

Perhaps the most striking characteristic of the book was the fact that it so definitely treated psychology as a natural science, in particular as a biological science. Psychology, of course, was being treated as a science elsewhere, notably by the experimentalists in Germany. But the psychology of James took a very different direction. James was interested in conscious processes not only in and by themselves, but as activities of the living organisms in which they occurred—

as activities that made a difference in their lives. It was his general scientific bent, of course, that made him turn from the speculative contemplation of the mind to the direct observation of immediate experience and its conditions; but it was his specific biological interest that made him see mental processes as activities of living creatures maintaining themselves in the world of nature—as activities, indeed, presumably useful to the creatures practising them. This view of mental life has had important consequences for American psychology. Indeed, in treating of mental processes as rooted in the needs and practices of living organisms, James was writing what has since proved to be a distinctively American psychology. He was expressing an attitude which, when made explicit, became that of the first characteristically American school of psychology, functionalism.

Closely related to his attitude toward mental life in general is the emphasis James placed on the non-rational side of human nature. Throughout the entire book, he never permits the reader to forget that the creature he is discussing is a creature of emotion and action as well as of cognition and reason. Even when he considers the intellectual processes themselves, he stresses the non-rational factors involved. He states with the utmost clearness, notably in his chapters on habit and association, his conviction that the intellect operates under definite physiological conditions. And he goes farther. Belief, he insists, is determined by emotional and volitional factors; conception and reasoning, arising under the influence of particular wants and needs, occur for the sake of action. Thought, as James describes it, is a mode of reaction developed by a creature concerned with the practical business of reacting to his environment. The human being who appears in James's psychology bears little resemblance to the rational man of earlier years.

And yet, for all his determination to treat psychology as

science and not as metaphysics, for all his unwillingness to overemphasize the rôle of the intellect in human nature, James did not escape, in his own person, the demands of the intellect for a conception of life that extends beyond that of science. It is repeatedly evident that the author of *The Principles of Psychology* is a man who is tremendously interested in metaphysical problems. Plainly discernible in his approach to psychology are the tendencies that were later to appear in his philosophy as pragmatism, pluralism, and radical empiricism. It is significant, however, that James kept his philosophy and his psychology apart; or rather, that when he introduced philosophy into his discussions, he recognized it as philosophy. As a consequence, it proved a distinct advantage to American psychology that James was a man with philosophical interests. It was, in fact, largely through James that American psychology made the transition from mental philosophy to science and made it, on the whole, with understanding. For James did not merely break with the past; he did not treat too lightly the more familiar ways of dealing with human material. He seriously considered the bearing of the psychology he was presenting on the philosophical ideas to which his readers were accustomed, and in doing so he made the passage to the new point of view intelligible and justifiable. Indeed, the thoroughness with which James dealt with those problems of mental philosophy which psychology as a science has a right to ignore—the problems of the soul and of mind-stuff, for example—is one of the reasons why it is unnecessary for treatises on psychology to cover that ground to-day.

Finally, the incompleteness, the tentativeness, the very inconsistencies of James's psychology were profoundly significant from the standpoint of the development of the science. His treatment, far more suggestive than conclusive, raised many more questions than it answered. Certainly James's teachings do not represent the form that psychology will take as a developed science. They necessarily lack the basis of hard, unequivocal facts which a mature science possesses, facts which ideally can be expressed in quantitative terms and submitted to experimental verification. But just as certainly James's psychology contains much of the unformed stuff of which science is made. At the very least, it is a psychology which has turned directly toward experience for the answers to its questions, and which is utterly faithful to its particular observations, whether or not they harmonize with each other or with a plan that is supposed to include them all. Perhaps it is this fidelity to particular facts which is the outstanding feature of James's psychology; certainly it is a feature which gives his treatment the character of authentic science. It is this fidelity to fact, too, which gives his psychology its tentative character, since admittedly not all the facts are available. It is therefore appropriate that James closes the book with a passage which refers immediately to the subject-matter of the last chapter, but which represents a far more general attitude in himself.

"Even in the clearest parts of Psychology our insight is insignificant enough. And the more sincerely one seeks to trace the actual course of *psychogenesis,* the steps by which as a race we may have come by the peculiar mental attributes which we possess, the more clearly one perceives 'the slowly gathering twilight close in utter night.' "

Chapter VI

FUNCTIONALISM AND THE UNIVERSITY OF CHICAGO

IN 1894, James Rowland Angell, then a young man of twenty-five, came to the new University of Chicago as director of the new department of psychology. In the same year John Dewey, ten years his senior, came to Chicago as professor of philosophy. Both men were versatile in their interests and abilities. Dewey, though primarily a philosopher, had worked in one of the first psychological laboratories in the United States, that of G. Stanley Hall at Johns Hopkins, and was already developing the line of thought that led to his work in education and in the social and political sciences. Angell had studied in several German universities, had been a pupil of William James at Harvard, and was now at Chicago combining administrative duties with his interest in psychology. Both men too were unusually effective as teachers—effective, that is, in stirring student thought to activity and in arousing genuine intellectual enthusiasm for their programs and points of view. Largely because of their combined influence, the University of Chicago rapi 'ly became a flourishing center of psychological study, and the capital of a new school of psychology, functionalism.

In functionalism, American psychology made its first definite and organized stand against domination by the Titchenerian, or Wundtian, school. As the name implies, functionalism was interested primarily in activities—in mental processes not merely as contents but as operations. Furthermore, it was interested in studying them in their natural setting and from the standpoint of their utility. Taking its cue from Darwin, and regarding mental processes as presumably useful to a living organism in the business of adapting itself to its environment, its approach, from the first, was distinctly biological. It had about it, too, an air of common sense, unabashed by academic taboos. In examining mental processes, it asked the questions of the practical man: "What are they for?" "What difference do they make?" "How do they work?" Obviously such questions cannot be answered by studying mental processes in and by themselves. However thoroughgoing such an analysis may be, the study of a process from the standpoint of content alone cannot tell what the process accomplishes. To answer that question, it is necessary to go beyond the process itself and consider the connections it makes: to investigate both its antecedents and its consequences, to discover what difference it makes to the organism, and to take into account its whole complex setting in the complex world in which it appears.

How widely such inquiries diverged from the official psychology of the day is almost immediately apparent. First of all, there was the functionalist's emphasis on process as process—as an event actually going forward. It is true that Wundt and Titchener had also emphasized this point, repeatedly insisting that mental elements must be regarded as processes. But apparently in the actual practice of conceiving elements as processes there is an all but insuperable difficulty. Elements have a way of being treated as things or static bits, whatever the protestations from the standpoint of theory; and this fact, together with the interest in conscious contents as such, gave to the orthodox psychology of the day, at least as it was unofficially interpreted, a static character and a granular feel. The functionalists, however, were eager to study mental processes not as elements entering into a composition, but as activities leading to practical consequences. Whereas structuralism deliberately and intentionally, in the interests of pure science, abstracted its material from its setting, functionalism just as deliberately and intentionally, in the interests of its chosen problem, kept its material in the natural environment in which it appeared. Implicit in this situation is the second marked difference between the two schools—the difference in their attitudes toward the applications of science. Functionalism, frankly joining hands with common sense, was from the first interested in utilities. Since its problem was "What do mental processes accomplish in the world?" it could hardly keep free of those considerations of value—in this case utilitarian —which Titchener so insistently maintained were outside the realm of pure science. It was inevitable therefore that functionalism should run over into applied science, and it actually did so almost at once, with Dewey's entrance into the field of education. All this meant a third great difference between structuralism and functionalism, a difference in their fundamental conceptions of subject-matter and method. Ever since the time of Wundt and Brentano it had been asserted that *functions* cannot appear in direct experience, and therefore cannot be objects of introspective observation. Besides, to inquire into the functions of mental processes meant taking into account much more than consciousness itself. In other words, introspection could no longer be considered the distinctive method of psychology, nor consciousness its special subject-matter. Thus even a preliminary survey of the program of functionalism shows wide departures from the established school.

It is interesting that neither Dewey nor Angell was at all ambitious to found a school. Certainly neither had the manner nor the temperament of the impassioned advocate of a new cause. Dewey, for all his power and originality, was meditative and deliberate. Angell, even in his most out-spoken protests against the old order, was gracious and tolerant. Yet the movement they sponsored plainly challenged authority, and flourished in the bracing atmosphere of combat with a worthy foe. Partly because its own statements openly sanctioned heresies, and partly because Titchener definitely excommunicated it, functionalism became a definite school. In a sense it has remained so down to the present. Psychologists trained at Chicago are distinctly conscious of their psychological lineage; they still think of their psychology in terms of comparisons and contrasts; and among them even to-day there is a solidarity of feeling second to that of no group in the country.

The phenomenon of a school growing up of itself, about leaders who were not at all eager to found a school, is in itself significant. Perhaps something in the atmosphere of the new University of Chicago was responsible for the fact. It is appropriate, surely, that the first distinctively American school of psychology arose at the new university that was itself an expression of so much that is characteristically American. The almost incredible feat of creating a great university outright—of actualizing a plan, of assembling a distinguished faculty, of bringing into being the whole complex organization, body and soul—gave the place an air of great things accomplished and about to be accomplished; and it is not surprising that a school of thought, starting in such circumstances, should thrive and grow.

But the local setting alone, however propitious, is not a sufficient explanation. The almost spontaneous generation of a new school of psychology meant primarily that much was in readiness for its inception. In many quarters in the United States, there was a feeling that psychology, as conventionally defined, was too narrow and cramped. As a matter of fact, the actual progress of psychology in America had not followed the lines laid down for it. Educational psychology, child psychology, animal psychology, the study of individual differences and of mental development—none of these movements could be forced into the conventional mold, yet all were getting under way. William James, of course, had always been a powerful influence outside the Titchenerian camp. G. Stanley Hall, though for a time a student at Leipzig, had never been too favorably impressed by Wundt; and his growing enthusiasm for genetic psychology, together with a temperamental predilection for what might be called psychology in the large, meant that psychology at Clark widely overflowed the conventional bounds. At Columbia, Cattell persevered in his interest in individual differences, and Thorndike undertook experiments on animals and human beings with little regard for the rules of Cornell. James Mark Baldwin was particularly outspoken against the strictures of the orthodox psychology. In his opinion, a young and growing science should not be limited to the procedures sanctioned by any one school, and his own interest in individual differences and mental development, together with a lively belief in the value of unrestricted theoretical discussions, doubtless contributed much to the strength of his conviction. He and Titchener clashed openly in a controversy on the interpretation of the difference between sensory and motor reaction-times, a controversy less important for the particular point at issue than for the clear opposition in which it placed the broader and stricter interpretations of psychology. These cases, moreover, are only indications of a general trend. Throughout the United States there was a widespread disposition to listen to the doctrine that the business of the psychologist is not necessarily limited to the minute dissection of states of consciousness. The peculiarly American enterprises in psychology, as distinguished from those in the German tradition, lent themselves readily to the program of functionalism. The tendencies were in existence, ready to be centralized and brought under a formulation that would unify and justify them. It was not only in the United States, however, that psychology as defined by Wundt and his school had failed to hold undisputed sway. In Germany, Brentano's act psychology, formulated almost simultaneously with Wundt's content psychology, had never been without influential adherents. Much of the French psychology, too, with its interest in mental abnormalities, lent itself readily to functional concepts. In England, James Ward, in his famous article "Psychology" in the *Encyclopædia Britannica,* not only recognized but emphasized the activity of the self or subject; and G. F. Stout, influenced by Ward, developed a psychology in which he regarded as the ultimate modes of being conscious three forms of activity—not contents, it is to be noted—cognition, affection, and conation. The Danish philosopher, Harald Höffding, also definitely treated psychological processes as modes of activity. In his *Outlines of Psychology,* he adopted the old tripartite division of mind into cognition, feeling, and will, thus utilizing a classification daringly reminiscent of faculty psychology. To Höffding, however, these categories meant neither "powers" nor "divisions" of the mind, but ways in which the whole mind operates on different occasions.

Functionalism at Chicago showed no disposition to minimize these anticipations of its teachings. On the contrary, it emphasized them, using them to show that its approach was one frequently taken by serious students, and thus to suggest that the conventional restrictions of the time were artificial. Certainly functionalism did not claim to have discovered something new under the sun. Angell always insisted that functionalism was not to be identified with psychology as it was taught at Chicago, and he even maintained that it did not properly constitute a school. In his opinion, the movement represented something broader than any scientific cult or sect. He believed that functionalistic principles had always been a part of psychology, and that structuralism, by setting up its own specifications, had really been the first school to separate itself from the main body of psychology. There can be little doubt that Titchener's paper, "The Postulates of a Structural Psychology," [1] sharpening as it did the contrast between the structural and functional points of view, and insisting that only the former was legitimate in a true science of psychology, did much to give the new enterprise distinctness and separateness.

But however the new school came into being, there can be no question that it grew and flourished, and that, despite Angell's protestations, functionalism came to be associated with the kind of psychology that was developing at the University of Chicago. From the first it received enthusiastic support there. G. H. Mead and A. W. Moore, both of the department of philosophy and both, like Dewey, interested in psychology, definitely took a stand for the new views. In 1902 Dewey himself became director of the School of Education in the University of Chicago, taking the opportunity, consistently enough, to put into practice the principles of both his philosophy and his psychology. After holding this position for two years, he went to Teachers College, Columbia University, as professor of philosophy. Charles H. Judd, who became director of the School of Education a few years after Dewey's departure, was also actively interested in the new movement. Though he had done the work for his doctorate at Leipzig and had thus received his training in the old school, his *Psychology*, published two

[1] See note 13, Chap. IV, p. 143.

years before he came to Chicago, was written so thoroughly
in the spirit of functionalism that his treatment of motor
reactions is often cited as an example of the functionalistic interpretation at its best. During this time, Angell,
as head of the department of psychology, had made it
one of the strongest in the country. He remained at Chicago for twenty-six years, and later became president of
Yale University. Since Angell's departure, Harvey Carr, the
second student to take his doctor's degree in psychology at
Chicago and the present head of the department, carried
on there the work that Dewey and Angell had begun.

It is significant that there is no one book or treatise
which represents functionalism as Titchener's *Text-book* represents his system, or James's *Principles* his psychology.
Dewey never wrote a systematic exposition of functional
psychology, though its principles are implicit in his many
writings. His *Text-Book of Psychology* was published in
1884, before he had worked out his characteristic psychological views and twelve years before he definitely launched
the functionalistic movement. Angell published his *Text-
Book of Psychology* in 1904 and his *Introduction to Psychology* in 1918, but though both books are written from the
functionalistic standpoint, neither has as its primary aim the
presentation of functionalism as a system. The same comment may be made on other general texts written in the
functionalistic vein. Besides, even if a systematic presentation
existed, no one book, no one product of functionalistic
thought, could adequately represent what was essentially a
movement and an activity. For functionalism, like its own
subject-matter, was a process with a function, an operation
on American psychology generally; and what it meant to
American psychology can best be discovered by following the
course of its formation and development. For convenience,
three phases of the movement may be distinguished: its

initiation by Dewey, its development under Angell's leadership, and its preservation as a definite influence by Carr.

Dewey's article, "The Reflex Arc Concept in Psychology," [2] published in 1896, marks the starting-point of functionalism as a definite movement. The import of this much-discussed paper is that psychological activity cannot be broken into parts or elements but must be regarded as a continuous whole. Like James, Dewey was attacking psychological atomism. James, it will be remembered, had shown that "simple ideas" as bits of consciousness have no existential reality. But Dewey believed that the fallacy of elementarism had simply retired to a new hiding-place. In the reflex-arc concept, with its distinctions between stimulus and response, between sensation and movement, between sensory, central, and motor portions of the arc, he saw the old tendency to think in terms of discrete units—the old atomism in a new form. It was Dewey's thesis that distinctions like that between stimulus and response are purely functional and are based not on actual differences in existing reality, but on the different rôles played by given acts in the total process.

Dewey stated his case by reference to the familiar example of the child who sees a flame, reaches for it, and burns its fingers. This activity is not a simple sequence of three events: seeing, reaching, and getting burned. It cannot be said that, in the first stage of the activity, seeing is the stimulus and reaching the response; that the sensation, seeing, comes first, and that the motor act, reaching, follows. The sensation does not *precede* movement, for seeing cannot be separated from looking. Motor adjustments of the head and eyes are involved in getting the sensation of light. Simi-

[2] John Dewey, "The Reflex Arc Concept in Psychology," *Psychological Review* (1896), 3, 357-370.

larly, reaching does not *follow* seeing and cannot be considered apart from it. Reaching cannot proceed unless seeing, persisting throughout, inhibits some motor reactions and initiates others, thus controlling the action. At the same time, reaching controls seeing, determining its direction throughout. Properly the activity is not merely seeing, but "seeing-for-reaching."

Then why has the distinction been made? If the activity is really a continuous process, why do we tend so strongly to think of it as composed of discrete parts? And why has the tendency become such an obdurate habit that we must continually be on our guard against it?

Stimulus and response have been distinguished, Dewey answers, because of the different rôles they play in the total coördination of reaching or maintaining an end or goal; because of their practical significance in adapting the organism to the situation of the moment. The distinction is a functional one, based on what the processes *do*, not an existential one, based on what the processes *are*.

This becomes clear if we compare two stages of adaptation: one a completed adaptation, such as a well-developed instinct; the other an adaptation in the process of formation, like the activity of the child learning not to touch the candle flame. In the completed adaptation, there is no question of stimulus *as* stimulus and response *as* response. There is simply an orderly sequence of acts in which one act may be regarded as the stimulus to its successor; but even this statement is true only if the coördination is considered as a whole and as a process toward an end or goal. Without reference to the goal, and without reference to the part they play in reaching the goal, the acts are simply a temporal sequence.

But in an act of adaptation not yet fully organized, such as that of the child reaching for the candle flame, there is

no fixed and certain order of events. Nothing has become
stabilized as stimulus or response. The problem, Dewey
says, is to discover or *constitute* the stimulus, quite as much
as to discover or constitute the response. In the child's previous experience, reaching for bright objects has sometimes
terminated in satisfaction, sometimes in pain. He is confronted now with the question: What sort of bright object
is this? The problem is to constitute the stimulus, and just
here the distinction between stimulus and response is made.
The reaching movements that have been initiated are now
inhibited by the imperfection in the coördination; the act
of constituting the stimulus, i.e., determining the nature of
the light, has to occur before reaching can proceed without
painful consequences. Attention is thus directed toward seeing, and that part of the coördination, therefore, becomes
distinct from reaching, not existentially but functionally, for
the practical purposes of the moment. The danger is that a
teleological distinction, developed in the course of a practical
act, may be taken to represent an existential fact.

It is the total coördination, then, not any part of it, that
the psychologist must take as his unit. This does not mean,
however, that Dewey merely substitutes a larger unit for a
smaller one. He does not believe that coördinations, placed
end to end, can explain behavior, any more than stimulus
and response, placed end to end, can do so. The total co-
ordination that one happens to be dealing with at the moment cannot be separated from its setting, any more than
the stimulus and the response can be separated from the
complete coördination in which they occur. The total co-
ordination is related to its past and its future and to the
total activity of the organism exactly as the different phases
of the reflex act are related to each other. There are no
partitions between the activities of the organism. When an

act displays unity and completeness, its unity is functional; it has no existential separateness.

Naturally enough, the first effect of this teaching is likely to be confusion; it obliterates habitual distinctions. The neat boundaries that separate one concept from another are shown to have no counterpart in the existential reality to which they are applied. There, all is continuity. Between stimulus and response, between one movement and another, between organism and environment, there are no real breaks. True, we may, and even must, introduce breaks in thinking of them; but we must never forget that the distinctions we use are of our own making, that they are not grounded in the nature of things but are convenient devices of creatures who invent them for practical purposes. The lines of demarcation that seem fixed and stable are really no more permanent than our own purposes; and the moment we confuse our functional distinctions with existing reality, the moment we expect the actual to be confined within the boundaries we have set up—as when we show surprise that the gulf we have made between thoughts and things is not impassable in nature—we are thoroughly misconceiving reality. We may legitimately use functional distinctions as practical devices, but we must never lose sight of the fact that they are mere devices, and that beneath these distinctions there is continuity.

This conception called for a far more thoroughgoing revision of psychological thought than is immediately apparent. First, it attacked psychological atomism in a peculiarly radical way. It is deeply significant that in his criticism of elementarism, Dewey chose as his target not elementary sensations and affections, but the reflex-arc concept—the very concept that had been introduced into psychology to accommodate the material which did not fit into the conventional pattern, the concept which seemed to lead away from the static, descriptive telling-off of elements in states of consciousness. Dewey showed, however, that so long as the reflex arc was regarded as a separate unit, or as an affair of disjointed parts, it was open to the same objections that had been leveled against the older psychology. His criticism was a hunting-down of the old enemy in a new and unlikely and apparently safe hiding-place.

Dewey's view also implied a change in attitude toward the mind-body problem. In his scheme, the old dualism disappears. Both the mental and the physical aspects of experience are recognized, but they are not treated as distinct, separate orders of events. There is no cleft between sensation and movement, between thoughts and things. The mind-body distinction is no more an existential distinction than is that between stimulus and response. Mental acts are not psychical events pure and simple; they are events in which both the physical and the psychical are present. Rising in the midst of the world of nature, they play their part in that world like any other natural events.

Dewey's teachings meant, too, an attitude of friendship toward applied psychology. They meant that mental processes cannot be disengaged from their conditions and consequences, that they are activities of creatures who are pursuing ends, entertaining purposes, engaging in enterprises literally "of consequence." The step to applied psychology was inevitable and Dewey himself took it when he became director of the School of Education. His influence, it need hardly be stated, has been as great in education as in psychology.

Of course, Dewey is primarily neither a psychologist nor an educator. He is a philosopher whose manner of looking at humanity and its problems has a way of leading him into special fields—into the political and social sciences as well as into psychology and education. His general mode of thought has been described as a habit of thinking of man "as an animal species finding his way about by the unique methods of the central nervous system on an insignificant planet with a very bad and variable climate." [3] Perhaps his two most influential books in psychology are *How We Think* and *Human Nature and Conduct.* In the former he emphasizes the place of thought in the world of the actual, calling attention to the fact that thought works back and forth without any actual difficulty across the "chasm" we have artificially created. In *Human Nature and Conduct,* emphasizing the close relationship between the individual and his surroundings, and using habit as the key to social psychology, he shows how habits are formed in the "interaction of biological aptitudes with a social environment."

During Angell's administration at Chicago, functionalism was embodied as an actual working school. It was no longer merely a hope and a theory, but a going enterprise visible in an active laboratory, in a growing body of research, in an enthusiastic teaching staff, and in an equally enthusiastic group of graduate students. It is curious that Angell's contribution to psychology, perhaps his chief contribution, should have taken just this form, for Angell always maintained that functionalism should not be identified with the Psychology of the Chicago school. Yet the rise of that school was of the greatest practical importance; for without a school, functionalism would have lacked the centralization that was one of the reasons for its effectiveness. Any movement is the better for having a local habitation as well as a name; and with a definite *locus operandi* functionalism became a solid actuality that could not be ignored. Under Angell the work at Chicago rapidly rose to promi-

[3] C. E. Ayres, "Philosophy au Naturel." *New Republic* (1925), 42, 129-131.

nence. In 1906, when he was made president of the American Psychological Association, he gave as his presidential address his now famous paper, "The Province of Functional Psychology." [4] Like Dewey's article on "The Reflex Arc Concept," Angell's address is one of the classic statements of the principles of functionalism. Dewey's article gave functionalism its first formulation; Angell's paper outlined its principles when the movement had been in progress more than a decade.

In Angell's article, three aspects of the movement are considered. First, functionalism is contrasted with structuralism. Structuralism addresses itself to contents; functionalism to operations. The structuralist's particular task is to analyze a state of consciousness into its elements; the functionalist's is to discover how a mental process operates, what it accomplishes, and under what conditions it appears.

Though it is unnecessary to dwell on the point, it should be noted that Angell's development of this topic is in part reminiscent of James's criticism of the "ideas" of associationism. The "moment of consciousness" that the structuralist analyzes is a perishable thing. A sensation or an idea, when not actually in experience, is non-existent. But mental functions persist. They are as enduring as the functions the biologist studies. Just as the same physiological function may be performed by different structures, so the same mental function may be performed by ideas that differ vastly in their content. We may never have the same idea twice; but an identifiable function may appear over and over again, each time represented in consciousness by an idea that, in existential composition, may be very different from the other ideas which at other times have served the same purpose. Angell draws an analogy between mental func-

[4] J. R. Angell, "The Province of Functional Psychology," *Psychological Review* (1907), 14, 61-91.

tions and the functions of undifferentiated protoplasm; in both cases a given function may appear repeatedly, though the temporary structures involved may never be twice the same. The functionalist's material is thus a more constant stuff than that employed by the structuralist.

Furthermore, even the mental content that the structuralist analyzes cannot really be dealt with as independent and isolated. The very state of consciousness that the structuralist studies—a sensation, for example—is dependent on the particular conditions in which it occurs, both in the experiencing subject and in the objective environment. In Titchener's terminology, the "what" is not really independent of the "how" and the "why." But to study the conditions in which an activity arises is to include the functionalist's task. Any really thoroughgoing inquiry into the structuralist's material requires the functionalist's point of view and procedure.

In the second place, functionalism may be regarded as a movement that is interested in the utilities of mental processes. Functionalism studies mental activity not in and by itself, but as a part of the whole world of biological activity, as part of the whole movement of organic evolution. As a rule, the structures and functions of a living organism are what they are because, in some way, they have enabled the organism to survive; because they have helped to adapt it to the conditions that constitute its environment. There is no reason why consciousness should be an exception to this rule. Since consciousness has survived, it presumably does something for the organism that would not otherwise be accomplished. Functionalism tries to discover precisely what this function is, not only for consciousness in general, but for particular processes like judging, feeling, and willing. From this point of view, the problem of functionalism may be defined as that of discovering the fundamental utilities of conscious activities. In commenting more specifically on the function of consciousness, Angell notes that both biologists and psychologists tend to treat consciousness as "substantially synonymous" with adaptive reactions to novel situations. It is when an organism is *forming* a habit, when the coördination is not yet under control, that consciousness most commonly appears. On the other hand, consciousness tends to desert a *fixed* habit; it is a commonplace that thoroughly learned reactions are likely to become automatic. And not only is consciousness regularly present when the organism is actually adapting itself to its environment, its characteristic sign in overt behavior is "the selective variation of response to stimulation." Taking his cue from these facts, the functionalist regards "selective accommodation" as the rôle of consciousness in general. Particular processes —perceiving, willing, feeling, and the like—may be classified variously, even from the functional point of view, since classification is always teleological. But all these processes will be found to show some form of "selective accommodation."

In the third place, functionalism may be regarded as a characteristic method of dealing with the mind-body problem. Regarding consciousness from the Darwinian standpoint, as having some utility in adapting the organism to its environment, functionalism assumes an interplay between the psychical and the physical. The possibility of an interplay between the two, of the same sort as the interplay between the forces of the physical world, is explained on the ground that there is no real distinction between the psychical and the physical. The functionalist regards the mind-body relation "as capable of treatment in psychology as a methodological distinction rather than a metaphysically existential one." That is, functionalism does away with the dualism which asserts that the physical and the mental are two different orders of events. It regards the distinction between mind and body as a convenience in our thinking, as a "teleological weapon," to use James's words, as a useful instrument for dealing with experience, but not as one that should prejudice us toward the belief that mind and matter are two really different entities. Indeed, the distinction between mind and body makes itself felt only after reflection; it is not present in the more primitive stages in experience. Besides, if taken as absolute and existential, it leads to metaphysical difficulties that are insoluble. For these reasons it is preferable to treat the mind-body distinction as methodological, to regard the physical and psychical as belonging to the same order, and to assume an easy passage from one to the other. This view commits one to no particular system of metaphysics, but is compatible with any one of a number of metaphysical interpretations.

Angell's address was given when functionalism was at the height of its influence, and the ease and clarity that mark his treatment are, in part, the consequence of the success which functionalism had attained since Dewey's criticism of the reflex-arc concept. Angell was speaking of an externalized movement; Dewey was developing the idea that was the germ of the movement. Dewey necessarily involved the reader in the stress and strain of refashioning working concepts. He turned the reflex-arc notion inside out to exhibit its inadequacies; and then, having deprived the reader of his accustomed tools, he invited him to the task of reconstruction. When Dewey wrote his account, it was necessary to take the reader into the very workshop where the fundamental concepts of the school were being forged; Angell could allow him to stand off from the movement and see it from the outside. At the time of Angell's address, functionalism was an established and growing enterprise, one in which youth and vigor were combined with achievement.

The work of Carr represents functionalism when it had settled down and become a recognized school, and was no longer a renaissance and a reformation. It is, in fact, one of the surest signs of the genuine vitality of the movement that it persisted after the excitement of combat had died down and that it steadily maintained its productivity in research. Carr's work, like Angell's, is inseparable from his duties as an administrator; the direction of the actual day-by-day activities of the department at Chicago forms one of his major contributions to psychology.

Earlier in the chapter, it was said that the textbooks written by functionalists do not as a rule present functionalism as a system. Carr's *Psychology* [5] is no exception to this rule; it is an expression rather than an exposition of functionalism. It is an expression, furthermore, by a man whose connection with the school has been long and intimate, and who has worked for years with functional concepts. As the papers of Dewey and Angell represent earlier stages of the movement, Carr's *Psychology* represents the functionalism of to-day.

In this book, Carr defines the subject-matter of psychology as mental activity. Mental activity is the generic term for such processes as perception, memory, imagination, feeling, judgment, and will. Mental activity is concerned with "the acquisition, fixation, retention, organization, and evaluation of experiences, and their subsequent utilization in the guidance of conduct." The conduct in which mental activity appears is called adaptive or adjustive behavior.

Here, in the sober, matter-of-fact terms of a school that has reached its maturity, are included the concepts which the functionalism of the nineties held in the teeth of an opposing tradition. The subject-matter of psychology is defined as activity, and the more specific description refers not

[5] Harvey Carr, *Psychology*, 1925.

to elements and content, but to processes like perceiving and feeling. The nature of mental activity is described in terms of what it accomplishes from the "acquisition" of experiences to their "utilization in the guidance of conduct." The kind of behavior in which mental activity occurs is characterized as typically "adaptive." All this is calmly set forth on the first page, not at all as a matter for argument, but simply as a statement of fact in a textbook.

The mind-body relation too is treated in a simple, uncontroversial manner. Mental activity is described as psychophysical. It is psychical in that the individual ordinarily has some knowledge of his activity, that he does not reason and feel and will without being aware of the fact; it is physical in that it is a reaction of the physical organism. No attempt is made to explain the connection between the physical and the psychical; the relationship is simply accepted as a characteristic of mental activity as it appears in experience. Carr makes it particularly plain, however, that mental acts are not to be identified with the purely psychical aspect of adaptive actions. The adjective "mental" refers to the whole process, psychical and physical. The psychical as a separate entity is nothing but an abstraction; it "has no more independent existence than the grin of a Cheshire cat."

Various methods of studying mental activity are accepted. Both introspection and objective observation are recognized. Experiment is mentioned as highly desirable, but complete experimental control of the human mind is admitted to be impossible. The study of social products is also included. Like Wundt, Carr believes that from the literature, art, language, inventions, and social and political institutions which the human race has produced, something can be learned of the mentality that produced them. He also believes that, since structure and function are so closely related, a knowledge of the anatomical structures and physio-

logical processes involved in mental acts is often most illuminating. Finally, he recognizes that common observation is
a means of arriving at psychological knowledge, though he
also recognizes that scientific psychology differs from common sense in being more careful and systematic, in using
the experimental method wherever possible, in gathering its
facts from a greater variety of sources, and in constructing a
more adequate systematic framework for organizing its data.
It is evident that, for functionalism, the approaches to psychological knowledge are numerous; that it is not associated
with a particular method as structuralism is with introspection. In actual practice, however, there has been a decided
leaning toward objectivity. Many pieces of research conducted at Chicago are carried on without recourse to introspection, and where introspection is used, it is checked by
objective controls. This procedure is, of course, determined
by the kinds of problems attacked; to study a process in its
setting and from the standpoint of its utility, it is necessary
to examine it from the outside. Practically, therefore, though
introspection has not been discarded, a marked shift in
emphasis has been made toward observation from the outside.

In the chapter entitled "Some Principles of Organic Behavior," Carr drives to the very center of his conception
of psychology. Here he considers first the reflex arc, but not
even in introducing the topic—and his book is intended as
a text for beginners—does he resort to the schematic simplicity that is sometimes used as an expository device. The
reflex-arc concept as he uses it implies three principles. The
first is that "all sensory stimuli must exert some effect on
the activity of the organism." The response need not be
obvious, nor appear necessarily as an overt movement; but
some response, perhaps a change in breathing or pulse rate,
or a shift in muscular tensions, always occurs. The second

principle is that "all activity, ideational as well as motor, is initiated by sensory stimuli." This point is introduced as an assumption. Just as there is no stimulus without its response, so there is no response without its stimulus. The stimulus, it is noted, is not necessarily in the external environment; it may be intraorganic, like the stimuli involved in hunger, thirst, and the sensations of muscular movement. The third principle is that there is "a continuous process of interaction between sensory stimuli and motor responses." Every movement, itself a response to a sensory situation, in turn modifies the subsequent activity. To take a simple illustration, a person may catch a glimpse of an object out of the tail of his eye and respond by focusing on the object directly. But this very action has altered the field of vision so that now the eyes are subject to a different set of stimuli; and since the stimulation is now different the response will be different, and so on indefinitely. Emphasizing, as he does, the continuous interplay between stimulus and response, and the complexity and subtlety of both stimulus and response, Carr is in little danger of making reflex action appear in a deceptively simple light.

These facts, however, do not explain *adaptive* behavior. They merely account for activity [6] in the sense that an organism endowed with reflex equipment will act in some way if it is placed in an environment capable of stimulating it. But such activity is not necessarily adaptive. A person who is trying to escape from a burning building may sneeze, but the sneeze is not an adaptive response. An adaptive act has three characteristics: "a motivating stimulus, a sensory

---

[6] Carr believes that it is not part of the psychologist's task to account for activity in the sense of explaining why activity occurs at all. The psychologist starts with an organism born into the world alive and acting. It is his business to account for the form and direction the activity takes, not for the fact that it occurs. Carr, *Psychology*, 72-73.

situation, and a response that alters that situation in a way that satisfies the motivating conditions." If a hungry man procures food and eats until his hunger is appeased, he is reacting in an adaptive manner. Here hunger is the motivating stimulus; food, a part of the sensory situation, is the stimulating object; and eating is the adaptive response.

A motive, it will be observed, is a stimulus. Carr defines motive as "a relatively persistent stimulus that dominates the behavior of an individual until he reacts in such a manner that he is no longer affected by it." Motives, Carr insists, are not essential to activity: they do not determine that activity shall occur; they simply determine the direction it shall take. In the illustration, hunger is the motive in the sense that it arouses activity of a particular kind. If the person were not hungry, he might respond to food in some other way—not by eating it.

The stimulating object, in this case the food, must also be considered, for the adaptive act is determined not only by the motive but also by the object toward which it is directed. This object is referred to as the incentive or objective or goal. An adaptive act is one that directly affects the stimulating object in some way.

The adaptive act, once aroused, is continued until its motivating conditions are satisfied and the stimulus is no longer effective. In the illustration, the act of eating appeases hunger, thus altering the motivating conditions and making the food ineffective as a stimulating object. But there are other ways in which an adaptive act may be brought to a close. The very continuance of an act may alter the motivating conditions; a child may stop playing because he becomes exhausted. Or the act may result in sensory consequences that disrupt it; a person who grasps a hot poker may drop it because of the pain in his hands. Always when the act ceases, it ceases because the situation has been changed in

such a way that the motivating conditions and the stimulating object are no longer effective.

But not for a moment must it be supposed that the
motivating stimulus and the stimulating object are the only
factors which determine the adaptive act. The total sensory
situation is involved. It makes a difference whether a bear is
seen in a cage or in the open. As a rule, a person makes an
adaptive response to only one aspect of the environment at
a time, chiefly because in most cases the entire musculature
of the body is involved, even in relatively simple reactions.
But though the response is made to one feature specifically,
it is not uninfluenced by the other features. Some elements
in the situation may act as distractions, impairing the efficiency of the act or even disrupting it. Others may inhibit
or profoundly alter the usual response to the stimulating
object. The very progress of the act repeatedly alters the
situation, and successively altered situations call for changed
reactions. The adaptive act is by no means simple; it involves a continuous interplay between complex stimulation
and complex response.

Furthermore, an adaptive act in higher organisms usually
involves two stages: a preliminary stage of attentive adjustment and a final stage of consummatory reaction to the
object. The preliminary stage includes such activities as the
initiation and maintenance of appropriate motor sets and
adjustments of sense-organs—activities that tend to shut out
distraction and to prepare the organism for the most efficient responses, motor and sensory.

Finally, in considering the adaptive act a distinction must
be made between two sets of consequences. One set has already been mentioned, the satisfaction of the motivating conditions. The other is the production of certain ulterior results. Eating not only satisfies hunger, it also nourishes the
body; and the two sets of consequences must not be con-

fused. The ulterior consequences of an act are not its motive. Neither are they its objective. Carr is very explicit in stating that an act cannot be explained in terms of its ulterior consequences. To say that we eat to nourish our bodies is not a scientific explanation. Eating, or any other adaptive act, must be explained not in terms of its consequences, but in terms of its proximate conditions, the motivating factors and the sensory situation. This point is important because it precludes the supposition, sometimes made, that because functionalism is interested in utilities, it explains mental acts teleologically.

In this account of the adaptive act, Carr pictures schematically his view of psychological material in general. The chief significance of his treatment lies in the fact that his idea is in every sense a *working* concept. In the course of the chapter, he reduces the functionalist's material—adjustive activity—to a detailed analysis which amounts practically to a plan of investigation, and which, in a sense, marks the progress of functionalism from revolt to industry. Furthermore, his conception of the adaptive act indicates the general point of view from which the factual material of psychology is presented in the rest of the book. Psychological processes are functions of living organisms engaged in the business of adaptation to the environment. These processes are determined by stimulation both from within and from without the organism. Organisms are active simply because they are born into the world alive and sensitive to stimulation, but their activity becomes adaptive only when a motivating stimulus determines the direction of an act that operates with reference to a stimulating object and produces effects which satisfy the motivating conditions. There are, between the organism and its environment, no breaks, no impassable gulfs; instead, there is a continuous and complex give and take. Psychology deals with events which are not reducible to static terms, and which, by serving and maintaining the organism, fit into the total scheme of biological activity.

Functionalism, of course, encountered many objections. Some of these, growing directly out of its clash with structuralism, quickly became disputes concerning the definition of psychology. A study of functions, utilities, values—none of which can be observed introspectively—is not, according to the structuralists, psychology at all. Obviously, if functions are by definition excluded from psychology, the study of functions is not psychology. But the matter can hardly be settled so simply. The very fact that the functionalists were quite aware of what they were doing, that they were open-eyed in their departures from the established conventions, meant that it was the definition itself that they were questioning. To assert that functionalism was at fault because it did not conform to the pattern it intentionally discarded was to leave the main point untouched, and in so far as structuralism carried out its campaign on that line, it was largely defending and explaining its own creed. The result was a direct confrontation of the two conceptions of psychology and a steadily increasing clarification of the points at issue.

On a somewhat different plane is the criticism that functionalism did not define its terms, that in particular it left vague its basic concept "function." Taking up the problem suggested by this situation, Ruckmick,[7] a pupil of Titchener, made a careful examination of English and American texts to discover how the term "function" is used in actual practice. He found two general classes into which the various uses of the word may be sorted. In the first, "function" is

    [7] C. A. Ruckmick, "The Use of the Term *Function* in English Text-Books of Psychology," *American Journal of Psychology* (1913), 2Q, 99-123.

used as synonymous with activity; perceiving and remembering are in this sense functions. In the second class, the term is used to denote the utility of an activity to the organism; thus it may be said that the function of ideation is to serve as an economical substitute for motor trial and error. This dual usage of the term has been cited by some critics as a sign of confusion and inconsistency; they have pointed out that it is apparently possible to speak of a "function of a function." But Carr, in a recent paper,[8] argues from the same facts in quite another vein. To him, the fact that all the uses of the term fall into these two classes seems to indicate considerable agreement. Claiming, further, that the two uses are not inconsistent, he notes that the same uses of the term are found in biology, where the word "function" sometimes denotes an activity such as breathing or digestion, and sometimes denotes the utility of an activity, as in the statement that the oxidation of the blood is the function of breathing. Furthermore, Carr finds that the two uses of the term can be reduced to one by employing the mathematical concept of function, which denotes a relation of contingency without further specifying that relation. To say that the oxidation of the blood is the function of breathing is to refer to one kind of relation, that of utility; to say that breathing is the function of the lungs is to refer to another kind of relation, that of a mode of operation to the structure which operates. Similarly psychology may speak of the function of reasoning to refer to the utility of reasoning in the whole organic scheme. Or it may refer to reasoning as a function in order to designate it as the operation of some structure; and when, as in the case of reasoning, the structures involved are not definitely known, it may use the term "function" to imply some relation to physiological con-

[8] Harvey Carr. "Functionalism," *Psychologies of 1930,* ed. by Carl Murchison, 59-78.

ditions. But Carr's analysis, it is important to notice, came after the fact. Functionalism used the concept first and defined it later; and this sequence of events is characteristic of the movement. For functionalism is primarily a trend in a general direction; it is not a definitely outlined and closely articulated system. Whether for good or for ill, functionalism has never been disposed to place definition and systematization in the foreground.

Functionalism has also encountered the criticism, sometimes merely a vague imputation, that it somehow falls short of the strictly scientific. This attitude, apparently, goes back to the old opposition between the act and the content psychologies in Germany—to the contrast between empirical and experimental methods, between extra-laboratory observation and controlled laboratory procedures, and to the belief on the part of content psychology that act psychology must of necessity be less rigorously scientific than itself. In America, however, this attitude is inapplicable. For American functionalists, as much as any other group, have been interested in experimentation. They do not, to be sure, use the standard procedures of the Titchenerian school, but they do investigate their problems under experimental conditions. In their studies of animals, for example, the investigator does not rely on mere general observation; he insists on a careful arrangement and control of conditions that will bring out the facts relevant to a definite problem. If the word "experiment" is given the meaning it has in science generally, and not the interpretation of a particular school of psychology, functionalism has no need to apologize for either the number or the quality of the experimental studies it has to its credit.

Added to these criticisms is the faint suspicion that functionalism, since it deals with utilities, is somehow tinged with teleology; and science has long looked askance at teleology when introduced into its explanations. To explain the eyes by saying that they are for seeing, the ears, for hearing, has proved less satisfactory than to discover the immediate conditions that account for the structure and operation of those organs. Whether or not teleological explanations are ever permissible in science is still a topic of lively discussion; but the question is irrelevant in the present connection because functionalism does not, as a matter of fact, use teleological explanations. It does, of course, employ teleological concepts in describing its data; it does so whenever it notes the utility of a process. But there is a difference between utility as an observed fact in experience and utility as an explanatory concept. It is entirely possible to note, for example, that an activity like eating is useful in maintaining the body, and at the same time to explain the mechanism of the activity without reference to that fact. Carr, it will be recalled, does precisely this.[9] He explains eating in terms of its immediate conditions—the internal stimuli of hunger and the environmental situation that includes food; and he carefully guards against confusing the ulterior consequences of eating with its motivating stimuli.

Of course functionalism has been accused, from the standpoint of pure science, of being mere technology, and therefore on a lower plane than the disinterested search for truth. Functionalism, it is true, has never attempted to keep clear of utility; it has shown little concern about keeping itself "pure," and it has never apologized for the fact that its knowledge may be turned to some use. In psychology, as in other sciences, the pros and cons of pure science as distinguished from applied science have always had their adherents; and in psychology, as elsewhere, the question is usu-

[9] This does not mean that Carr regards explanation and description as fundamentally different. He subscribes to the view that explanation is itself description of an unusually thorough sort.

ally decided on the basis of temperamental preference. In this connection, however, Carr makes an interesting comment on the attitude of pure science. If pure science is really "disinterested," he says, it can have no concern whatever whether or not its discoveries are useful; it can feel neither sorrow that its discoveries are useful, nor pride that they are useless in the highest degree. A preference for results that are strictly non-utilitarian is itself a violation of the spirit of pure science, which knows no preferences. After all, Carr points out, it is adherence to scientific method that makes a study scientific—not the subject-matter it deals with nor the setting in which it is carried out. Certain researches conducted in industrial laboratories admirably illustrate the spirit of science, some of them even of pure science; and theoretically it is quite possible to get useless knowledge of the uses of organic functions. If functionalism has tended to be interested in utilities, this interest has occasioned no violation of scientific principles. Whether they are found in pure or applied science, the essentials of scientific procedure are the same.

But functionalism, on the whole, has shown less interest in making effective rejoinders to its opponents' criticisms than in getting its own program under way; and it is by giving its principles this positive expression that it has exerted its greatest influence on American psychology. Titchener, it will be remembered, defined the subject-matter of psychology as "the world with man left in"; and it is largely because of the success of functionalism that American psychology now deals with "man left in the world." To study functions is to study activities that are connected with the world at both ends, activities which typically are initiated by external stimuli and which terminate in operations on the external world. Thus the outstanding contribution of functionalism is its conception of psychological processes not as something remote and detached, but as rooted in the conditions in which they are actually found; effective in the sense that other biological activities are effective, making some difference in the world by their operations, not merely reflecting or keeping step with the procession of events they accompany.

Nevertheless, functionalism does not, at present, stand out in American psychology as a distinct school and system. It did so only in its beginnings, when it had the conspicuousness of a new movement—in particular, of a movement opposed to structuralism. Several circumstances account for the fact that it has lost its former prominence. For one thing, newer and more aggressive movements have claimed attention. Behaviorism, which made a point of being radical, and *Gestalt* psychology, which enjoyed the prestige of an importation, have crowded it away from the center of the stage. More important, perhaps, is the fact that functionalism is not easily popularized; that it does not lend itself to the modes of thought that common sense has made habitual. Curiously enough, functionalism, starting from a common-sense interest in the utilities of mental processes, found it necessary to modify certain common-sense conceptions. Its interest in activities compelled it to think of processes as processes—not only theoretically but in practice; and ever since the time of Heraclitus, process considered as the basis of experience has seemed to make experience disappear into nothing. Common sense prefers something it can take hold of, something substantial, something it can treat as an element in the sense that a brick is an element in a brick wall. Besides, the attitude of functionalism toward the mind-body question somewhat obscured the mind-body distinction that is at present deeply embedded in human thinking. Though functionalism is dualistic in the sense of recognizing both psychical and physical aspects of experience, it is not dualistic in the sense of separating them in the manner that common sense has inherited from the past. It defines its material neither as psychical nor as physical, but as psychophysical, and to many persons this definition seems obscure. It is easy, because it is habitual, so think in terms of mind and matter, or of mind or matter, and functionalism by abandoning this mode of thought severs a bond of understanding with common sense. But whatever the difficulties of conceiving its materials theoretically, functionalism has proved by achievement that its approach may lead to profitable results; and this fact, curiously enough, is the chief reason why it does not stand out as a separate school. Its methods and point of view have been so generally accepted that they now exist simply as a part of the common property of psychology; they are no longer the special possessions of a particular school.

For in functionalism, American psychology passed through a phase of its development in which it brought together and organized many tendencies already in existence, utilizing them so successfully that they passed into general practice. To treat of mental activities as well as contents, to think in terms of adaptations and adjustments, to observe psychological processes in relation to their setting, to regard man as a biological organism adapting itself to its environment—all these procedures have been so widely accepted in psychology that they no longer attract special attention.

Still, there is a tendency in some quarters to think of functionalism as something that has passed, and in a sense this point of view is justifiable. As a school and as a system, functionalism, though it has retained something of its old *esprit de corps,* has lost its novelty and much of its distinctness. But if the functionalists were trying not to establish a school, but to make legitimate certain modes of thought and research and thus to widen the range of psychological investigation, they have accomplished precisely what they set out to do. They have seen their problems and methods enter so completely into psychology as no longer to be distinguishable as the property of a single school. From the standpoint of the basic principles of the system itself, there could be no happier ending.

Chapter VII

BEHAVIORISM

IN 1903, the University of Chicago conferred its first doctoral degree in psychology [1] upon John Broadus Watson,
who ten years later became the founder of behaviorism.[2]

In the eyes of behaviorism, functionalism is a timid, half-
hearted, half-way measure, confusing and ineffectual. It
made terms with an enemy who should have been slain. For
behaviorism is opposed to all psychology that deals with
consciousness. It sees the whole concept of consciousness as
useless and vicious, as nothing but the survival of medieval
superstition about the soul, and as utterly unworthy of
scientific consideration. Its proposal is as simple as it is
severe. Psychology must break with the past, discard the
concept of consciousness altogether, begin at the beginning,
and construct a new science.

It would be difficult to exaggerate the singleness of vision
with which the orthodox Watsonian sees the present situation
in psychology. On the one side is behaviorism, on the other
"traditional psychology." Non-behavioristic psychologies
may differ among themselves, but beside the one staring fact
that they are all mentalistic, their differences are negligible.
They are tarred with the same brush, they are all dualistic,

[1] The first psychologist to receive a doctor's degree in the University
of Chicago was Helen Thompson Wooley, who took her degree in the
department of philosophy.

[2] The behaviorism described in this chapter is Watsonian behaviorism.
There are of course many variants of behaviorism, but the discussion
in this chapter refers to the one promulgated by Watson.

they deal with mind and matter, and hence they cannot possibly be scientific. For mind, to Watson, plainly means something extranatural; and the dualist, to him, is one who tries to mix the natural and the non-natural, and who therefore commits the unpardonable sin against science of not carrying through his account in wholly naturalistic terms. If psychology is ever to become a science, it must follow the example of the physical sciences; it must become materialistic, mechanistic, deterministic, objective. To obtrude the mental is to make an opening for the mystical and the magical. Because behaviorism seeks to make psychology a science in the strictest sense of the term, it insists that the notion of mind be unequivocally discarded.

It is important to realize the vehemence and thoroughness with which the concept of consciousness is rejected.[3] Mental processes, consciousness, souls, and ghosts are all of a piece, and are altogether unfit for scientific use. The existence of consciousness is a "plain assumption." It cannot be proved by any scientific test, for consciousness cannot be seen, nor touched, nor exhibited in a test-tube. Even if it exists it cannot be studied scientifically, because admittedly it is subject only to private inspection. Finally, a belief in the mental is allied to modes of thinking that are wholly incompatible with the ways of science. It is related to the religious, the mystical, and the metaphysical interpretations of the world. The notion of consciousness is the result of old wives' tales and monks' lore, of the teachings of medicinemen and priests. Consciousness is only another name for the soul of theology, and the attempts of the older psychology to make it seem anything else are utterly futile. To admit the mental into science is to open the door to the enemies of science—to subjectivism, supernaturalism, and tender-

[3] See especially Chap. I of Watson's *Behaviorism*, either the 1925 or the 1930 edition.

mindedness generally. With the simplicity and finality of the
Last Judgment, behaviorism divides the sheep from the
goats. On the right hand side are behaviorism and science
and all its works; on the left are souls and superstition and
a mistaken tradition; and the line of demarcation is clear
and unmistakable.

Perhaps all this seems somewhat emotional, but it would
be a mistake to suppose that behaviorism made its way on
mere emotionalism. From the first it had definite achievements to support its claims and a practical program of action
to offer. For behaviorism, though iconoclastic, is not merely
iconoclastic. Fundamentally, it stands for the positive and
constructive measure of extending the methods and point
of view of animal psychology into human psychology; and
in 1913, when behaviorism was officially inaugurated, animal
psychology had attained a position that commanded respect.

The origins of animal psychology, however, are hardly
above reproach, for the most important of them lie in the
special pleadings of the early Darwinians, who, in their eagerness to show that there is no break between the human and
the animal species, uncritically attributed complex mental
processes to animals. At that time, animal psychology relied
mainly on the anecdotal method, but it gradually outgrew
this questionable practice. Under the influence of Lloyd-
Morgan, it was subjected to the discipline of the law of
parsimony, and investigators soon learned to be wary of at-
tributing ideas to animals so long as it was possible to explain
their behavior in simpler terms. Besides, Lloyd-Morgan, dis-
satisfied with the anecdotal method, developed a form of
observation approximating the experimental. Requiring animals to perform tricks or tasks in especially arranged situations, he carefully noted what they could do, and also what
they could not do, under specified conditions. The next important advance in method was made by Thorndike, who

took animal problems into the laboratory and devised situations like mazes and puzzle-boxes, which made it possible to
observe, record, and even measure the animal's performance
in some detail. Later the work of Pavlov and Bechterev
began to attract the attention of psychologists, and eventually—in America, however, mainly after the rise of behaviorism—students of animal behavior enthusiastically added the
conditioned-reflex method to the other devices that they had
taken over from the physiological laboratories. In the United
States, interest in animal psychology was especially keen and
the work of Margaret Floy Washburn and Robert M. Yerkes
did much to sustain it. Methods of studying animal activity
steadily gained in precision and in the adequacy of experimental control, and by 1913 animal psychology was well
under way.

The outstanding advantage of using animals in psychological research is the possibility of more complete control
of the conditions of experimentation. It is more nearly possible in animals than in man to regulate diet, hours of rest
and activity, and living-conditions generally. Then too, because animals are presumably less complex in organization,
the number of complicating factors in the experiment is
automatically reduced, and a problem can be made more
nearly to approximate the simplicity that favors clarity
and exactness of treatment. It is even possible to study the
whole life-span of the animal and, in short-lived species, to
study the same process in generation after generation. Besides, it is possible in animals to resort to procedures that
cannot be practised on human beings: for example, to im-
pair sense-organs or parts of the brain in order to determine
their rôle in specified performances, or to submit the organism to other possibly harmful influences in order to discover their effects on subsequent behavior. Animal psychologists, as a rule, are proud of the resemblance of their

methods to those of the physical sciences; and some of them are more than a little scornful of their brother psychologists who are content to deal with "intangibles" and "imponderables."

Much of the distinctive character of behaviorism is due to its close connection with animal psychology. Animal psychology is perforce objective in the sense that the observer, like the astronomer, the physicist, or the botanist, necessarily stands outside the material he studies. True, so long as psychology was defined as the science of consciousness, animal consciousness was customarily inferred from motor behavior; but even then the facts about behavior—about learning, about native reactions, about responsiveness to various kinds of stimulations, and the like—were the points that most of the investigators found really interesting; the speculations about animal consciousness were likely to be perfunctory. And fundamentally it is the attempt to study human animals as other animals are studied that constitutes the true originality of behaviorism. The materialism which it sometimes flaunts as radical is after all a very ancient philosophy. There is nothing new in saying that man is dust, or even that man is an animal; but when the behaviorist says it, he is saved from mere empty repetition of an age-old saw by the fact that he is advocating a very specific and practical way of perceiving and studying human nature. His statement means that man must be regarded as an animal species, simply as one among the many species of the animal order, in no fundamental sense constituting a special case. It implies further a willingness to study human reactions exactly as other events in the natural world are studied —as a mechanic inquires into the operations of a machine, or a physiologist into the functions of a dog's adrenal glands. It means, too, that the student must see man as a complete reacting organism, and that he must study him in relation to the natural world. And as seen against the background of "traditional" psychology, this means that the psychologist must put aside the dissection of states of consciousness and study the human being as a whole living organism reacting to his whole natural environment, both physical and social.

That American psychology was ready for such a program had been made abundantly plain by the hospitality it had shown functionalism. For the same conditions that ensured for functionalism an interested hearing paved the way for behaviorism's more spectacular victory. Practically, behaviorism did what functionalism did, and did it more dramatically. It cut the Gordian knot, which functionalism had merely loosened to give psychology a wider tether. Watson himself, to be sure, objects to all attempts to link behaviorism with functionalism; but however much the two movements may differ in temper and in basic conceptions, they are alike in demanding a wider range for psychological research. The simple fact is that American psychologists had grown restive under conventional restraints. They were finding the old problems lifeless and thin, they were "half sick of shadows," and turning gladly toward something that seemed more alive and substantial, they welcomed a plain, downright revolt. For behaviorism was far more satisfactory than functionalism as a release from repression. It called upon its followers to fight an enemy who must be utterly destroyed, not merely to parley with one who might be induced to modify his ways.

Watson was a graduate student in the University of Chicago in the days when functionalism was in the heyday of its powers. His chief interest even then was in animal psychology.[4] He himself started the animal laboratory, and

[4] Watson's doctoral dissertation is entitled, "Kinæsthetic and Organic Sensations: their Rôle in the Reactions of the White Rat to the Maze," *Psychological Review* (1907), 8, Monograph Supplement No. 2, 1-100.

after receiving his degree he remained a year at Chicago as
a member of the staff to take charge of the work in animal
psychology. In 1904 he went to Johns Hopkins University as
professor of psychology.

It was while he was at Chicago, however, and in connection with his work in animal psychology, that he developed
the basic conceptions of behaviorism. As has already been
said, Watson himself objects to any attempt to look for the
origins of behaviorism in functionalism. To him, the difference in their attitudes toward the recognition of consciousness separates, profoundly and essentially, the two points
of view. Yet it was distinctly characteristic of functionalism
to look at man as an animal reacting to his environment,
and this attitude is one that behaviorism takes for granted.
It was this attitude, too, that made functionalism so hospitable to animal psychology, the soil in which behaviorism
grew.

In his studies of animals, Watson became more and more
firmly convinced that animal psychology is a science in its
own right, entirely capable of standing on its own feet and
under no obligation whatever to translate its findings into
mentalistic terms. He became convinced, further, that the
methods of animal psychology might profitably be applied to
human psychology; that human psychology indeed would be
vastly improved if, discarding all reference to consciousness, it studied its subjects as animals are studied. He first
formulated his views in conversations with his colleagues.
Angell, then head of the department at Chicago, though
thoroughly in sympathy with some of Watson's views, ad-
vised him not to take a stand for a human psychology without consciousness. Watson, however, maintained his position, and in 1912 announced his views in a series of lectures
at Columbia University. The first published statement of
his position appeared in 1913 in an article entitled "Psy-

chology as the Behaviorist Views It." [5] A paper, "The Image and Affection in Behavior," [6] soon followed—an important addition because image and affection, conceived as remote alike from external stimulus and overt response, were considered the strongholds of introspectionism. Watson, by reducing images to implicit language responses, and affection to slight reactions set up by tumescence and detumescence of the genitals, maintained that both might be studied as bodily movements, and that there was therefore no portion of the subject-matter of psychology to which the methods of behaviorism were not adequate.

Inevitably Titchener pronounced on this position. In one of his decisive polemics,[7] he took the stand that findings not formulated in terms of consciousness are simply not psychology. They may be interesting, they may be important, they may be valuable to psychology; but they are not, in themselves, psychology. Watson replied that the only psychology worthy of the name of science is to be derived from such findings; that a psychology of consciousness is mere pseudoscience. And so again, as in the case of functionalism more than a decade before, Titchener gave distinctness and dramatic significance to the movement he opposed, by taking a decisive stand against it.

The course of behaviorism, as it developed in Watson's thought, may be traced most objectively through his three general treatises. The first of these, *Behavior, an Introduction to Comparative Psychology,* appeared in 1914. In this book, by his marshaling of the experimental work in the field, he demonstrates with impressive success that animal or comparative psychology has an independent place among the sciences.

[5] *Psychological Review* (1913), 20, 158-177.

[6] *Journal of Philosophy, Psychology and Scientific Method* (1913), 10, 421-428.

[7] E. B. Titchener, "On 'Psychology as the Behaviorist Views It,'" *Proceedings of the American Philosophical Society* (1914), 53. 1-17

His next book, published in 1919, was *Psychology from the Standpoint of a Behaviorist*. Here very definitely the principles of animal psychology are extended into human psychology. The main thesis of the book is that the human creature and all his activities can be explained by one who regards him as a stimulus-response machine. Terms that imply consciousness are scrupulously avoided. The book is notable, too, for its inclusion of accounts of the research that Watson had just conducted on the native reactions of human infants and on their first acquisitions through experience. The prominence given to this material marks the recognition by behaviorism of the importance of infancy in human development and of the genetic method of studying human reactions.

Watson's third book, *Behaviorism*, appeared in 1925.[8] Though it is a more popular presentation of his point of view, in purpose it is no less serious than its predecessors. "Every effort," the author writes in the preface, "has been made to present facts in unmutilated form and to state theoretical positions with accuracy." The book differs from the earlier presentation in two main respects. The first is that the approving attitude toward applied psychology is noticeably more marked than before. Even in 1919, by stating his problem as the "prediction and control" of behavior, Watson unequivocally took a stand for a psychology that works in practice; but in the book published in 1925, he shows a still greater interest in the practical applications of psychological knowledge. Not content with merely understanding the human machine, he offers suggestions for altering and improving it.[9] The second new position taken in this

[8] A revised edition was brought out in 1930.

[9] In 1920, Watson became professionally identified with applied psychology. He left Johns Hopkins University and took up work in the psychology of advertising.

book is the stand on heredity. Flatly denying the existence of instincts, native intelligence, and native "gifts" of all sorts, Watson asserts that what are ordinarily called instincts, special gifts, and native abilities are really the results of environment and training. This attitude of course enormously emphasizes the importance of infancy and early childhood as the most important formative period in human life.

The outlines of behaviorism are diagrammatically clear. The subject-matter of psychology is behavior—not conscious contents, not mental functions, not psychophysical processes of any sort, but movements in time and space. Behavior is the activity of the organism as a whole, just as digestion, respiration, and secretion are activities of its particular organs. As physiology studies the functions of stomachs, lungs, and livers, psychology studies the activities of whole living bodies. The lungs breathe, the whole body behaves. Both breathing and behavior are activities of physical structures and as such can be studied by the objective methods that characterize all science.

Only objective methods are accepted as valid. Introspection is completely rejected; its elaborate pretense of careful observation is futile and hopeless from the start. Even if there are states of consciousness for the introspectionist to observe—and their existence can never be scientifically proved—it is forever impossible for two observers to see the same thing. No one can see the thoughts and feelings of another person, and nothing that is open only to private inspection can possibly give rise to objective knowledge.

Psychology has several objective methods at its disposal. Observation is, of course, fundamental to all procedures, and scientific observations may be made either with or without instruments. The former may be illustrated by the photographic studies of eye movements in reading, the latter by Fabre's classic work on insects. Psychological tests are also recognized, but with no enthusiasm, and with the definite understanding that they are not "mental" tests—that they do not test "intelligence" or "special abilities" as aspects of "mind." When a behaviorist uses tests, he regards them simply as measures of behavior—of the subject's responses, verbal or otherwise, to the objective situations that the tests present. Behaviorism even salvages some of the methods of the older psychology. The measurement of reaction-time, for example, is accepted as entirely objective. So are the memory experiments, for Ebbinghaus and his followers studied the formation, retention, and decay of associations in terms of objective performances and situations. The admission of the memory experiments is of course accompanied by the inevitable warning that there is nothing "mental" about "memory"; that memory simply means the reinstatement of reactions after a period during which they have not been practised. Behaviorism acknowledges, too, the methods of applied psychology, both educational and industrial, since such problems as determining the returns on advertising, and measuring the efficiency of learning or of industrial operations in given conditions, can be investigated by correlating definite objective performances with specified objective situations. Even "verbal report" is recognized as a source of information, but at the hands of the behaviorist, the subject's comment on his own condition or performance receives exactly the same treatment as do any other overt reactions. Certainly they are not regarded as representing states of consciousness. If a person says, "I feel sad," his statement is noted, along with his drooping posture, as possibly symptomatic of the condition of his total reaction system. It is never accepted as a report on a "mental" condition.

One objective method, however, is so important in the behavioristic conception that it must be singled out for special attention. This is the conditioned-reflex technique developed by Pavlov and his pupils. The mention of the conditioned reflex is the announcement of a theme that rapidly becomes dominant in behavioristic psychology. For the process of "conditioning" not only reveals a new means of investigating behavior; it is also largely responsible for the character of behavior itself.

A response is "conditioned" when it becomes attached to a stimulus that did not originally arouse it. An experiment from Pavlov's laboratory has become the stock example. In dogs, the salivary response is originally aroused by the presence of food on the tongue; that is, food is the "adequate stimulus" to the response of salivation. In the experiment, a bell is rung every time food is presented, and after a number of repetitions, the bell alone, without the food, arouses the response. In other words, a stimulus that originally did not elicit the response does so after having been repeatedly a part of the situation to which the response was made. This experiment, though it involves a very simple case of the conditioned reflex, illustrates the principle in all conditioning. Sometimes, as in the example given, the response remains the same and a new stimulus is substituted. At other times, the stimulus remains the same and a new response is substituted, as when a child, instead of pointing to an object, learns to call it by name. But in each case a modification of behavior has occurred; in each case the original stimulus-response connection has been altered.

From the standpoint of method, the process of conditioning is important because it provides an objective way of analyzing behavior. On the assumption that behavior is composed of simple units like reflexes, and that all larger behavior units are integrations of stimulus-response connections, it is theoretically possible through the technique of conditioning to study the very process by which behavior is built up and torn down. It should be possible, too, by means of conditioning, to attack some of the problems that at first sight seem inaccessible to any method but introspection. Sensation has always seemed a stronghold of the introspectionist, but the possibility of conditioning suggests a way of investigating even so "subjective" a problem as discovering how far out into the red and violet ends of the spectrum the human eye can see. Watson suggests the following procedure:

"We start with any intermediate wave length and by the use of the electric shock establish a conditioned reflex. Each time the light appears the reflex occurs. We then increase the length of the wave rather sharply and if the reflex appears we again increase the wave length. We finally reach a point where the reflex breaks down, even when punishment is used to restore it—approximately at $760 \, \mu\mu$. This wave length represents the human being's spectral range at the red end. We then follow the same procedure with respect to the violet end ($397 \, \mu\mu$). In this way we determine the individual's range just as surely as if we had stimulated the subject with monochromatic lights varying in wave lengths and asked him if he saw them." [10]

The great advantage of the method is its complete objectivity—an important consideration in the early days when behaviorism was eager to show that there was no province in psychology, not sensation itself, that it found inaccessible. In actual practice, however, the conditioned reflex has not proved a sufficiently stable unit of behavior to fulfil its promise as an instrument of research. But the suggestion that it be used is itself significant as an illustration of the uncompromising stand that behaviorism takes in favor of objective methods of research.

The general problem of psychology, as the behaviorist sees

[10] J. B. Watson, *Psychology from the Standpoint of a Behaviorist*, 35-36.

it, is to predict and control behavior. More specifically, the task of psychology is to determine the stimuli that occasion any given response, and the responses occasioned by any given stimulus. Ideally the psychologist should understand the human animal as an engineer understands a machine; he should know what the body is made of, how it is put together, and how it works. And since behavior is the activity of the organism as a whole, the psychologist is interested chiefly in three sets of apparatus: the receptors or sense-organs, through which the organism receives all the stimulation that sets it going; the effectors, or muscles and glands, which are the organs of response; and the nervous system, through which all connections are made between receptors and effectors.

The proper starting-point for the psychological study of the human organism is birth. It is necessary first to find out what reactions are possible to the human infant through its native constitution, and then to discover how, bit by bit, other reactions are added; or more properly, how original reactions are "conditioned," and how, through conditioning, more and more complex forms of behavior are "built in." Behaviorism finds that the original reaction-equipment of the human animal is extremely limited as compared with his later activities. The human infant has at its disposal a number of reflexes; it can make bodily movements of a random (though not uncaused) sort; and it has the use of its various bodily tissues and organs, for example, glandular secretion and muscular contractility. In other words, it has inherited only its bodily structures and their modes of functioning. It has inherited no "mental traits." It has inherited neither general intelligence nor special abilities, neither gifts nor talents. It has not even inherited any "instincts." Watson emphatically denies that any human being is equipped with instincts, with native intelligence, with innate gifts or talents, with a specialized tendency to proficiency of any sort. It is in this connection that he makes his much quoted statement:

"Give me a dozen healthy infants, well-formed, and my own specified world to bring them up in and I'll guarantee to take any one at random and train him to become any type of specialist I might select—doctor, lawyer, artist, merchant-chief and, yes, even beggar-man and thief, regardless of his talents, penchants, tendencies, abilities, vocations, and race of his ancestors." [11]

Very early, in fact in infancy, conditioning sets in. Conditioning is the simplest form of learning; it is, indeed, the elementary process to which all learning is reducible. Out of the few simple responses that the infant has in its repertoire, largely through learning or conditioning, but partly through growth or maturation, all the complicated activities that the adult displays are built up. The so-called instincts are products of this sort. Pugnacity, self-assertion, curiosity, and the like—all the activities we commonly call instincts—are exceedingly complex integrations of reactions which, through conditioning, have been knit together and attached to certain stimuli. The process, often very elaborate, is one in which the social environment plays a large part, and in which the period of infancy is of crucial importance. But through and through, the process is one of learning. The "instincts" are not inherited.

Emotions, too, are largely learned reactions. Three kinds of emotional responses, and only three—fear, rage, and love—can be aroused in the infant previously to learning, simply by the application of the appropriate stimuli. It is understood, of course, that the terms "fear," "rage," and "love" refer to nothing "mental." Emotions are not matters of feeling or affective quality; they are bodily reactions. They are distinguished from other bodily reactions by the fact that

[11] J. B. Watson, *Behaviorism*, 82.

they are predominantly visceral, involving chiefly the glands and smooth or "involuntary" muscles like those found in the walls of intestines and blood-vessels. Emotional responses, too, are subject to the same kind of conditioning that occurs in striped or "voluntary" muscle like that in the arms and legs and hands. Exactly as he acquires his motor skills—typewriting, skating, playing the violin—a person acquires his complex emotional responses, his loyalties and aversions, his vague dreads and unreasoned sympathies. His viscera learn as his hands, arms, and legs do, and possibly more rapidly. Complex emotions are built up on the basis of the few unlearned reactions. Natively, fear may be aroused in an infant by loud noises, but the fear so aroused may be attached to an originally "inadequate" stimulus like a rabbit, if the child hears a loud noise every time he sees a rabbit. Through transfer and spread, the fear may become attached to other furry or hairy objects, to the room in which the rabbit was seen, to the person who held the rabbit. The original fear-responses themselves—starting, crying, withdrawing—may become greatly modified by the substitution of other reactions through conditioning. But however wide the ramifications, however intricate the connections, the complex emotional pattern is a product of learning or conditioning.

So too are the complicated systems of habits and motor skills that Watson refers to as "manual habits." Manual habits are distinguished on the one hand from the "visceral" or emotional activities, and on the other from the "laryngeal" habits that are commonly called thinking. Manual habits include such specific skills as writing, typewriting, painting, and driving an automobile, and such generalized modes of behavior as make a man punctual, orderly, and persevering. Manual habits are built up on original "random" movements of the trunk, arms, legs, hands, and fingers. While admitting that much of the process of motor learning remains as yet unknown, Watson firmly believes that the whole process is reducible to th econditioned-response mechanism. For example, in an activity like playing scales on the piano, each separate response is at first made to a visual stimulus, either to the piano-key or to the note in the printed score. But as the activity is practised again and again, the movement of one finger becomes the stimulus to the movement of the next, and eventually the whole scale can be run off without the visual stimulus of notes or keys. Each movement has been conditioned to the preceding movement and the visual cue is no longer necessary. The result is that reactions at first distinct from each other have been knit together to form a unitary pattern. If both hands are used, the connections become more complex, and if chords are struck with both hands, still more highly organized systems of connections are formed. But the unit is always the conditioned reaction. Furthermore, the mere frequency and recency of the exercise are sufficient to explain the formation of habit. Watson is altogether opposed to the theory that "pleasure" or "satisfaction" tends to fix successful reactions and "annoyance" or "dissatisfaction" to eliminate unsuccessful ones. His criticism of the theory involves several technical points, but his main objection rises from the fact that "pleasure" and "satisfaction" seem to him to imply the intervention of a mental force. Learning, whatever its precise nature, is a thoroughly material and mechanical affair.

"Laryngeal habits" is the behaviorist's phrase for thinking. Laryngeal habits are developed from random, unlearned vocalization, in exactly the same way as manual habits are developed from random movements of the limbs and trunk. Language is at first overt. By a process of conditioning, the child acquires words; and words, because they may be substituted for things and concrete situations, give him the power of manipulating his environment without making the actual overt movements. This is all that is meant by thinking. A man thinks—that is, makes implicit verbal reactions —just as a rat makes overt muscular movements in a maze. The man's words and the rat's scurryings through the maze are both activities by which the animal achieves an adjustment to a situation to which at first he lacks the adequate response. The great advantage of thinking is that it is more economical, partly because it involves a much smaller part of the bodily musculature, and partly because a course of action may be tried out implicitly without the risk, expenditure of time and effort, and possible disaster that actual trial in overt behavior might bring. Again the inevitable warning is sounded; there is nothing mysterious about thinking. Its operations, to be sure, are internal and therefore invisible to the onlooker, but there is nothing inside the body that is essentially different from the external world—certainly nothing "mental" and immaterial. Furthermore, speech only gradually becomes internal or "implicit." At first the child uses the overt movements of spoken language; then, largely because of his social environment, he learns to repress his overt speech and to substitute implicit movements. But the movements go on, subvocally and implicitly, and these movements constitute all that is involved in thought.

Though a distinction has been made between laryngeal and manual behavior, the distinction is not absolute. The function of speech may be carried on by any bodily movement—by a shrug of the shoulders, a frown, a gesture, a nod of assent, a general resistant stiffening of the muscles; by any movement at all, if only it stands for an object or situation as a word or phrase does. It is, in fact, the rule rather than the exception for the whole body to be involved in an activity. Behaviorism raises the question "Is thinking exclusively a matter of language mechanisms?" The answer is "No" if the phrase "language mechanisms" refers to speech alone, with the manual and visceral activities ruled out. But if the phrase is used to contrast thinking with mental activity, if it refers to any bodily movement which fulfils the function of speech, to any movement which, like a word, is substitutable for some object or situation, the answer is emphatically "Yes." Furthermore, manual reactions do not ordinarily go on without implicit verbalization. It is verbalization, in fact, that brings them under control. We can direct our actions when we can supply verbal cues; we "know" what we are doing, and how we do it, when we can talk about it, implicitly or overtly. As a rule, the three streams of activity, the manual, the laryngeal, and the visceral, go on simultaneously. When the laryngeal is absent, the activity is out of control; hence the presence of verbalization is of the utmost practical importance.

There are two classes of reactions, however, from which verbalization is regularly absent—emotional responses and the behavior of infancy and early childhood. Obviously verbalization cannot occur before language has been acquired; and even as adults, since language was developed largely with reference to the external world, human beings lack terms for most of the events inside their own bodies, especially those vague and not easily localized reactions which constitute the emotions. Thus there develops a system of unverbalized reactions, mainly infantile and visceral, which, because they are unverbalized, influence their owner's behavior in a manner that he cannot control. To this system belong vague aversions, dreads, preferences, longings, prejudices, all sorts of attitudes, childish and emotional, that may be intellectually unjustifiable and even unrecognized, but which are no less tenacious and certainly no less potent on that account. In Watson's terminology, the "unverbalized" corresponds to Freud's "unconscious" without the aura of the mystical that clings to the Freudian concept.

All these reactions put together—verbal, visceral, and manual, actual and potential—constitute the personality. There is, of course, nothing mysterious about the personality. Personality is not an "indefinable something," but a system of responses, the sum total of an individual's reactions and tendencies to reaction. Often the term personality is used to refer especially to the social effect of an individual; in such cases it is characterized by words like "dominating," "charming," "repellent," "magnetic," or "weak." But this aspect of personality, like all others, is explicable in terms of stimulus and response. The dominating personality, for instance, is one that through its own traits and behavior—through an authoritative way of speaking, an air of assurance, an imposing stature, a dignified bearing—arouses in others the responses of submission which in childhood they made unthinkingly to adults. Because personality is nothing but a system of reactions, it can be studied by the matter-of-fact methods of science. That it cannot be studied very completely at present is the result of the fact that adequate methods have not yet been developed; there is nothing in the personality that of necessity eludes scientific treatment. To know a personality is to possess specific information about the individual's habits of work, education, attitudes, achievements, dominant emotional trends, social adaptability, favorite recreations and sports, sex life, reactions to conventional standards, special peculiarities, and compensations for unsatisfactory adjustments. Not that it is possible to analyze the personality once and for all. The personality changes as old reactions are discarded and new ones are acquired. In the behaviorist's psychology, personality does not subsist and persist through the vicissitudes of life in the manner of the theological soul. But the dominant habit-

systems at any given period constitute the personality at
that time.

The whole system of behavior, then, the complete personality, is built up out of a few simple reactions by the process
of conditioning. A limited repertoire of native responses,
the process of conditioning, the stimuli provided by the body
and by the environment, social as well as physical—these are
all that the behaviorist needs. His account, he maintains,
omits no part of human activity. He can explain thought and
emotion as well as overt bodily movements. In the end he
exhibits a complete human being, in Watson's words, "an
assembled organic machine ready to run."

This is behaviorism in its bare essentials; but almost as
important in accounting for its career and its influence are
the secondary characteristics with which its author sent it
into the world.

One of these is a special attitude toward the nervous
system. In Watson's opinion, conventional psychology has
given an inexcusably exaggerated importance, as futile as it
is overweighted, to this one bodily structure. Actually, little
is known about the operations of the nervous system. The
"puzzle pictures" in the textbooks and the accompanying
legends are for the most part products of gratuitous speculation, conveniently made to fit the facts they purport to explain. The nervous system, Watson says, is a "mystery box,"
a place into which a mentalistic psychology pushes its problems in order to create the illusion that they have been
explained. Besides—and this objection is strongly characteristic—preoccupation with the nervous system is sheer overemphasis; it is the habit of a psychology concerned with
minds and presumably with what goes on in the head and
brain. But one of the most emphatic teachings of behaviorism
is that psychology must study the whole body—smooth

and striped muscles, viscera and glands, receptors and con-
nectors, flesh, blood, and bones. It must study the nervous
system, of course, but merely as one of the structures of the
body, not as the dominant structure. If there is any set of
organs that the behaviorist singles out for special attention,
it is the muscles and glands, for the effectors are the organs
of behavior *par excellence.* It is profoundly significant that
Watson explains associative learning in terms of events in
the muscles rather than in the brain. If one muscular movement becomes the stimulus for the next, the whole trans-
action seems to him aboveboard—less inaccessible and hence
less mysterious than connections made inside the brain.
Watson is tremendously concerned, too, that the smooth
muscles and glands, the organs of emotion, shall receive
their fair share of attention; human beings, he says, are
"terribly at the mercy" of their glands. His refusal to
emphasize the nervous system is, indeed, an expression of
some of his fundamental attitudes. One of these is his conviction that psychology must study the organism as a
whole; another is his distaste for anything invisible and inaccessible, even if it is made invisible and inaccessible by
something so material as the human skull.

Behaviorism also has a special attitude toward heredity.
In 1919, in *Psychology from the Standpoint of a Behaviorist,* Watson, in common with most psychologists of the day,
recognized emotion and instinct as hereditary behavior, in
contrast with habits or learned behavior. But even then,
again in common with most psychologists, he showed a
lively skepticism toward regarding any of the more elaborate
patterns of behavior as hereditary. He recognized only three
emotions, fear, rage, and love, as native; and he counted
as instinctive reactions only such simple coördinations as
those involved in nursing and a few primitive defensive
movements. Soon after the appearance of his book, however,

the whole concept of instinct was subjected to unprecedented criticism. The question was asked, "Are there any instincts?" Z. Y. Kuo,[12] taking a position on the extreme left, maintained that the concept of instinct should be discarded altogether, urging among his arguments against it that the theory of instinct was based on the old exploded doctrine of innate ideas, and that it implied the operation of a mental or spiritual force. Kuo held that all so-called instincts are learned behavior and that even reflexes are learned reactions acquired in the uterus. In his next book, *Behaviorism*, Watson came out strongly for a psychology without instincts. He had always been critical of the concept of instinct, and once he saw it as allied with mentalism and an outworn tradition, he was whole-heartedly opposed to it. Besides, to one interested in the prediction and control of behavior, a psychology without instincts has definite advantages. The less there is natively "given" in the organism, the better the chances for understanding and improving it; for understanding it by studying complex reactions as they are built up or torn down bit by bit; for improving it by adding and eliminating and combining reactions, thereby making the organism a better machine.

This last point suggests another characteristic of behaviorism, its interest in the practical management of human affairs. For all its disdain of anything but the severely scientific, behaviorism has not a trace of the scorn with which pure science sometimes regards applied science. Behaviorism is distinctly interested in the welfare and salvation— the strictly secular salvation—of the human race. The behaviorist does not survey his material with the detachment that ignores values; he knows good from evil. Watson, for

[12] Z. Y. Kuo, "Giving up Instincts in Psychology," *Journal of Philosophy* (1921), 18, 645-663; "How Are Our Instincts Acquired?" *Psychological Review* (1922), 29, 344-365.

example, is not content merely to observe children's fears and to note the conditions in which they are acquired and lost; he sees most of those fears as avoidable mishaps, and he seeks ways and means of removing them. Nor does he observe with disinterested calm that there are false prophets in the land—character-readers, psychoanalysts, and pseudo-psychologists who receive pay for their pseudo-services. He regrets in italics that it is so, and it becomes his business and his pleasure to expose them. Of course, in a thoroughly disinterested study of human behavior, neither the coward nor the bigot, neither the introspectionist nor the fraud, would arouse the slightest tremor of disapproval or compassion. But behaviorism does not pretend to be a disinterested psychology. It is frankly an applied science, seeking to bring the efficiency of the engineer to bear upon the problem of reform. It is true that the precise direction of the reform is not altogether settled. Sometimes, with the worldly wisdom of the practical man, behaviorism seems to say that society has set the patterns to which humanity must conform; but sometimes it suggests that those patterns themselves have been set in blind ignorance of the limitations and possibilities of the human machine. Occasionally the belief in the improvability of human ways rises to astonishing heights. In the closing paragraph of *Behaviorism,* a book in which the author has repeatedly denounced the folly of beliefs not grounded on the tested facts of science, Watson says:

"I am trying to dangle a stimulus in front of you, a verbal stimulus which, if acted upon, will gradually change this universe. For the universe will change if you bring up your children, not in the freedom of the libertine, but in behavioristic freedom—a freedom which we cannot even picture in words, so little do we know of it. Will not these children in turn, with their better ways of living and thinking, replace us as society, and in turn bring up their children in a still more scientific way, until the world finally becomes a place fit for human habitation?"

But if human beings are to be improved, a beginning must be made early in life, and the recognition of the importance of infancy is another of the prominent characteristics of behaviorism. Infancy is interesting to behaviorism partly from the standpoint of methodology. By observing infants, the student may see behavior in the making; he may note the repertoire of reactions a human being has at birth and discover the ways in which they are modified. But infancy is also important from the standpoint of practical control of behavior, for in infancy the very foundations of behavior are established. In his earliest years, certainly before he is six years old, a person is made or marred. It is during these years that he learns to meet the world with fear or confidence, with hostility or friendliness, to succumb to difficulties or to master them, to expect success or defeat; these years, in short, are the period during which he acquires the attitudes and habits, largely visceral and largely unverbalized, which will always constitute the core of his personality, and which form the foundations of the powerful "unverbalized" part of his being. Watson's own interest in the field is unmistakable. Some of his most influential research has been on the reactions of infants, and his book *The Psychological Care of the Infant and Child* is dedicated to the parents who first rear a happy child.

But underlying these particular features of the system is a characteristic so pervasive that it attaches specifically to no one doctrine. Perhaps it may best be described as a withdrawal reaction, amounting almost to a shuddering away from anything suggesting the word "mental." This attitude is more than a calm conviction that psychology has been hampered by an interest in consciousness and introspection;

it is an active distaste for the whole concept of mind. For the mental, to Watson, means the non-natural if not the supernatural. It represents a way of looking at things entirely antithetic to that of science. It means souls and animism and miracles and mystery. It suggests credulity and wonder, not skepticism and investigation; an unseen world, not facts of observation; speculation and verbalism, not downright experimentation. The moment Watson sees a theory as implying the mental, he sees it as doomed. He does not, of course, dispense with evidence and the critical weighing of evidence. But there is no escaping the impression that his onslaughts against consciousness, image, affection, and instinct are determined first of all by the fact that he sees them as involving something immaterial and therefore supernatural; and that the point is really settled for him in the crucial instant when he sees the concept as somehow involving an acceptance of the mental.

Because of this attitude behaviorism has become more than a mere school of psychology; it has become a crusade against the enemies of science, and in this rôle it has taken on, even more than have most schools of psychology, something of the character of a cult. Its adherents are devoted to a cause; they are in possession of a truth that not all men have the courage or the wit or the knowledge to accept; and much of the strength of behaviorism as a living movement is derived from this fact. For most American youths have come under the influence of fundamentalism in some form, obvious or subtle, and some of them in their revolt against it have found the greatest sense of freedom in accepting the clean-cut, hard-headed, unequivocal creed of orthodox behaviorism. It is interesting in this connection to note that words, to many behaviorists, take on something of the importance they assume in primitive cults; in particular that certain of them have been placed under a taboo. All science, of course, is careful of its terminology; but there is more than the usual attempt to avoid confusing connotations, more than the prosaic demand for exactness, in the zeal with which the behaviorist keeps his terminology pure. He is willing to resort to all sorts of circumlocution to avoid such words as "consciousness," "sensation," "idea," "will," "pleasure," and "image"; and if in an extremity he is forced to employ them, he scrupulously surrounds them with the ceremonial of quotes. It is, indeed, one of the curious and significant facts about behaviorism that it has acquired some of the emotional attitudes usually associated with the conception of life that it regards as its arch-enemy. Its prohibitions are not merely the precautionary measures of science; they are defenses against a discarded view of life.

But the dominant tone of behaviorism is hardly one of restraint. Behaviorism is above all things expansive and aggressive. Armed with the buoyant assurance that comes from seeing the world in blacks and whites, it accepts or rejects; it does not compromise. And what it lacks in subtlety, it gains in power, in the ability to throw itself into tasks without reservation. Ranging right on the one side and wrong on the other, behaviorism has achieved a system with sharp, clean outlines. As a conception it has the firmness and definiteness that characterized structuralism, and partly for this reason it has become, like structuralism, an indispensable point of reference in American psychology.

There are, of course, behaviorisms and behaviorisms. What has been said applies to Watsonian behaviorism, but modifications of the system have appeared on all sides. As a matter of fact, few psychologists call themselves behaviorists without qualification. Some heartily approve the dismissal of consciousness but refuse to accept Watson's views on heredity. Some question the doctrine of building in by conditioning but believe that none but objective methods should be used. Occasionally there is an attempt to out-Watson Watson, and acceptances and rejections have been tried in all sorts of combinations. As a consequence, behavioristic psychology merges gradually into psychology in general, and strange to say, the result is not confusion. Thanks to the distinctness of Watson's teachings, they form a definite, though not unchanging, standard by which all deviations may be measured. The outcome is rather a communication between behavioristic and non-behavioristic psychologies that has resulted in enormous conquests on the part of behaviorism by peaceful penetration. For not even behaviorism, with all its boldness and picturesqueness, has taken psychology by storm. It captured the imagination by violence, to be sure; but its influence on the actual practices of the science has been achieved by a process far more effective in bringing about lasting changes—the steady infiltration of customs.

Behaviorism indeed has overflowed the bounds of psychology proper. It has figured in editorials, literary criticism, social and political discussions, and sermons. It has attracted the attention, in some cases the favorable attention, of philosophers. Holt has supported it in *The Freudian Wish,* Santayana has contrasted it favorably with "literary psychology," and Russell, impressed by the fact that self-observation gives so little insight into the self, is interested, though he criticizes the epistemology implied in the system, in the attempt to study human behavior from the outside. And more than any interpretation of psychology, with the exception of the psychoanalytic theory, behaviorism has awakened popular interest in the United States. In particular, its program for bettering humanity by the most efficient methods of science has made an all but irresistible appeal to the attention of the American public.

Within American psychology itself, the rise of behaviorism has been both conspicuous and important. As a means of focusing discussion, of putting problems, of stimulating research, of stirring enthusiasm, there has been nothing to compare with it since the introduction of the first laboratories and the publication of James's *Principles*. For a time behaviorism almost dichotomized American psychology into the behavioristic and non-behavioristic camps, and even today the shortest and surest way of defining a psychological position in America is to state it with reference to behaviorism. Whether for better or for worse, behaviorism has profoundly affected the folk-ways and *mores* of American psychology.

The most direct line of influence of behaviorism has been that which grew out of its insistence that only objective methods be used. Behaviorism, of course, did not introduce objective methods into psychology. Ever since the time of Fechner and Helmholtz, objective methods have held a place of honor, and they did so even in the days when introspection was proclaimed as the distinctive method of psychology. Certainly behaviorism does not stand merely for more brass instruments; there were plenty of brass instruments in the older psychology. But by insisting on objective methods and on the exclusive use of objective methods, behaviorism has brought about a shift in emphasis that amounts to a revolution. It has cut so deep into the prevailing customs as to alter the very problems that arise in psychology. With its origins in animal psychology, and with its habit of observing the whole organism in action, behaviorism has seized upon problems that are more obvious, of larger scope, and far more likely to appeal to most people as vital, than the increasingly minute dissections of states of consciousness to which the introspectionists were devoting their best efforts. Even in its narrowness and intolerance, behaviorism has been influential; for it not only justifies new problems, but flaunts old ones as ridiculous. Taking the stand of robust common sense, it congratulates itself on having something better to do than making doubtful discriminations between shades of blue, and determining whether or not there is a glassy effect in images. Frankly proud of keeping within the realm of observations open to all—of dealing with seen and recorded movements, with tracings on kymograph sheets, and with pointer readings that any one can see—behaviorism is glad to limit its studies to material which arouses the immediate conviction that there is "something there." As a consequence of its aggressive attitude, even those studies which still make liberal use of introspection show marks of the behavioristic influence. Indeed, one of the signs of the vigor of this extraordinarily vigorous movement is the way in which it has managed to get its attitudes recognized by those who oppose its fundamental doctrines. Even its taboos are heeded, these perhaps especially. There is a tendency, even among psychologists who firmly believe in their right to take consciousness into consideration, to stress the objective records of their findings, and sometimes to explain that, though in their own thinking they include consciousness, their statements hold equally for behavior with consciousness left out. Since the rise of behaviorism, introspection and the results of introspection are less likely to stand alone; they are supplemented and even supported by objective data. Not only among its adherents, but in American psychology generally, behaviorism has enormously increased the emphasis on objective methods in research.

There is one set of experiments that stands out with special prominence in relation to behavioristic theory, those of K. S. Lashley, Watson's most distinguished pupil. These experiments, constituting the most extensive body of re-

search put out by a behaviorist on a single problem, bear
directly on Watson's assumption that simple reactions like
the reflex, conditioned or unconditioned, are the units of
which behavior is composed.

Lashley's research centers about the cortical activities
involved in learning. His general plan was to train animals
—he generally used rats—in some specified performance such
as running a maze or making visual discriminations; then
to destroy a part or parts of the cortex; and finally, after
the animal had recovered from the operation, to determine
to what extent and in what manner the performance had
been impaired. Throughout the experiments, the performances of the experimental animals were checked against
those of suitable control groups. These studies, on the border-
line between physiology and psychology, required the use of
the techniques of both sciences; and many psychologists, impressed by the ready use of the resources of physiology by
one of their number, seem inclined at times to overlook the
fact that from the standpoint of method, the distinctive
feature of the study is the experimental and quantitative determination of the animal's *behavior* throughout the investigation—a practice derived from psychology. The point is an
important one because in many of the older studies the investigators were content to rely on general observation for
their accounts of behavior; to note, for example, that an animal seemed clumsy, or listless, or faltering. But in Lashley's
studies, general observation was replaced by the experimental methods of animal psychology and by quantitative methods similar to those used in the objective measurement of intelligence. It is especially important to notice that the
methods were quantitative as well as experimental. For
through the definite measurements of behavior throughout
the research, it was possible to determine mathematically the

relationships between loss or impairment of specified abilities and the location and extent of the correlated brain injuries.[18]

The outcome of these researches was a mass of evidence indicating that in most cases a given part of the cerebral cortex is not invariably associated with a particular performance; in other words, that strict localization of function is not the rule. To Lashley, this meant that it was no longer possible to conceive of the nervous system as a structure in which the reflex arc is the unit, as a system in which fixed and definite nervous pathways connect particular points of stimulation with particular organs of response. To be sure, some pathways are more likely to be involved in a given activity than others—pathways that are in a sense more convenient —but there is as a rule no necessity about the arrangement. If those pathways are destroyed, their functions are not permanently lost but are apparently taken over by other parts of the brain. Instead of strict localization of function in the cortex, there is equipotentiality of its various parts for the activities in which it is involved. There is, however—and this is the positive side of Lashley's contribution—a relation between the *amount* of the cortical area destroyed and the degree of deterioration in behavior. A slight brain injury as a rule gives no observable impairment in performance, but as the injury increases in magnitude, the performance becomes progressively more disturbed. Furthermore, more complex performances require a larger amount of brain tissue than do simpler tasks. On the basis of this evidence Lashley concluded that the cortex acts as a whole rather than in separate parts; he stressed mass-action rather than piece-by-piece

[18] Lashley was not the first investigator to make careful experimental determinations of the animal's behavior during experiments involving extirpation. The investigations of Shepherd Ivory Franz, which began in 1902, are considered the pioneer work in this field. Lashley, however, emphasized the quantitative side of the data more than Franz did.

conduction, equipotentiality of function rather than strict localization.[14]

The relation of Lashley's work to behaviorism is interesting from several points of view. First of all, it definitely discredits the particular conception of neural activity that Watson assumes throughout his thinking; it denies that behavior is "built in" or constructed bit by bit on the conditioned-reflex plan. But at the same time it leaves unshaken the basic behavioristic contention that only objective methods should be used; it is in fact a brilliant demonstration of the value of such methods in psychological research. From this point of view, Lashley's relation to behaviorism is somewhat like that of Külpe to the doctrines of Wundt, for both Lashley and Külpe, by using the distinctive methods of their respective schools, came upon facts contrary to the teachings of those schools. In this sense, they illustrate the function of schools and systems in actual practice. The work of both men shows that research stimulated by a system and controlled by the scientific method may reveal facts which are at variance with the system; that a system puts definite problems and stimulates investigations, but that it does not determine the outcome of the investigation.

So far, however, little has been said on the point that to most people is the fundamental, and certainly the most interesting, issue raised by behaviorism: the possibility of a psychology without consciousness. A few specialists, absorbed in their research, may consider behaviorism important chiefly

[14] This does not mean that Lashley rules out specific localization absolutely. He has discovered, in fact, that the function of pattern vision is specifically localized in the cortex. He believes that such facts of localization, along with facts indicating mass action, must be taken into account in interpreting cortical activity. The general tendency of his own work, however, has been to bring into the foreground the theory of mass action. K. S. Lashley, "Mass Action in Cerebral Function," *Science* (1931), 73, 245-254.

from the standpoint of methodology; but to the world at large, and to most psychologists as well, the deepest significance of the behavioristic conception lies in the claim that it has no place, and no need, for consciousness. And strangely enough, the moment this fundamental issue is directly focused, the system begins to lose the clarity which at first glance seems preëminently to characterize it. For behaviorism does not, as a matter of fact, actually give an account of psychology that dispenses with the individual's awareness of his own actions. Its purpose, of course, is to do so, and in doing so to divest psychology of its last shred of metaphysics and subjectivism. Behaviorists commonly assume that any one who objects to their views does so because he thinks that behaviorism has gone too far, that it has insisted too strongly on the rigors of a severely scientific point of view. They seem not to have considered that their position might be open to attack from another quarter; that behaviorism might be criticized as not going far enough in the direction of science, as not being whole-heartedly objective and empirical, as not being sufficiently disentangled from a metaphysical attitude toward the mind-body problem.

If this statement of the case seems a contradiction in terms, that fact bears witness to the strong association behaviorism has established between the conception of a strictly scientific psychology and its own point of view. Behaviorism, it is repeatedly asserted, is scientific psychology. Any position that is contrasted with it is by implication less scientific. To ask that a psychology become more scientific, is simply to ask that it become more behavioristic.

And yet, at the basis of the behaviorist's thinking is the mind-body distinction in the metaphysical sense—not as a convenient classification of facts of experience, but as a division between appearance and reality. Embedded in the very core of the behaviorist's doctrine is the Platonic distinction between mind and matter; and behaviorism, like Plato, regards the one term as real and the other as illusory. Its very case against dualism is stated in terms of that distinction and is made by the classical metaphysical procedure of reducing the one term to the other. This metaphysical distinction, rather than empirical evidence, is the basis on which behaviorism accepts or rejects data for scientific consideration and on which it forms conceptions for dealing with them. Thought-processes, for example, are said to be language mechanisms, not because there is experimental evidence to prove the assertion, but because as language mechanisms they conform to the preferred concept, matter. Behaviorism has adopted a metaphysics to end metaphysics.

Perhaps it will be objected that the materialism of behaviorism is merely a working hypothesis; that it is not intended as a comment on the ultimate nature of reality and hence has nothing to do with metaphysics. But there are signs more convincing than direct declarations that behaviorism does not take its stand on the mind-body problem merely as a matter of methodological convenience. One of them is the emotional urgency with which the thoroughgoing behaviorist takes his beliefs and taboos. Another is his attitude toward psychologists who study consciousness. For to the behaviorist, the examination of immediate experience is not merely trivial, not merely a superficial and inefficient method of studying the human animal, not merely off the main line of vital human problems, though of course it is all that; it is an empty gesture in the empty air. The behaviorist's attitude toward introspectionists is not at all the same as his attitude toward other scientists whose work does not especially interest him—as it might be toward conchologists, for example, since from the standpoint of the basic problems of behaviorism, the labors of the conchologist are as trivial, as unimportant, as irrelevant to the vital problems of human beings as are those of the introspectionist. But the behaviorist believes in the conchologist's shells as he does not believe in the introspectionist's consciousness; he does not regard the conchologist as the dupe of an illusion. The same belief in the deeper reality of the material is implied as an underlying assumption in some of the theoretical discussions of behaviorism. In Lashley's one theoretical paper, "The Behavioristic Interpretation of Consciousness," [15] the bulk of the discussion is devoted to the task of showing that every characteristic which has ever been assigned to consciousness can be explained in terms of bodily mechanisms; and the implication is that since everything which has been called mental can be reduced to the physical, the concept of consciousness is superfluous. But unless one regards the material as more real, this conclusion does not inevitably follow. Without that assumption, the close correspondence might mean any one of a number of things—among the more obvious, that the material can be reduced to the mental in the manner of Berkeley and the German idealists; or, on a less ambitious and more empirical level, that descriptions from the standpoint of consciousness and behavior, being so closely in agreement, complement and corroborate rather than oppose each other.

Since science is not concerned with the ultimate nature of reality, it makes no difference, from the purely scientific standpoint, what kind of metaphysics a scientist holds so long as his metaphysics does not prejudice his science. But the moment a scientist gives his metaphysical concepts precedence over the facts of experience, he is departing from the scientific code. For the ideal of science is to construct concepts that will stand the test of experience; and the distinctive characteristic of the scientific method is that it

[15] *Psychological Review* (1923), **30**, 237-272, 329-439.

supplements the appeal to reason with the appeal to experience, refusing to acknowledge the validity of the concepts it has forged until they have been checked by the data of observation. And this rule of the code behaviorism violates; it passes judgment on factual data by applying as a touchstone the metaphysical concept of matter. When confronted with accounts that purport to deal with such happenings as images, ideas, or feelings of satisfyingness, it knows in advance that they are wrong. Since these purported facts of experience do not conform to a preferred mode of conception, there is no need to examine them.

But how did behaviorism, which is determined above all things to be scientific, fall into this mode of thought? By making the entirely legitimate demand that psychological knowledge be objective knowledge; by insisting that without objectivity of knowledge, psychology can never be taken seriously as a science. Watson was clearly appalled by the differences of opinion in psychology, by the lack of a reliable body of knowledge that compels assent, such as that found in the physical sciences; and apparently assuming that objective knowledge is knowledge about an external physical world which by its very nature is open to the inspection of all, he tried to remedy the evil by discarding from psychology all consideration of mental processes.

But is objective knowledge necessarily knowledge about a physical world? Does the objectivity of the knowledge of the physical sciences depend, as Watson seems to imply, on the fact that they deal with a material world? And is there any assurance that that world is open to the inspection of all? The answer to these questions requires a closer examination of the word "objective."

The word "objective," as applied to the physical world refers, of course, to the distinction between the experiencing subject and the experienced object, the self and the not-self, and to the organization of all experienced events about those two poles. Some events, such as thoughts and feelings, are referred to the self; others, such as trees and snowstorms are referred to a world external to the self. This external world, furthermore, is regarded as independent of the self; it is not considered the property of any one self, but is thought of as an object common to all selves. Its events are public. To be sure, the distinction between the subject and the object is by no means absolute, but that fact may be ignored for the present, since the physical world as it is ordinarily conceived, is a typical object in the sense indicated.[16]

When the world "objective" is applied to knowledge, its meaning is similar though not identical. As applied to knowledge, the distinction between subjective and objective is the distinction between opinion and fact, between belief that is influenced by the accidents of the personal and private and assertions that hold true for all. Objective knowledge, like the objective world, is impersonal and public; it is not determined by peculiarities in the nature or circumstances of any one self; it is uninfluenced by the wishes, hopes and prejudices of the self. Common sense has certain rough and ready tests for the objectivity of knowledge, such tests as agreement among different observers, consistency with other items of knowledge, practical efficacy when applied to actual situations. And science, refining and extending the methods of common sense, has developed the whole procedure that it calls the scientific method as a means of ensuring the objectivity of its concepts.

It goes without saying that scientific knowledge is ob-

[16] The word "objective" has been used, up to this point in this chapter, with reference to the distinction made in this paragraph. Objective observations, for example, are observations of things and events in the external world; objective methods are directed toward the objects and happenings in a world outside the self.

jective knowledge in the sense that it is independent of private opinion and preference, of peculiarities of interpretation, of personal idiosyncrasies of all sorts. The method it employs is a device for making it so. But that method is based on no assurance whatever that two or more observers see the same object, or that any object exists independent of their perception of it. Not even in physics is the objectivity of knowledge based on the assurance that two or more observers actually see the same object. A physicist, noting the position of a pointer on a scale obviously cannot see a pointer independent of his own perception of it. Neither can he perceive immediately the perception of any other observer and compare it directly with his own. If twenty physicists are noting the position of a pointer on a scale, no one of them can see directly a fellow worker's pointer reading any more than he can experience directly the loves and hates of the other nineteen. In this sense the physicist is as restricted to private perception as is the psychologist. It is as difficult to prove the existence of an independent physical world as of states of consciousness in humanity in general, and the physicist does not even try. He does not consider it necessary to try. The whole problem is one which, as a scientist, he has abandoned, and has abandoned wittingly and deliberately. The objectivity of his knowledge is based not on any proof that it is derived from an objective world, but on the way in which it meets the regular tests of science. It is not the source of knowledge but its verification that determines its objectivity in science. The physicist does not pause at length to ask: Do these events which I observe exist only in my perception? He asks: Do they lead to communicable judgments based on repeated and verified experience? No more than the psychologist does he have direct assurance that his observations represent something outside his own experience. And if physics is not cut off from the possibility of obtaining objective knowledge by this lack, neither is psychology—that is, if psychology is content with the scientific criteria of objectivity and does not judge its data by applying a metaphysical theory of reality.

This discussion does not imply, however, that psychology should cling to the notion of the mental, either as an explanatory concept or as a description of its subject-matter. Rather it suggests that the mind-matter distinction has been far too greatly emphasized by psychology. As a matter of fact, neither the concept of matter nor that of mind seems to be adequate to the needs of the present situation in science. It has often been observed that they are being discarded by physics and psychology, the two sciences that, at first thought, we judge should find them most useful. Physicists no longer deal with matter in the sense of little balls or solidities of substance, and psychologists—non-behaviorists and behaviorists alike—no longer deal with the minds Watson so vehemently denounces. Long before the rise of behaviorism students of consciousness had ceased to employ the crude conception of the mental attributed to them by Watson.[17]

Nevertheless, there is an important difference between the way in which physics has met the situation and the course that behaviorism is urging upon psychology. When physicists discovered the limitations of thinking in terms of the concrete mechanical models, which were once regarded as the ideal of explanation, they turned to a new type of explanation made to suit the facts observed. Instead of mechanical models, they used mathematical formulas that gave quantitative statements of observed relations. In other words, physics pushed on to a new way of conceptualizing its data. But when behaviorism became convinced that the concept of

[17] Titchener's criticism of the "manikin" of common sense, reported in Chapter IV of this book, is a single illustration of this fact.

mind was inadequate to the task of psychology, it did not, like physics, make the adjustment in method suggested by the data themselves. Rather, it retained and utilized the mind-matter distinction. Finding the one term inapplicable, it merely substituted the other, assuming that if the one did not apply the other must. Instead of doing away with the mind-body distinction, behaviorism emphasized and preserved it.

The reasons for this course are not hard to discover. First, there is the greater ease of thinking in habitual terms, of using concepts already at hand instead of devising new modes of thought. And since the problems of animal psychology, from which behaviorism arose, lent themselves readily to the concept of matter, there was little in the situation to stimulate radically different modes of thought. In the second place—and this is probably the more important consideration—the study of the physical world has been associated, habitually and historically, with the impersonal and unbiased method of science. From this point of view, there is indeed a practical justification for thinking exclusively in terms of matter. If a person has been so conditioned, emotionally and intellectually, that he inevitably associates with matter all the attitudes of science, then as a means of maintaining the scientific attitude it is entirely legitimate for him to conceive all psychological data in physical terms before attempting to operate on them scientifically. But in that case, the practice becomes a precautionary measure for those who need it, not an essential part of scientific procedure. If a psychologist can contemplate a wish or a thought, as it immediately appears to him in first-hand experience, simply as a natural event in the natural world—as he regards a thunder-storm or indigestion, for example, when he is considering them from an impersonal, scientific point of view—it is unnecessary for him to try to strengthen that attitude by assuring himself that all such happenings conform to a concept for which physics has found a limited use. There is no more reason why all psychologists should go through this procedure than for all bricklayers to go through the movements that efficiency experts found some of the most skilful members of that craft performing habitually but needlessly.

Perhaps these considerations seem very remote from the problems with which behaviorism or any other system of psychology is immediately concerned. But the preservation by behaviorism of the distinction between matter and mind as a distinction between the real and the illusory—the virtual though unavowed preservation of that distinction—has had some very real effects on its actual practices.

One of them is a tendency to indulge in feats of translation, and apparently at times to regard the translation as an explanation. It is difficult, when reading some of the behavioristic accounts, to escape the impression that the writers regard it as an explanation to say that a wish is an organic set, that a meaning is a bodily attitude, that thoughts are language mechanisms. Yet little is added to the knowledge of wishes, meanings, and thoughts by these statements, which after all consist largely in taking over what is known about these happenings from common sense and the older psychology and devising, often not on the basis of known facts, some possible physiological account of them. Such procedures may easily create the illusion of explanation when there is none, and by giving psychology a stock of verbal formulas with which to answer its questions, conceal the fact that it does not know the answers. In many cases, of course, the procedure is not intended as an explanation, but merely as a preliminary step toward explanation, that of treating the data in such a way as to make scientific explanation possible. In such cases, the practice is the previously mentioned precautionary measure for ensuring the scientific treatment of the problem. In other cases the procedure has a more positive value. It is sometimes used as a means of seeing the facts under a new guise that suggests hitherto unsuspected relationships and new possibilities of explanation. The procedure then becomes definitely productive, and there is, of course, no objection whatever to its use. But whenever translation is substituted for explanation, psychology is immediately exposed to the dangers that arise from having on hand a stock of ready verbal formulas with which to meet specific inquiries as they arise.

Another consequence of the behavioristic attitude toward the mind-body problem is that behaviorism has difficulty in dealing with facts that do not lend themselves to explanations of the mechanical-model type. Classical behaviorism, taking its cue from classical physics, conceives the human being as an organic machine, and seeks to analyze all human reactions into specific stimulus-response connections. In their intentness on this problem, many behaviorists have fallen into the way of thinking that unless a reaction can be thought of in terms of definite physiological processes, unless it can be analyzed at least imaginatively and tentatively into particular muscular and glandular activities, it is somehow unreal, or at least less real than the particular muscular and glandular reactions themselves. Even in their own field of animal learning, there is something of this attitude. Often behaviorists are so immensely impressed by the importance of relating their findings to physiological knowledge that they forget that physiology has a similar obligation to the facts of psychology; that the physiologist who undertakes to explain the action of the nervous system and muscles must explain, among other things, how those structures operate when the animal learns; and that his explanation must take into account the facts of learning as determined by competent psychologists, as surely as the psychologist must take into account the facts about sense-organs, muscles, and nerves as determined by competent physiologists. Nor is the psychologist's account merely a temporary makeshift, to be used only so long as physiological knowledge is incomplete, something that will disappear into physiology when accounts of sense-organs and nerves and muscles and glands are complete to the last detail. Even if every muscular contraction, every sensory reaction, every stimulus-response connection, were completely known, the total course of the animal's learning would be a necessary part of the account. Each term—the psychological and the physiological—puts a part of the problem; each acts as a check on the other; neither can be considered more important to knowledge than the other; both are indispensable. The behaviorists may declare that they have recognized this fact all along, and that, in defining behavior as the activity of the organism as a whole, they have brought its recognition into the very center of psychology.[18] But it is all the more significant that, in spite of this fact, so many behaviorists in their actual practice regard their findings as scientifically respectable only when they can think of them in terms of definite physiological operations. Clearly there is a strong association between the behavioristic conception of the subject-matter of psychology and the mechanical-model type of explanation.

And if this habit of thought appears in the work in animal psychology, it is far more prominent in the attitude toward studies that do not even pretend to offer explanations of the

---

[18] Watson defines behavior as the activity of the organism as a whole. He states distinctly that behaviorism is interested not merely in "muscle twitches," but in long-range activities such as "taking food," "writing a letter," and "building a house." But it is clear that he thinks of such activities as integrations of component processes, and as eventually reducible to particular stimulus-response connections.

mechanical-model variety. An instance is the lukewarm, if not scornful, attitude of many behaviorists toward the work on intelligence. Since intelligence cannot as yet be stated in terms of specific bodily processes, the whole notion of intelligence is, according to the standards of the behaviorists, vague and nebulous even when defined without reference to consciousness. On the other hand, psychology has been equally unsuccessful in the attempt to analyze intelligence into mental components. The problem of intelligence is, in fact, an excellent illustration of the kind of situation in which psychology has had to devise methods dictated by the actual demands of the data instead of relying on existing techniques and systematic formulations.

It is highly significant that the whole movement toward the testing and measuring of intelligence developed without the backing of any particular school or system, growing largely out of demands of practical situations. It is also significant that psychology, when confronted with this problem, spontaneously developed the mathematical-equation type of explanation. To be sure, investigators at first tried the more conventional analytical procedure. Binet, in his earlier work on intelligence, attempted to measure separately and then to summate what he believed might be component processes, and Cattell based his researches on the same plan. But success came only when Binet, putting aside temporarily the problem of content and analysis, attempted to measure intelligence in general in terms of its relation to other facts. It is important to notice that in devising tests of intelligence a psychologist does not first decide what constitutes intelligence and then arbitrarily apply his definition. He tries a number of tests, presumably requiring activities commonly considered intelligent, and from this number selects as tests of intelligence only those which give results that vary quantitatively with outside criteria of what is generally meant by intelligence—maturity, ability to do school-work, the judgments of qualified persons, occupational standing, and the like. Consequently he defines intelligence not in terms of its content or composition but in terms of its relations with other facts. In other words, he is using a conception of the mathematical-equation sort, not of the mechanical-model type. Psychology must regretfully admit, it is true, that much of the work in measuring intelligence and other traits is not above reproach; but the really respectable work in that field has demonstrated at the very least that it is possible to measure a reaction, the contents of which are not specified, in such a way as to give constant and reliable results statable in terms of quantitative relations to other facts.[19]

The data that come out of such studies can be, and are, interpreted variously by different investigators; and since one of the obvious interpretations is that intelligence and the other complex activities measured mathematically are elaborate bodily reactions, the behaviorists, if they are so inclined, can formally make room for this part of psychology in their system. But they are likely to do so somewhat grudgingly, with the attitude that such work is not first-rate, or at least that it cannot be considered "fundamental" research. Yet studies of this sort violate no part of the behaviorist's code: they are not concerned with consciousness, they make no use of introspection, and they deal with observable activities of whole living organisms. Still the facts they yield do not seem to the behaviorists as real as facts

[19] Mathematical procedures, of course, were not introduced into psychology by the testing movement. Ever since the time of Fechner, psychology has used quantitative methods. But the attempt to measure intelligence has led to an increasing use of mathematics as a tool, has revealed more and more possibilities in its use, and has brought distinctly to the fore the possibility of defining psychological terms by means of their quantitative relationships to outside criteria.

about muscles and glands. Behaviorism, with its leaning toward mechanical models, finds it difficult really to assimilate this large portion of psychology which, logically, it cannot exclude.

There is still another difficulty, and a more serious one, that grows out of the behaviorist's attitude toward the mind-body problem: the inability to state precisely what is meant by the rejection of consciousness. Sometimes behaviorism seems to deny flatly that conscious events occur, to assert that any one who believes in them is the victim of an illusion. But sometimes it seems to say that the question of whether or not conscious events occur is beside the main issue—that they may or may not exist, but that if they do, they are essentially unamenable to scientific investigation, and that they can, therefore, have no place in a scientific psychology. By adopting the second alternative, the behaviorist can keep his science wholly free of consciousness; but in doing so he commits himself to a dualism and an indeterminism that run counter to the basic principles of his thinking. If he admits that there is something in the human make-up that is essentially—not merely temporarily and in the absence of technique—inaccessible to scientific inquiry he asserts a duality in human nature by saying that human activity is of two different sorts, one of which is subject to scientific investigation and one of which is beyond the reach of scientific inquiry. But this admission is all that the most ardent advocate of freewill needs. With a component, however minute, of the human make-up that science can never know, he has at his disposal something not subject to the laws of science, something which the scientist cannot predict and control. And this is an outcome which the behaviorist obviously does not intend.

The alternative is to deny consciousness outright, to say that the human organism lives and moves without any awareness of what it is doing. But if the behaviorist accepts this alternative, he finds it extremely difficult to explain what he means by some of his terms. When he says that thinking is merely a matter of language mechanisms, or emotion an affair of visceral and glandular responses, he is at a loss to tell where he gets the terms "thinking" and "emotion." He cannot get them from his own awareness of his own inner speech or disturbed heart-beat, for, by hypothesis, such awareness is impossible. The heart and the larynx, to be sure, belong to the physical world, but one's immediate awareness of their action can be based only on one's personal and private sensations. Does the behaviorist mean, then, that a person cannot be aware of his own anger except by means of kymograph tracings, or blood-analysis, or some other evidence of his bodily reactions that is accessible to others as well as to himself—by catching sight of his flushed face in a mirror, for example, or by seeing directly his own clenched fist? But the behaviorist admits that he does not yet know specifically the patterns of bodily reaction that constitute thoughts and emotions. And more, according to the strict interpretation of his hypothesis, awareness of the external world—the ability to read kymograph records, for example—would be as inexplicable as an immediate awareness of inner speech or of muscular contractions or of heart-beats. But behaviorism raises no question about the validity of observations of the external world. It does not rule out the exteroceptors, particularly the eyes, as sources of information. In actual practice, behaviorism rejects awareness that arises through the interoceptors and proprioceptors; awareness which arises through the exteroceptors it accepts without question.

In this fact lies the clue to the acceptances and rejections that characterize behaviorism. The behaviorist, like any other scientist, is dependent on his own immediate experi-

ence. But experiences that are referred to an external object
are accepted on the assumption that such objects can enter
into the experience of all observers and can, on that account,
give rise to knowledge that has objective validity. Experiences that are referred to the self are rejected because they
cannot be observed by any one but the person who immediately experiences them, and because it is assumed that they
cannot, therefore, give rise to knowledge that is public and
objective. Some events inside the body can be made public
by records that represent them. Various mechanical devices
give records of respiratory changes, muscular contractions,
pulse-rate, and the like, and chemical devices give information of another variety. All of these behaviorism is glad to
accept. But there are some events that can be made public
only through verbal descriptions [20] given by the person who
experiences them, or by some prearranged signal such as
releasing a reaction key to indicate their presence. Are such
records acceptable as scientific data? From the standpoint of
science, the answer to the question should be determined by
the same criteria by which mechanical devices or any other
means of investigating experience are judged fit or unfit for
scientific use. Do they give consistent results that can be
verified by repeated observations and which produce agreement among qualified observers?

But this is not the question behaviorism asks. At this
point, instead of using the scientific tests for the objective
validity of knowledge, it brings in the distinction between
the physical and the mental which it employs as a distinction
between reality and illusion. Events like immediately felt

[20] The "verbal report" that behaviorism recognizes as a method does
not include such descriptions. The behaviorist treats a verbal report simply
as an overt reaction, not as an account of something not itself. To accept
a verbal report as an account of an experience which the reporter has
observed would be to recognize consciousness of an experience not
accessible to an outside observer, and to employ a form of introspection.

sensations and fluctuations of attention are classified as mental, and by the behaviorist's own statement, the mental is regarded as objectionable because it connotes the mysterious and the supernatural. But only because the mind-body distinction is used in a prescientific sense do such connotations arise. Without those reverberations from a past that behaviorism has avowedly discarded, the facts of experience would be all of a piece, though classifiable in different ways from different points of view. Primarily they would all simply be happenings in experience, and it would be a matter of secondary importance whether they involved exteroceptors or interoceptors and proprioceptors; whether they were referred to a common external world or to a private and internal experience; or even whether they were classified, for convenience, as physical or mental. If something like a dread of the supernatural did not lurk in the background, there would be no reason why such events as sensations and emotions and thoughts, in the form in which they immediately present themselves to the person who has them, should not be conceived simply as natural events in the natural world. And in that case there is no reason why a scientist should not utilize them as sources of information, or why he should find any datum of experience at all disconcerting; why he should not view a thought or a feeling of pleasantness with the same calm detachment with which he has learned to regard earthquakes, fevers, and glandular secretions. Only those who believe in ghosts are afraid of them. It is true that some of the facts of experience, such as thoughts and emotions, are far more difficult to observe than others; and that at present, in the absence of suitable techniques, they are accessible only to methods that, from the standpoint of science, are far from satisfactory. It is true, too, that the problems they present may seem utterly uninteresting and utterly unimportant to particular scientists,

who in that case are under no obligation whatever to investigate them. But this does not mean that the experiences
themselves are uninvestigable or that they cannot possibly
reward careful study.

Neither does it mean that the attempt to study such
processes would amount to a mere restoration of the *status
quo* in psychology, a return to the custom of the day when
psychology considered its main business the examination of
conscious processes. The importance of studying the organism as a whole, and of studying it from the outside, has been
so triumphantly demonstrated that there is no need to dwell
on that point. The question is not whether psychology is to
be swamped by mysticism and supernaturalism, but whether
it is to extend the methods of science into regions that
mysticism and supernaturalism are likely to claim as their
own. It would be a curious and ironical turn of events if the
school that has fought so stoutly for a thoroughly scientific
study of psychological processes should, by denying or ignoring the existence of some of them, become an obstacle to a
scientific mode of conceiving them, or deny psychology the
use of tools and methods by which a scientific approach to
them may be made possible.

But it would be an absurd and flagrant error to leave
the impression that the influence of behaviorism has been
chiefly restrictive. On the contrary, it is precisely because
behaviorism has won such enormous prestige through its
successful fight for enlarging the scope of psychology that
even its secondary, and perhaps unintended, effects are important.

The immediate and outstanding and undeniable achievement of behaviorism was to free American psychology from
a cramping tradition. Like functionalism, and far more force-
fully than functionalism, it refused to be bound by the re-

strictions of a science of consciousness. Under the influence of behaviorism, American psychology strengthened its habit of looking at psychological processes in relation to their biological setting, became increasingly aware of the importance of studying the organism as a whole, and recognized more clearly than ever before the advantages of extending into human psychology the point of view and methods of animal psychology. Above all, behaviorism kept insistently in the foreground its demand that only objective knowledge be accepted as scientific.

Behaviorism, however, determined objectivity by reference to the metaphysical concept of matter, not by the application of the tests actually used in science. Instead of getting rid of the mind-body distinction, behaviorism placed it in the very center of its thought and made its inclusions and exclusions on that basis. As a consequence, it was forced to deny admittance to certain data, the absence of which makes its account incomplete and even unintelligible. But the situation so created is not really an *impasse*. It remains an *impasse* only so long as the mental is conceived as extranatural, and only so long as the distinction between the mental and material is used not as a convenient classification of facts of experience, but as a metaphysical distinction between reality and illusion. By taking all the facts of experience simply as data, as happenings in the natural order, and by determining the objectivity of its knowledge by the tests science regularly applies, psychology can keep its knowledge thoroughly objective without being forced to make embarrassing exclusions.

It is possible that part of the service of behaviorism has been to confront psychology with this situation. It is possible that, in attempting to force a choice between two alternatives, matter and mind, it has brought psychology to a realization that it is not obliged to take these concepts, either separately or together, as final modes of dealing with its subject-matter; but that it, like physics or any other natural science confronted with a situation to which its habitual modes of thought are inadequate, must revise its concepts and devise new ones in ways determined by the data themselves rather than by preëxisting formulations.

Chapter VIII

DYNAMIC PSYCHOLOGY AND COLUMBIA UNIVERSITY

DYNAMIC psychology, as interpreted by Robert Sessions Woodworth, is a modest, matter-of-fact, unaggressive system, first formally presented in a series of lectures which when published made an unpretentious volume of barely more than two hundred pages.[1] Unlike most systems, dynamic psychology is not grounded on a protest; it does not derive its motive power from what it is against. On the contrary, nourished by the contributions of many schools, it developed within the field of psychology, appreciative of work undertaken from many points of view and grateful for the results of sound scientific endeavor wherever they are to be found. And yet the system is not merely eclectic. Its tolerance is derived not from the lack of a definite and distinguishing point of view, but from the fact that it discerns in the many activities included in psychology, often opposed and apparently irreconcilable, a common interest and aim. It finds that psychologists, despite expressed differences, have actually been tending in the same direction; that their work hangs together in spite of disagreements. The object of this

[1] The lectures were given in 1916-7. The book, *Dynamic Psychology*, which appeared in 1918, though the first published statement that applies the author's working principles to the total field of psychology, was by no means his first announcement of those principles. In his article "Dynamic Psychology" (*Psychologies of 1930*, 327-336), one finds the phrase "Dynamic Psychology, as I have used the words for twenty years."

common interest and aim Woodworth designates by the
phrase "the workings of the mind." [2]

This phrase, taken over from the psychology of the past,
is reminiscent particularly of the inquiries of Locke, Berkeley, and Hume. These men, according to Woodworth, differ
from the scientific psychologists of to-day less in their intention than in their method. Their method was that of basing
conclusions on the experiences they had chanced to accumulate; whereas science, though it may derive hypotheses from
casual past experience, draws conclusions only when the
hypotheses have been tested by experiments especially arranged to bring out the relevant information. But in spite
of this difference, the psychologists of yesterday and those
of to-day are united by their interest in the same class of
facts. So also the many schools existing at present, though
apparently opposed, are united by a common attempt to
understand the same problem, "the workings of the mind."

The characterization of its subject-matter by this phrase
from the past calls attention to another distinctive feature
of dynamic psychology; it makes no claim to novelty. Not
only has it set itself to destroy no enemy; it has no new
plan of salvation to offer. Having discovered that psychology has followed a constant course in the past, and believing
that it has accomplished and is accomplishing results of scientific value, dynamic psychology tries to make explicit the
principles that have guided psychology all along. It is therefore conservative in the literal sense of the term. Its purpose
is not to found a new school, but to make plain what psychology has always been doing. Most systems of psychology
arise as attempts to start something new. Their founders,
feeling that they have learned from the past primarily
what not to do, are chiefly interested in innovations

[2] R. S. Woodworth, "Dynamic Psychology," *Psychologies of 1925*,
111-126.

that are to be tested by the experience of the future. Dynamic psychology, on the other hand, attempts to bring together the contributions of the past, and to conduct its researches on the basis of principles that have already been found profitable. It is not a system of youth, by youth, and for youth. It is a system that has drawn on a fruitful experience, an interpretation based on a hope that has been both tempered and fortified by past achievements.

Specifically, dynamic psychology is the psychology of cause and effect. This is the concept which Woodworth makes fundamental to the system and which he calmly and steadily defends. What the psychologist really wants to know, he maintains, is why people do the things they do—how they learn and think, why they feel as they feel and act as they act. In order to understand these activities from the standpoint of cause and effect, it is necessary to get as complete a view as possible of the process to be studied—to follow it through its entire course, to discover both its minute details and its broad tendencies, to examine it both from within and from without, and on the basis of this knowledge to note uniformities and to formulate laws. Only knowledge of this sort makes it possible to say that one event is the cause of another.

Any one who states his system in terms of cause and effect is sure to be reminded that in the sophisticated science of to-day these concepts are no longer utilized. Woodworth considers this point specifically.[3] It is hardly necessary for him to say that he is not seeking ultimate causes; it is a commonplace that science deals only with proximate causes. The objection he has to meet is that science no longer uses the concept of cause at all. Woodworth admits that in a complete description of the universe as an all-inclusive sys-

[3] R. S. Woodworth, "Dynamic Psychology," *Psychologies of 1930*, 328-329.

tem, there would be need neither for the notion of cause nor for the related notions of force and explanation. He observes, however, that no such description is as yet at hand; and that in their actual work scientists still utilize something very like those outworn concepts, even though they define force as the product of mass and acceleration, refer to causes as stimuli and conditions and situations, and regard explanation as merely an uncommonly complete description. In physics, for example, though force is defined in terms of motion, and in thus being treated as motion seems to disappear as force, nevertheless the force acting in a given system, A, is not defined in terms of the changes in *that* system, but in terms of the changes in *another* system, B. The crux of the matter lies in the fact that for any given system, a force is something acting on that system from without. This treatment savors strongly of cause and effect; and Woodworth believes that any one who deals with systems that are not self-contained—systems which vary with the varying conditions in the environment—will actually think in terms of cause and effect, however he may purify his terminology. And the psychologist is always dealing with subject-matter that is not complete and self-contained. If he works with the organism as a whole, he must consider the environment; if he studies a particular activity, like learning, he cannot ignore a concurrent activity, like hunger. For this reason, Woodworth feels justified in retaining the concept of cause and effect, and he prefers, on the whole, to do so without resorting to altered terminology. He believes, it is clear, that the immediate problems of psychology can be pursued without too much regard for the revolutionary discoveries of physics and astronomy. The broad-mindedness of dynamic psychology toward the many schools of psychological thought is accompanied by a tough-mindedness in sticking to problems as they present themselves in concrete terms and in their present and actual stage of development. A dynamic psychology is likely to be called on, too, to take a stand on the questions of mechanism and vitalism, of freewill and determinism.[4] But Woodworth believes that the science of psychology has nothing to do with either of these questions. The question of mechanism versus vitalism, in so far as it is a scientific question at all, concerns the life-processes of cells, and it will be solved, if any science solves it, by cell physiology. Psychology, Woodworth says, "does not come within shooting distance" of it. And the question of freewill versus determinism, in so far as it involves the question of purposivism as a philosophy of nature, is a metaphysical problem and is therefore quite outside the province of psychology or of any other natural science. What dynamic psychology attempts is the more modest and more immediate task of tracing observable sequences of cause and effect within its special field.

Obviously, in studying a system which assumes that psychology has had an honorable past, and which regards that past as something to be utilized rather than discarded, it is important to know the background from which the system emerged. Dynamic psychology was developed at Columbia University, but it is not related to Columbia as is structuralism to Cornell, or functionalism to Chicago.

Psychology at Columbia is not easy to describe. It stands for no set body of doctrine, taught with the consistency and paternalism found in more closely organized schools. Yet it shows definite and recognizable characteristics. A graduate student in psychology cannot spend many weeks at Columbia without becoming aware of the immense importance in that atmosphere of curves of distribution, of individual differ-

[4] R. S. Woodworth, "Dynamic Psychology," *Psychologies of 1925*, 115-12Q

ences, of the measurement of intelligence and other human capacities, of experimental procedures and statistical devices, and of the undercurrent of physiological thought. He discovers immediately that psychology does not lead a sheltered life; that it rubs elbows with biology, statistics, education, commerce, industry, and the world of affairs. He encounters many different trends of thought, and he frequently comes upon the same ones from different angles. But the separate strands of teaching are not knit together for him into a firm and patterned fabric. No one cares how he arranges the threads that are placed in his hands; certainly there is no model which he is urged to copy. Columbia students are as definitely marked as those of any other group, but the mark itself is straggling and irregular. The same units—the same "identical elements"—tend to appear in each member of the group, but in arrangement they vary enormously from person to person, and only rarely do they form a true design.

In the early days of psychology at Columbia, the dominating figure was, beyond question, James McKeen Cattell. Cattell, it will be remembered, was one of Wundt's first students at the Leipzig laboratory. It has almost passed into legend that, at his own suggestion, he became Wundt's first assistant, and that in Wundt's laboratory, where the object of study was the generalized human mind, and where Wundt regularly assigned students the problems for their doctoral dissertations, Cattell suggested his own problem and included in his plan a study of individual differences. Wundt pronounced the program *ganz Amerikanisch,* and it is of great importance to psychology in the United States that Cattell remained *ganz Amerikanisch* and at the same time an active member of the Leipzig group. His persistent attention to individual differences meant, among other things, that he became immensely interested in Galton's approach to psy⌐

chology. For a year, during which he was lecturer at Cambridge University, he was personally associated with Galton, and thus added to his first-hand experience with experimental psychology at Leipzig a first-hand acquaintance with the Galtonian methods.

It is not surprising, therefore, that when Cattell founded a psychological laboratory at Columbia, the study of individual differences became prominent. At first, this work consisted chiefly in measuring, in successive classes of Columbia College freshmen, particular capacities like visual acuity, reaction-time, and association-time, in an attempt to arrive at measures of scholastic ability. But the success of the Binet tests brought about a thoroughgoing innovation. Cattell's tests, attacking the problem analytically by measuring separate capacities separately, gave results in which there was no correspondence with student ability. Binet, abandoning the attempt to analyze intelligence into its components, and presenting a number of tasks that presumably required general intelligence for their execution, produced a scale which actually did differentiate between various grades of intelligence in children, when intelligence was judged by the available criteria outside the tests themselves. The success of the Binet scale suggested that the way to measure intelligence, at least for the time, was to go at it in the large, not piece by piece. The Binet method, therefore, was taken up enthusiastically at Columbia, and Teachers College became one of the most active centers of the testing movement in America.

The work in tests, however, reveals only one side of Cattell's influence. His interest in experimental psychology in the more restricted sense is represented not only by his own researches, principally in reaction-time, in association, and in psychophysics, but by the work of his students. Even since Cattell's departure, there has continued to emerge from the Columbia laboratory a steady stream of experimental studies; and if they have made less stir in the world than has the testing movement, theirs is but the usual fate of studies in which the practical value is not obvious and is perhaps non-existent. But in Cattell's hands even the classical experimental problems took an unconventional turn. Introspection was not treated as a sacrosanct discipline, statistics bore more and more of the burden of checking and organizing results, and individual differences were duly noted and considered even in studies that employed the methods developed at Leipzig for the investigation of the generalized human mind. Experimental psychology as Cattell saw it was not an esoteric discipline that must brace itself against common sense. As early as 1904, about a decade before behaviorism made its official appearance, Cattell, in an address *to* the International Congress of Arts and Sciences, made the following statement concerning the rôle of the "trained introspectionist" in psychology:

"I am not convinced that psychology should be limited to the study of consciousness as such. . . . There is no conflict between introspective analysis and objective experiment . . . on the contrary, they should and do continually coöperate. But the rather widespread notion that there is no psychology apart from introspection is refuted by the brute argument of accomplished fact. It seems to me that most of the research work that has been done by me or in my laboratory is nearly as independent of introspection as work in physics or zoology." [5]

This is but a single instance of the fact that in America, as at Leipzig, Cattell's approach to psychological problems was marked by independence and directness. Alert to his environment, keenly responsive to it, participating actively

[5] J. McK. Cattell, "The Conceptions and Methods of Psychology," *Popular Science Monthly* (1904), **66,** 176-186.

in the happenings about him, he nevertheless maintained his special interests and his characteristic ways of doing things. As a consequence, the Cattell tradition at Columbia stands for a certain independence, a certain unorthodoxy and latitudinarianism in dealing with psychological material. This does not mean, however, that Cattell encouraged a large vagueness in psychological thought and practice, nor that his personal opinions lacked definiteness or incisiveness. The hushed tales told by former students of his dealings with what he considered lapses from scientific rectitude contain not the slightest suggestion of overgentleness in the face of such transgressions.

It might be added parenthetically that Cattell's influence extends beyond that of his own researches and of his immediate contacts with students—in fact, beyond the borders of psychology. His abilities as an organizer and administrator, together with his interest in clearing the way for the advancement of science in general, have drawn him into executive and editorial work not always directly connected with psychology.

In the next academic generation at Columbia, the first person to rise to prominence was Edward Lee Thorndike. Thorndike's originality asserted itself early. In 1898, when he was twenty-four years old, he published his classical monograph *Animal Intelligence*. This work is important partly because it reported the first systematic study of animal intelligence by means of laboratory experiments, and partly because it led to a theory of learning that played a part of great consequence in subsequent research and theory. In this study Thorndike interprets the behavior of his animals not in terms of ideas, but in terms of the "stamping in" and "stamping out" of neural connections between stimulus and response—the strengthening and fixing of some bonds and the weakening and elimination of others until a pattern of behavior is formed that meets the situation. Strengthening and weakening are explained in terms of two major laws: the law of exercise and the law of effect. According to the first, the more frequently, the more recently, and the more vigorously a bond is exercised, the more effectively it is stamped in; and conversely, the less it is exercised, the more likely it is to be weakened and eventually eliminated. According to the second, the law of effect, responses that lead to satisfying states tend to be retained, and those that lead to annoying ones tend to be eliminated; in other words, the neural connections are influenced by the *effects* of the reaction. The tendency of the theory as a whole is to explain learning mechanistically; and the conception by which it does so is so definite and concrete, and bears so directly on a crucial problem that it has become one of the established points of reference in the actively worked field of learning and intelligence. Thorndike himself extended the theory to human intelligence, which he explained, as he had explained animal learning, in terms of specific bonds of connection between stimulus and response. Later he recognized different dimensions of intelligence, altitude, width, area, and speed, and also different sorts of intelligence, such as abstract, social, and concrete intelligence. Still later, he recognized a principle of "belonging together," over and above mere "togetherness" in time and space.[6]

Thorndike's original conception, it will be observed, has undergone considerable development, but it is still fundamentally a theory of specific bonds. Like the theory of learning with which it is related, his theory of intelligence has been stimulating not only to research, but also to contro-

[6] Thorndike's more recent views on human intelligence and learning may be found in *The Measurement of Intelligence* (1926), *Adult Learning*, with E. O. Bregman, S. W. Tilton, E. Woodyard (1928), and *Human Learning* (1931).

versy. Its most distinguished opponent is Charles Spearman, who upholds the theory [7] that there is a general factor in intelligence in addition to the specific factors. The resulting controversy on the organization of intelligence has been one of the most animated psychology has known and, what is more important, one of the most productive in actual research.

Thorndike has been interested, too, in measurement in education, not from the standpoint of tests of intelligence only, but also from that of measuring the results of education generally. Evidently Thorndike is temperamentally opposed to vagueness and indefiniteness. Any problem that passes through his hands is almost automatically reduced to concrete and quantitative terms. When he became interested in education, therefore, he immediately sought to discover just what and how much was accomplished by the attempt to educate. It seemed obvious to him that the problems involved in individual differences, mental fatigue, learning, and the transfer of training required quantitative and experimental treatment. Even before intelligence tests came into vogue, Thorndike had adopted the practice of measurement in education and had taken his problems into the laboratory. The three volumes of his *Educational Psychology,* published in 1913 and 1914, summarize the results of his early work in this field. But though his method was essentially experimental, both his problems and his temperament led him away from experimental psychology in the conventional sense of the term. Instead of the minute introspections of a few trained observers, he studied the performances of large numbers of subjects, obtaining results that could be tabulated and treated statistically by the experimenter. Thus

[7] C. Spearman, *The Nature of Intelligence and the Principles of Cognition* (1923), and *The Abilities of Man: Their Nature and Measurement* (1927).

under Thorndike's influence, as under Cattell's, the psychological experiment stepped aside from the beaten path, and as a result there grew up not only an altered conception of the psychological experiment but also an atmosphere of positivism and engineering efficiency in educational research. True, the cult of the quantitative in education has not been an unalloyed blessing. It has led, at times, to pieces of research in which the zeal for the quantitative, accompanied by a curious lack of insight into the situation investigated, has expressed itself in a blind and almost militant faith that no factor which is not amenable to existing methods of measurement can possibly be important. But on the whole, education has profited by the attempt to measure its products and thus to substitute exact knowledge for the vague hope that somehow good will be accomplished.

It is hardly necessary to add that in this atmosphere the applications of psychology were not scorned, and that fields other than education were soon invaded. H. L. Hollingworth and A. T. Poffenberger were among the first to work actively in vocational psychology, the psychology of advertising, and the problems of applied psychology in general. Columbia, however, does not stand for applied psychology, as Cornell, for example, stands for pure psychology. It simply recognizes applied psychology, along with pure psychology, as a legitimate field for scientific inquiry.

As a consequence, the psychological scene at Columbia presents a motley aspect, which to any one accustomed to a closer organization must seem casual and even disorderly. Animal psychology, the psychology of tests and measurement, the various kinds of applied psychology, the orthodox and unorthodox varieties of experimental psychology, theoretical discussions of learning, of intelligence, of measurement, and of the bearing of psychology generally—all are represented, and all go their separate ways. The different projects are not always harmonious; they jostle each other— sometimes intentionally—but they all persist. Some of them may appear to the onlooker decidedly less valuable than others, but they all maintain themselves somehow as parts of psychology.

This is the immediate academic background of Woodworth's dynamic psychology; but the system is neither the summing-up of the tendencies in its environment nor the authorized interpretation of psychology in its world. Certainly it is not taught as the official psychology of the university. It is hardly an exaggeration to say that it is not taught at all, that it is simply encountered as one of the many forms in which psychology expresses itself at Columbia. Yet in so far as it takes cognizance of the many trends in psychology, both past and present, and finds something of value in all, dynamic psychology represents the temper of the world of which it is a part, a world where many enterprises are going forward and where none has gained sufficient ascendancy over the others to be able to maintain that its road alone leads to scientific truth.

For Woodworth himself, the road to psychology—or rather, a very important stretch of it—lay through physiology. From the first, he was interested in the phenomena of movement; his doctoral dissertation was entitled *The Accuracy of Voluntary Movement*.[8] It is significant too that his contributions to the imageless-thought controversy were at first incidental to his study of movement; that the attempt to discover the cue to voluntary action first led him to the evidence that the images and sensations required by the orthodox theory of the higher mental processes did not appear in the actual experiences of his subjects. Indeed, his whole approach to this problem is strongly characteristic.

[8] *Psychological Review* (1899), Monograph Supplement.

Like many psychologists, Woodworth tends to think in terms of stimulus and response, but he prefers to begin with the response rather than the stimulus, and then to investigate the conditions antecedent to it. Early in his career, he studied with the English physiologist Sherrington, and the work of Sherrington has deeply influenced his thinking. Woodworth regularly utilizes such concepts as stimulus and response, preparatory and consummatory reactions, facilitation, inhibition, and integration. His psychology is very definitely a psychology of reactions. A knowledge of stimulus-response relations he regards as a "base line that is essential in any accurate survey of the whole field of activity," and he holds this opinion in spite of the criticisms to which the stimulus-response concept has been subjected—criticisms with which, in many cases, he is in entire agreement, and some of which he himself has made. Dynamic psychology, though a psychology of stimulus and response, is by no means a crude translation of stimulus and response into cause and effect.

There are, in fact, three main points which Woodworth believes must always be considered in thinking in terms of stimulus-response connections. The first is that the stimulus is not the cause of the response, but only a part of the cause. The structure of the organism, its stores of energy, the activities going forward, its general condition—all these are involved in determining the response. Even in a machine like a loaded gun, the action is not determined solely by the stimulus (the blow of the trigger); the structure of the gun and its stored energy (the gunpowder) must also be taken into account. In the human organism, as in the loaded gun, a stimulus, corresponding to the blow of the trigger, is necessary to start action; but the nature of the action is determined quite as much by the structure and condition of the organism itself as by the stimulus that initiates it. The organism that intervenes between stimulus and response is never ignored in Woodworth's psychology.

A second point which must be recognized clearly is that no stimulus-response reaction can be considered as an isolated, discrete event. Sometimes the reflex, or some other simple reaction, is treated for convenience as if it were the only event occurring in the nervous system at the time, or at least as if it ran its course entirely uninfluenced· by othe events. Actually, nothing so simple occurs. Any neural event is subject to the influence of the multitude of other neural events that precede and accompany it. No stimulus acts upon an organism in which there is no other stimulation at work. No reaction occurs in an organism in which there is no other activity in progress. Hence psychology must always be on its guard against the specious simplicity of the reflex-arc concept taken in the abstract. Woodworth heartily agrees with the protests [9] against the tendency to consider a reaction-arc apart from its setting, as a discrete event occurring in an otherwise inactive organism.

His third point—and this is one of Woodworth's characteristic criticisms—is that the reaction-arc is not an *indivisible* unit. Not only is the reaction not discrete from its surroundings; its internal unity is not absolute. It can be broken in the middle. According to Woodworth, there is an advantage in thinking in terms of half-arcs, especially in regarding the response or the motor side of the reaction as a convenient unit, and in thinking of each response as evocable by several stimuli and approachable by several paths. Sherrington has shown that even reflexes do not involve a fixed

---

[9] He mentions especially C. S. Sherrington, *The Integrative Action of the Nervous System;* J. Dewey, "The Reflex Arc Concept in Psychology" (see this book, Chapter VI); and L. L. Thurstone, "The Stimulus-Response Fallacy in Psychology," *Psychological Review* (1923), 30, 354-369.

and invariable stimulus-response connection but that each motor reaction has a rather wide receptive field. The scratch reflex, for example, can be elicited by stimulation over a rather large area of the flank. The studies of the conditioned reflex point in the same direction. A response such as salivation, which at first is elicited by a sapid substance on the tongue, can through training be aroused by an associated stimulus such as a blue light. If the original connection were fixed and unalterable, if the reaction-arc were really an inflexible unit, if there were no possibility of making new connections in the middle, such conditioning simply could not occur. Psychology is at fault, therefore, if it attempts to explain complex behavior as a building-up or building-in of complex units of behavior in which complete reaction-arcs figure as units. Woodworth believes that changes are made within the arcs themselves, within the central nervous system rather than at the periphery.

And yet, in spite of the dangers lurking in its neighborhood, Woodworth believes that the stimulus-response concept, when taken with the proper precautions, is the most useful tool psychology can employ for analyzing its material. This does not mean, however, that there is nothing more to psychology than the analysis of behavior into stimulus-response connections. Even if it were possible, in studying a comparatively simple activity like seeing a pin and picking it up, to trace every stimulus-response connection in minute detail from the impinging of light on the retina through all the sensory, neural, muscular, and glandular reactions involved in approaching the pin, bending the body, and stretching out the arm, to the opposition of thumb and forefinger and the straightening of the body, that knowledge would not give psychology all it wants to know. The most detailed knowledge is not necessarily the most complete knowledge. Already, in describing the activity as seeing and picking up a pin, one has left the level of detailed stimulus-response connections. On that level, there are only minute sensory, nervous, muscular, and glandular events, one leading to another, working together in tandems and in teams, facilitating and inhibiting each other. If an observer actually confined himself to that level, he would never know that any one had seen a pin and picked it up.

Or, to use Woodworth's own illustration:

"A chimpanzee, let us say, joins together two sticks of bamboo and uses the jointed pole for reaching a banana. This is a psychological description; much more and finer detail might be added and the description still remain at the psychological level. Now the physiologist may undertake to describe this same series of events, in terms of the action of different muscles, of separate muscle fibers, synapses in localized nerve centers, and so on. He would be describing the same real process—not a 'parallel' process—but his description would employ different concepts and would be, in general, very different from the psychologist's description. It would be much more minute than the psychologist's description, but not necessarily any truer. It would not include the relationships observed by the psychologist, and would not be so useful for purposes of prediction and control, if we wished to know what the chimpanzee would *do* in a given situation." [10]

In other words, some knowledge remains inaccessible when observation is restricted to the most detailed relationships; some knowledge is discoverable only when observations are extended over a wider range. Knowledge of the chemical formula for water, for example, does not exhaust our knowledge of water. The most complete understanding of its chemical composition, of the elements and their relationships, does not acquaint us with such facts as that water quenches thirst, cleanses bodies, falls as rain, flows in rivers, ebbs and

[10] R. S. Woodworth, "Dynamic Psychology," *Psychologies of 1925*, 120.

swells as tides, wears away rock, and turns machinery. Yet these facts about water are as real and as important as the facts of its composition. The tendency to regard the most detailed knowledge as the most fundamental knowledge is in part an illusion. Not that Woodworth objects to detailed analysis or has the slightest tendency to minimize its importance; he does hold, however, for the legitimacy and also for the necessity of observations that deal with other than the most minute relations observable. The science of geology will serve as an illustration. Geology is not a "fundamental" science; it reduces its findings to the terms of other sciences, physics and chemistry. Yet geology discovers facts that physics and chemistry do not disclose. So psychology, though it turns to physiology for a further analysis of its data, brings to light facts that physiology does not reveal—facts, furthermore, which are as real and as important and as self-contained as those which physiology studies.

This means that the subject-matter of psychology cannot be distinguished from that of physiology in terms of the stuff of which it is made. The terms "mental process" and "mental life," as Woodworth uses them, do not refer to an order of events different from that which forms the subject-matter of the physical sciences; the psychologist and the physiologist study "the same real process," not "parallel" processes. With the ultimate nature of this process neither the psychologist nor any other scientist, as a scientist, has any concern. It is enough to say that dynamic psychology is interested in sequences of cause and effect involving relationships wider in range than those studied by physiology and narrower than those studied by sociology.

What Woodworth means by the subject-matter of psychology becomes clearer when he defines his position with reference to the two schools that American psychology habitually contrasts with each other, introspectionism and behaviorism.

The subject-matter of dynamic psychology is neither con-sciousness nor behavior; it includes both. The important point in tracing a causal sequence is to get an unbroken series of events, and in order to do so both the facts of consciousness and the facts of behavior must be taken into account. Through observations of behavior, it is possible to discover both the external stimulus that initiates a reaction and the overt response in which it terminates; but what hap-pens between the two ends of the process is known, at least for the present, largely through introspection.

Toward introspection Woodworth's attitude is one neither of flat rejection nor of enthusiastic acceptance. In this case, as in others, there is little of the all-or-none character in his response. Regarding the simpler kinds of introspection, he entertains no serious doubts. He believes that when a person is asked, "Which of these two colors appears to you the brighter?" the observation is no different, essentially, from the observation of an event in the external world. But the more complex kind of introspection is a different and far more difficult affair. Here the observer is, in effect, required to do two things at once—to go through a mental process and to observe the process at the same time; or, since this is an extremely difficult and perhaps impossible feat, to cap-ture in a quick retrospective glance the content and character of the process he has just completed. Woodworth believes that this kind of introspection is not above suspicion, but he observes that some results have come out with such regularity that they command general assent. There is, for example, the observation that consciousness tends to desert a practised act as the act becomes more habitual, until at last the performance is automatic. Woodworth finds it hard to withhold assent from such findings and believes that "in their hearts even the most extreme behaviorists believe them." Introspection in his eyes is neither infallible nor worthless; what it does accomplish it can accomplish. The experimenter must not expect too much of it; he must not require of it too refined an analysis, and wherever possible, he ought to apply objective checks. Introspection is a method that dynamic psychology accepts as having distinct uses and distinct limitations.

Woodworth accepts introspection, then, as a legitimate method, but not as the distinctive method of psychology. Certainly he does not subscribe to the view that psychology is properly a study of consciousness by the method of introspection. He believes furthermore that this doctrine was not present in experimental psychology in the beginning; that it was not an essential part of the "new" psychology; and that the rôle of the psychologist as a "trained introspectionist" began to be emphasized in the nineties when men like Titchener and Külpe, interested in making a place for psychology among the sciences, were eager to assign it a distinctive method and a field of experience not claimed by any other natural science. But the actual history of psychology, Woodworth believes, gives little support to their point of view. He points out that much of the early work in experimental psychology was not an introspective study of consciousness, and he cites as evidence Fechner's experiments in psychophysics, the reaction-time studies, and the work on memory, practice, individual differences, heredity, mental development, and abnormal conditions. If there is a characteristic method in psychology, Woodworth believes it is the "success measuring device," which consists in the "assignment of a task and the measurement of the success with which the task is performed; with variation of the conditions and observations of the resulting changes in the performance of the task." [11] Whether the process studied is

[11] R. S. Woodworth, *Dynamic Psychology*, 31.

consciousness or behavior, the point is to relate a given performance to its conditions—in other words, to discover the relationships we ordinarily refer to as cause and effect.

With behaviorism Woodworth is distinctly sympathetic, perhaps, on the whole, more so than with introspectionism. Certainly behaviorism fits in with his tendency to consider the movement of the organism and to discover the conditions determining particular movements. But he cannot agree that it is necessary to renounce the introspective method and all its works. He sees the rejection of introspection not as the inevitable outcome of a fundamental incompatibility between the study of consciousness and the study of behavior, but as the consequence of a local feud—of the special set of circumstances in which behaviorism was forced to gain recognition. For so long as psychology was defined as the science of consciousness, the students of animal behavior were by definition not psychologists; and the behaviorists, not content with revising the definition to include their own work, retaliated by asserting that their psychology alone was genuine and that the older psychology was mere pseudoscience.

The ensuing battle was conspicuous, but according to Woodworth, aside from the main line of psychological development. Seeing the problem of psychology as he did, as an attempt to discover cause and effect sequences in mental activities, he regarded both introspectionism and behaviorism as incomplete. Even if it were possible to give an exhaustive description of consciousness, there would be gaps in the knowledge of the workings of the mind, for the reason, if for no other, that consciousness does not accompany all mental events. Similarly behavior considered as a series of motor reactions to external stimuli does not, taken by itself, give a complete account; it leaves out what happens in the organism between the external stimulus and the motor response. Eventually a detailed analysis of the intervening process may be made by physiology, particularly by brain physiology; but in the meantime, much is to be learned by following the activity from beginning to end, using observation of both behavior and consciousness. It would be beside the point, therefore, to define psychology either as the science of consciousness or as that of behavior.

Thus it happens, curiously enough, that dynamic psychology, which is essentially conservative, finds little use for the conventional categories in defining its material. The facts they stand for, when seen from its standpoint, fall into a different perspective. Dynamic psychology is not dualistic. Such phrases as "mental life" and "the workings of the mind" do not refer to some special stuff, different from the material that other natural sciences investigate. They denote such activities as learning, thinking, and feeling, which are, by common consent and without much inquiry into their essential nature, recognized as the subject-matter of psychology. As a matter of fact, Woodworth is not greatly concerned with the definition of psychology; he regards the definition of a science as neither essential to its development nor its proper starting-point. The best definition of a science, he says, is a description of the problems it is actually investigating. The identification rather than the definition of its subject-matter is the actual starting-point of a science, and the material psychology actually works with can be identified without being formally defined.[12] After all, the question

---

[12] To deal with psychological material in this way requires that it be conceived either very abstractly or very concretely. If abstractly, events must be dealt with simply as events, without reference to their content. If concretely, they must be taken as they occur in experience, with as few presuppositions as possible as to their ultimate constitution. The extremes are not so far apart as they seem; both rest on the willingness to ignore, for the purposes of the moment, the deeper questions of what is being dealt with.

dynamic psychology asks concerning its subject-matter is not "What is this?" but "How does it work?"

All this discussion has had to do with the framework of psychology rather than with psychology itself; and it has given far more emphasis to such matters than Woodworth himself usually places there. Woodworth is likely to get down as quickly as possible to what he considers the real business of psychology—to the particular problems its subject-matter presents.

When he takes up his special task of tracing causal sequences in actual behavior, he makes a distinction between two kinds of events, mechanisms and drives. The problem of mechanism is the problem of *how* a thing is done; the problem of drive is the problem of *why* it is done. The action of the baseball pitcher serves as an illustration. "The problem of mechanism is the problem of how he aims, gauges distance and amount of curve and coördinates his movements to produce the desired end. The problem of drive includes such questions as to why he is engaged in this exercise at all, why he pitches better on one day than on another, why he rouses himself more against one batter than another and many similar questions." [13] Or, if the distinction is applied to a machine, the drive is the *power applied,* the steam or electricity or water-power that makes the machine go. The mechanism is that which is *made to go;* it is the structure driven by whatever power is employed.

Thorndike's cats, in their struggles to escape from puzzle-boxes, illustrate both mechanism and drive. Their clawings, scratchings, bitings, and pushings are mechanisms—modes of reaction that the animal has at its disposal when stimulated in certain ways. The drive is hunger. The external stimulus—perhaps a bit of fish outside the cage—does not

[13] R. S. Woodworth, *Dynamic Psychology,* 36-37.

invariably provoke a burst of activity in a cat that, locked inside, sees and smells it. A sated cat may curl up and sleep. The mechanisms are set in motion not only by the external stimulus but also by the internal drive.

The formal reaction-time experiment also illustrates mechanism and drive. Here the mechanism is the finger movement that releases the reaction-key in response to a specified signal, such as a flash of light. The drive is the neuromuscular set toward that movement which is aroused in the subject by the instructions. Here again the external stimulus alone does not produce the response; a flash of light does not regularly lead to a particular finger movement. The drive—in this case a highly artificial affair hardly to be encountered outside the laboratory—is in many respects very different from the thoroughly "natural" state of hunger, yet its relation to the ensuing activity is precisely the same. It creates conditions favorable to the action of the appropriate mechanisms; without its presence, the mechanisms would not operate.

Outside the laboratory, human drives are of far greater complexity, but even a highly complex activity like reading the *Critique of Pure Reason* may be explained in terms of mechanism and drive. Obviously, the reader has acquired the necessary mechanisms, the complicated set of reactions known as reading. The printed page supplies the stimuli and reading is the response. But again the response is not invariably elicited; the mere presence of the *Critique of Pure Reason* does not arouse reading in all literate persons. Once more it is necessary to consider the drive. A person may read the *Critique of Pure Reason* because he is a student with an examination to pass, or because he is a philosopher who wants to adduce new proofs that Kant was wrong, or because he has heard that the book is hard going and wants to see what he can make of it, or because of any one or more of a hundred reasons. He may be moved by ambition, by curiosity, by self-assertion, by interest, by his present mood, or by the total plan of his life-work. The drive that makes him read the *Critique of Pure Reason* may operate through large sections of his life and may determine a wide variety of activities. If it does so, it resembles most human motives, for motives commonly operate over fairly long stretches of time. Behavior comes in lengths, Woodworth says, not in separate stimulus-response bits; the question of drives involves the long-range as well as the short-range activities of life. It brings in the problems of needs and cravings and wishes and purposes, from their simplest and most obvious to their most complex and subtle forms.

Perhaps all this seems somewhat remote from the simple stimulus-response formula with which dynamic psychology started. And yet it is an essential part of Woodworth's thesis that the greatest complexities of human behavior, including motives and purposes, have a place in the regular chain of cause and effect, and especially that they fit into the stimulus-response pattern.

In maintaining this thesis, Woodworth points out first that the distinction between mechanism and drive is not absolute. This point is an important one in his system. It means first of all that the drive is itself a mechanism, a response of the living organism. A drive is not a *deus ex machina,* an inexplicable something that directs the organism from without. It is not even a *deus in machina;* it is part and parcel of the organism itself. A drive may be an organic state like hunger, or fatigue, or euphoria, which predisposes the organism to act in a certain way. It may be a neuro-muscular set like that in the delayed-reaction experiments; [14]

[14] The delayed reaction is a response made after an interval of time has elapsed between the presence of the physical stimulus and the initiation of the overt response. Experimental investigation of this type of

or, if one prefers an illustration from daily life, like that of the runner on his mark, crouched and ready to go at the crack of the pistol. It may also be a set of a much less obvious and peripheral sort—a political ambition or an interest in mathematics—a set which can hardly be maintained by an appropriate bodily posture, but which is nevertheless represented by processes in the organism, among which those in the nerve-centers presumably play the leading rôle. But in every case, the activity itself is a response to a stimulus and is a drive by virtue of its function—by virtue of the fact that it facilitates some mechanisms and inhibits others.

But a mechanism is also a drive. Even when it is most undeniably a mechanism, when it is most patently driven by something else, a mechanism is only relatively passive; its own nature determines the nature of the response. The clawings of a cat driven to escape from a puzzle-box are actions determined in part by the mechanisms at the animal's disposal—by the structure of its bones and muscles and nervous system. Even if human and feline hunger were precisely the same, the behavior of men and cats would differ in the same circumstances, because the sensory, neural, glandular, muscular, and skeletal mechanisms are different in the two species. Furthermore, a mechanism may run on its own drive. Reading-reactions have been cited as mechanisms, but once acquired, they tend to get into action and demand expression on their own account. They may even serve as the drive to other activities, such as buying books, seeking quiet places with good light, or haunting libraries. Woodworth believes that, with the exception of a few simple reflexes, any mechanism may acquire the power to run on its own drive, or may become a drive to other activities.

behavior was initiated and greatly stimulated by a study by W. S. Hunter. "The Delayed Reaction in Animals and Children," *Animal Behavior Monographs* (1913), 2, 1-86.

The business man who is miserable when he retires from business is an excellent illustration. His daily activities have become so thoroughly a part of his being that they demand expression on their own account.

Mechanisms and drives, then, are fundamentally alike in being responses of an organism—an important point in fitting them into the stimulus-response scheme. It will be remembered that, even at the reflex level, Woodworth is cautious about oversimplifying the stimulus-response relation; that he is always on his guard against leaving the organism out of his calculations. His scheme is not simply stimulus-response, but stimulus-organism-response; not S-R, but S-O-R.

The way in which mechanism and drive fit into this pattern may be illustrated by an everyday occurrence like feeling hungry and seeking food. Here the drive is hunger, something that is itself an organic response to a stimulus—or rather to a number of stimuli—and which constitutes a set of the organism toward the particular group of mechanisms involved in eating. But the mechanisms involved in eating do not occur simply because the drive has been aroused, because the organism is hungry; they do not occur unless the stimuli to the specific mechanisms involved in eating are present. Chewing and swallowing movements are not ordinarily made unless there is food in the mouth. Therefore a number of preparatory reactions must first be made to bring the organism into the presence of the stimuli that arouse the consummatory reactions of eating. But each of these preparatory reactions must also fit into the stimulus-response scheme. Suppose that the hungry man walks to the pantry, and opens doors and boxes until he finds something to eat. All these reactions (the mechanisms) are facilitated by hunger (the drive); but the drive alone does not account for his specific activities. Each preparatory reaction requires a stimulus of its own—a floor to walk on, a knob to turn, a door to open. The stimulus-response pattern runs through the whole activity. The drive itself is a response to stimuli; the preparatory and consummatory reactions are responses to stimuli; and all are integrated into a unit of behavior by the persistent action of the drive. Even so simple an occurrence shows a highly elaborate organization, but the whole unit is reducible to responses to stimuli.

This S-O-R scheme is adequate, Woodworth believes, to even the most complex cases of motivation. All motives are either organic states or reactions in progress, and, as such, they facilitate some reactions and inhibit others, just as all going reactions do. His purpose is to show that all human behavior, even in its most complex and subtle forms, can be explained in terms of mechanism and drive.

In undertaking this task, Woodworth directly faces a problem that psychology on the whole has tended to avoid— the problem of why people do the things they do; the problem of motives, of the sources and springs of action. Science, he observes, tends to shy off from the question "Why?" For science has given up trying to account for the ultimate nature of things, and the question "Why?" always leads to another "Why?", whereas the answer to the question "How?" is complete as far as it goes. Psychology accordingly has occupied itself chiefly with problems of mechanics, as opposed to dynamics; with such questions as *how* associations take place, *how* learning progresses, *how* reaction-time is affected by various conditions. But in animal activities, and especially in human behavior, the question *why* certain things are done is so insistently present to common sense that sooner or later it must be observed by science. And Woodworth attempts to show that a recognition of the question "Why?" and of the facts of motive and purpose need not lead the questioner to seek forces outside the world of cause and effect, outside the natural order.

Woodworth, however, was not the person chiefly responsible for raising this question in contemporary psychology. When he gave his lectures on dynamic psychology, the question of the springs of action was already in the air. William McDougall had brought it prominently into the foreground in his *Introduction to Social Psychology*,[15] a book that advocated a theory of instinct which immediately commanded attention.

On the negative side, McDougall's doctrine was an emphatic denial of two notions: the conception of the rational man utilized in conventional social and political theory; and the idea that psychology as it existed—the mechanistic psychology, for instance, which devoted itself to the detailed operations of association—had any contribution to make to the problem of the springs of action. His positive teaching was that the instincts are the great driving forces of human activity. In human beings there are seven primary instincts: flight, pugnacity, curiosity, disgust, parental behavior, self-assertion, and self-abasement. In addition, there are tendencies like gregariousness and imitation, which lack some of the characteristics of primary instincts but which are nevertheless native springs of action. There are also sentiments like loyalty and patriotism, which are complex products of instinct, intellect, and emotion, and which derive whatever motive power they possess from their instinctive components. Each of the primary instincts is paired with a primary emotion, for example, flight with fear, pugnacity with anger. The instinctive and the emotional in human nature are thus intimately connected. The emotion, in a sense, is the unchanging core of instinctive behavior. The perceptual inlets to instinctive action may be changed, the motor response

[15] See especially the first four chapters.

may be altered, but the emotional tone retains its distinctive character.

The most challenging point in McDougall's theory was his insistence that the instincts are the great driving forces of human conduct; that directly or indirectly they are the prime movers of all human activity, not excluding the intellectual; that only at the life-giving touch of the instincts are the human mechanisms stirred to action. Conation—purposive striving toward a goal, purposive striving that is not itself reducible to mechanism—is for McDougall the fundamental category in psychology.

Woodworth is in complete agreement with McDougall's conviction that it is necessary to consider the drives, the urges, the moving agents in human behavior. But he disagrees profoundly with the theory that there is a special set of activities, the instincts, which necessarily furnish the drive for all human behavior; that a few powerful urges constitute the basis of all human activity. It is Woodworth's contention that there is no special class of activities which necessarily furnishes the motive power for behavior; that the distinction between mechanism and drive is purely functional; that any mechanism (with the exception of some of the simple reflexes) is capable of becoming the drive for other mechanisms; and that the drive is itself a mechanism which, only by virtue of its functional relations to other mechanisms, has in turn become their drive. Whereas McDougall regards the instincts as possessed of a unique driving power, Woodworth believes that drives are endowed with no power peculiar to themselves, but that they are mechanisms distinguishable from other mechanisms only in terms of their functional relations.

Woodworth's disagreement with McDougall's theory begins to emerge when, in *Dynamic Psychology,* he gives his inventory of native human reactions. In this book, his general plan, after stating the groundwork of his system, is first to take stock of the human being's unlearned reactions and then to show how, on the basis of this original equipment, the rest of his behavior develops. IIe begins by listing the more detailed processes: the sensitivity of the receptors, the contractility of the muscles, the reflexes, certain coördinations of reflexes, and organic functions such as respiration and digestion. He then goes on to mention broader activities such as emotions and instincts, and though his inventory of the instincts and McDougall's do not coincide exactly, nothing in that fact marks a fundamental disagreement. Even here, however, there is a general characteristic of Woodworth's inventory that is significant. No break occurs in his list between such detailed reactions as swallowing and vocalization, and the powerful impulses that McDougall lists as primary instincts. Instead, there is a gradual increase, from one end of the list to the other, in the complexity and in what might be called the amplitude of the reactions. But when Woodworth includes "native capacities" in his list, relates them to the intellectual side of human nature, and maintains that they too are drives to action, his disagreement with McDougall stands out distinctly and unmistakably.

By native capacities Woodworth means "aptitudes" or "gifts" for making certain responses or for dealing with certain classes of things. A person with a gift for music or for mathematics is peculiarly responsive to special kinds of objects. That these capacities are native, Woodworth concludes from such evidence as that they tend to run in families, that they crop out in individuals separated by a generation or more from other members of the family who possessed the gift, and that some individuals are more responsive than the general run of humanity to training in a particular line and display a stronger interest in such training than is usually aroused. Native capacities differ from instincts in that they are less fully developed, less ready for execution. No matter how gifted a person may be in music or mathematics, he was not born with the mechanisms for excellent performance in either activity. What he was born with is a responsiveness to a certain class of materials that makes him quick and eager and efficient in acquiring the mechanisms for dealing with those materials. Another point that Woodworth makes in regard to native capacities is that they are not particular "faculties," such as perception, or imagination, or reasoning, but responses to particular things or relations. In a gifted person, there are ready responses to particular classes of objects—to musical sounds, or mathematical relationships, for example. Finally, and most significantly, capacities are related to the intellectual side of man's nature rather than to the emotional and conative, and they are, therefore, outside the realm of the instinctive as McDougall describes it.

It is here that the difference between Woodworth's theory and McDougall's becomes most striking. The native capacities, since they are largely intellectual, belong to that side of human nature which McDougall regards as impotent without the instincts, as apparatus that would be inert unless galvanized into life by their powerful driving force. But Woodworth regards these gifts or capacities as sharing, with any other native reaction, the motive power necessary to get into action. He writes:

"This it the chief point at which the present discussion takes issue with McDougall—indeed, disagreement on this point is the chief element of contention in this whole book. The great aim of the book is, that is to say, to attempt to show that any mechanism—except perhaps some of the most rudimentary that give the simple reflexes—once it is aroused, is capable of furnishing its own drive and also of lending drive to other connected mechanisms.

"The question is, whether the mechanisms for the thousand and one things which the human individual has the capacity to do are themselves wholly passive, requiring the drive of these few instincts, or whether each such mechanism can be directly aroused and continue in action without assistance from hunger, sex, self-assertion, curiosity and the rest." [16]

That the major instincts furnish drive for other activities, that one can get increased activity out of a subject by arousing his self-assertive or mastery motive, or his curiosity, Woodworth unhesitatingly admits. But to say that the major instincts may reinforce the exercise of a native gift is quite different from saying that they are the only sources of power by which such activity can be set going. Woodworth believes that the driving power of the instincts cannot account for some of the outstanding characteristics that the exercise of a gift exhibits. For one thing, it does not account for the specialization so noticeable in the gifted; it does not explain, for instance, why a child's mastery motive may be active in one field, that of numbers, and not in another, that of music. Neither does it explain why the mastery motive either remains inactive or can be rationalized away if an attempt is made to put the child on his mettle in some activity that has nothing to do with his special gift. Finally, it does not account for the *absorption* of an individual in a particular activity. To this characteristic Woodworth attaches a great deal of importance, for its presence strongly suggests that the activity is a consummatory reaction. Furthermore, without absorption, without complete attention to the matter in hand, there is no first-rate accomplishment. At the height of performance, any extraneous interest, any consciousness of the mastery motive or of hunger or of sex, is a distraction. A mathematician works best when he is interested in mathematics alone. And yet, if the instincts are the only springs of

[16] R. S. Woodworth, *Dynamic Psychology*, 67.

action, their involvement should facilitate the reaction, and what is more, should be necessary to its exercise. But Woodworth's point is that the activity may go on on its own account; does in fact, go best on its own account. Once started, the performance carries itself along. The motive is not something above or apart from the going activity. It is part and parcel of the activity itself.

This attitude toward the exercise of native capacity is but a special case of Woodworth's attitude toward activity in general. He does not consider it necessary always to call on powerful drives like the instincts to explain the activity of a living organism. The well-fed, well-rested infant, kicking and crowing and waving its arms, does not seem to him to be under the influence of a powerful drive; it seems to be acting because there are stimuli in the environment and in its own body that arouse mechanisms which constitute part of its equipment; and a similar statement may be made of the more highly developed mechanisms, native and acquired. Indeed, any mechanism, with the possible exception of the simpler reflexes, once aroused, not only furnishes its own drive but may also act as a drive to other mechanisms—any mechanism whatever, it should be noted, not only those which are emotional or instinctive.[17] This means that dynamic psychology, as Woodworth uses the term, is not limited to a particular class of psychological activities, but that it includes the whole of psychology. The concepts of mechanism and drive apply to activities like learning, memory, and association, as well as to emotion and instinct. It is highly significant that in one of his papers [18] Woodworth uses the facts of perception to illustrate the principles of

[17] The phrase "dynamic psychology" is sometimes used to denote the affective and conative processes particularly. It should be noted that this is not the sense in which Woodworth uses the term.

[18] R. S. Woodworth, "Dynamic Psychology," *Psychologies of 1925.*

mechanism and drive, and indeed of his whole conception of dynamic psychology.

All this leads again to the statement that there is no absolute difference between mechanism and drive. All human activity is of a piece. The distinction is useful because it makes possible a clear statement of the problems of psychology, particularly the difficult problems of motivation. But the basis of the distinction is functional: a mechanism is a drive if it facilitates or reinforces another mechanism. There is no one set of activities that invariably serve as drives. The same principles are at work in all kinds of behavior. The most complex activities can be explained in terms of the S-O-R pattern. All sorts of responses, not only those related to instinct and emotion, are capable of becoming drives. There is an unbroken continuity from the kind of facilitation and reinforcement observable in spinal reflexes to the most complex and inclusive cases of purpose.

The greater part of *Dynamic Psychology* is an attempt to demonstrate the adequacy of the concept of mechanism and drive to the whole field of human behavior. The approach is genetic. As has been said, Woodworth begins by making an inventory of native reactions as the basis of all subsequent development. He then takes up in succession the problem of learning, or the way in which the individual modifies and extends his native equipment; the problem of control, or how, in a given situation, out of many possible responses some are selected and produced and others discarded or deferred; the problem of originality, or how out of his stock of equipment and modes of reaction the individual produces novel responses; the problems of abnormal behavior, or how in accordance with the same laws that give rise to normal responses abnormal reactions are developed; and the problems of social behavior, or how the complex reactions that rise from, and give rise to, social situations are developed. To Woodworth, the particular problems that come under these headings constitute the real business of psychology, and the consideration of any one of them will show the concepts of dynamic psychology actually at work on psychological material.

His treatment of the topic of learning will serve the purpose of illustration as well as any. Here the problem is to account for the enormous addition that the individual makes to his original equipment through practice and experience. Or perhaps modification is a better word than addition, for the person acquires new reactions through the alteration of his native stimulus-response connections as he responds to the stimuli in the environment.

It should be noted in passing that, according to Woodworth, both heredity and environment are involved. Since learning is a reaction *of* the organism *to* the environment, both the organism and the environment play a part in determining the response. Native behavior may be modified in five ways: a natively given stimulus-response connection may be strengthened and stabilized through exercise; a new stimulus may be attached to a given response in the manner of the conditioned reflex; a new response may be attached to a given stimulus in a similar way; an existing stimulus-response connection may be broken through pain, failure, or negative adaptation, so that the stimulus no longer arouses the response originally attached to it; and a number of separate responses may be supplanted by a single unitary response as in the formation of "higher units" in typewriting—a "higher unit" in this case being the writing of a whole word or phrase in a single coördinated act, instead of striking the letters one by one in a series of single and separate movements.

Several points in this treatment of learning are especially

noteworthy. One of these is the interpretation of the "higher units"—the "word habits" and "phrase habits" of the skilled typist which displace the "letter habits" of the beginner. According to Woodworth, the organism acquires a "higher unit" by making a single unitary response to a plurality of stimuli. The skilled typist writes the word "and" by a single coördinated act, not by simply making more rapidly the three separate movements necessary for striking the letters a, n, and d. Whereas in the beginner each letter requires a separate movement, in the skilled operator the three letters (the plurality of stimuli) arouse the serially organized movements for striking a-n-d (the single unitary response). The important feature of this explanation is its emphasis on *response;* the close association of the formerly distinct movements is explained not in terms of the characteristics of the associated items—such as contiguity in time and space—but in terms of the activity of the organism itself. This, however, is only a special case of the application of the stimulus-response formula, as conceived by dynamic psychology, 'to the facts of association. For it is not only in motor acts that association is explained in terms of response. Activities like perception and memory are similarly interpreted. The perception of a table, for example, is a higher organization of sensory processes—not a mere collection of them—standing in the same relation to the primary sensory responses as do "word habits" to "letter habits." Perception in short is an active response, not something "imprinted on the senses," not a mere collection of sensory elements. It is of special interest that Woodworth calls attention to the fact that the separate items of a perception need not come first —that a printed word, for example, may first be seen as a whole, and the letters analyzed out later. In this respect and in others—in his recognition, for instance, of the wholeness and unity of the higher motor units—he is dealing with some of the facts on which *Gestalt* psychology places great emphasis. But to Woodworth, these facts do not require the thoroughgoing revision of psychology that the *Gestalt* school considers necessary.

Another characteristic of Woodworth's treatment is his insistence that learning is the same in both drives and mechanisms. In anger, for instance, the primitive emotional responses may be attached to new stimuli; they may be detached from the stimuli that originally aroused them; they may be modified in overt expression; or they may be organized into such "higher units" as sentiments of indignation and loyalty. Again mechanisms and drives behave alike. Furthermore, in discussing the relation of drives and learning, Woodworth finds occasion, as he did in his treatment of special capacities or gifts, to emphasize the specificity of drives; to assert again that a particular activity may generate its own drive; to insist that it is not necessary to assume a few major trends or instincts without which the organism cannot be thrown into action. He observes, too, that it is characteristic of the living organism to respond to increased difficulty by increased effort—that activity becomes especially interesting when, though it is within one's abilities, it is not so well under control, not so easy, as to be automatic. It is at this point that the activity becomes interesting for its own sake; in other words, begins to run on its own drive.

The treatment of these topics shows how Woodworth applies the concepts of dynamic psychology to some of the special problems of learning. The other major problems—those involved in control, originality, abnormal behavior, and social behavior—are similarly treated, and in the end the whole field of psychology appears schematically outlined in terms of mechanisms and drives. In his analysis, Woodworth faces some of the more complex problems of human behavior; and throughout he attempts to show that these problems may be adequately dealt with by means of the everyday, working concepts of psychology.

The system, it is plainly apparent, rises to no climax. It offers no novel and revolutionary synthesis, and it leads to no vantage-ground from which the facts of psychology appear in a new and suddenly significant perspective. On the contrary, occupied with the everyday business of the workshop of science, it attempts only to show that a unifying principle has always been present in psychology and has always figured in its achievements. Dynamic psychology, promising nothing but the slow gains of science, remains unpretentious and undramatic to the last.

It is not even involved in the excitement that comes from taking sides on the conventionally opposed alternatives in psychology. Behaviorism and introspectionism, heredity and environment, the part and the whole, freewill and determinism, mechanism and vitalism—on none of these questions does it stand unreservedly for one side or the other. Woodworth has often been criticized on this point. To most people there is something straightforward and satisfying in a statement that comes out flatly for or against a given proposition—perhaps because it reduces the situation to the clear-cut terms of combat. But to Woodworth, the situation is not one of combat. The point is not to achieve a victory but to pursue an enterprise, and the alternatives as they have arranged themselves historically happen not to be pertinent to the enterprise. To take sides would be to abandon his task and to be drawn into the irrelevant. And he does not abandon the task. The refusal to take sides is indeed a necessary consequence of the enterprise he has undertaken and of his whole conception of psychology. Taking as his starting-point the concrete, particular, observable activities of living organisms, he has pledged himself to get as complete an account as possible of the workings of these processes in terms of cause and effect—not to stand through thick and thin for consciousness as opposed to behavior, for heredity as opposed to environment, for vitalism as opposed to mechanism, or for any other hypothesis that is off the main line of his inquiry. It is true that some of the most brilliant achievements of science have been accomplished by the method of combat—by championing a hypothesis against every kind of opposition until it is proved right or wrong, or partly right and partly wrong. But this is only one of the ways in which science wins its successes. Sometimes it gains its victories through the workers who are so interested in the particular problems of a particular class of facts that they deliberately postpone or ignore, for the time, the consideration of the more remote and far-reaching implications of those problems.

Indeed, in his interest in the particular processes he is studying, Woodworth is following the procedure that has always characterized science as contrasted with metaphysics. More often than not, the logically opposed alternatives that have confronted each other through long ages, make their appeal to human interest either directly or indirectly through the metaphysical implications which surround them. But whatever progress science has made has come through deliberately turning its attention away from the problems of the ultimate. For this reason psychology in particular, all the more because it is a young science and was very recently a part of philosophy, is on its guard against metaphysics; so much so, in fact, that a system of psychology may adopt, either deliberately or unintentionally, a metaphysics to justify its dismissal of the problems it considers metaphysical. But Woodworth assumes that a scientist has a right, as a scientist, to follow his problems wherever they lead him in the world of experience, without offering a metaphysical justification for the practice. In this respect his psychology shows more freedom from the domination of metaphysics than do those systems which more vehemently profess their freedom.

Probably this attitude, this interest in the concrete particulars of a new science, also accounts for another characteristic of Woodworth's psychology. His is in no sense a closed system. It is a psychology that, even more than most, recognizes the incompleteness and tentativeness of the science, and imposes no finality and no premature harmony and simplicity on its heterogeneous facts. Consequently, it is not a system that stands out in arresting outlines. It is a system, in fact, in which there is always danger of not seeing the forest for the trees; certainly the attention is repeatedly invited to particular trees and to particular clumps of trees. It is even easy to lose sight of the author's distinctive contributions. Woodworth plainly believes that there is a science of psychology independent of any man's system, a body of knowledge reasonably well established and generally accepted by psychologists, and it is this body of knowledge which is the object of his interest. There is in consequence a particularly close interplay between his own thought and that of psychology in general. The result is that his contributions, even in his own writings, are interwoven with the texture of psychology as a whole; they do not stand out as something apart from it.

Naturally a system of this sort does not serve as a rallying-point either for defense or for attack. Its temper reflects the possibility of the progress of science not by revolt but by growth, not by drastic correction but by the gradual accumulation of knowledge and the emergence of new principles and points of view. Among the many warring systems in the psychology of to-day, this temper, too, has its place. For science often finds itself guided by converging lines of evidence toward neither extreme of a clear-cut alternative but toward a position, not necessarily between them, from which it finds that both have been partly right.

Chapter IX

GESTALT PSYCHOLOGY

IF two lines, not too far apart, are exposed instantaneously and successively at a determined optimal rate, the observer will see not two lines, but a single line moving from the position of the first to that of the second. In the external object, there is neither movement nor continuity; the two lines are stationary and are discrete in time and space. What the observer sees, however, is unmistakably a movement—and what is more, a movement that is visibly present, not merely inferred; something as immediate and actual as anything directly perceived by the senses. Besides, a single change in the external conditions completely alters the character of the perception. If the time-interval is sufficiently reduced, the subject sees simultaneously two motionless lines side by side; if the interval is sufficiently lengthened, he sees first one line, then another, separated by time as well as space.

The attempt to explain these apparently trivial happenings was historically the starting-point of *Gestalt* psychology. The phenomena themselves are commonplace enough; they occur wherever moving pictures are shown. Naturally psychologists had known for some time that the perception of movement presented a problem, but in 1910, Max Wertheimer, working with situations like those described, saw the problem in such a light as to lead him to a radical questioning of the very foundations of the science. He became strongly convinced that the conventional explanations

in terms of sensory elements and their combinations were
grossly inadequate; that whatever the experience of perceived movement might be, it was not a composition of visual
sensations, not a mosaic of parts compounded, blended,
fused, or associated in any way. He was particularly struck
by the fact that the conventional explanations did not do
justice to the psychological datum as it is immediately given;
that they did not take into account the singleness, wholeness,
unjointedness, fluidity, of the immediate experience. To
Wertheimer it seemed that the psychologists who found the
existing explanations satisfactory were blinded by customary
modes of thought; that, starting as a matter of course with
the idea of elementary sensations, they failed to account for
the actual character of the experience before them in their
preoccupation with a theory that had become so habitual as
to be unquestioned. In order to guard himself against a similar error, Wertheimer decided to give the experience he was
investigating a special name. He therefore called the impression of apparent movement the phi phenomenon, partly to
single it out as a unique fact to be explained, and partly to
designate it by a neutral term that did not entangle him in
existing theories.

His problem, furthermore, had physiological implications.
Having questioned the explanation of perception as a sum of
sensations, he also questioned the conception of the corresponding physiological process as a sum of the activities
in discrete neural units. To Wertheimer it seemed that neither
the psychological nor the physiological process, neither the
perception nor the neural excitation, could be conceived as a
mere sum of parts; that the brain-process, like the perception, must be a unified whole, no more an integration of
separate activities of distinct neural units than the perception is a composition of discrete sensations.

Two psychologists who served as subjects in Wertheimer's

study, Wolfgang Köhler and Kurt Koffka, became as convinced as the experimenter that the older psychology was totally inadequate to the facts of the case—and in Germany in 1910, the "older psychology" meant the experimental psychology that bore the Wundtian stamp. The three men were fully aware that in taking this stand they were opposing a powerful academic tradition. They knew that in attacking the practice of explaining psychological phenomena in terms of elements and their combinations, they were striking at the very foundations of the science. Thus *Gestalt* psychology in Germany, like behaviorism in America, rose consciously as a psychology of protest.

The protest was neither mild in character nor limited in scope. The new school demanded nothing short of a complete revision of psychology. The leaders of the movement were quick to see that the problem involved in the phi phenomenon was present in other common cases of perception. For example, we are continually seeing certain objects as rectangular—table-tops, picture-frames, doors and windows, sheets of paper; but only in a really exceptional case is the image projected on the retina actually rectangular. We see a black object in the sunlight as black, and a white object in the shadow as white, even when conditions have been carefully arranged so that physically the same amount of light is reflected from both objects. We see a man as having the same height whether he is five or ten yards away, though in the one case the retinal image is four times as large as in the other. In all these cases, as in the phi phenomenon, and in literally thousands like them, the obvious and almost pictorial difference between the character of the actual perception and that of the local sensory stimulation throws into sharp relief the problem that, in the opinion of the Gestaltists, the old school had utterly failed to meet. And the same instances show with the utmost clearness the dependence of the perception on the totality of the stimulating conditions. Naturally the Gestaltists seized upon cases of this sort to drive home their point that the old explanations had fallen into a disastrous error; that they had failed to take into account the very qualities they purported to explain—the actually perceived motion, the rectangularity, the difference in brightness, the constancy in size. Surely, the Gestaltists maintain, the actual experience in none of these perceptions is immediately given as a collection of elements or as a sum of parts. The perception itself shows a character of totality, a form, a *Gestalt*, which in the very attempt at analysis is destroyed; and this experience, as directly given, sets the problem for psychology. It is this experience that presents the raw data which psychology must explain, and which it must never be content to explain away. To begin with elements is to begin at the wrong end; for elements are products of reflection and abstraction, remotely derived from the immediate experience they are invoked to explain. *Gestalt* psychology attempts to get back to naïve perception, to immediate experience "undebauched by learning"; and it insists that it finds there not assemblages of elements, but unified wholes; not masses of sensations, but trees, clouds, and sky. And this assertion it invites any one to verify simply by opening his eyes and looking at the world about him in his ordinary everyday way.

The *Gestalt*, it is important to notice, is a whole that is not merely the sum of its parts. It is primary to the parts and fundamental to them. The *Gestalt* cannot be conceived as a composition of elements, a statement which the Gestaltists immediately sought to demonstrate by experimental evidence. Their first investigations were in the field of perception, but they soon extended their research into other territory. Learning, memory, insight, and motor reactions were all studied as activities that were not mere integrations of part-activities. The whole subject-matter of psychology was swept into the movement; and the school that started as an attempt to do justice to a particular problem in visual perception ended by demanding a thoroughgoing revision of the fundamental principles of the science. It did not, indeed, stop with psychology itself but extended its principles into the physical sciences.

There is no word in English that exactly corresponds to the German *Gestalt*. Several translations, among them "form," "shape," and "configuration," have been suggested, but none of these has been accepted with whole-hearted approval. "Shape" has been criticized as suggesting a too limited field, the visual. "Configuration" has been used, but very warily, perhaps because its derivation suggests, though rather remotely, a composition of elements that is the very antithesis of the *Gestalt*. "Form" is evidently the least objectionable, and is coming into fairly general use; but in doing so it is taking on new connotations derived from the German *Gestalt*.

According to Köhler, *Gestalt* is used in two ways in German. Sometimes it denotes shape or form as a *property* of things; sometimes it denotes "a concrete individual and characteristic entity, existing as something detached and *having* a shape or form as one of its attributes." [1] Both these uses require some explanation.

As a *property* of things, *Gestalt* is used of such characteristics as squareness or triangularity in geometrical figures, or of the distinctive spatial appearance of concrete objects such as tables, chairs, and trees. It is also applied to the characteristics of temporal sequences like melodies, or of sequences that are both spatial and temporal, like dancing, walking, creeping, or jumping. In this sense, *Gestalt* refers

[1] W. Köhler, *Gestalt Psychology*, 191-194.

to the less specific properties of things, to qualities expressed by such adjectives as "angular" or "symmetrical" as applied to spatial figures; "major" or "minor," to musical phrases; "graceful" or "awkward," to movements like walking or dancing. Such properties, it is important to notice, cannot be present in a "punctiform" experience. They are supralocal; they imply extended wholes of some sort.

In the second sense, as applied to the entity that *has* form, the term *Gestalt* refers to triangles and squares as opposed to triangularity and squareness, and to tables and chairs as opposed to the characteristic forms of those objects. In this sense, *Gestalt* refers to any segregated and circumscribed whole. According to Köhler, there is a tendency to prefer this meaning of the term, since the same underlying process that accounts for the formation of wholes also explains the properties of wholes. Again it must be noted that the application of the term is not limited to the visual field, or even to the sensory field as a whole. Learning, thinking, striving, acting, have all been treated as *Gestalten*. The concept has invaded the whole field of psychology. It has even been extended beyond the borders of psychology. Köhler sees *Gestalten* in biological processes like ontogenesis and in physical processes like the polarization of an electrode. In the evolution of organic structures from undifferentiated protoplasm, and in the patterning of an electric field about positive and negative poles, he finds evidence that physical nature, like psychological experience, is figured and "formed."

Wertheimer's paper [2] on the perception of apparent movement, which was brought out in 1912, was the first publication of the *Gestalt* school and Wertheimer is therefore regarded as its founder. But Köhler and Koffka, both closely associated with the movement from the start, have been no

[2] M. Wertheimer, "Experimentelle Studien über das Sehen von Bewegungen," *Zeitschrift für Psychologie,* 61, 161-265.

less active than he in working out the *Gestalt* concepts and in putting the new school on its feet. Koffka immediately directed his efforts and those of his students to problems in the visual perception of movement. He also applied the principles of *Gestalt* psychology to the problems of mental development. Köhler is probably most widely known in America for the study reported in his book *The Mentality of Apes*. This study was made on the island of Teneriffe, where he had been sent for this investigation by the Prussian Academy, and where he was marooned during the four years of the World War. The conditions on the island were extremely favorable for a thorough study of the nine apes who were his subjects, and a mass of information about their ways was brought to light. But perhaps the outstanding contribution of the study, certainly its most challenging feature from the standpoint of contemporary psychology, was the application of the *Gestalt* concept to the higher mental processes in animals—to the manner in which the apes solved problems, and more particularly to their "insight" into problematical situations. Köhler is known, too, for his extension of the *Gestalt* theory to biology and physics.[3] Besides, both men have been remarkably effective in getting the new views before the English-speaking public. Koffka published several articles in English. One of his papers in particular,[4] a review of the experimental literature of the *Gestalt* school, was noticeably influential in arousing the interest of American psychologists. Indeed, it is largely due to Köhler and Koffka that the present interest in the movement exists in the United States. Both men have lectured in America, and Koffka is at present engaged in research at Smith College. The three

[3] W. Köhler, *Die physischen Gestalten in Ruhe und in stationaren Zustand*, 1920.

[4] K. Koffka, "Perception: an Introduction to the *Gestalt-theorie*," *Psychological Bulletin* (1922), **19**, 531-585.

most widely read books on the subject in America are Koffka's *The Growth of the Mind,* and Köhler's *The Mentality of Apes* and *Gestalt Psychology,* the last-named a general exposition intended for the layman as well as for the professional psychologist.

Naturally the problems that gave rise to the *Gestalt* school had not completely escaped the notice of earlier psychologists. It has, in fact, become something of a fashion to discover anticipations of *Gestalt* psychology in the work of earlier writers—and for that matter, anticipations of behaviorism and psychoanalysis and the rest. It is not at all surprising that such anticipations should have occurred, that the problems directly focused by a given school should have attracted the attention, though sometimes vaguely and peripherally, of other workers in the same field. Anticipations, in a sense, point to the genuineness of the problem itself, to the fact that there is really something there. Besides, quite apart from their significance from this point of view, anticipations of a concept often clarify that concept in the light of similarities and contrasts. Of two of the anticipations of *Gestalt* psychology this is particularly true.

One of them centered about the question of "form-quality" or *Gestaltqualität,* a problem that aroused considerable attention in the latter half of the nineties and even led to the growth of a school of psychology, the Graz school. The idea of form-quality really goes back to 1885, to Ernst Mach's book *The Analysis of Sensations.* Mach's main thesis was that sensation constitutes the basis of all science, both physical and psychological; but in the present connection, the significant point in his teachings is that he recognized *sensations* of space-form and *sensations* of time-form. That is, Mach included among sensations spatial patterns like geo- metrical figures, and temporal patterns like melodies, which are independent, as regards form, of any of the particular sensational qualities, like color and pitch, in which they appear. This idea was developed by von Ehrenfels, who in 1890 gave it the formulation in which it is most widely known. Von Ehrenfels made it clear that there are qualities in experience not accounted for by the properties of the generally recognized sensations. These qualities he called *Gestaltqualitäten* or form-qualities. The stock example is the melody, a temporal form or pattern that is independent of the particular sensational elements of which it is composed. In other words, a melody may be played in different keys, on instruments that differ in timbre, in different intensities of sound, and still remain the same melody, distinctly recognizable through all change. The melody is therefore "transposable"; it is independent of the particular sensations in which it occurs; it may appear in another set in which not one element of the first set is present. The same holds true of spatial pattern. A triangle, like a melody, is "transposable." The lines of which it is composed may be short or long; they may be black or red or blue; and yet the figure remains a triangle. The problem of form is thus definitely presented. Form unquestionably *is*, but *is not* in any of the sensational elements. To von Ehrenfels and to the Graz school, which took up the problem, this meant that form is itself an element, but an element that is not a sensation. It is a new element created by the intellect operating on the sensational elements. The sensational elements are themselves indispensable. Out of them the intellect creates the form. To the Graz school, therefore, form was a new *element,* an element built on the basis of the sensations, a creation by an act of the intellect. The psychologists who adopted this view solved the problem not by discarding elements but by adding a new one, derived in a different way. They differed from the Wundtians not in denying elements, but in adding elements that the Wundtians did not include, and which were produced by mental acts that the Wundtians did not recognize.

Another anticipation of *Gestalt* psychology occurred in William James's protest against elementarism. It is not necessary to dwell on the fact that James regarded the elements of the associationists as artificial abstractions, and that in his insistence that consciousness is a stream, not a train or a mosaic, he emphasized not only the continuity of experience, but also the fact that the continuity is primary. To James, the distinctions are secondary. "Things" are extricated, for partial and practical purposes, from the flux of experience, which is originally "a big, blooming, buzzing confusion." James's conception is thus very different from that of von Ehrenfels. Von Ehrenfels started with elements and ended with new elements; James started with continuity and ended with objects cut out from their context by the practical needs and purposes of life.

With both these interpretations *Gestalt* psychology emphatically disagrees. It disagrees with the Graz school because it is opposed to elementarism entirely. Though quite in accord with the contention that form is essentially different from the generally recognized sensational elements, that it is transposable, and that it cannot be reduced to the elements themselves, *Gestalt* psychology does not solve the problem by adding new elements. It disagrees with James in his belief that things, objects, units of all sorts, are created by being torn out of their context. It believes in wholes, but in *segregated* wholes—in segregated wholes that are there from the first. When we look out upon the world, the Gestaltists say, we see definite objects like trees and stones, and these objects are perceived as distinct from their surroundings as immediately as green is perceived as different from gray.

But these differences of opinion are merely by the way. It is the experimental psychology of the Wundtian sort that the Gestaltists see as their chief enemy, and it was with reference to this enemy that they first announced their independence and formulated their program. They saw in the "meaning theory" of that school an excellent illustration of its vices, and in consequence one of the best ways of understanding the point of view of the Gestaltists is to consider the objections they urge against that theory.

The case of constancy of form in perception will serve the purposes of illustration as well as any single example. As every one knows, a person seated at a rectangular table actually sees the table-top as rectangular, as he also does when he is standing beside it, or looking at it from across the room. But in none of these instances is the retinal image itself a rectangle. It can be demonstrated in the laboratory that the retinal image is, in every one of these cases, an irregular quadrilateral, and that it varies in form with the position of the eye in relation to the table. Psychology, then, has to answer the question: How is the actual perception related to a retinal image so different from itself?

According to the meaning theory, the core of the percept is the mass of sensation corresponding to just this irregular quadrilateral of retinal spots included in the image projected point for point on the retina by the object. But the table-top is not actually seen as an irregular quadrilateral because such visual sensations have been repeatedly associated with other experiences; because the person has learned, through countless occurrences of the same sort, that objects of that apparent shape, situated in just that relation to the eyes, are really rectangular. Eye movements, tactual impressions, gross bodily movements, and hundreds of other happenings have made their contributions. Experience has been heaped upon experience until the separate items have become so intimately interconnected, and so immediately associated with a particular sensory stimulation, that the whole mass is touched off when the central core of sensation is aroused. Still, the whole affair is one of elements and associations. The core of sensation has acquired an elaborate context; that context is meaning; and meaning gives the percept its character.

All this, according to the Gestaltists, is an excellent illustration of what perception is not. Their first objection is directed against the doctrine of elementarism. *Gestalt* psychology takes an unequivocal stand against the idea that elements, as real existences, are the stuff of which a perception or any other psychological experience is made. It flatly denies that elements pieced together, blended, fused, or associated in any way give the perceptions we actually experience. A core of sensations, forming the center of a cluster of images or of any other elementary processes, simply is not what we immediately perceive. Wertheimer used the term "bundle hypothesis" to characterize the theory that experience is a composition of elements; and the Gestaltists directed a large part of their attack, especially in the early stages of their struggle, against that conception. The elements, they have asserted repeatedly, exist only as products of analysis. Instead of appearing immediately as the primitive stuff that makes up experience, they are discovered only after sophisticated reflection, and as the outcome of what is admittedly a special attitude, that of the trained introspectionist. A direct examination of experience does not disclose elements at all—in Köhler's words, "minute local things which nobody ever sees." Besides, the concept of elements is objectionable because it blinds us to the situation as it actually exists. So intent do we become on reducing the perception to its elements that we alter it, destroy it, rob it of its fullness and uniqueness, in the attempt to make it harmonize with a preconceived scheme. Not only does elementarism give us a picture that is false; it gets in the way of our direct observation of what is actually before us.

A second protest, really implied in the first, is directed against associationism. The bonds of connection, like the elements themselves, are unreal. The "bundles" are held together by mere verbal cords, by mere "and-connections," to use another of Wertheimer's phrases. The error of elements has as a necessary consequence the error of associations. If experience is broken into artificial bits, some artificial means must be devised of putting it together again, and bonds of associations are the result. With the denial of elements and association, the meaning theory is of course rejected; or rather when deprived of its content, elements and connections, it inevitably collapses.

Since elements and associations and the bundle hypothesis have been rejected, it is not surprising that the Gestaltists are keenly alive to the dangers of analysis. The intellect, operating upon our experience, can break it into parts; but it does not follow that the experience has therefore actually been made of the parts into which it has been broken. On the contrary, the Gestaltists insist, the product of analysis is not at all the same as the original experience. Analysis alters the datum it sets out to examine; it destroys the very thing that it is the business of science to explain. The total character and uniqueness are lost in dissection, as a muscle is no longer a muscle when it has been sliced into sections to be studied under a microscope. And even if a muscle is less artificially divided, if it is dissected into real or natural parts, into the muscle fibers that can be seen as actual parts of the structure, it ceases to be a muscle. No one would attempt to explain a muscle as derived additively from such parts, artificial or natural, put together in the original order. Yet something very like such an attempt is made by a psychology that explains its material as actually composed of the elements into which it can be broken.

A fourth protest can hardly be formulated apart from the others because it underlies and includes them. This is the attack upon the "constancy hypothesis." According to the *Gestalt* school, the constancy hypothesis pervades psychological thinking without being specifically recognized. It assumes a strict localization in sensory stimulation, a one-to-one relation between peripheral stimulation and the immediate experience. So long as there is a correspondence between the two, it is assumed that there is nothing to explain; and when a discrepancy occurs, an explanation is evolved that preserves the correspondence by some intervening connection.

In *Gestalt Psychology,* Köhler with the utmost care exposes the constancy hypothesis. As delicately as a surgeon probing a critical wound, he dissects the tissue of thought where the constancy hypothesis lies buried. Again the rectangular table may be used as an illustration. This object, as has been said so often, usually looks rectangular, and yet it is entirely possible to see the table-top as the irregular quadrilateral described by the introspectionist. Which of these is the real or true sensory experience? Of course both are real in the sense that both actually occur in experience. Certainly it is possible to see the table either as common sense sees it, or as the trained introspectionist sees it. But which is more real? Which is the true psychological experience? The question might almost be put: Which is real and which is illusory?

According to the trained introspectionist, the true sensory experience is that which he arrives at by means of his special attitude: the core of sensation to which the secondary contributions of meaning adhere. But surely, Köhler points out, from the standpoint of common sense it is precisely such experiences that are exceptional. We see the table as rectangular literally thousands of times to the one time we see it as an irregular quadrilateral, and these thousands of experiences are the ones we actually use in our dealings with tables. Besides, the introspectionist's table is secondary in the sense that it is derived from the perception which immediately and spontaneously occurs, from the kind of experience that common sense and science alike must take as their starting-point. Not that common sense objects to the meaning theory. On the contrary, it accepts it at once as entirely reasonable. It even suggests it itself when confronted with the facts. Common sense is not at all surprised that the explanation should take this form; it is surprised only that there is so great a difference between the everyday experiences it knows so well and the character of the "true" sensory stimulation that underlies them.

This surprise Köhler considers extremely significant. Evidently it is very natural to suppose that there is a one-to-one correspondence between the immediate experience and the peripheral stimulation—so natural that when a difference between the two is demonstrated, an explanation is immediately sought that restores the correspondence. It is this tendency which expresses itself as the constancy hypothesis; and, rooted as it is in a basic disposition in our thinking, the constancy hypothesis has been taken for granted. It exists in psychology as an untested assumption, and to find an untested assumption at the basis of a science is to uncover a scientific scandal.

There is really no evidence, Köhler insists, at least in the vast majority of cases, that the experiences explained by the meaning theory occur because they have actually acquired meaning. True, there are a few cases where it is possible to show that meaning has been added to some central core.

The symbol + undeniably looks like "plus," and this fact is clearly due to learning. But cases of this sort are not the rule. The meaning theory has never been demonstrated of the thousand and one perceptions in everyday life to which it is unhesitatingly applied. An enormous amount of learning would have to take place, if the meaning theory were true, before a complex object like the human face could be recognized as the same from all points of view and in all possible conditions of light and shade; yet the human face is one of the first objects the infant shows signs of recognizing. And this is but one illustration among many. The meaning theory has been accepted not because it is supported by evidence but because no need for evidence has been felt.

But when this situation is presented to the introspectionist, he is almost certain to show signs of resentment; and, to Köhler, the resentment of introspectionism is as significant as the surprise of common sense. Both mean that the foundations of conviction have been touched. Traditional psychology has accepted the meaning theory with all its implications simply because it is based on a very natural tendency in human thinking, a tendency which, when made explicit, is formulated as the constancy hypothesis. That hypothesis itself has been accepted without being questioned —even without being recognized—and the whole superstructure that has been erected upon it rests upon a foundation which has never been tested.

A fifth objection that *Gestalt* psychology urges against its rivals is directed against their physiology. It is, in a sense, an objection to the application of the constancy hypothesis to the activity of the nervous system. For along with elementarism, associationism, the meaning theory, and the constancy hypothesis, there goes the conception that treats the nervous system as a complicated mechanism of separate conductors. According to this theory, neural currents run from definitely localized points of stimulation in the sense-organs to particular organs of response, along definite pathways in the nervous system in which the lines of conduction are fixed and determined throughout. In other words, the nervous system is conceived on the analogy of a man-made machine with "rigid arrangements"—the phrase is Köhler's—in which each part is capable of only one kind of action. This conception is admirably suited to a psychology that deals with elements and associations, which expounds the meaning theory, and which assumes the constancy hypothesis. The Gestaltists quite naturally discard it along with the psychological theories it accompanies. The physiological explanations that the Gestaltists propose to substitute can best be considered after their positive teachings have been more completely presented.

But before proceeding to these positive teachings, it is well to note that the objections just discussed are, appropriately enough, all interrelated; that they are all parts of the one great and primary objection to the practice of explaining psychological experience piecemeal. They are parts of a protest that is more than their sum, a protest which must be recognized as of the utmost importance in *Gestalt* psychology. For much of the character of the *Gestalt* movement, certainly in its early years, was determined by the fact that it was proclaiming a revolution. Its first task was to expose the inadequacies of existing psychology, and the marks of insurgency were strong upon it. At almost exactly the same time that behaviorism sounded its challenge in America, *Gestalt* psychology rose against the established tradition in Germany. Like behaviorism, it had a genuine fight on its hands in making its way against the solid strength of an entrenched tradition. And just as behaviorism defined its position very largely in terms of what it opposed,

Gestalt psychology struck the key-note of its campaign by declaring that it was against the established order. Its program included the posting of a proscription list, and at the top of the list were elementarism, associationism, the constancy hypothesis, the meaning theory, the reliance on analysis, and the conception of the nervous system as a mechanism of rigid arrangements in which definite and fixed pathways connect definite and fixed points.

It is evident, however, from this mere list of protests that *Gestalt* psychology does not come with the appearance of plain, practical, common-sense directness that has given behaviorism much of its popularity. The man in the street understands at once what it means to regard the human being as a machine, and what it means to make it a better machine by a better adjustment of its parts. He needs only to use the habits of thought already in his possession, after discarding those which deal with consciousness. But *Gestalt* psychology can resort to no such simple measures. Though it calls psychology back to ordinary experience, to the plain observations of everyday life, it immediately begins inquiring why that experience is what it is, and thus steps out of the plane of common sense in its attempt to comprehend and explain it. It is true that behaviorists and Gestaltists alike start with the world as it appears to ordinary observation, not as it appears to the trained introspectionist. Both call psychology back to the familiar level of common sense, to the world of ordinary perception. The difference is that *Gestalt* psychology begins to examine and explain it, behaviorism to manipulate and operate upon it. Consequently *Gestalt* psychology is more likely than behaviorism to plunge the reader into the unfamiliar technicalities of a laboratory problem—into unfamiliar technicalities, it is to be noted, for behaviorism too has its characteristic techniques and is as insistent as *Gestalt* psychology on laboratory research. The

Gestaltists, for example, are enormously interested in problems of perception, and if there is anything the average person takes for granted it is the objects he sees and the sounds he hears. The problem of how and why these commonplace things appear as they do strikes him as either abstruse or foolish. Certainly the procedures of the behaviorist seem more practical and more intelligible. Even when he deals with problems of perception, the behaviorist proceeds in a way that immediately commends itself to common sense. If he wants to know by what sense-organs (or receptors) a rat finds its way through a maze, he deprives rats of their receptors, set by set, and in various combinations, and notes in each case how the performance is affected. If he wants to know whether a certain part of the brain is involved in seeing, he removes or impairs that part and finds out what happens. He does not, like the Gestaltist, occupy himself with subtle phases of human perception in slightly varied conditions that seem to the practical man to make no difference in the world. Besides, *Gestalt* psychology has an awareness of epistemology that behaviorism considers it a virtue to lack. Behaviorism solves its epistemological problems by crashing through them, assuming the realism of common sense. But *Gestalt* psychology picks its way deliberately through the mazes of epistemology, giving reasons for the faith that is in it. It exercises considerable care in establishing its right to its position; or rather, in showing that, from the standpoint of epistemology, its position is no worse than that of the physical sciences.[5] Finally, the fact that *Gestalt* psychology asks the reader to discard his old habit of thinking in terms of part joined to part, leaves him

[5] It is interesting to note that in Germany *Gestalt* psychology has frequently been criticized for its lack of epistemological sophistication, in the United States for a too serious concern with epistemological problems.

with the sense of bewilderment that naturally follows a change of old ways of doing things. In this respect especially, *Gestalt* psychology demands a change that is probably more fundamental and intimate than anything suggested by behaviorism. It demands an alteration in ways of perceiving and conceiving. The radicalism of behaviorism is chiefly practical and moral, but the *Gestalt* view requires an intellectual readjustment. And demanding, as it does, a change in habitual modes of thought, *Gestalt* psychology lacks the immediate intelligibility of a conception that simply requires a new and striking rearrangement of old ways of thinking.

When the Gestaltists present the positive side of their case, they again appeal to immediate experience, to the world as it is given in ordinary perception.

Any one who looks at the world about him, the Gestaltists declare, will see in the visual field a number of objects, perhaps tables and chairs and windows and doors, perhaps trees and stones and water and clouds. But in any case he will see *objects,* and there are two implications in this simple fact. The first is that he does not see clusters of sensations, but unified wholes. The second is that the wholes are separate and distinct from a background. They are not only wholes, but segregated wholes.

The same facts may be demonstrated in even simpler terms, where the units are not objects as the word is ordinarily used.[6] An example is the arrangement of lines in Figure 1.

[6] The following drawings have been adapted from figures used in Wertheimer's "Untersuchungen zur Lehre von der Gestalt," *Psychologische Forschung* (1923), **4**, 301-350, and also used by Köhler in "Some Tasks of Gestalt Psychology," *Psychologies of 1930*, 143-160. The discussion in the text, though based on the accounts of Wertheimer and Köhler, does not purport to be a condensed reproduction of their expositions. It has been modified to suit the purposes of the present book.

FIGURE 1

Here the observer, spontaneously and without suggestion, sees the lines in groups of two; but whether the grouping is determined by spatial nearness or by the property of in-closing space cannot be determined from this single case. There is no question, however, that the tendency to form groups, and just these groups, is very strong. If the observer tries to form other groups, he discovers how strong a tendency is working against him. It is fairly easy to form a single pair of two of the more distant lines, but most people find it impossible actually to *see* this grouping over the entire field.

It can easily be shown that such grouping is closely related to the perception of wholes and of objects. If other lines are added, as in Figure 2, the phenomenon of grouping becomes more pronounced. The groups stand out more

FIGURE 2

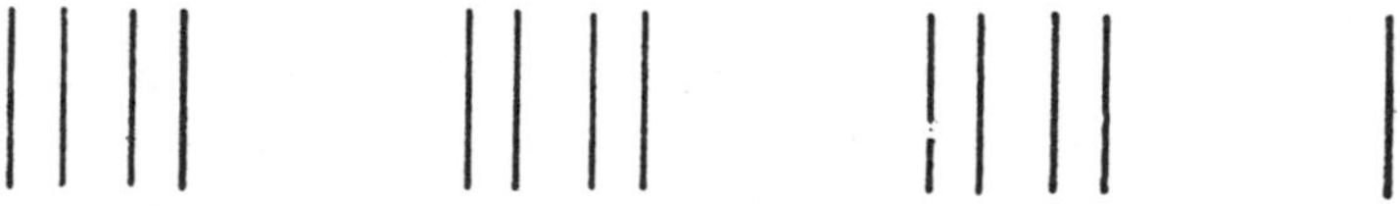

distinctly as units. If the spaces are so completely filled with lines that the shading is continuous, as in Figure 3, there is no question that the shaded areas are units; and if the rectangles they form are projected forward so that they become solids, they at once become objects in the common meaning of the term.

FIGURE 3

FIGURE 3

But suppose that Figure 1 is altered not by filling in the spaces, but by adding horizontal lines as in Figure 4.

FIGURE 4

The perception is now changed. There is a distinct tendency to treat as units the wider spaces, bounded by the more distant pairs of lines, and to see the brackets that face each other as forming rectangles. This phenomenon illustrates the principle of "closure." Not only is there a tendency to "form" in our reactions, but the tendency is so strong that when the external situation is incompletely "formed," the psychological reaction tends to complete it. "Closure" is a special case of the "law of pregnancy," according to which experience, whether spatial or temporal, and whatever the sensory department, tends to assume the best possible form, so that forms tend to become more precise and more sharply defined—to become more completely, more typically, what they are.

Figure 4 also illustrates another fact. It shows that the formation of wholes is not an affair of a single set of factors. In this case, both spatial nearness and the property of inclosing space are involved. For most people, the tendency to form inclosed spaces is dominant, in this situation, over spatial nearness. That it is not invariably dominant, however, is shown by the fact that it is possible to see three groups of figures like the following] [. Figure 5 shows an arrangement where still another factor determines the grouping. Here neither spatial nearness nor inclosed space is decisive; the groups are determined by the qualitative similarity of their members.

FIGURE 5

} } } o o o } } } o o o } } } o o o } } }

Plainly perception is fluid and plastic, and the conditions that determine the formation of groups are varied.

Any of the arrangements presented in these five figures illustrates another fact noted by *Gestalt* psychology, that of figure and ground. Even in Figure 1 the pairs of lines with their inclosed spaces are figures as contrasted with the rest of the space, which is background. The phenomenon becomes more pronounced as the grouping becomes more stable, and it is most noticeable of all in complete forms like the rectangles in Figure 3. In some patterns, figure and ground are reversible—a fact that is illustrated by many decorative designs. Often the total effect is very different when figure and ground are interchanged. Figure and ground show characteristic differences. Figure looks more solid; it "stands out." Ground is simply empty space. Only figure is "formed." For example, in Figure 3 the rectangles are seen as forms, and the background as mere expanse. The background is not seen as a plane surface with rectangles cut out of it, as is geometrically possible.

Groups loose and stable, figures complete and incomplete, geometrical forms and solid objects—all are *Gestalten;* and even these very simple cases show the principles that underlie experience. Fundamentally, there is the tendency for experience to be "formed"; for members to fall into groups; for incomplete figures to be completed and made more definite and precise; for the total field to be organized—one might almost say stratified—into figure and ground. It is as if a process were working toward a state of equilibrium, a state in which forms reach the maximum of stability and in which the total organization is most complete. The process is not one involving the composition of elements. The forms that appear cannot be explained in terms of bit added to bit. The fact that two lines are seen as a pair cannot be explained by taking the lines singly nor by analyzing them into parts. It is the disposition of the total field that determines that they shall be seen in twos. That the total configuration determines the experience can most readily be seen when the addition or alteration of a single part changes the character of the whole perception. *Gestalten* are not rigid structures composed of rigid units; they show different degrees of stability. It is this kind of experience which psychology must explain—not elements juxtaposed in time and space, but experience in which "formed" wholes appear and tend to appear.

Perhaps it seems forced to draw so much doctrine out of a few lines and figures. But *Gestalt* psychology, it must be remembered, is always on guard against the meaning theory, and in using illustrations as clear of meaning as possible, it is avoiding the criticism that its materials exhibit the characteristics they possess because meaning has first given them those characteristics. The common objects of life are loaded with meaning as simple lines and spaces are not. Besides, the Gestaltists, having exhibited their principles in this meaningless medium, are never at a loss to show that

the same principles are at work in everyday experience.[7]
Any object is a segregated whole. It is not a collection of
parts, not an indistinguishable portion of an undifferentiated
continuity; it is a unit and discrete and it is immediately
sensed as such. Any object with its background shows figure and ground, and in some cases the characteristic differences between figure and ground are particularly striking.
Köhler points out that the sky visible between the buildings
in a street is ordinarily not seen as "formed." Yet with the
definite outlines that surround it, the sky might perfectly well
constitute a "figure" geometrically, though psychologically it
rarely does so. Commonly the buildings are seen as forms, the
sky as background. A maritime chart, too, shows the importance of figure and ground. Most people, when first looking
at such a chart of the Mediterranean Sea, do not recognize it
as the Mediterranean. The outline is, of course, exactly the
same as that given on a land map; but it is not recognized
because, in the maritime chart, the sea is presented as the
form, not as mere background as in the ordinary land maps
of the Mediterranean world. Here the reversal of figure
and ground so completely alters the perception that a familiar outline is not recognized. The *Gestalt* psychologists
are interested, too, in cases of embedded form, such as those
found in puzzle-pictures in which a dog, a doll, or any common object is to be discovered somewhere in the drawing.
In the eyes of the Gestaltists, these embedded forms show
the triumph of the immediate sensory organization over
meaning; for such forms have all that the meaning theory
requires, and yet they are not immediately recognized. They
have outlines repeatedly given in experience; they have acquired a mass of associations; yet in the given situation they
are lost.

[7] Most of the illustrations that follow are taken from Köhler's *Gestalt
Psychology* and Koffka's *The Growth of the Mind.*

Grouping, too, is shown in countless ways in everyday life. It is not necessary to specify the many cases in which the grouping of common objects follows the principles shown in the figures illustrated—relative distance, the inclosing of space, the completion of suggested forms, and so on. Grouping may occur in more subtle and yet no less real ways. If three men are engaged in an argument, two against one, the two will be seen as one group and the third as a unit separate from them. The activity of debate may determine the perception of the whole scene, and may be dominant over other conditions such as spatial nearness or similarity in race or age.

The formation of a *Gestalt* that is both temporal and spatial is illustrated by the patterning of experience which occurs when one is getting acquainted with a city never before visited. Not even the first landmark is seen by itself but appears in relation to a vague extent. Soon a few other landmarks stand out, a few localities become distinct, and gradually the whole field gains in distinctness and articulation until a definite organization is attained.

Most of these examples involve visual perception, but *Gestalten,* of course, are not limited to the visual field. A simple pattern of taps, — — $\underline{/}$ — — — $\underline{/}$ — — — $\underline{/}$ — —, illustrates in the auditory realm several of the principles just discussed: the phenomenon of grouping, in that the sets of threes are heard as segregated wholes; the phenomenon of figure and ground, in that the groups of taps are the figures and the intervals of silence the ground; the phenomenon of "closure," in that there is a tendency to add a tap to the last group to make a complete whole. Incidentally, the translation of the visual pattern to the auditory field, a translation that is made without the slightest difficulty, illustrates the "transposability" of the form and demonstrates its independence of any particular set of elements.

Koffka's work on mental development gives some very significant illustrations of *Gestalten* not primarily perceptual. The reflexes involved in eye movements, for example, are explained not in terms of end-to-end neural connections, as in the typical reflex-arc scheme, but as activities in a single physical system in which special structures, like the retinas and muscles, are not independent pieces of apparatus, but members of a whole in which all the parts are intimately related and responsive to each other, and in which no part is uninfluenced by what is going on elsewhere. Instincts, too, are *Gestalten*. An instinctive action, Koffka insists, is not a chain of reflexes, not a mere succession of part-activities, but a continuous process, a unified whole in which every part-activity is determined not only by its immediate predecessor, but also by the total activity and by every phase of the total activity—particularly by the nature of the act that terminates the process. One of the conspicuous characteristics of instinct, its tendency toward an end or goal, gives a particularly good illustration of "closure" in a temporal *Gestalt*.

Köhler's studies of apes show that *Gestalten* occur in the process of solving problems. The solving of a problem, Köhler finds to be a continuous action—not at all like Thorndike's stamping in and stamping out of definite, preëxisting bonds,[8] but an activity directed toward an end, an activity that is a continuous whole, and one in which every part-activity falls into place in the total pattern that alone gives it significance. This fact is apparent from the animal's overt behavior. In genuine problem-solving, the bodily movements themselves form a temporal sequence that definitely shows continuity, direction toward a goal, and closure. But even

[8] A criticism of Thorndike's theory of learning representative of the *Gestalt* point of view may be found in Koffka's *The Growth of the Mind*, 163-174.

more important is the fact that the crucial point in the solution of the problem, the "insight" into the situation, is also
conceived as the formation of a *Gestalt*. Insight is a patterning of the perceptual field in such a way that the significant
relations are apparent; it is the formation of a *Gestalt* in
which the relevant factors fall into place with respect to the
whole. To put the matter more specifically, an animal has
insight into his problem when he perceives a box as something that he can climb upon, and which he can place under
the fruit that is suspended out of reach; or when, happening
to place two sticks in line with one another, he sees them
joined to make a single stick long enough to procure the
fruit that either stick alone is too short to reach.

Finally, *Gestalten* are found in processes outside the psychological field altogether. In biology, the process of ontogenesis shows striking examples. Here the orderly development of definite organic structures from the primitive
germ-layers gives both spatial and temporal *Gestalten* remarkably similar to those found in psychology. They show
the same orderly sequence, the same continuity, the same
progress toward a given end, the same relation of particular
processes to the whole in which they are involved. Physics,
too, shows *Gestalten*. Every one knows that oil and water
do not mix, and every one who has seen the two substances
remain distinct from each other has seen the formation of
physical *Gestalten*, in this case through the interaction of
physical forces at the boundaries of the two liquids. Another
illustration shows even more strikingly the formation of a
physical *Gestalt*. If a loop of silk thread is thrown upon a
soap-film so lightly that the film is unbroken, and if the
area enclosed by the loop is pricked with a pin, the resulting
hole will take the form of a circle, no matter what the original shape of the loop. Here a regular form is invariably
brought about through the interaction of the physical forces

set going by the pin-prick. The whole solar system, indeed,
may be regarded as a *Gestalt,* no part of which is independent of the whole or of any other part, and the whole of
which shows in both temporal and spatial patterning a high
degree of organization that is maintained by the interaction
of physical forces. And in all these cases, in the solar system
as in the punctured soap-film, in the growth of the organs
of the body as in the unmixed oil and water, the process is
ordered and the form achieved without any visible machinery
for doing so—without any of the special arrangements of
mechanical structures that we see in man-made machines.

Without special arrangements, it must be particularly
noted. The phrase is important because it gives the clue
to the explanatory principles which the Gestaltists propose
to substitute for those they discard. *Gestalt* psychology is at
pains to show that physical *Gestalten* may be accounted for
through the interaction of physical forces themselves, that
the rigid structures which characterize man-made machines
are not essential. The rejection of mechanism is usually
thought of as implying an acceptance of vitalism; but *Gestalt*
psychology, it is expressly stated, is as much opposed to
vitalism as to mechanism. Both mechanism and vitalism ignore the field of dynamics, the department of physics that
studies the interaction of physical forces themselves; and it
is in this field of physical science that *Gestalt* psychology
finds the possibility of explaining its phenomena. A physical
explanation, the Gestaltists point out, is not necessarily a
mechanical explanation; a non-mechanical explanation is not
necessarily a mystical explanation. A psychology that cannot
accept the old notion of the nervous system as a machine—
as an arrangement of fixed conduction units—is not driven
out of the natural sciences in search of an explanation. It
has the whole field of dynamics at its disposal.

In the machines that men make there are two sets of factors involved; the forces which make them go, and the special arrangements which make them go in a particular way. In the steam-engine, the force is the pressure exerted by the steam; the special arrangements are the cylinder and the piston that fits into the cylinder. The steam-engine is typical of man-made machines in that the force is guided by rigid arrangements which make action possible in only *one* direction.

Human beings are likely to think that the forces of nature —the "blind" forces, they call them—if left to themselves produce only chaos and destruction. Reasoning on the analogy of their own machines, they assume that if natural forces are to produce any kind of order, they must be directed along fixed lines marked out by special arrangements. Men find it hard to believe that the forces of nature interacting upon each other can, in and by themselves, produce harmony and order.

And yet man-made machines are only a special case of physical systems in general. In all physical systems there are two sets of factors: the forces themselves, and those properties of the system which may be called the constant conditions of its action. Rigid arrangements such as those found in a machine are but a special class of constant conditions; and in the physical systems actually found in nature, there is an enormous variation in the relative influence of the actual forces and the constant conditions. Sometimes the one predominates, sometimes the other. Man-made machines are a limiting case in which the rigid arrangements are tremendously important because they exclude all possibilities of action but one. In contrast, there is the order of the solar system, which is maintained by the interaction of physical forces; here there are no rigid arrangements—no "crystal spheres" like those of Aristotelian astronomy, no structures at all, in fact—to keep the planets in their courses. And when two atoms unite in the formation of a single molecule, they form an orderly whole, again without special arrangements, through dynamical interaction alone.

Corresponding to the machine theory is the conception of the nervous system as a set of isolated conductors by means of which neural impulses are conveyed from definite point to definite point along fixed pathways. A system so conceived is obviously an affair of special arrangements; and as in man-made machines, the special arrangements—particular fiber-tracts, particular nerve-centers, and the like—are the decisive factors. It is this conception which the Gestaltists oppose. *Gestalt* psychology maintains that the experience which observation reveals, patterned, plastic, and "formed" as it is, cannot be obtained from such rigid arrangements; in the interplay of physical forces themselves, rather than in machine-like structures that exclude all possibilities but one, it sees the clue to the situation. *Gestalt* psychology assumes in the nervous system an interplay of forces analogous to the kind of dynamical interaction which, without special structures to restrict its paths of action, produces organization in the atom and in the solar system. The Gestaltist does not think in terms of systems of fibers connecting particular sensory areas with particular motor organs through fixed pathways in the central nervous system. He believes that no matter how elaborate and numerous the possibilities of connection become, they are inadequate to explain experience as it is. He thinks rather in terms of patterns of shifting stresses and strains like those which make the hole in the soap-film a circle. The nervous system, he insists, or rather the nervous system and its appendages, must be taken as a whole. What happens on the retina, for example, can never be considered in and by itself; for the retina is simply one of the surfaces of the nervous system, and anything that happens there influences and is influenced by the total course of events in the

nervous system. It is highly significant that the formation of
Gestalten in immediate experience is determined by factors
like relative distance and the relations of qualitative properties—as is demonstrated in the simplest terms by the pairs
of lines and other figures given earlier in the chapter; for
it is just such factors that physics finds to be decisive in
the interplay of forces. To the Gestaltists the conception of
nervous action in terms of dynamical interaction seems not
only to be demanded by the character of immediate experience but also to be supported by the facts of the physical
sciences. The details of the conception have not been worked
out, but the contrast between a theory of dynamical interaction and one of machinelike arrangements is clear and unmistakable.[9]

Possibly all this seems overambitious. Surely the Gestaltists have gone fast and far. Beginning with particular phenomena in perception, they have extended their concepts
throughout the whole field of psychology and even beyond
into biology and physics. The question inevitably arises: Is
there any evidence to support these speculations?

No one could be more soberly aware of the pertinence of
this question than the Gestaltists themselves, for however
zealously they present their case, their school is not one that
spends itself in exposition and argument. Taking its rise in
an experimental study, *Gestalt* psychology has never claimed
that its problems can be settled in any other way than by
an appeal to scientific evidence. From the first the Gestaltists
have applied themselves assiduously to experimentation.
Some of their most important research has been in percep-

[9] The theory just outlined is a brief report of Köhler's account in
Gestalt Psychology, Chap. IV. Wertheimer likewise opposed the old
theory, substituting one of cortical short-circuiting.

tion, and, unfortunately from the standpoint of exposition, much of this work has been rather technical. But one experiment in perception, which is as simple in technique as it is characteristic in general method, will illustrate the mode of attack.

Köhler, experimenting with hens, trained them to take grains from a paper of a certain gray. Two shades of gray were used, on both of which grains were scattered. When the hens took grains from the darker gray they were permitted to swallow them; when they pecked at grains on the lighter gray they were driven away. Sometimes the darker gray was to the right of the lighter shade, sometimes to the left. Eventually the hens learned to take the grain from the darker gray.

This part of the experiment was merely preparatory. A test series followed that put the crucial question. Again grains were scattered on papers of two different shades of gray, but the gray that had been the darker of the two in the preliminary series was the lighter of the two in the test series. If the hens now pecked from this paper, they would be reacting to a specific element, to a particular gray; if they sought food on the darker gray, they would be reacting to a total situation, to a relation, to the darker side of a pattern. The hens answered the question by pecking, as a rule, at grains on the darker of the two grays, not on the particular gray to which they had learned to respond in the training series. Their behavior was a response to relative brightness. This account gives only the barest outline of the experiment and does not do justice either to the manner in which the conditions were systematically varied and controlled or to the consideration given to subsidiary problems. It does show, however, the general plan that is typical of many of the experiments in perception. Conditions are arranged in which it is possible to react either to a particular element or to the total *Gestalt,* and the reactions of the subjects decide in favor of one of the alternatives.

Following the šame general plan, experiments on recognition have been undertaken to determine whether a particular element or the total situation is decisive. In memory in general, the *Gestalt* school has tried to show, both by its own experiments and by the reinterpretation of the older studies, that the total organization, rather than specific associations between particular elements, determines whether a given content is reiained and reproduced. Köhler's work on apes is the classic experiment on the higher processes involving insight. Kurt Lewin has contributed studies on action and behavior. The concept of figure and ground, which the Gestaltists have adopted, grew out of the work of Edgar Rubin. From first to last, active research has always played an important part in the program of the *Gestalt* school.

It is significant, furthermore, that the Gestaltists have found evidence corroborative of their theories outside the field of psychology itself. American psychologists have been especially interested in the fact that some of the recent work in biology—work undertaken quite independently of the *Gestalt* school and with no reference whatever to its teachings— has given results in line with its theories. The work of Child, for instance, indicates that the establishment of a physiological gradient is of the utmost importance in determining the pattern of the developing organism; that the pattern may be altered by altering the gradient. This means, to use the terminology of the Gestaltists, that the development of the organism is a matter of shifting stresses and strains—of dynamical interaction rather than of rigid arrangements. The work of Coghill touches the problems of psychology even more directly. Studying the motor behavior of developing organisms as correlated with neural growth, Coghill discovered in amblystoma that movements of the entire body appeared first, and that precise and restricted movements like reflexes came later, the more restricted movements being differentiated out of the larger movements in the course of development. Minkowski and others found indications of the same course of development in the human fetus. By examining the reactions of aborted fetuses, they discovered that the activity of the smaller and younger specimens is diffuse, involving the organism as a whole, but that in organisms representing a more advanced stage of development, well-differentiated reflexes can be elicited.

Then too, the studies of Franz and Lashley indicate, both by the method of extirpation in animal brains and by the method of retraining soldiers suffering from brain lesions, that the destruction of limited areas in the brain does not permanently prevent the behavior ordinarily attributed to those portions of the brain; or, again to use the phraseology of the Gestaltists, that there are no "rigid arrangements" necessarily and invariably involved in the performance of given acts. It is particularly interesting to notice, in this connection, that it was the examination of immediate experience, rather than direct research on the nervous system itself, that led the Gestaltists to their theory of the nature of neural activity. Having noted certain properties in immediate experience—its organization, its responsiveness to the total constellation of stimuli—which they thought the machine theory inadequate to explain, they developed a new theory in harmony both with their own observations and also with known physical laws. In other words, the Gestaltists preferred their theory primarily because it gave a better account of the facts of immediate experience, not because they had experimented with the nervous system itself.[10] In working in

[10] This does not mean, of course, that the Gestaltists proceeded with no regard for the work on the physiology of the nervous system. In particular, the German studies based on the victims of the war gave

this way, they played a part in one of the most interesting convergences of opinion in psychology. The similarity between the *Gestalt* interpretation of neural activity and that advocated by Lashley, between "dynamical interaction" and "mass-action," is immediately apparent, as is also the fact that the evidence contributed from the two sources is complementary. It is highly significant that two lines of work so differently motivated and arising from such different problems and points of view should come so close together; that a theory of neural action based on what ought to be the case according to the observation of immediate experience should agree so closely with a theory that, based on direct experimentation with the nervous system itself, likewise rejected the theory of definite localized action along rigidly determined pathways and substituted the concept of mass-action.

From the preceding discussion it is obvious that *Gestalt* psychology recognizes both behavior and consciousness, and that it has no hesitation whatever about directing its observations toward either the physical world or immediate experience. But to American students, any account of the school will seem vague and indefinite until it expressly states the position of the Gestaltists with respect to the two points of reference that have become so habitual, structuralism and behaviorism.

In different ways, *Gestalt* psychology is opposed to both. The traditional experimental psychology of Germany, of which Titchenerian structuralism was the American representative, was, of course, the arch-enemy in the eyes of the Gestaltists; and even to-day, twenty years after their declaration of independence, if any noticeable animus creeps into

support to their views. Their own specific contributions, however, came from the experimental studies of the psychological processes themselves.

their words, it is more likely to be found in their attacks upon this school than in any other connection. Their objection, it is hardly necessary to say, is to the elementarism of the school and to the habits of thought its elementarism implies, not to the attempt to study consciousness. *Gestalt* psychology accepts immediate experience as factual data not a shade less questionable than the raw data of the physical sciences. It does object, however, to the limitations that the older psychology places on the scientific study of direct experience. It objects to the exclusive use of the kind of observation developed in the "trained introspectionist"; it objects to the exclusive use of a technique in which a special laboratory attitude is assumed, and in which experience as it is given in everyday observation (the rectangular table as it ordinarily looks) is discarded in favor of "corrected" experience (the irregular quadrilateral that the introspectionist describes). The Gestaltists emphatically insist that the naïve experience of common sense has a right to a hearing in psychology. They believe in the "uncorrected" kind of observation called phenomenological. And more, they believe that the introspectionist rules out the more urgent and more significant problems of his science by considering as "true" psychological data only such experiences as result from his special attitude. *Gestalt* psychology has no objection whatever to the examination of direct experience. Its case against the trained introspectionist is against the artificiality of his method, not against his attempt to examine consciousness.

To behaviorism, the *Gestalt* school has two chief objections. One is that the behaviorists needlessly discard consciousness—needlessly, because consciousness is a fact of experience neither more nor less justifiable, logically and epistemologically, than the physical world. It is significant that in *Gestalt Psychology,* a book written in English for publication in America, Köhler, addressing himself to what he calls the fundamentalism that behaviorism has established in America, devotes the whole of the first chapter to pointing out the inconsistency between the "healthy naïveté" of the behaviorists in accepting the physical world, and their "epistemological purity" in rejecting consciousness. In this chapter, beginning with naïve experience as the starting-point of all science, he shows how the distinction between the objective and the subjective is made, and explains that it is as impossible to prove the existence of an independent physical world as of the consciousness of one's neighbor. And since physics has proceeded in spite of this fact, he argues that it is possible for psychology to do likewise; that it is better to adopt a "healthy naïveté" than to be bound by the scruples of "epistemological purity." The second objection to behaviorism is that it employs exactly the same procedure that characterized the older psychology in so far as it builds up larger wholes from elementary processes. For though behaviorism does not evolve complex states of consciousness from elementary sensations and affections, it builds up complicated patterns of behavior by the integration of simple reactions. And the result, the Gestaltists find, in behaviorism as in the older psychology, is a lamentable sterility so far as the production of positive concepts is concerned. *Gestalt* psychology sees in behaviorism nothing really new; nothing but the same monotonous formula, $S - R$; nothing but reflexes, conditioned and unconditioned, brought together in more and more complex forms.

Besides, *Gestalt* psychology disagrees with both behaviorism and structuralism in that it refuses to model its procedures slavishly on those of older and better-developed sciences, such as physics. One of the characteristics of a highly developed science like physics is the exactness with which it makes its determinations. But after all, the Gestaltists observe, psychology is a young science, and much of its striving for exact measurement and precise determination is inappropriate to its present stage of development. The immediate concern of psychology is with preliminary problems; it must first establish general modes of reaction; it must make the first rough draft of its problems as physics did long ago. Köhler attempted to do this in his study of apes; and he regards it as characteristic of the prevalent mood of psychology that one criticism of his study was that it failed to reduce its observations to quantitative terms. Such a procedure, according to Köhler, would have been entirely beside the point. His purpose was to discover what *kinds* of activity would occur; and the significant results, far from being clearer, would even have been obscured if he had presented them in the form of tables and graphs. To force an immature science into ways that are unsuited to its stage of development is itself unscientific. The Gestaltists believe that psychology is not yet ready for many of the exact quantitative determinations it is attempting, and that much of its work on measurement is wasted because it does not yet know what it is measuring.

But nothing must be permitted to obscure the fact that the chief objection of *Gestalt* psychology to both behaviorism and structuralism is to their practice of taking their material piecemeal, of assuming that their larger units are nothing but smaller ones put together in specific combinations. After all, *Gestalt* psychology is not primarily interested in such questions as whether consciousness or behavior is the subject-matter of psychology, or whether introspection or objective observation is its proper method. Its main contention is that by means of the concept of *Gestalt* it has called attention to characteristics of experience that have been ignored and that cannot rightfully be ignored; and all its differences from other schools are incidental to its position on that crucial point.

Any movement that attacked the existing order as the *Gestalt* school did, would naturally provoke opposition, and *Gestalt* psychology has had whatever advantages are to be gained from vigorous and varied criticism.

First there is the almost inevitable objection that *Gestalt* psychology is not really new. This objection is immediately sustained if it refers to the general way of thinking of the whole as not equivalent to the sum of its parts, of form and organization as characteristics of experience not explicable in terms of elements. In that sense, *Gestalt* psychology, as the Gestaltists admit, is at least as old as Heraclitus and Anaxagoras, and it cannot even claim to have rediscovered the problem in modern times. Writers like James and Dewey have protested against elementarism as vigorously as any Gestaltist. But if *Gestalt* psychology is taken in a more specific sense, as introducing particular concepts that have brought to light definite problems obscured by the practices of the time, it has as good a claim to novelty as any movement can have; for it introduced into the psychology of the day a way of looking at things and a way of doing things which were not being tried, or which were, at least, not recognized. In that sense *Gestalt* psychology is new as fresh customs are new, or fashions in taste or morals, or changes in government, or the invention of industrial machines, or any other innovation that is not novel in an absolute sense but which nevertheless changes the course of events at the time. After all, from the standpoint of the progress of science, the important question is not whether an idea is new, but whether it is relevant to the needs of the existing situation. And the way in which *Gestalt* psychology has suggested problems and lines of investigation to workers who are outside the school, or even opposed to it, constitutes one of the best possible pieces of evidence that its insights have made a difference in the actual practices of the science.

There is, however, another and somewhat more subtle form in which the objection that there is nothing really new in *Gestalt* psychology occasionally appears. It is sometimes said that the Gestaltists have greatly overemphasized the doctrine of elementarism as upheld by the older experimental school; that they have really attacked a man of straw. One statement of the case runs as follows:

"Nor must it be thought that orthodox psychology had ever taken its credo about elements any too seriously. It was accustomed to do homage to elements and their attributes, as it were, on Sunday, and then to play with what were really *Gestalten* all through the week. The strength of *Gestalt* psychology in this regard was that it asked every one to do what he had for the most part been doing, and that it wished, therefore, to affirm the psychology of actual research rather than to remake it." [11]

But if this is the case, it is a distinct advantage that the situation has been brought into plain view, if only by demolishing a straw man. After all, science cannot seriously approve of not letting the right hand know what the left hand is doing. Science, of course, is not above muddling through. Scientific practice often runs ahead of theory; it often proceeds unwittingly and unintentionally on assumptions that it discovers only after it has used them. But the justification for this procedure is that in the actual business of acquiring and interpreting its data, those assumptions eventually do come to light. Somewhere along the line there is a point where the scientist encounters recalcitrant facts that force him to examine the assumptions to which they refuse to conform. Such a point is always an important one in the development of science. As psychology itself teaches, it is the most natural thing in the world for habitual assumptions to retire from notice, and yet subterraneously influence one's

[11] E. G. Boring. *A History of Experimental Psychology*, 577.

procedures. If *Gestalt* psychology has done nothing more than to bring into the open assumptions that are implied in the practices of psychology and which are not definitely recognized, it has justified its existence. Whether its teachings are right or wrong, and whether they are new or old, they have helped to clarify the situation.

The Gestaltists' position on the constancy hypothesis has been criticized in a somewhat similar vein. Is it true, some have asked, that the constancy hypothesis is at the basis of the thinking of the older psychology? Certainly much of the work in sense physiology and in psychophysics grew out of the repeated evidence that there is no obvious one-to-one correspondence between the peripheral stimulation and the psychological experience. In a sense, this may mean that psychology has always known that the constancy hypothesis does not hold; at least that psychological experience is not a faithful copy of local sensory stimulation. But in another sense, it may mean that the constancy hypothesis simply retired to a deeper level. If local stimulation and psychological response do not correspond in an obvious and pictorial way, then the correspondence must be preserved in some other fashion. Total situations must be broken into elements, and through the elements, some aroused by immediate sensory stimulation and some by association, a correspondence with local stimulation is retained in its essentials. The conception of the nervous system as an elaborate set of connecting fibers is entirely in line with this view. So also are the mechanical explanations of the operations of the sense-organs which occupied workers on the border-line between physiology and psychology. The paths of connection may be extremely circuitous, the mechanical operations extremely intricate, but the correspondence is preserved by structural connections throughout the process. The old constancy is there, though achieved by less obvious means.

But this line of reasoning suggests that even in the explanations of *Gestalt* psychology, the constancy hypothesis appears. It has been suggested indeed that, in some form or other, the constancy hypothesis is not only a very natural tendency in thinking, as Köhler points out, but even a necessary tendency in scientific thought. *Gestalt* psychology itself began as an attempt to account for experience as it is immediately given in relation to the conditions of stimulation. It was, in fact, because Wertheimer did not find the expected correspondence—expected, that is, from the point of view of the older explanations—that the new line of thought was developed. What the first Gestaltists sought to do was to find a really adequate way of showing how immediate experience, in all its fullness, is related to the stimulating conditions; and to do away with the specious explanation that accounted for the connection only by losing sight of some of the characteristics of immediate experience. *Gestalt* psychology has found that the connection between the two can be more adequately explained in terms of some form of dynamical interaction. But may not dynamical interaction be merely a more subtle form of connection—a connection that does not involve structural bonds, but which involves an organization, the result of which is a truer correspondence between the immediate experience and the conditions of stimulation? Has *Gestalt* psychology not merely substituted more subtle lines of connection for the obvious ones visible in concrete mechanical structures? And in doing so, is it not using the constancy hypothesis?

Yes, if the constancy hypothesis is taken to mean any attempt whatever to trace lines of relation between experience and its stimulating conditions, between one situation and another. In this extremely general sense, *Gestalt* psychology is employing a method always used in psychology, and in every other science. But the term "constancy hypothesis," as used by the *Gestalt* school, has a far more specific meaning. It refers definitely to a "constancy" between immediate experience and definite local stimulation, to a theory that is associated with the conception of the nervous system as a structure of "special arrangements," and with the conception of immediate experience as composed of elements. If the constancy hypothesis is taken in this sense, *Gestalt* psychology, by calling attention to it, has placed a clear-cut alternative before the science. On the one side are mental elements and associations, and a nervous system of special arrangements; on the other are *Gestalten* and dynamical interaction. In the concrete, the contrast is definite and clear. It makes little difference to what extent novelty enters the situation; it makes little difference whether there is a basic similarity in the thought underlying the constancy hypothesis and the theory of dynamical interaction. The point is that by calling attention to the constancy hypothesis in a specific sense, *Gestalt* psychology has brought an important issue into the open, has compelled psychology to examine some of its assumptions, and has to that extent forced it to clarify its thinking.

This point, however, suggests that *Gestalt* psychology has itself been accused of lack of clearness in some of its fundamental concepts. The central concept, that of *Gestalt,* has been cited as the most flagrant example. Critics have pointed out that the term has been applied to the most varied phenomena—to visual patterns both spatial and temporal, to immediate experience in other sensory fields, to memory and thought, to instinct and to other forms of overt motor behavior; they note that, in addition, *Gestalt* has been used to refer to wholeness, unity, and organization; and that with the bringing together of so much material under the same general heading, there has been a tendency to generalize from one field to another, not always cautiously. In the early days of the movement this criticism was heard more frequently than it is now, for as experimental problems have been put, the conditions in which particular phenomena occur have been more definitely determined and statements have increased in precision. The charge of vagueness has also been made against the physiological theories that the *Gestalt* school proposes. Certainly *Gestalt* psychology offers no picture of nervous activity that can be visualized and diagrammed as can the conception it opposes, a conception according to which it is theoretically possible to trace a given excitation from beginning to end by means of pathways that become enormously complicated, but in which the principle is always the same, that of conduction units placed end to end. If vagueness means inability to present a definitely outlined and completely filled-in picture, *Gestalt* psychology must plead guilty to the charge. It frankly admits that its knowledge of the nervous system is inadequate to the task of tracing in detail the dynamical interaction it assumes. The Gestaltists are aware too that the problem of dynamical interaction presents more difficulties than do the older concepts. They also admit that they have inferred this process from psychological phenomena and from the principles of dynamics and that the evidence from physiology is merely corroborative. They believe, however, that it is entirely legitimate to follow this procedure. Furthermore, to the Gestaltists the fact that their explanation is necessarily incomplete does not mean that, so far as it goes, it is vague. The direction in which it tends is clearly marked; and they see no reason why, especially as workers in a very young science, they should refuse to follow the suggestions of their data, even if those data indicate that most of their problems lie before them.

Gestalt psychology has also been criticized for its stand on analysis. Can the Gestaltists seriously mean to discredit analysis as a method of scientific investigation? Sometimes they seem to do so in their statements that analysis destroys the very reality it seeks to explain; that to reduce a thing to its elements and study it piecemeal is to lose sight of the thing itself. Such statements were part of the Gestaltists' attack against elementarism, and of their insistence that the whole is not merely the sum of its parts. Naturally critics lost no time in pointing out that without analysis experimental science could not exist, and that even the *Gestalt* school must use analysis in experimentally isolating, varying, and controlling different sets of factors. Altogether there was much confusion as to what, precisely, the Gestaltists meant by their attacks on analysis. In some of their earlier warnings against the dangers of analysis, they evidently overshot the mark. Recently, however, Köhler has taken up the point specifically. He explains that *Gestalt* psychology, by its emphasis on wholes, does not intend at all to abandon analysis as a scientific method. He points out that the Gestaltists definitely recognize *segregated* wholes, and that they thus employ a mode of analysis which deals in genuine parts, however emphatically they may refuse to have anything to do with sensational elements that have no existence as discrete bits of experience. For example, whenever they deal with a field in which there are segregated wholes and subwholes, such as a group in which there are several members, the Gestaltists utilize such analysis. Then too, *Gestalt* psychology recognizes a form of analysis in which, through the adoption of a definite attitude by the observer, a selection of some parts of the field and a suppression of others occurs—a kind of analysis that may bring about a change in the organization of the field, so that the total impression is distinctly altered. But this kind of analysis is also sensibly present in actual experience. Finally, *Gestalt* psychology even admits an analysis that does not deal in real parts,

This is a kind of "differential" analysis in which the material studied is broken into convenient parts with the definite understanding that the parts are not real and that they will disappear in the final results, as they do in the method of the differential calculus. This analysis is recognized as a necessary procedure in scientific work, entirely innocent so long as it is recognized for what it is—an intellectual tool. The analysis opposed by *Gestalt* psychology is the analysis that reduces experience to mental elements which are products of abstraction rather than data of observation, and which then treats them as the real materials, the real units, of which experience is composed. This view is sometimes expressed by saying that the Gestaltists object not to analysis, but to synthesis.

Among many American psychologists, however, the fundamental objection to *Gestalt* psychology has little to do with its stand on any of these questions; it grows rather out of a general suspicion that the teachings of the Gestaltists are somehow tainted with metaphysics or are at least related to a kind of psychology they have definitely put behind them. Because of the tremendous influence of behaviorism in America, there is an undercurrent of feeling that to deal with matter is the proper pursuit of science, and that to deal with mind is to become involved in metaphysics. The behaviorists, having dispelled ghosts, are wary of this school which freely and without apology refers to direct experience. And when a Gestaltist accuses them of "epistemological purity" in their refusal to have any dealings with consciousness, they frankly do not understand. Neither do they attempt to answer argument with argument. They simply stand their ground, refusing to be taken in by anything that sounds so medieval, all the while suspecting that this is the kind of psychology from which they have won their freedom. They are interested, it is true, in *Gestalt* experiments in animal psychology, for these they find unimpeachably objective. They are willing and even eager to try the new problems in that field which the *Gestalt* doctrines have suggested. They are, in fact, disposed to give respectful consideration to any aspect of the subject that does not involve them in an acceptance of consciousness, in anything they regard as mysterious. But they are in no mood to be convinced by a plausible stranger who comes bearing arguments from epistemology in his hands. To them such arguments, however skilful, seem far less real than the plain and palpable and undeniable matters of fact with which they are accustomed to operate.

These are by no means the only objections urged against *Gestalt* psychology, but they represent some of the major issues. In the meantime there can be no question that the school has made its mark upon the science. It has caused many psychologists to question the fundamental assumptions on which they were working, and to examine critically certain formal restrictions that, partly because of academic tradition and partly because they were being taken for granted, were growing unduly powerful. It has suggested problems so genuine and significant that they have aroused the active interest of psychologists both within and without the school. Above all, *Gestalt* psychology stands for definite hypotheses and methods of experimentation and is directly and indirectly responsible for a vast amount of research. Like other schools that revolted against an established order, the Gestaltists have had a refreshing influence on psychology as a whole. Fundamentally their attempt has been to call psychology from a set professionalism to a first-hand, open-eyed view of experience. School after school has in some manner made the same attempt; and it is indicative of the difficulties of observation inherent in psychology that the fresh attempt has always been needed.

Chapter X

FREUD AND THE PSYCHOANALYTIC MOVEMENT

TO turn to the psychoanalytic interpretation of psychology is to turn to a movement strikingly different from those considered so far. The systems just reviewed, whatever their disagreements, are alike in being academic. They breathe the atmosphere of libraries and laboratories, of seminars and lecture-halls. Either they are pure science or its nearest kin. Even those which most zealously justify the applications of science have themselves arisen in close association with the attempt to see the subject-matter of psychology with a certain detachment, freed for the moment from the necessity of doing anything about it. Not one of them had its actual source in applied science. All of them were born in academic halls, and all formed their habits and characters by early associations with the academic world. But psychoanalysis is neither academic nor pure. With its roots in the soil of clinical practice, it is, both in origin and in main intention, an attempt to accomplish what Titchener so vehemently denied was a proper pursuit for scientific psychology—the cure of sick souls.

The founder of the movement was Sigmund Freud. Freud began his career by studying medicine in Vienna and for a time found his chief interest in physiology, especially in the physiology of the nervous system. Eventually he took up the practice of medicine, associating himself with a somewhat older man, Dr. Josef Breuer. Soon Freud became interested in neurotic disorders, and it was in his actual dealings with cases of this sort—Freud stresses this point particularly—in first-hand observations extending over years of experience, that he gradually worked out the practice and theory of psychoanalysis. For though Freud firmly and sometimes bitterly maintains that he, and he alone, is the founder of psychoanalysis, he never claims that he arrived at his conception either by sudden insight or by outright creation. He repeatedly refers to the long experience that little by little and in unconnected fragments revealed to him the human personality as he has come to see it.

In 1885, Freud went to Paris to study under Charcot, then the outstanding authority in Europe on mental disorders. Freud was immensely impressed by Charcot and was particularly interested in his treatment of hysteria. Charcot believed that hysteria and hypnosis are intimately associated; that true hypnosis indeed is essentially a hysterical phenomenon and can be induced only in hysterical patients. Naturally enough, he advocated its use for both the investigation and the treatment of hysterical conditions. This general idea was not new to Freud. Largely because of Charcot's prestige, the treatment of hysteria by hypnosis was widely known, and Freud himself had become acquainted with the practice in his work in Vienna.

There was one incident, however, apart from Charcot's regular instruction, that stood out with memorable distinctness in Freud's experiences as a student in Paris. One evening at a reception, he heard Charcot discussing a case that had come up in the day's practice. Speaking with the greatest possible emphasis, Charcot declared that in such conditions there was *always* a sexual involvement. "Always, always, always," he repeated.[1] Freud was astonished, not only

[1] Charcot denied having made the statement. Freud reports both the statement and the denial in his paper on "The History of the Psychoanalytic Movement." *Psychoanalytical Review* (1916), **3,** 406-454. The

by the content of the statement, but by the fact that Charcot did not disclose this knowledge if he had it in his possession. Later, when his own practice was leading him to his theory of the sexual basis of the neuroses, he recalled Charcot's statement, evidently regarding it as an expert opinion that corroborated his own findings.

But even before he went to Paris, Freud had caught sight of an idea that, like the theory of the sexual basis of the neuroses, was to become one of the fundamental doctrines of psychoanalysis. One of Breuer's cases seemed to him especially significant. The patient was a young woman whose hysterical symptoms had grown out of an incident in her earlier life. Obviously the incident had impressed her violently, yet she had completely forgotten it. The treatment of her condition was essentially a catharsis, a release of pent-up emotion effected by having her recall and reproduce under hypnosis the experience that lay at the root of her trouble. The interpretation given by both Freud and Breuer was that the original experience had aroused an emotional disturbance that had been prevented from expressing itself in the direct and normal way; and that the emotion, finding its natural outlet blocked, had sought another channel and expressed itself in the symptoms. This process Freud called conversion, and he referred to the symptoms as the conversion of the original effect. The case is important in the development of psychoanalytic theory because it points to the underground workings of psychic tensions. The discovery that an incident, unconscious and long forgotten, was nevertheless the source of marked disturbances in behavior not only called attention to the rôle of the unconscious, but suggested that the unconscious is strongly dynamic.

And yet this case, though highly significant in the develop-

history of the development of psychoanalysis given in this chapter is based principally on this account written by Freud.

ment of the theory, did not involve genuine psychoanalysis. Hypnosis had been used, and, according to Freud, true psychoanalysis begins only when hypnosis has been discarded. Freud had studied this patient, it will be remembered, before he had gone to Paris, and the development of true psychoanalysis came much later. On returning to Vienna after studying with Charcot, Freud again associated himself with Breuer and again adopted the practice of hypnosis along with the cathartic procedure. But he did not find the method entirely satisfactory. It was successful enough in removing the symptoms, but in the long run it did not effect a cure. Many patients who had been dismissed as cured returned later, often with different symptoms. Further investigation usually led to the discovery that the real cause of the difficulty had not been unearthed; that it lay buried much deeper in the patient's past than the first investigation had penetrated. These experiences made Freud regard the hypnotic method as superficial, as an inadequate tool for digging down to the true roots of the difficulty.

In the meantime, both Breuer and Freud had been developing, rather informally, a method of Breuer's invention in which the patient was encouraged to talk himself out to the physician—a procedure sometimes called the talking method. The patient was kept in the ordinary waking state —that is, he was not under hypnosis—and was urged to express himself as freely as he pleased, to say whatever it came into his head to say, and to keep back nothing because it seemed embarrassing or trivial, or because it would not ordinarily be mentioned. In these conversations the patients sometimes recalled long-forgotten experiences that constituted important clues to their difficulties.

At first both hypnosis and the talking method were used, but as time went on Freud came to depend more and more on the latter. In particular he considered it a tremendous advantage to work with the patient's active coöperation and knowledge. For under hypnosis the patient was literally not all there. Only a dissociated fragment of his personality was present; the rest was lost in hypnotic sleep. On waking he might be completely unaware of what had happened during the treatment, and in consequence he was not really made whole. To Freud the hypnotic method seemed a far less thorough procedure than that in which the patient, under the guidance of the physician but on the basis of his own contributions, was led to see the true source of his difficulty. This procedure was the beginning of the psychoanalytic technique. Catharsis was included as essential, but hypnosis was discarded as superficial, and the talking method, or as it was called later, the free-association method, was substituted for it. This description does not imply, however, that the development of the psychoanalytic technique consisted merely in sorting and fitting together procedures that happened to be available. Psychoanalysis was evolved slowly and tentatively, and it achieved its mature form only after it had conquered stubborn difficulties.

But the difficulties themselves were enlightening. Two of them Freud regarded as especially significant. The lesser he called transference. This term refers to the fact that the patient, during the long, intimately personal conversations in which his emotions are being probed and stirred, develops a strong affective attachment for the analyst—either falls in love with him quite plainly and without indirection, or else develops a negativistic and hostile attitude that Freud regards as merely the obverse of falling in love, and basically the same kind of response. When Breuer became convinced that transference was regularly aroused, he felt obliged to reject the analytic procedure. He also objected to Freud's emphasis on the rôle of sex in the causation of the neuroses. He gave up, therefore, the method that he had been so influential in starting, and the two men went their separate professional ways.

To Freud the occurrence of transference constituted additional evidence of the sexual nature of the patient's difficulties. It meant that the emotion stirred up by the analysis had attached itself to the analyst. Transference became in his opinion a necessary part of the process—so necessary as to be one of the distinguishing features of genuine psychoanalysis. But the condition, though indispensable, was properly only temporary. It was part of the task of the skilful physician to detach the emotion from himself and redirect it into channels where its presence would be appropriate, and where it would be conducive to the patient's mental health.

The other difficulty was the resistance that the patient is sure to develop in the course of the analysis; for the process of free association in psychoanalysis is anything but an easy drifting from memory to memory until the cause of the difficulty is encountered. Sooner or later a point is reached where the patient is unwilling or unable to go on: unwilling, because he has come upon something too painful or hideous or shocking to face; unable, because his mind has become a blank and he is completely at a standstill. Unwillingness and inability to go on are simply two degrees of resistance, the latter the more serious. Both are ways in which the patient is protecting himself from pain, and the presence of pain means that the analysis is probing a real wound. Resistance, therefore, shows that the treatment is going in the right direction, is reaching a critical point, and must be continued along the line it has taken. No matter how intense his sufferings, the patient must bring himself face to face with the situation that has been covered or evaded or distorted. Only by seeing it as it actually is, with all its hidden implications, only by reacting to it fully and without equivocation, can he find release for his pent-up emotions. In the course of a complete analysis, resistance is encountered not once but often, and each time it must be overcome relentlessly. Furthermore it must be overcome without hypnosis. It would be easier, it is true, for both patient and physician if the painful memories could be reinstated under hypnosis. The lost incidents would then be reproduced without making connection with the conscious personality, and therefore without arousing resistance. But Freud's experience made him increasingly skeptical of hypnosis as a means of penetrating to the really deep layers of the personality. Besides, the basic purpose of psychoanalysis is to bring the rejected content back to conscious experience, to close the gap its rejection has created, and thus to heal the wound that divides the personality against itself. This can be accomplished only when the patient consciously faces the situation in its unmitigated plainness; there is no other way of obtaining true release.

The discovery of resistance was also the discovery of repression—or rather, the occurrence of resistance led Freud to the theory of repression as its only adequate explanation. The theory of repression is, briefly, that a troublesome but forgotten experience, whether it be a memory or a wish, is unconscious not because it has merely lapsed or passively slipped out of consciousness, but because it has been forced out. And having been pushed out, it is held down by violence. For the repressed experience is not an idea or memory in the ordinary sense of the term; it is charged with emotion and desire. But desire is essentially impulsive; it tends strongly to overt expression; and the repressed content is by no means dead. It lives on in the unconscious, exerting its influence covertly, twisting conduct into unusual forms. The conscious self or ego cannot kill it nor even render it inactive; the ego can only keep it in the unconscious. "The theory of repression," Freud says, "is the main pillar upon which rests the edifice of psychoanalysis." [2] Implicit in it are the distinctive features of the psychoanalytic view—the conception of the unconscious as active and striving, and of warfare between a conscious self, the ego, and unconscious desire.

Psychoanalysis as a technique was now well under way, and the basic lines of the theory were laid down. Free association was accepted as the method; resistance and its significance were understood; and the patient's insight into his predicament, and catharsis through the attendant emotional release, were recognized as the essentials of therapy. But while the technique was still in the making—in fact before Breuer and Freud parted company—Freud had begun to suspect that the dreams of his patients were significant. The theory of dreams, like the technique of psychoanalysis itself, evolved slowly, but by the time Freud had thoroughly developed the conception, he regarded it as another of the essentials of the psychoanalytic theory. It is not at all surprising that Freud should take this stand, for just as the concept of repression emphasizes the activity of the unconscious, the theory of dreams points to its indirection. In dreams the repressed forces are discovered circumventing resistances by tortuous ways and by hook or crook achieving forbidden satisfactions.

According to Freud, the dream is essentially a disguised satisfaction for desires that have been repressed during waking life. Dreams are far more meaningful and far more elaborate than they seem. Every dream has both a manifest and a latent content. The manifest content is the story one tells in recounting the dream—the dream at its face value; but the latent content holds its true significance. The manifest content may be supplied by the happenings of one's waking life—is, in fact, usually taken from the experiences of the

[2] S. Freud, "The History of the Psychoanalytic Movement," *Psychoanalytical Review* (1916), **3**, 413.

previous twenty-four hours; but, for all that, the dream is
no simple, casual play of matter-of-fact association. The
manifest content is mere material that the repressed psychic
forces employ. The desires that have been thrust into the
unconscious during the day have a chance to express themselves at night when sleep relaxes the vigilance of the
"censor," Freud's figure of speech for the inhibitions that the
ego imposes on the unconscious. But even when the ego
sleeps and censorship is relaxed, the banished desires dare
not express themselves openly. If they were frankly sexual
the sleeper would be shocked awake; in fact, when the meaning of the dream becomes too obvious, he does awake.
Therefore the forbidden desires adopt disguises and slip past
the censor into consciousness, unrecognized.

The disguises are various and ingenious in the extreme.
One of them is symbolism. The persons, objects, and events
that figure in the manifest content of the dream really stand
for something else. The public festival that one patient enjoyed in her dream represented the funeral of her husband.
Terrified flight from a foe regularly stands for the longed-for
pursuit by a lover. Some symbols derive their significance
from particular personal experiences of the dreamer; others
are common to all humanity and always have the same
meaning. Gardens, balconies, and doors signify the female
body, and church spires, candles, and serpents the male
genitals.

Symbolism, however, does not perform the dream-work
alone; there are other ways of concealing the dream's true
meaning. Apparently there are no limits to the ingenuity of
the unconscious in its devices for eluding the censor. The
significant item may be made to seem a trivial part of the
whole, yet in reality be the basic reason for the dream. Or
the significant emotion may be attached to a seemingly neutral object. And even when the dream has been thoroughly

disguised, the dream-work is not done. When the dreamer awakes he must not know what he has really been doing. Therefore secondary elaboration occurs. In remembering and reporting his dream, the dreamer unconsciously throws it into logical and coherent form, so that it bears some resemblance to a connected story or actual event. But in the dream itself, logic and coherence are neither present nor felt to be wanting, for dreaming is an expression of a deep and primitive form of thinking on which the logical and critical modes of thought have not yet been imposed. Thus dreams reveal not only the elaborate indirection of unconscious thought but also the alogical character of its operations.

It was also during the formative period of psychoanalysis that the theory of infantile sexuality was developed. Freud's practice had thoroughly convinced him of the sexual basis of the neuroses; and though the open declaration of his belief brought him the greatest unpopularity and something very like professional ostracism—a circumstance to which he was deeply sensitive—he held fast to the theory and even felt obliged to push it farther. Gradually, but more and more firmly, he became convinced that sexual strivings operate powerfully before the age of sexual maturity; eventually he concluded that they are at work even in infancy.

The evidence upon which Freud based this conclusion has been mentioned in passing. He had given up hypnosis in his practice because he felt that it failed to get at the underlying cause of the patient's difficulty. The fact had repeatedly been forced upon his attention that each psychic wound or trauma had a history. A thorough investigation always led the patient farther and farther back into the past, and eventually he referred his difficulty to a seduction in childhood. But side by side with this discovery came another that seemed a flat contradiction. In most cases, further investigation revealed the fact that the seductions were mere fantasy; that they simply had not occurred. For a time Freud was completely baffled. Analysis invariably led back to sexual shocks in childhood, and investigation showed that the sexual shocks had no objective existence. Then it occurred to him that if his patients so regularly imagined seductions, that fact itself was important; to have produced fantasies of seduction seemed to him as significant in its way as to have experienced actual seduction. To Freud, the situation meant that the child's sexual desires were gratified by autoerotic practices, and that these practices, forbidden and already regarded as shameful, were screened from the conscious self by fantasies of seduction that shielded the self from all blame. This interpretation gave him his clue to the importance of the sexual life of the child; and the theory of infantile sexuality was built into the foundations of his system along with the doctrines of repression and the unconscious. No school has emphasized more strongly than have the psychoanalysts the tremendous importance of infancy and childhood in determining adult character.

With these discoveries, the theory as well as the technique of psychoanalysis had completed the formative stage. But it must not be supposed that the actual process of development was either so systematic or so coherent as an account written after the event might lead one to suppose. Freud repeatedly comments on the periods of doubt and bewilderment through which he passed, on the fact that he did not foresee the theories to which his observations were leading him. Still, little by little the major concepts took form and fell into line with one another. The unconscious was conceived as active, striving, and powerful. Repression was regarded as an indication of conflict between the ego and the unconscious desires. The indirection of the unconscious and its primitive, alogical character were both indicated by dreams. The importance of sexual desires, even from infancy, was acknowledged. These views Freud regards as the first, fruits of analysis; and he always insists that they are the hard-won results of direct observation, not mere imaginings and speculations.

The psychoanalytic theory may be regarded as a construction to account for these and subsequent discoveries. Freud's teachings, however, have never been a fixed and rigid body of doctrine. Freud himself is continually modifying and supplementing them, and continually explaining that they are not complete and final. Still, the main outlines have remained fairly constant and may be briefly indicated.

The psychic life of human beings consists of two main parts, the conscious and the unconscious. The conscious is small and relatively insignificant. What a person knows about his own motives and conduct gives but a fragmentary and superficial aspect of his total personality. Beneath the conscious self is the vast and powerful unconscious, the source of the great concealed forces that constitute the real driving power behind human actions. Between the conscious and the unconscious is the preconscious,[3] which merges gradually into both, but which resembles the conscious rather than the unconscious in content and character and is accessible to consciousness without emotional resistance. The preconscious does not consist of material that has been actively discarded and repressed; consequently its contents can be summoned by the ordinary processes of association. The censor is usually located in the preconscious.

Both the conscious and the unconscious are conceived as active. Freud evidently regards it as a matter of plain everyday observation, certainly as a fact needing no proof, that conscious selves are creatures of wishes and desires; and it is

[3] Sometimes called the foreconscious, the name by which it was formerly known.

one of the distinctive characteristics of his theory that the unconscious too is conceived as active and striving. In this sense Freud anthropomorphizes the unconscious. He speaks of it as if it were distinctly personal, as personal as the people we meet in everyday life. He describes the unconscious not primarily in terms of neural traces or engrams, not as habit systems, not as split-off, depersonalized fragments of personality—to mention a few of the less anthropomorphic conceptions that have been used by students of the unconscious—but as an active, wishing, striving agent, very much like the persons common sense recognizes and understands. The unconscious, as Freud sees it, is through and through dynamic; the whole psychic structure, whether conscious or unconscious, is fundamentally a tissue of striving and desire.

Between the conscious and the unconscious, there is incessant warfare. A human being learns, literally from infancy, that anything associated with the sexual life is shameful. From the first, society imposes powerful taboos, and the conscious self responds by shutting all manifestations of sex from sight, by forcing them down into the unconscious as disgraceful. But beneath the level of consciousness, the desires live on, and though frustrated, they strive with all their might and with all their cunning to circumvent the prohibitions of the ego. The psychic life is thus organized about two centers: the ego or conscious self, which develops "conscience" as an expression of social approval; and the unconscious or libido, which harbors the powerful sexual desires, some of which the ego does not even suspect to exist, and some of which it banishes but cannot destroy.

Freud's attention was at first directed mainly to the libido. He has always considered the influence of the sexual drive an absolutely crucial point in his theory. Any attempt to evade the issue he sees as a weak attempt to make the truth less intolerable, as a timid concession to conventional ways of thought and feeling. This is essentially the accusation he brings against Jung and Adler, both former pupils and associates, and both founders of schools that have diverged from his own. Jung considers the great driving force to be a general vital urge, not to be identified with the specifically sexual, though it has a large and important sexual component. The rôle that Freud gives to sex, Adler assigns to the desire for mastery, to the longing "to be a complete man." Both these views Freud denounces as weak and vicious evasions; he leaves no doubt whatever that he considers the sexual motive of overwhelming importance in human conduct.

Freud uses the word "sex" in a very general sense. He includes in it not only the specifically sexual interests and activities, but the whole love life—it might almost be said, the whole pleasure life—of human beings. The list of activities that he and his followers have seen as having a sexual significance is almost inexhaustible; but its range and variety may be indicated by the fact that it includes such simple practices as walking, smoking, and bathing, and such complex activities as artistic creation, religious ceremonial, social and political institutions, and even the development of civilization itself.

The struggle between the libido and the ego begins in infancy. The earliest pleasure of the new-born babe is that of nursing, and this pleasure Freud regards as sexual. From the cradle, the child is in love with his mother; but society sees to it that the sexual interest is neither expressed nor recognized as sexual. Certainly the child's enjoyment of his mother does not proceed without check. For one thing, the father has claims on the mother and is in this respect the child's rival. The outcome is the Œdipus complex: the child loves his mother and hates his father. It is true, the child may also love his father, in which case his attitude is ambivalent—he both loves and hates the same person. The corresponding complex, developed somewhat differently, is present in the girl: [4] she is in love with her father and either hates her mother or develops an ambivalent attitude toward her. The whole situation, with its violent loves and jealousies, with its inevitable conflicts and repressions, involves an enormous amount of psychic stress and strain that may be the source of endless emotional disorders.

Of course the sexual life of the child differs from that of the adult. At first it is autoerotic; the satisfactions are centered in the child's own body and are derived from the stimulation, at first accidental, of the erogenous zones. Between infancy and puberty, there is a latency period, during which the sex desires are expressed in forms of affection that society approves, and during which the child spends much of his time with companions of his own age and sex. At adolescence, the sex interest again becomes prominent and is definitely directed toward persons of the opposite sex.

Normal development regularly shows these successive stages, but normal development may not occur. All sorts of complications arise from the fact that the human child is "polymorphous perverse"—that is, his sex impulse is not strictly delimited; it may express itself in a great variety of forms, and attach itself to a great variety of objects. A possible and very common consequence of this situation is homosexuality; the libido finds its object in a person like the self in sex. A mild form of homosexuality, indeed, may even be considered a phase of normal development, forming an easy, or at least a convenient, transition from autoerotic practices, which require only the self, to genuine heterosexuality, which

[4] For a time the girl's entanglement was called the Electra complex, but at present, because the underlying principle is the same in both sexes, the term Œdipus complex is applied to both. The development of the girl's Œdipus complex is more indirect and involved than that of the boy's.

requires a person of the opposite sex. There are other ways, too, in which the regular development of the emotional life may be interfered with. "Fixation" may occur at any level. A given adjustment may be so completely satisfactory that the next stage is not attempted; at least it may be preferred to the enterprise and risk involved in meeting a new situation. A boy may be so devoted to his mother and so satisfied with the relation, especially if her love is centered on him, that he fails to become interested in other women; or a girl may become so engrossed in her girl companions, so absorbed in the emotional ups and downs supplied by her school-girl crushes, that she does not make the transition to the love of men. These phases may or may not involve physical intimacy, and they may be transient or lasting. Every transition is made with some difficulty; consequently a timid person, or one oversensitive or physically wounded, may find it on the whole more to his liking to remain at a given level than to summon his forces for a new adjustment. Even a person who has successfully negotiated a transition is not safely established on the more mature level. There is always the possibility of "regression" to an earlier and easier stage. A child who cannot get on with his child companions may withdraw into himself, or seek the comforting shelter of the family circle. A disappointed lover may return to the companionship of his own sex or to his mother's love, or he may withdraw into his own thoughts and feelings.

No one, not even the most fortunate, can escape the conflict between desire and repression. Every one born into human society is doomed to have some of his impulses thwarted; and consequently the conduct even of normal persons gives evidence of clashes and tensions. The psychology of everyday life shows this to be true, and Freud is never at a loss to find evidence for his theories in the commonplace incidents we dismiss as insignificant or attribute to chance. Slips of the tongue and slips of the pen, forgotten names and forgotten appointments, lost gifts and mislaid possessions, all point to the rôle of wish and motive. Such happenings, Freud insists, are by no means accidental. The woman who loses her wedding ring wishes that she had never had it.[5] The physician who forgets the name of his rival wishes that name blotted out of existence. The newspaper that prints "Clown Prince" for "Crown Prince" and corrects its error by announcing that of course it meant "Clown Prince," really means what it says. Even untutored common sense has a shrewd suspicion that forgetting is significant; one rarely admits without embarrassment that he failed to keep an appointment because he forgot it. Events of this sort are always determined. They are even over-determined. Several lines of causation may converge on the same mishap, and physical as well as psychical determinants may be involved. Errors in speech, for example, may be due in part to difficulties of muscular coördination, to transpositions of letters, to similarities in words, and the like. But such conditions do not constitute the whole explanation. They do not explain why one particular slip and not another was made—why just that combination of sounds and no other was uttered. A young business man, for example, striving to be generous to a rival, and intending to say "Yes, he is very efficient," actually said, "Yes, he is very officious." Obviously he was slipping into an easy confusion of words, but he was also expressing his real opinion. Desire and indirect fulfilment are at the basis of normal as well as abnormal conduct, and motive determines even those happenings we attribute to chance.

Furthermore, normal people dream, and dreams, it need hardly be repeated, give abundant evidence of the machina-

[5] Most of these illustrations given in this paragraph are taken from Freud's *The Psychopathology of Everyday Life*.

tions of the unconscious. Day-dreams as well as night dreams are common among normal people, and, like night dreams, they are forms of wish-fulfilment and of primitive modes of thinking. Day-dreams, in fact, give the clue to one of the most interesting of the Freudian theories: the interpretation of the rôle of the intellect in human affairs.

At the hands of Freud the intellect receives scant respect. The notion of "reason enthroned" disappears into myth, and the rational man collapses in the midst of Freudian desires. Thought and reason are anything but dominant forces in man's nature; they exist only to serve the great primal urges and desires that are the real masters of human conduct. The intellect is their servant, and a corruptible servant, not above twisting and concealing and manipulating the truth in the interests of its powerful masters. Always reason is motivated by affective needs; it exists to do their bidding; directly or indirectly it works to procure their satisfactions. True, in order to serve effectively, the intellect must learn to deal with the world as it is, to cope with actual facts, and therefore to take on the critical, logical, realistic ways we recognize as genuine thought. But these are secondary modes of reaction forced upon primitive and alogical thought by the fact that the instinctive cravings, if they are to obtain real satisfaction, must operate in a real world. Even the most logical and realistic thought is determined by personal and primitive desire.

Besides, the intellect does not always heed the lessons it has learned. Sometimes, shirking the difficulties of adjustments to real situations, it provides imagined joys and triumphs that cannot, at the time, be achieved in reality. Bleuler gave the name "autistic thinking" to this kind of intellection, of which the day-dream is the best possible illustration. In contrast with realistic thinking, autistic thinking is uncritically wishful, stopping with immediate and imagined satisfactions that can be obtained without the cost and risk of actual engagement with a real world. Autistic thinking, plainly motivated by the pleasure principle, reveals the intellect in unmistakable subjection to instinct and desire.

Another practice that indicates the secondary rôle of the intellect is one which Ernest Jones calls rationalization. Rationalization consists in finding *good* reasons for a deed, when the doer is unwilling to reveal or recognize the *real* reason—or when, as is entirely possible, he does not himself know what the real reason is. The occurrence of rationalization means that we do things primarily because we want to, and find reasons secondarily. The man who really *wants* to play golf can find plenty of good reasons why he should do so, both in and out of business hours. Golf is good exercise; it clears his head for business; he often clinches a deal on the golf-course; all work and no play make Jack a dull boy. Human beings like to think of themselves as ruled by reason, and rationalization is a device that fosters the illusion.

But all this, it may be objected, is rather trivial. Slips of the tongue and lapses of memory, dreams and blunders, irregularities of thought such as day-dreaming and rationalization, are after all not the major activities of life. Can the principles of psychoanalysis explain the more serious problems of human conduct?

Certainly the Freudians do not shirk the task. The neuroses can hardly be considered trivial, and psychoanalytic theory has as its very source the attempt to understand and cure the neuroses. According to the Freudians, exactly the same forces are at work in normal and in abnormal behavior, but in abnormal conduct those forces are exaggerated and their effects are more conspicuous. Neurotic symptoms are indirect expressions of repressed desires. Hysterical blindness may be an escape from an intolerable duty; a soldier who cannot bear either to fight or to flee may solve his problem by becoming blind—a poor solution certainly, but one that at least resolves the conflict between conscience and desire without loss of self-respect. Hysterical paralysis may be a defense against an appalling temptation; members that cannot move may keep their owner out of harm's way. An apparently senseless mannerism or eccentricity of conduct may be a substitute satisfaction for a longing that has been denied; in one case, the stereotyped motor habit of a neurotic girl represented the occupation of the lover she had lost. Not that the road from desire to symptom is simple and straightforward. Typically the patient does not know what he is doing. The mechanisms [6] are in the unconscious, and the unconscious, acting with characteristic indirection, makes the true state of affairs bewilderingly difficult to discern. But, always, at the bottom of the trouble is desire—desire denied direct expression and tortured into some malformation of conduct.

Freud himself, as a physician, treated the neuroses and the psychoneuroses. But his followers have extended his interpretations, often with additions of their own, into the more marked departures from the normal that are classified as psychoses. The first to make this extension was the Swiss psychiatrist, Bleuler. Bleuler explained schizophrenia, the most baffling of the psychoses, as a splitting or "fragmentation" of the personality, as the consequence of a conflict so

[6] The word "mechanisms" is employed by the psychoanalysts to refer to the specific processes by which the unconscious operates. Healy, Bronner, and Bowers, in *The Structure and Meaning of Psychoanalysis*, 193, suggest the adoption of the term "dynamism" in place of the word "mechanism." "Psychiatry," they say, "and especially psychoanalysis, is particularly interested in the dynamics of mental life, in moving forces and the laws which relate to them. Then, as a physicist might formulate it, a dynamism is a specific force operating in a specific manner or direction."

severe that it tore the personality into shreds. Bleuler's lead was followed enthusiastically by other members of his profession; and to-day there is hardly a corner of abnormal psychology into which psychoanalytic interpretations have not penetrated. No symptom is too trivial, no disorder too formidable, for the zeal, the industry, and the all but incredible ingenuity of those who try to fit the Freudian key into every lock.

The serious concerns of normal behavior, too, have been explained in terms of Freudian mechanisms. Obviously the life-work, which bulks so large in everyday affairs, can be overlooked by no theory that attempts an adequate explanation of human conduct. The Freudians have considered this problem from several points of view. One theory is that the urge for achievement, for success, for distinction of all sorts, is basically the desire for a mate; that beneath all striving for power or wealth or fame is the desire to attract the favorable notice of the other sex. Through the labors of the artist, the scientist, the statesman, the captain of industry, runs the motive of exhibitionism—a sublimated and redirected exhibitionism, to be sure, but fundamentally a primitive desire to be seen. More specific explanations have been offered in abundance. The scientist, it has been suggested, is a *voyeur*. His search for truth, however disinterested and impersonal it may seem, has its origin in the thwarted sexual curiosity of childhood, which persists and attaches itself to objects not obviously connected with the situations that first aroused it. An enormous amount of attention has been directed toward the arts, but probably the most famous single attempt to account for the artist's production in terms of psychoanalytical concepts is Freud's *Leonardo da Vinci*. To Freud, there could be no more perfect illustration of the Œdipus complex than that displayed by this man, an illegitimate son, devoted to his unhappy mother, even in manhood haunted by her face, and representing it again and again in his paintings. A somewhat different way of applying the Freudian principles is shown in Freud's comments on Jensen's novel *Gradiva*. Here a single literary production is used to reveal not the motive of the author's work, but the psychoanalytic interpretation of the situation he describes. The character and conduct of the young archæologist who is the hero of the novel, even his interest in archæology, are shown to be expressions of unconscious desires.

And the same underground forces that operate in individuals are at work in society as a whole. In countless ways the sex energy is sublimated—directed into channels that society approves. Myth, religious ceremonial, tribal taboos, social institutions—all of them, through symbolism or some other disguise, bespeak the gratification of forbidden desire. The practices that attend them, however much conventionalized through use and repetition, are rooted in the unconscious and charged with emotion. The whole fabric of civilization is marked with the Freudian pattern—with conflict, repression, the interposition of resistances, and circuitous routes to satisfaction.

So far, a fairly simple opposition has been assumed between the conscious and the unconscious, between the ego-trends and the sex-trends. But of late, Freud has advanced theories which picture that opposition as far less simple and clear-cut than it seemed. Turning his attention to the ego-trends, he was impressed by the large libidinal content he discovered there; by self-love expressing itself in a manner far more complex and subtle than that found in simple autoerotism. The result was a new theory of the organization of the psyche, centering about three concepts, the id, the ego, and the superego. The relation between the new theory and the old has not been clearly worked out. Freud seems to regard both as aspects of the same reality, as views of the psyche seen from slightly different angles of vision. He frankly acknowledges that the relationships between them are obscure, but he believes that the obscurity is due to incomplete knowledge; moreover, he feels strongly that a desire for consistency should not prevent the recording of insights that an existing system—especially one which is admittedly incomplete—does not readily accommodate.

Of the three concepts, the id (the Latin *id*) is probably the least revolutionary. It corresponds rather closely to the old notion of the unconscious. Some analysts, indeed, believe that it has supplanted the concept of the unconscious, though others regard it as a supplementary interpretation. The id is the deepest and most primitive part of the personality. It is profound, obscure, unconscious, and powerful. It contains as its largest component the instinctive sexual urges, but it includes also habit tendencies that the individual has suppressed, and a kind of blind wisdom inherited from the race. The id, though powerful, is quite without perception; it is unmoral, unenlightened, imperious, and rash. Seeking only the pleasures of the moment, it demands its satisfactions insistently but blindly.

The ego develops out of the id through the contact of the self with external reality, and becomes the mediator between the self and the external world. The ego knows reality as the id does not—perceiving where the id craves blindly. Perception, together with a capacity for manipulating the environment and regulating the id with reference to it, is the distinctive activity of the ego. The ego of the new theory is in fact far less the blind oppressor than the ego of old. Though it curbs the id, often standing out sternly against its demands, the ego, either by seizing or making opportunities, contrives whatever genuine satisfactions the id receives. In these activities the ego becomes something of an opportunist, even something of a diplomat. It also becomes an object of love to the id. Freud finds in self-love a libidinal component that the id directly supplies.

By far the most striking of the new conceptions is that of the superego. Perhaps the best way to describe the superego is to say that it is Freud's conception of conscience, and then to add immediately that it is a conscience which is infantile, unenlightened, largely unconscious, and powerful in the extreme. The superego is formed when the child, in his early contacts with the world about him, incorporates into himself the parent ideal—an ideal in which both parents are somehow represented—and adopts as part of himself the prohibitions enforced by the parents in infancy and childhood. The superego has been described as the "heir of the Œdipus complex." It grows out of the infantile attempt at self-discipline, at fortification against forbidden acts by the establishment within the self of the standards of the parents' world. The superego, therefore, includes the emotions that characterize the Œdipus complex and is organized about "Thou shalts" and "Thou shalt nots" that are derived from the unreasoned, uncomprehended, confusedly emotional moral situations of childhood. In its emotional intensity and in the blind insistence of its demands, it resembles the id more than the ego; it communicates with the id more freely than can the ego. And yet, very early, the superego acquires tremendous power over the ego; it is capable of severity to the point of cruelty in inflicting punishment for violations of its code. A curious arrangement sometimes exists in which the superego permits the ego departures from the code at the price of agonies of remorse and suffering afterward. The superego, in short, is the unconscious morality of the individual, which, often at variance with his conscious beliefs and principles, inflicts suffering and demands expiation for deeds of which the person does not consciously know he disapproves. The situation enormously increases the chances for conflict; Freud believes that an incalculable amount of psychic energy is wasted by the entanglements in which the superego is involved.

It must be remembered, too, that Freud is not alone in revising and developing his system. Modifications of his teachings have sprung up everywhere, often bitterly opposed to each other. Some of the suggestions of his followers have been accepted by Freud, but others—notably those of Jung and Adler—have been denounced and rejected. It is surprising that, in the luxuriance of doctrine which has developed, Freud's principles stand out as clearly as they do. For in spite of the changes that he is continually introducing, and in spite of the alterations and extensions—as often as not unofficial—which others have made in his name, the main outlines of his conception are clearly discernible. There is always the basic pattern of a self at war with unconscious desires, though the relations between them are intricate and not always clear. Currents of striving and repression run through the whole psychic structure—lines of resistance, of the circumvention of resistance, and of the indirect fulfilment of desire.

At the threshold of any attempt to evaluate the doctrines of psychoanalysis is a curious and significant difficulty. If the theory be true, the prosaic business of considering pros and cons may itself be an expression of unconscious motives, and any objections that rise to a critic's attention may be unconscious defenses against unwelcome revelations.[7] In that

---

[7] To be more specific, if the critic rejects the theory, he may be acting in self-defense. If he is friendly toward the theory as a whole, reserving his objections for one or two points, he may simply be employing a more subtle defense, attempting to protect his most sensitive wounds by conceding points that do not greatly concern him. Even if he gives good reasons for the stand he takes, he can never be sure he is not

case, the objections themselves constitute evidence of the system's essential rightness; for their occurrence means that the critic finds the import of psychoanalysis objectionable and is protecting himself in the manner predicted by the theory. This possibility should be stated and recognized at the outset.

This situation, in fact, is a special case of a logical difficulty which confronts any attempt to evaluate the theory from the standpoint of science: it is impossible either to prove or to disprove the psychoanalytic theories on the basis of scientific evidence. It is, in fact, impossible to prove them *because* it is impossible to disprove them. Science in the end appeals to experimental evidence, and a crucial experiment is one that gives a yes or no answer to some question. The experiment, therefore, must be put in such a way as to make possible an answer of either "Yes" or "No"; or of "Yes—in a given percentage of cases." It is for this reason that science insists on counting negative cases. But the psychoanalytic theory, as it is now formulated, makes a negative case impossible. For example if the analysis discloses a sex complex, the theory is confirmed. If it does not, it has failed to do so because the analysis has encountered a stubborn resistance, hence a particularly serious sex complex; and again the theory is confirmed. This illustration is less subtle than many that might have been chosen, but it indicates the essential nature of the difficulty.

From the standpoint of science, this question of evidence constitutes the most serious obstacle in the way of judging the theory. Attempts have been made, to be sure, in some cases by psychoanalysts but for the most part by academic psychologists, to submit some of the concepts of the system to the experimental and statistical procedures of science.

rationalizing. And the critic cannot be sure that he is not adopting such devices, because his motives may be deep in his unconscious.

The free-association experiment is one device that has been used for the purpose. This experiment, one of the stock procedures of Wundt's laboratory, was carried over by Jung into the field of psychoanalysis; and though free association under psychoanalysis and free association in the laboratory are admittedly somewhat different, the method has been seized upon by many psychologists as a possible means of putting some of the problems of psychoanalysis experimentally. Animal psychology suggests other lines of attack. For example, an attempt has been made to determine the relative strength of hunger and sex as drives by arranging conditions that will show for which of two alternatives, food or a mate, an animal is more likely to endure painful electric shocks. With human beings, questionnaires and rating scales have been used to discover to what extent specified conditions are present—for example, boys' preference of the mother to the father—but such data even when positive are indirect, and at best they are merely corroborative. Besides, there is a feeling not at all uncommon among psychoanalysts that such studies are futile and even objectionable. To many of them it seems patently impossible to include the really vital factors in a laboratory experiment or in a questionnaire; and it seems not only beside the point but positively misleading to consider statistical averages and curves of distribution and to ground conclusions on tabulated data quantitatively treated. Such practices, they insist, obscure the individual; and the individual, whose minutest idiosyncrasies may be important, must always be kept in the center of attention.

All this means that the psychoanalysts offer a different kind of evidence from that accepted by science. It does not mean that they offer *no* evidence. Their evidence, however, is the kind accumulated in experience as it happens to come, not in situations especially prepared to test the propositions in questions. The psychoanalysts pin their faith to what they have directly observed in their analyses and to what they have accomplished in practice. It is as if they simply said, "Look and see," assured that any one who sees what they have seen must be convinced as they have been convinced. Inevitably, in attempting to consider psychoanalysis from the scientific point of view, the critic is confronted by two kinds of evidence: on the one hand, immediate "untreated" observations that have accumulated and that have produced conviction in the course of practical, everyday experience; on the other, observations submitted to procedures especially arranged to test the hypothesis to which they are relevant. Of course the fact that the evidence offered in support of the psychoanalytic theory is not strictly scientific does not mean that the theory is false. It does not even mean that scientists have refused to accept it, for it is one of the remarkable facts about this remarkable theory that it has made its way even among scientists without the backing of evidence which is strictly scientific. It simply means that when a belief in the psychoanalytic theory is held, it is held on other grounds than scientific proof. It means that the belief is based not on systematically verified evidence, but on a feeling that there is something there; that the theory explains plausibly the things people actually do; that the bizarre speculations, wild as they seem, fall in convincingly with common observation, and help to make coherent and intelligible the otherwise chaotic and meaningless activities that make up so large a part of human behavior. Any one who accepts or rejects the psychoanalytic theories does so by means of the same kind of reasoning that gives him the thousand and one judgments he is forced to make in everyday life on the basis of insufficient or inadequate evidence—the kind of judgments, in fact, that he is forced to live by, but which have no standing in science. Such estimates, growing out of a multitude of impressions and interpreta-

tions, guesses and insights, often result in unshakable convictions, convictions which may be right or wrong but which,
from the standpoint of science, cannot be recognized as either
proved or disproved.

Aside from these criticisms of the general nature of the
evidence, objections have been made to specific points in
the psychoanalytic theory. The most frequent of these is that
Freud enormously overemphasizes the rôle of sex. Occasionally one hears the baseless objection that Freud reduces
everything to sex—baseless because it is not true to the
facts. Freud has never claimed that the sex motive is the
only drive to activity. He has always recognized the self-
preservative tendencies, and from the first he has implied in
the ego forces that are capable of repressing sex desires.
But the sex drive, he points out, is subjected to strong and
repeated repression, and because of this fact it has led to
marked disturbances in conduct. All this, however, does not
alter the fact that Freud assigns to sex the major rôle in
human conduct, and that his doctrine of its pervasive and
tremendous potency is one of his most conspicuous working
concepts.

Freud's answer to the objection that he overemphasizes sex
is too obvious to require statement. It was chiefly because
Jung and Adler tried to alter his teaching in this respect that
he became so bitterly estranged from both of them. But
Jung and Adler, each substituting a general urge for the sex
interest, are much closer to Freud than are most of his
critics. To many psychologists it seems a mistake to assume
that the wide and varied range of human activity is so
largely dependent, as Freud believes, on any single, general
motive, whether it be self-preservation, self-assertion, the
sex drive, or a life-force in general. Such a practice seems
to them to tempt to large, loose speculations, to an easy and
stereotyped reference of any specific line of conduct to the

one accepted source. They note that psychology, like any other science, has progressed in direct proportion to its discovery of the particular conditions that determine particular events. They prefer therefore to begin more naïvely by taking apparent differences at their face value, and to try to discover the special circumstances that occasion the conduct attributed by common sense to a variety of more specific motives—fear, anger, curiosity, revenge, a desire to dominate, and a host of others. They believe strongly that a genuine explanation involves an account of the particular circumstances which lead to a particular action; and that the ever-present availability of a general explanation—the permanent possibility of saying of any action, "It is due to the sex motive"—may easily discourage the investigation of particulars.

It will immediately be objected—and rightly—that the Freudians do not, as a matter of actual fact, stop with general expositions; that they insist on the importance of knowing with full particulars how the troublesome condition arose in a given person. But there is an enormous difference between investigating the particulars that connect a given condition with a cause which in its general nature is known and investigating the particulars that surround that condition in order to determine the nature of the cause itself. Besides, Freud's extension of the term "sex" far beyond the commonly accepted usage has been criticized as confusing. It is difficult to know, when an activity has been characterized as sexual, to what extent the involvement of the specifically sexual is intended. And yet, in spite of these objections, it is not at all regrettable that Freud places as much emphasis on sex as he does. The topic was conspicuously neglected by academic psychologies; and Freud's overemphasis is quite possibly a necessary step toward giving sex its rightful place in an account of human behavior.

Nevertheless it may be questioned whether Freud's evidence on infantile sexuality, even as he himself presents it, leads necessarily to his conclusions. The theory, it will be remembered, grew out of the fact that in his early analyses he kept discovering that an apparently finished analysis was not really complete; that it had to be pushed farther and farther back into the patient's history until it reached the period of early childhood or infancy, where it commonly terminated in the discovery of an imagined seduction. But does this sequence necessarily indicate infantile sexuality? May not a succession of failures to reach the root of the difficulty mean quite simply a succession of failures? And was it not necessary to change the meaning of the term "sexual" as the analysis was extended farther back into childhood? And since the seductions in infancy turned out to be fantasies, is it not possible that something in the procedure of analysis suggested their production or magnified their significance to the patients? At least interpretations of the data other than that given by Freud are possible. This does not mean, of course, that Freud himself was not honestly convinced nor that his conviction was not based on evidence. But it is entirely possible that his conviction was the result of a mass of impressions so subtle that they could not be separately noted and formulated. It is possible that the real bases of his convictions escaped his own observation and report, and that his conclusions were the outcome of an unconscious summation of responses in an unusually acute observer. It is a commonplace in psychology that convictions arise in this way, convictions on scientific matters as well as on others. But the basis of such conviction is private and personal, and the proposition that expresses it cannot be recognized as scientific knowledge until it is supported by evidence demonstrable to others. Again the old difficulty raises its head; the evidence is of a different order from that recognized by science.

Closely connected with this problem of the relation of evidence and conviction is the criticism that the free association employed in psychoanalysis is not really "free." It has been noted that, no matter how carefully the analyst effaces himself, no matter how he strives to refrain from suggestions that may influence the course of the patient's reflections, the patient must somehow be given to understand that, in letting his thoughts lead where they will, he must not try to withhold anything which seems trivial or embarrassing, or which is not ordinarily mentioned. But that understanding, it is asserted, constitutes a set toward a definite trend of thought. Furthermore, from time to time during the analysis the physician intervenes, sometimes to suggest interpretations, sometimes to help the patient overcome a resistance, sometimes to aid in the problem of transference. This situation makes it possible for the investigator to exert an influence against which it is peculiarly difficult to establish safeguards. The analysts themselves are aware of these difficulties and have devised various methods by which they try to cope with them. And certainly it must be said in fairness to Freud that his willingness to alter his published opinions indicates that in his case at least theoretical convictions have not been impervious to impressions made by facts brought out by actual dealings with patients.

The system has also been criticized for internal inconsistencies and obscurities. The Œdipus complex in particular has come in for a large share of attack. How does the newborn child learn to repress his libidinal desires? Exactly how is the attitude of the social environment communicated to him? Whence comes his power of repression? From the ego-tendencies? Are they then stronger than the libido? Just what is the relation between sexual desires and the ego?

Freud's new theories on the ego-trends, pointing as they do to a complex interplay between the ego and the libido, and to a self-love in which the libido is involved, make the distinction between the two less clear than before. Such considerations, however, do not seriously disturb the psychoanalysts. They regard it as a virtue in their leaders that they show no haste to crystallize beliefs into final systems; that they preserve, instead, a responsiveness to facts as they see them, even if the facts are apparently inconsistent; and that they maintain a readiness to recognize tendencies which they are convinced are in operation, even if the exact interrelations of those tendencies cannot be represented in diagrams. They believe that many of these difficulties are temporary and that some of them are artificial; that furthermore they seem unduly important to those whose academic habits of thought make their possessors uncomfortable until they have achieved a neatly articulated framework for their working conceptions. They believe, too, that to those who have had first-hand experience with psychoanalysis—again the appeal is to direct and intuitive observation—the imperfections, inconsistencies, and incompleteness of the system seem insignificant beside the immediately apparent relevance of the theory as a whole to the facts that present themselves in human life.

Thus the difference between academic psychologists and psychoanalysts repeatedly comes back to differences in habits of thought developed by their respective problems. Certainly much of the wariness of the academic psychologists has its roots in a dislike for what they consider a lack of directness —of plain matter-of-fact literalness—in the Freudian statements. The cloud of mythology and personification that hovers over the concepts of the school has been particularly distasteful. Figures of speech like the "censor" or the "Œdipus complex," or even those implied in "conflict," "repression," "dream-work," and the like, seem strangely out of place in scientific explanations. Every science, of course, has recourse to terms that are not quite literal. The physicist does not mean by an atom a little hard lump of matter; and Freud does not mean by the censor an actual manikin sitting at a trap-door that opens down into the prison of the unconscious. There may even be an advantage to the psychoanalyst, from the point of view of actual practice, in personifying the psychological forces with which he deals. After all, he deals directly with people, and his attitude toward his patients may be subtly affected by the fact that he thinks of their difficulties in terms not of impersonal stresses and strains, but of strivings and failings of human creatures. But to science, the whole atmosphere created by this practice seems one of riot and confusion. For science puts little trust in figures of speech; it fears that essentials may be confused with features which are merely incidental to a particular mode of expression, and that important problems may be obscured. For example, so long as the libido is considered a vast reservoir of power that can flow indifferently through various channels, the possibility of its manifold expressions presents few problems. Only when the attempt is made to think in terms of actual bodily structures and sources of energy do the particular difficulties of the concept become apparent.

And yet, in spite of the objections they have heaped upon psychoanalytic theory, academic psychologies have not been able to ignore it. In a measure, some of them have even accepted it. Behaviorism has been extremely hospitable to some of the Freudian concepts, when it has translated them into terms of bodily mechanisms and submitted them in some cases to corrective operations. Upon both social and abnormal psychology, also, the concepts of psychoanalysis have been tremendously influential. They have even found their way into many textbooks for beginning students, though often they have lost much of their original character in the course of that process. And all this has happened, it is important to notice, in the absence of evidence that is strictly scientific. Wherever the Freudian theories have been accepted outside the psychoanalytic fold, they have been received not because they carry the credentials of exact, verifiable evidence, but because they have aroused conviction as convictions are aroused in everyday life—by the feeling that they represent keen observation and shrewd speculation which, in the main, square with the facts.

Because of the fundamental disagreement on the validity of the evidence, the arguments for and against the Freudian theories can be continued indefinitely. It is, in fact, this disagreement on the question of what constitutes evidence that gives the psychoanalytic theory its chief interest to the student of schools and systems. For the Freudian theories represent a creative stage in scientific thought in which the hypotheses that can later be tested critically are being worked out. They form a psychology in the stage of inklings and guesses that will later be confirmed or rejected, a psychology which at present is enormously intent on the observation of its material, but which is as yet without adequate means of safeguarding its observations. It is enlightening to compare psychoanalytic psychology with structuralism, in this respect its antithesis. Structuralism, equipped with a highly developed scientific method, and refusing to deal with materials not amenable to that method, admirably illustrates the demand for exactness and correctness by which science disciplines untutored curiosity. Psychoanalysis, with its seemingly inexhaustible curiosity, at present lacks the means, and apparently at times the inclination, to check its exuberant speculation by severely critical tests. But what it lacks in correctness, it gains in vitality, in the comprehensiveness of its view, and in the closeness of its problems to the concerns of everyday life. For, it cannot be repeated too often, psychoanalytic psychology does not dispense with observation; it makes use of observation that is intuitive rather than critical. It is, therefore, through its vitality, its first-hand contact with its material, its scope, its common-sense shrewdness, that psychoanalytic theory has influenced psychology in general. It is as if academic psychology, confronted with a theory which it could neither prove nor disprove, but which it could not ignore, matched intuition with intuition and risked a judgment. Its collective verdict has been something like "two-fifths genius and three-fifths sheer fudge," with the fractions not accurately determined. Academic psychology, though it has shown a strong desire to wield Occam's razor and to remove the wealth of imaginative construction that surrounds the theory, has nevertheless been impressed by some of its interpretations. Many psychologists find the concepts of conflict and repression fruitful hypotheses, and many find mechanisms like rationalization, autistic thinking, and the various forms of indirect wish-fulfilment abundantly illustrated in everyday life. Most of them recognize the value of Freud's influence in calling attention to the problems of the personality as a whole, and grant him an important place in the general movement that, steadily undermining the notion of the rational man, emphasizes the tremendous importance of the conative and affective sides of human nature. Most of them also grant his importance in emphasizing the much-neglected psychological problems of sex. Freud's doctrines concerning the importance of infancy and early childhood have been received—often after the subtraction of most of his teachings concerning the sexuality of the child—partly because, in their general drift, they are in accord with many of the findings of the academic psychologists themselves. It is also acknowledged rather generally that Freud, despite his penchant for the vague and the mystical, has in the main promoted a more naturalistic view of man. Finally, Freud's fundamental conception of the importance of the unconscious, his conviction that the things human beings are aware of doing throw little light on the deeper layers of their nature, is recognized as raising fundamental problems concerning the methodology and the basic structure of the whole science of psychology.

Chapter XI

AFTERTHOUGHT

PERHAPS behind its array of systems the psychology of the present makes a sorry showing. System after system announces its principles, each imposes its order on the facts that arrest its attention, and each puts its case with a degree of plausibility. The difficulty is that they all do so and that they are all more or less at odds with each other. It is significant, too, that the more definitely a system draws the lines of its pattern, the more rigidly it selects its facts; that the clearest and most consistent systems are those most given to denials and exclusions. Besides, no system, not even the most aggressive, can or does claim that it is as yet fully established by fact. And when it is remembered that the systems just considered are only a few of those current in psychology, the confusion grows and multiplies. Yet this is the situation after more than half a century of effort: systems in plenty, but no one interpretation of the facts of psychology to which all psychologists, or even a majority, agree.

To many, this lack of harmony means that the whole enterprise of psychology is one of the wasted and hopeless efforts of the human race. In some, it strengthens a conviction that the attempt to make psychology a science is essentially futile; not merely that efforts have failed but that they will always fail, that the task is by its very nature an impossible one, either because the human intellect is incapable of the feat or, what amounts to the same thing, because the subject-matter is so complex or so elusive as to defy scientific treatment. Many who look upon the field, whether from within or from without, find little there worthy to be called science. They see fragments of fact, or at best scattered lines of consistent evidence, but nowhere the unified, coherent structure of knowledge they expect a science to achieve.

It is easy enough to fall into these reflections, and nothing can be gained by refusing to recognize in all soberness that psychology, for all its effort and ambition, may fail. But it would be equally unwise to refuse to recognize that the opposite possibility also exists. After all, the view of psychology as seen through its divergent systems is only one aspect of the whole and, as such, it is partial and to that extent unjust. For there is more in psychology than systems, more even than scattered facts. Running through its factual content, even as seen through the eyes of rival systems, are converging lines of evidence that point to the same conclusions. The most impressive are those marked out by workers who, starting from very different theoretical bases, meet on common ground in the discovery of common facts—or rather, of facts that call for a common interpretation. There is nothing in psychology more promising than the trends of agreement in independent pieces of research that different systems have inspired, trends which may be the beginning of a solid groundwork on which a factual science of psychology will be founded. Systems may thus serve as the basis of operations which reveal facts that are independent of systems.

Perhaps the most striking case of agreement is that between workers in behaviorism and *Gestalt* psychology on the inadequacy of the conventional way of conceiving neural action. Lashley, dealing directly with the nervous system and with overt behavior, cast the most serious doubt on the reflex and conditioned-reflex conception of the organic machine, and on the whole notion of behavior as built up of smaller and relatively stable units of reaction. The Gestalt-ists, starting with problems in perception as immediately experienced by the perceiving subject, became convinced that such experience could not be explained by the activity of a nervous system of isolated conductors. Even on the positive side the theories are remarkably similar. Both in Lashley's theory of mass-action and in Köhler's conception of dynam-ical interaction, the nervous system is regarded as a struc-ture in which the action of the whole is of inescapable im-portance and in which far more subtle lines of influence are at work than those involved in the operation of separate part on separate part.

Another line of agreement has emerged several times. Külpe and his pupils extending the methods of the Wund-tian laboratory, Binet occupied with the testing of intelli-gence, Woodworth seeking the cues to voluntary movement, all arrived independently at the conclusion that thought is not an affair of images and sensations variously combined; that it cannot, in fact, be described in terms of structural content. There is an evident connection, too, between this discovery and the one just mentioned; another vote is cast against the mosaic theory. Many psychologists, however, were skeptical of this unlooked-for result and, undertaking further studies of the higher thought-processes, discovered there—sometimes in the apparently "contentless" stretches of thought—kinæsthetic sensations and images of a sort easily overlooked. Though the occurrence of such content was differently interpreted by different investigators, its pres-ence drew attention to the motor side of human behavior. The evidence that kinæsthesis is part of the thought con-sciousness brought into prominence the conception of thought as something that cannot be considered apart from the activity of the physical organism in which it occurs.

This aspect of the studies of the higher thought-processes suggests still another line of agreement that runs through the several schools, a growing recognition of the importance of the motor side of human activity. The apparently obvious fact that psychological processes take place in creatures who act and move gained only slowly the foreground of attention in psychology. In ancient times and in the early modern period, though movement and action were indeed considered at times, the emphasis was decidedly on the side of cognition. But as soon as systematic laboratory observation was developed, as soon as psychologists deliberately set themselves to examine processes actually going on before them instead of reflecting on experiences recalled from the past, evidences of motor reaction began to obtrude themselves conspicuously. Significantly enough, the possible importance of the motor side of human activity was revealed very early by introspection. The outstanding case is the recognition by Müller and Schumann of the "motor set"—the discovery that in comparing lifted weights, the judgment is the outcome of immediately felt muscular sensations, not of higher intellectual processes in which present sensations are compared with images representing the past. Later, the introspective studies of the higher thought-processes again emphasized the possible significance of muscular activity. The motor side of activity became still more prominent in studies of learning, where the acquisition of motor skills was often used as the material to be studied and where introspective data, when used, were supplementary to records of progress in the motor action itself. The climax of attention to the movements of the organism was reached in behaviorism, which maintains that behavior or movement, implicit and explicit, is the proper subject-matter of psychology. An important consequence of this whole tendency to consider movement and action was that psychology acquired the habit of looking

at its material from the outside as well as from within, and
of regarding man as an animal reacting to his environment
as other animals do. Man, thus placed in the phylogenetic
and evolutionary series, was exposed to the revealing light
of comparative psychology, and as a consequence psychology
was freed from the idea that human beings constitute a
unique and special case in the order of nature.

Still another movement in which psychologists of many
schools have participated is the gradual modification of the
notion of the rational man. For some reason human beings,
when they become reflective, tend strongly to regard man's
rational nature as peculiarly and essentially himself. Certainly the Greek philosophers did so; and the schoolmen of
the Middle Ages, though different from the Greeks in temper
and intention, exalted reason no less than they. The same
tendency is present in the early modern period; for the
psychology of the seventeenth and eighteenth centuries was
preoccupied, if not with reasoning processes in the strict
sense of the term, at least with cognition in general. And
yet even in this movement, there were signs that the conception of the rational man must be modified. Locke
and Hume were asserting even then that the products
of thought are largely affairs of habit and custom and of
experience "imprinted on the senses" from without. And
when experimental studies of thinking were undertaken, the
evidence pointed almost at once to a conception of thought
as an activity far less severely rational than it had seemed.
Perhaps the most telling experiments of this group are those
which, adapting the methods of animal psychology to the
examination of human thought, have repeatedly revealed the
large amount of "typically animal" trial and error in human
thinking under these conditions, and have repeatedly emphasized similarities rather than differences between human

and animal performances. From the opposite standpoint—from the standpoint, that is, of the occurrence of insight rather than trial and error—Köhler's study of apes has also indicated the continuity of human with animal intelligence. And not only have the intellectual processes themselves been conceived as less rational than they seemed; such as they are and whatever they are, they have come to be viewed as far less decisive than they were formerly thought to be in determining human conduct. The psychoanalysts, of course, have been most emphatic on this point, but academic psychologists have tended in the same direction. From their various points of view, James, Dewey, and McDougall have all militated against the exaggerated notion of the potency of reason in human conduct; and Watson, calling attention to the importance of visceral and glandular activities, has taken essentially the same stand. There is a notable agreement among psychologists that the rational and cognitive sides of human nature have been enormously overemphasized in the past.

Along all these lines both opinion and practice have converged, and in consequence psychology to-day is addressing itself to a material very different from that which formed its subject-matter a century or even a half-century ago. The human beings psychology now studies are creatures who have a definite place in the animal series and in the world of nature generally, and who are studied both through the onlooker's observation of their overt actions and through their own reports of activities not visible to a spectator. They are creatures in whom emotion and impulse are powerful factors in determining conduct and in whom reason seems less decisive than was long supposed. They are creatures, too, who seem not to be put together according to any very obvious mosaic plan of construction, whether of conscious elements or of motor reactions. It is not enough to study their reactions piecemeal; it is necessary to take into account the organism as a whole.

All these points of similarity have been found in connection with fairly concrete factual material, but even in the theoretical bases of systems, in the very characteristics that distinguish them from each other, traces of agreement may be discovered.

Strange to say, there is a fundamental sameness of attitude toward that bugbear of psychology, the ever-recurring problem of the relation of mind and body. Perhaps this attitude is best described as an attempt to come to terms with the question in some fashion so that it will not be continually getting in the way. More positively and more specifically, the attitude is one of regarding the subject-matter of psychology not as constituting a world apart but as taking its place in the natural order. Historically psychology began as the study of mind or consciousness, and that circumstance put the problem of bringing the facts of psychology into relation with those of the physical sciences. Some systems have attempted to solve the problem by adopting a general formulation which they hope will once and for all serve the purpose. Others have simply noted whatever relationships they find in experience, assuming that a scientist, by the very nature of his problem, is not obliged to account for those relationships in metaphysical terms. Moreover, this common attitude, this tendency to bring the facts of psychology into relation with those of the natural sciences in general, is present whether or not the system is "dualistic" in the sense of regarding the mental and the physical as two distinct orders. In one way or another a connection is made. Structuralism, for example, by the doctrine of psychophysical parallelism, makes it possible to distinguish between the mental and the physical orders and yet to state observed relationships between them. Behaviorism, by reducing the mental to the physical, maintains that the relation is one of identity. Functionalism declares that its views and practices are compatible with any one of a number of metaphysical interpretations. Every system either devises a way of justi-fying its procedures or asserts that no justification is needed. There is, in fact, a growing tendency to disregard the metaphysics of the mind-body problem, a tendency which is one of the surest signs that psychology is becoming a science. For since science by definition limits its inquiries to the world of experience, there is no reason why the mind-body relations as they are observed in experience should not be treated as are other observed relations—as, for instance, they actually are treated in sense physiology. From the em-pirical standpoint the mind-body relations are no more unin-telligible, and no less so, than the relations encountered in other sciences; and if they seem to constitute a peculiarly sig-nificant problem, they do so because personal concerns and emotional values have singled them out as a special case. Eventually every natural science arrives at facts and rela-tions that it cannot explain—and that it does not even at-tempt to explain. And this does not mean that science is per-vaded with mystery. On the contrary, science gets on with its work precisely because it accepts certain empirical facts and relations as given and as constituting the practical limits of its inquiry, without pausing to ponder at length how they can possibly be so.

As a science, psychology is in the same situation. No more than any other science is it obliged—or qualified—to pro-nounce on the ultimate nature of its data. No more than any other science is it required—or permitted—to recognize any-thing outside the natural order in its explanations. Its busi-ness, again like that of any other science, is to determine the relationships it observes in experience and to account for its material in terms of such relationships. This is such a commonplace in scientific thought that it may seem superfluous to state it. And yet from points of view other than the scientific, the events usually classified as mental are so often regarded as utterly unique that it is sometimes necessary to state explicitly that they may be taken simply as happening in the natural order. But the habit of seeing the difference between mental and material events in the same light as one sees other empirical differences, of regarding both kinds of events as facts of experience that may be differently classified and between which it is possible to determine empirical relationships, of looking upon the most intimate and intricate thoughts and feelings, however they may be named, as parts of the same natural order as tides and planets and muscular contractions—this habit marks the attainment of the scientific attitude. And this habit psychology is now acquiring. For every one of the systems studied, in so far as it has dealt with the mind-body problems at all, has adopted a formulation which has made possible the treatment of its chosen subject-matter as part of the natural world, and which has made that subject-matter amenable to the regular procedures of science.

Similarly, as to definitions of the subject-matter of psychology, the disagreements between systems are neither so profound nor so disorganizing as they seem. For the most part differences in definition involve differences in the selection of facts; they do not imply denial of the facts themselves. Titchener in his polemics against behaviorism and functionalism did not deny the existence nor even the value of the materials brought forward for recognition; he merely denied that they were psychology. Neither does *Gestalt* psychology deny the facts with which the introspectionists are occupied; it merely asserts that these facts are the outcome of a special attitude and denies the right of that special attitude to determine the limits of psychology. Not even behaviorism expressly denies that consciousness exists—though unofficially it comes very near doing so and certainly maintains that science cannot recognize consciousness, since there is no scientific evidence of its existence. The position of behaviorism seems to be that consciousness (if it exists) cannot be subjected to scientific observation and therefore has no place in a psychology that pretends to be a science. Such catholic psychologies as those of James, Angell, and Woodworth are far more interested in inclusions than in exclusions; and the psychoanalysts and the academic psychologists in general have objects of investigation that are complementary rather than mutually exclusive. Practically, this means that different sets of workers are pursuing different sets of problems—a state of affairs hardly to be deplored in a growing science. And if some schools are so zealously bent on their own enterprises that they consider others a waste of time or worse, that situation too has its advantages. The definitions of psychology upheld by the various systems as they actually work themselves out in practice are statements of particular problems in an incomplete science. They are delimitations, temporarily convenient and practically necessary, of a field so wide and so little explored that something must be done to bring down its dimensions to workable size.

On questions of method the situation is much the same. Actually psychologists are not so far apart as they seem. Few methods are rejected root and branch and on principle by any set of workers. Behaviorism, of course, absolutely rules out introspection, but other schools show less animus, or none, in their attitude toward it; without giving it the exalted position once claimed for it, they accept it with varying degrees of enthusiasm and give it leave to accomplish what it can. The technique of psychoanalysis is dismissed by many as unsound for scientific investigation, and it certainly has not been adopted by academic psychology as a regular method of experimental research. But aside from these two modes of inquiry, the methods of psychology tend to be transferable from school to school. Besides, there are techniques, experimental and statistical, that have been developed outside of any system—the devices, for example, used in industrial psychology and in the testing and measuring of mental traits. Though these have been submitted to a bombardment of criticism, they have survived in part, have been improved and supplemented, and have even been extended to situations very different from those which gave rise to them. Methods, of course, are determined by problems; and a particular psychologist, once his main interests are settled, does not as a rule run the whole gamut of available procedures in his work. Naturally, too, differences of opinion, such as are bound to occur in any science, arise concerning the relative merits of various techniques. But more and more, criticism is tending to fasten upon specific weaknesses and limitations in a technique, less and less on its alliance with a given school or system. Very steadily psychology is developing a common stock of methods; and it is no longer surprising to see modes of experimentation and measurement devised by one school adapted to the problems of another.

It would be quite possible, indeed, to write an account of systems which, instead of emphasizing the characteristics by which they are distinguished, would stress their underlying similarities; which would show that, despite their differences, they are all directed upon the same class of facts; which would even suggest that their very disagreements arise from a jealous concern that that class of facts shall be seen aright. It would be possible, indeed, to base such an account on the statements in which systems expressly mark themselves off from other systems—on Titchener's papers excommunicating functionalism and behaviorism, for instance, and on Watson's and Wertheimer's declarations of independence. It is interesting to consider how much extra-systematic psychology is left standing after the attacks of opposing schools have done their worst; how much groundwork is implied in the fact that they can make their criticisms significant to each other. Not the least enlightening aspect of such controversies is the fact that the antagonists, when pointing a difference, use terms and refer to facts that imply admissions on both sides. They meet on common ground to make their disagreements clear.

On the other hand it would be possible, and perhaps more obviously possible, to take the systems with all their differences upon them and trace a continuity of development; to show that even revolutionary movements derive something of their form and much of their strength from the systems they revolt against; that successive protests have led to the extension of the field of psychology, not to the annihilation of any of its actual achievements; to show, in short, that the rise and fall of schools and systems form not a chaos, but a pattern. It would be possible, too, to show that psychology is becoming increasingly aware of these facts about itself. Of late there have been histories of psychology, accounts of its outstanding experiments, syntheses of its materials in particular fields, and surveys of contemporary schools and theories, which, taken together, indicate that psychology is taking on reflective ways, pausing apparently to take stock of itself, to see what its zest and enterprise have accomplished. Possibly this reflectiveness means disappointment or weariness or disillusion; possibly it means that the first youthful confidence has been shaken, or that originality and creativeness are temporarily spent. But it may also mean that psychology is assembling its resources for a longer and harder struggle than at first seemed necessary. Thus it might be maintained in sober earnest that psychology is tending toward harmony and stability. But such a contention would be profoundly false if it pretended to express more than the partial truth it contains. The whole argument for the case sounds specious and forced the moment it ceases to be accompanied by the never-to-be-forgotten warning that there is another side to the story. Psychology, it is true, has definite acquisitions to its credit, and to ignore them is both foolish and unjust. But it is equally foolish and equally unjust to pretend that they are greater than they are. Nothing could be more misleading than to pretend that psychology is more mature than it is, or that it has as yet achieved an integration of the materials in its grasp. For the significant fact about psychology as it now exists is not so much that it is discordant; that it is inept; that its work is at sixes and sevens; but that it is young and that it may be growing, that it has both the rawness and the promise of youth, and that it is in the very midst of the struggle for that command of tools and materials which is characteristic of a mature science.

Psychology is, in fact, interesting, if for no other reason, because it affords a spectacle of a science still in the making. Scientific curiosity, which has penetrated so many of the ways of nature, is here discovered in the very act of feeling its way through a region it has only begun to explore, battering at barriers, groping through confusions, and working sometimes fumblingly, sometimes craftily, sometimes excitedly, sometimes wearily, at a problem that is still largely unsolved. For psychology is a science that has not yet made its great discovery. It has found nothing that does for it what the atomic theory has done for chemistry, the principle of organic evolution for biology, the laws of motion for physics.

Nothing that gives it a unifying principle has yet been discovered or recognized. As a rule, a science is presented, from the standpoint of both subject-matter and development, in the light of its great successes. Its verified hypotheses form the established lines about which it sets its facts in order, and about which it organizes its research. But psychology has not yet won its great unifying victory. It has had flashes of perception, it holds a handful of clues, but it has not yet achieved a synthesis or an insight that is compelling as well as plausible. And no one does psychology a good turn by pretending that the situation is otherwise. Surely it is a doubtful compliment to credit psychology with characteristics it does not possess. For psychology has no more need to apologize for itself than a youth has for not being a man, or an apprentice for not being a master. Only when it pretends to be something it is not does psychology become unconvincing and at times ridiculous. Its ways are justified not by glozing the facts but by exposing them exactly as they are.

Certainly it is from this condition of psychology—its incompleteness, its youth, its striving toward a still distant goal—that systems derive their significance. As final accounts of psychology, they do not stand; they do not pretend to stand. But as programs of action and instruments of morale, they at once become intelligible and important. Their very variety becomes significant, suggesting that the situation has provoked the varied reaction of trial and error by which human intelligence regularly attacks problems in unfamiliar fields. Their tentativeness, too, explains and justifies some of their secondary characteristics, among others the emotionalism that sometimes attends them and that often seems strangely out of place in the austere pursuits of science. Indeed, something very like biological utility is discernible in the emotionalism that systems at present call forth. For though a securely established fact neither provokes nor requires ardent championship, a theory that may possibly be true but has not yet been proved true may be sustained, through the critical period when it is being tested, by an emotionally determined preference or aversion. The tentative character of systems accounts also for their tendency to run in schools. Social support, like emotion, fortifies convictions not yet established as true; and it is difficult to imagine a better social instrument for maintaining morale than a recognized school, composed of workers devoted to a common cause, stirred by common hopes and loyalties and distastes, bent on the overthrow of a common enemy. It is not surprising, therefore, that psychology is largely organized about schools; and it is a fairly satisfactory practical definition of a school to say that it is a group of workers who are giving a particular idea or a particular set of ideas considerably more than its share of attention and emphasis.

Again it must be said that there is nothing at all discreditable in this situation; that systems are, on the contrary, among the legitimate and appropriate and practically indispensable tools by which a scientific psychology is being produced. At the very least, they give definiteness and direction to an enterprise so vast and ambitious and as yet so formless, that artificial limitations imposed on endeavor are apparently among the necessary conditions of producing any results at all. Actually most of the facts in the possession of psychology have grown up about schools and systems. Even the most conspicuous exception to the rule—the research in applied psychology, educational and industrial—is one that proves it; for here delimitations like those imposed by a system are secured by the demands of a practical problem. Besides, not even the dissensions among schools are altogether disadvantageous. Rivalry may add zest to effort and so multiply achievement. The most intolerant schools are often the most productive; and loyalties, aversions, and strongly emotional prejudices may operate in the production of impersonal truth. For the product of scientific thought is identifiable neither with the means nor with the conditions of its production; and it is the product that is impartial and impersonal. The scientific method is a device for making it so, regardless of the conditions that motivated its acquisition. Perhaps the most impressive evidence of the effectiveness of the scientific method, in this respect, is that found in the work of investigators who, as adherents of a particular school, conduct researches which bring to light facts at variance with the teachings of that school. In their very clashes, furthermore, schools correct themselves and each other. Without exception, they recognize that the test of a doctrine, whether one they are advocating or one they are attacking, is experimental verification; and it is their recognition of this fact that makes systems of psychology more than mere speculations in the air. By making actual trial of assertions—their own and each other's—the various schools have made whatever acquisitions they have to their credit. And if a stable science of psychology is brought into being, these acquisitions and others like them will form its factual content.

Naturally in taking leave of schools and systems, there is an impulse to sift and sort their offerings. But the attempt to do so would be premature at best, and at worst would suggest an illusory conclusiveness in so far as it gave the appearance of rounding off an enterprise. To measure a system in some way against other systems and to detect signs of its influence on psychology in general is possible, of course, and even necessary to understanding it. It is enlightening to note the acquisitions it has made, the checks it has encountered, the enterprises it has promoted, the opposition it has stimulated, the alliances it has made—in short, to determine as definitely as possible its place in the pattern that psychology forms at present. But that pattern itself is only a part of a whole as yet inadequately indicated. Any sifting and sorting undertaken on that basis—anything of that nature implied in the foregoing chapters, for example—must be regarded in exactly the same light as are the systems themselves: as giving a temporary and tentative interpretation of a set of facts that is admittedly incomplete. Besides, the attempt to sift and sort is superfluous as well as premature and uncertain. Far more effectively than it can be done in any other way, the schools and systems are themselves accomplishing the task; and they are doing so not by speculation and argument alone, but by the evidence they are steadily accumulating about their beliefs. When this evidence is sufficient in bulk and solidity, it will itself determine the form of psychology and constitute its substance. At that time systems will no longer be needed; they will have fulfilled their purpose. But that time has not yet come. At present they are at the full height of their vigor and usefulness. It is better, therefore, to keep the picture one of unfinished action, and to leave schools and systems of psychology in the very act of producing the structure that, if they are successful, will make their own existence unnecessary.

REFERENCES

The following list of titles does not constitute a complete bibliography. It includes articles and books specifically referred to in the text and it also gives a few other references that will be helpful to the student. For convenience, the list has been divided according to chapters, though there is, of course, considerable overlapping of the reading matter for the different chapters.

Chapters I, II, III

Boring, E. G., *A History of Experimental Psychology* (New York, The Century Co., 1929).

Brett, G. S., *A History of Psychology* (London, G. Allen and Unwin, 1912, 1921).

Dessoir, Max, *Outlines of the History of Psychology* (New York, The Macmillan Co., 1912).

Hall, G. S., *Founders of Modern Psychology* (New York, D. Appleton & Co., 1912).

Klemm, O., *History of Psychology* (New York, Charles Scribner's Sons, 1914).

Lewes, G. H., *The Biographical History of Philosophy* (London, John W. Parker and Son, 1857).

Murchison, Carl, ed., *Psychologies of 1925* (Worcester, Mass., Clark University Press, 1925).

——————, *Psychologies of 1930* (Worcester, Mass., Clark University Press, 1930).

Murphy, Gardner, *An Historical Introduction to Modern Psychology* (New York, Harcourt, Brace, and Co., 1929).

Pillsbury, W. B., *The History of Psychology* (New York, W. W. Norton & Co., 1929).

Rand, Benjamin, *Classical Psychologists* (New York, Houghton Mifflin Co., 1912).

Rogers, A. K., *A Student's History of Philosophy* (New York, The Macmillan Co., 1913).

Vaihinger, H., *The Philosophy of "As If"* (New York, Harcourt, Brace, and Co., 1924).

Warren, H. C., *A History of Association Psychology* (New York, Charles Scribner's Sons, 1921).

Weber, Alfred, and Perry, R. B., *A History of Philosophy* (New York, Charles Scribner's Sons, 1925).

Woodworth, R. S., *Contemporary Schools of Psychology* (New York, The Ronald Press, 1931).

Chapter IV

Bentley, Madison, "The Psychologies Called Structural; Historical Derivation," *Psychologies of 1925*, 383-393.

——————, "The Work of the Structuralists," *Psychologies of 1925*, 395-404.

——————, "The Psychological Organism," *Psychologies of 1925*, 405-412.

Boring, E. G., "Edward Bradford Titchener," *Amer. J. Psychol.*, 1927, **38**, 489-506.

Titchener, E. B., *An Outline of Psychology* (New York, The Macmillan Co., 1896).

——————, *Experimental Psychology: Qualitative, Instructor's Manual; Qualitative, Student's Manual; Quantitative, Instructor's Manual; Quantitative, Student's Manual* (New York, The Macmillan Co., 1901-05).

——————, *A Primer of Psychology* (New York, The Macmillan Co., 1898-99).

——————, *Lectures on the Elementary Psychology of Feeling and Attention* (New York, The Macmillan Co., 1908).

——————, *Lectures on the Experimental Psychology of the Thought Processes* (New York, The Macmillan Co., 1909).

——————, *A Text-Book of Psychology* (New York, The Macmillan Co., 1909-10).

——————, "The Postulates of a Structural Psychology," *Philos. Rev.*, 1898, **7**, 449-465.

Titchener, E. B., "Structural and Functional Psychology," *Philos. Rev.*, 1899, **8**, 290-299.

——————, "On 'Psychology as the Behaviorist Views It,'" *Proc. Amer. Philos. Soc.*, 1914, **53**, 1-17.

——————, *A Beginner's Psychology* (New York, The Macmillan Co., 1915).

——————, *Systematic Psychology: Prolegomena* (New York, The Macmillan Co., 1929).

——————, Colleagues and former students of, *Studies in Psychology* (Worcester, Mass., L. N. Wilson, 1917).

Chapter V

Bard, P., "The Neuro-Humoral Basis of Emotional Reactions," *The Foundations of Experimental Psychology*, ed. by C. Murchison (Worcester, Mass., Clark University Press, 1929), 449-487.

Cannon, W. B., *Bodily Changes in Pain, Hunger, Fear and Rage* (New York, D. Appleton and Co., 1929).

——————, "The James-Lange Theory of Emotions: a Critical Examination and an Alternative Theory," *Amer. J. Psychol.*, 1927, **39**, 106-124.

James, Henry, Jr., "A List of the Published Writings of William James," *Psychol. Rev.*, 1911, **18**, 157-165.

James, William, *The Principles of Psychology* (New York, Henry Holt and Co., 1890).

——————, *Psychology: Briefer Course* (New York, Henry Holt and Co., 1892).

——————, *The Varieties of Religious Experience* (New York, Longmans, Green and Co., 1902).

——————, *The Will to Believe and Other Essays in Popular Philosophy* (New York, Longmans, Green and Co., 1897).

——————, *Talks to Teachers on Psychology: and to Students on Some of Life's Ideals* (New York, Henry Holt and Co., 1899).

——————, "Does Consciousness Exist?" *Essays in Radical Empiricism* (New York, Longmans, Green and Co., 1912), 1-38.

James, William, *The Letters of William James*, ed. by his son, Henry James (Boston, The Atlantic Monthly Press, 1920).

——————, and Lange, C. G., *The Emotions*, including a trans. by I. A. Haupt of Lange's *Über Gemuthsbewegungen* (Baltimore, Williams and Wilkins Co., 1922).

Santayana, George, *Character and Opinion in the United States* (New York, Charles Scribner's Sons, 1920).

Sherrington, C. G., *The Integrative Action of the Nervous System* (New York, Charles Scribner's Sons, 1906).

Chapter VI

Angell, J. R., *Psychology* (New York, Henry Holt and Co., 1904).

——————, *Introduction to Psychology* (New York, Henry Holt and Co., 1918).

——————, "The Province of Functional Psychology," *Psychol. Rev.*, 1907, **14**, 61-69.

Ayres, C. E., "Philosophy au Naturel," *New Republic*, 1925, **42**, 129-131.

Carr, Harvey, *Psychology* (New York, Longmans, Green and Co., 1925).

——————, "Functionalism," *Psychologies of 1930*, 59-78.

Dewey, John, *Psychology* (New York, Harper and Brothers, 1887).

——————, "The Reflex Arc Concept in Psychology," *Psychol. Rev.*, 1896, **3**, 357-370.

——————, *How We Think* (Boston, D. C. Heath and Co., 1910).

——————, *Human Nature and Conduct* (New York, Henry Holt and Co., 1922).

Höffding, Harold, *Outlines of Psychology* (New York, The Macmillan Co., 1896).

Stout, G. F., *A Manual of Psychology* (New York, Hinds and Noble, 1899).

——————, *The Groundwork of Psychology* (New York, Hinds and Noble, 1903).

Chapter VII

Diserens, C. M., "Psychological Objectivism," *Psychol. Rev.*, 1925, 32, 121-152.
Kuo, Z. Y., "Giving up Instincts in Psychology," *J. of Phil.*, 1921, 18, 645-663.
————, "How Are Our Instincts Acquired?" *Psychol. Rev.*, 1922, 29, 344-365.
Lashley, K. S., "The Behavioristic Conception of Consciousness," *Psychol. Rev.*, 1923, 30, 237-272, 329-353.
————, *Brain Mechanisms and Intelligence* (Chicago, University of Chicago Press, 1929).
————, "Basic Neural Mechanisms in Behavior," *Psychol. Rev.*, 1930, 37, 1-24.
————, "Mass Action in Cerebral Function," *Science*, 1931, 73, 245-254.
Roback, A. A., *Behaviorism and Psychology* (Cambridge, University Bookstore, 1923).
Russell, Bertrand, *Philosophy* (New York, W. W. Norton and Co., 1927).
Washburn, M. F., "Introspection as an Objective Method," *Psychol. Rev.*, 1922, 29, 89-112.
Watson, J. B., "Kinæsthetic and Organic Sensations: Their Rôle in the Reactions of the White Rat to the Maze," *Psychol. Rev.*, 1907, 8, Mon. Supp. No. 2, 1-100.
————, "Psychology as the Behaviorist Views It," *Psychol. Rev.*, 1913, 20, 158-177.
————, "Image and Affection in Behavior," *J. Phil. Psychol. and Sci. Meth.*, 1913, 10, 421-428.
————, *Behavior, an Introduction to Comparative Psychology* (New York, Henry Holt and Co., 1914).
————, *Psychology from the Standpoint of a Behaviorist* (Philadelphia, J. B. Lippincott Co., 1919).
————, "Recent Experiments on How We Lose and Change Our Emotional Equipment," *Psychologies of 1925*, 59-81.
————, "Experimental Studies of the Growth of the Emotions," *Psychologies of 1925*, 37-57.
————, "What the Nursery Has to Say About Instincts," *Psychologies of 1925*, 1-35.

Watson, J. B., *Behaviorism* (New York, W. W. Norton and Co., 1925, 1930).

————, and R. R., *The Psychological Care of the Infant and Child* (New York, W. W. Norton and Co., 1928).

————, and McDougall, William, *The Battle of Behaviorism* (London, K. Paul, Trench, Trubner and Co., 1928).

Chapter VIII

Cattell, J. McK., "The Conceptions and Methods of Psychology," *Pop. Sci. Mon.*, 1904, 66, 176-186.

————, Students of, "The Psychological Researches of James McKeen Cattell," *Arch. Psychol.*, 1914, No. 30.

Hunter, W. S., "The Delayed Reaction in Animals and Children," *Animal Behav. Monog.*, 2, 1913, 1-86.

McDougall, W., *Introduction to Social Psychology* (London, Methuen and Co., 1908).

Spearman, C., *The Nature of Intelligence and the Principles of Cognition* (New York, The Macmillan Co., 1923).

————, *The Abilities of Man: Their Nature and Measurement* (New York, The Macmillan Co., 1927).

Thorndike, E. L., "Animal Intelligence," *Psychol. Rev.*, 1898, 2, Mon. Supp. No. 4, 1-109.

————, *Animal Intelligence: Experimental Studies,* including the monograph, "Animal Intelligence" (New York, The Macmillan Co., 1911).

————, *Educational Psychology*, 3 vols. (New York, Teachers College, Columbia University, 1913, 1914).

————, with E. O. Bregman, M. V. Cobb, E. Woodyard, *The Measurement of Intelligence* (New York, Bureau of Publications, Teachers College, Columbia University, July, 1927).

————, with E. O. Bregman, S. W. Tilton, E. Woodyard, *Adult Learning* (New York, The Macmillan Co., 1928).

————, *Human Learning* (New York, The Century Co., 1931).

Thurstone, L. L., "The Stimulus-Response Fallacy in Psychology," *Psychol. Rev.*, 1923, 30, 354-369.

References   437

Woodworth, R. S., "The Accuracy of Voluntary Movement,"
    Psychol. Rev., 1899, **3**, Mon. Supp. No. 2, 1-114.
———, "A Revision of Imageless Thought," *Psychol.
    Rev.*, 1915, **22**, 1-27.
———, *Dynamic Psychology* (New York, The Co-
    lumbia University Press, 1918).
———, "Dynamic Psychology," *Psychologies of 1925*,
    111-126.
———, "Dynamic Psychology," *Psychologies of 1930*,
    327-336.
———, "Four Varieties of Behaviorism," *Psychol.
    Rev.*, 1924, **31**, 257-272.
———, *Psychology* (New York, Henry Holt and Co.,
    1921; rev. ed., 1929).

Chapter IX

Allport, G. W., "The Standpoint of Gestalt Psychology,"
    Psyche, 1924, **4**, 354-361.
Calkins, M. W., "Critical Comments on the Gestalt-Theorie,"
    Psychol. Rev., 1926, **33**, 135-158.
Child, G. M., *Physiological Foundations of Behavior* (New
    York, Henry Holt and Co., 1924).
Coghill, G. E., *Anatomy and the Problem of Behavior* (Cam-
    bridge, The University Press, 1929).
DeLaguna, G. A., "Dualism and Gestalt Psychology,"
    Psychol. Rev., 1930, **37**, 187-213.
Helson, H., "The Psychology of Gestalt," *Amer. J. Psychol.*,
    1925, **36**, 342-370; 1926, **37**, 25-62; 189-223.
Hsiao, H. H., "A Suggestive Review of Gestalt Psychology,"
    Psychol. Rev., 1928, **35**, 280-297.
Kantor, J. R., "The Significance of the Gestalt Conception
    in Psychology," *J. Philos.*, 1922, **22**, 238-240.
Klüver, Heinrich, "Contemporary German Psychology," in
    G. Murphy, *An Historical Introduction to Modern Psy-
    chology*, 1929, 426-434.
Köhler, Wolfgang, *The Mentality of Apes* (New York, Har-
    court, Brace, and Co., 1925).
———, "Intelligence in Apes," *Psychologies of 1925*,
    145-161.

438 References

Köhler, Wolfgang, "An Aspect of Gestalt Psychology," *Psychologies of 1925*, 163-195.

———, "Some Tasks of Gestalt Psychology," *Psychologies of 1930*, 143-160.

———, *Gestalt Psychology* (New York, H. Liveright, 1929).

Koffka, Kurt, "Perception: an Introduction to the Gestalt-Theorie," *Psychol. Bull.*, 1922, 19, 531-585.

———, "Introspection and the Method of Psychology," *Brit. J. Psychol.*, 1924, 15, 149-161.

———, *The Growth of the Mind* (New York, Harcourt, Brace and Co., 1924).

———, "Mental Development," *Psychologies of 1925*, 130-143.

———, "Some Problems of Space Perception," *Psychologies of 1930*, 161-187.

Line, W., "Gestalt Psychology in Relation to Other Psychological Systems," *Psychol. Rev.*, 1931, 38, 375-391.

Ogden, R. M., "The Gestalt-Hypothesis," *Psychol. Rev.*, 1928, 35, 136-141.

Rignano, E., "The Psychological Theory of Form," *Psychol. Rev.*, 1928, 35, 118-135.

Spearman, C., "The New Psychology of 'Shape,'" *Brit. J. Psychol.*, 1925, 15, 211-225.

Washburn, M. F., "Gestalt Psychology and Motor Psychology," *Amer. J. Psychol.*, 1926, 37, 516-520.

Wertheimer, Max, "Experimentelle Studien über das Sehen von Bewegungen," *Zsch. f. Psychol.*, 1912, 61, 161-265.

———, "Untersuchungen zur Lehre von der Gestalt," *Psychol. Forsch.*, 1923, 4, 301-350.

Chapter X

Adler, Alfred, *The Neurotic Constitution* (New York, Moffat, Yard and Co., 1917).

———, *The Practice and Theory of Individual Psychology* (New York, Harcourt, Brace and Co., 1924).

Freud, Sigmund, *Psychopathology of Everyday Life* (New York, The Macmillan Co., 1914).

References 439

Freud, Sigmund, *A General Introduction to Psychoanalysis* (New York, Boni and Liveright, 1920).

——————, *The Interpretation of Dreams* (New York, The Macmillan Co., 1913).

——————, *Beyond the Pleasure Principle* (New York, Boni and Liveright, 1924).

——————, *Leonardo da Vinci* (New York, Moffat, Yard and Co., 1916).

——————, *Totem and Taboo* (New York, Moffat, Yard and Co., 1918).

——————, *Wit and Its Relation to the Unconscious* (New York, Moffat, Yard and Co., 1916).

——————, *The Ego and the Id* (London, The Hogarth Press, 1927).

——————, *The Problem of Lay-Analyses* (New York, Brentano's, 1927).

——————, "The History of the Psychoanalytic Movement," *Psychoanal. Rev.*, 1916, 3, 406-454.

——————, *Delusion and Dream*, a study of Wilhelm Jensen's novel, *Gradiva* (New York, Moffat, Yard and Co., 1917).

Healy, W., Bronner, A., and Bowers, A., *The Meaning and Structure of Psychoanalysis* (New York, Alfred A. Knopf, 1930).

Holt, E. B., *The Freudian Wish* (New York, Henry Holt and Co., 1915).

Jung, C. G., *Psychology of the Unconscious* (New York, Moffat, Yard and Co., 1916).

——————, *Psychological Types* (New York, Harcourt, Brace and Co., 1926).

——————, *Two Essays on Analytical Psychology* (New York, Dodd, Mead and Co., 1928).

Wohlgemuth, Adolf, *A Critical Examination of Psychoanalysis* (London, Allen and Unwin, 1923).

INDEX OF NAMES

INDEX OF SUBJECTS